ANGELINA

ANGELINA

An Unauthorized Biography

ANDREW MORTON

ST. MARTIN'S PRESS ❧ NEW YORK

www.stmartins.com

Library of Congress Cataloging-in-Publication Data

Morton, Andrew.
    Angelina : an unauthorized biography / Andrew Morton. — 1st ed.
      p. cm.
    ISBN 978-0-312-55561-0
   1. Jolie, Angelina, 1975– 2. Motion picture actors and actresses—United States—Biography. I. Title.
   PN2287.J583M67   2010
   791.4302'8092–dc22
   [B]   2010020454

First Edition: August 2010

10 9 8 7 6 5 4 3 2 1

To Craig, Dave, and Max

ANGELINA

PROLOGUE:
THE IVORY TOWER

One of the pitfalls of childhood is that one doesn't have to understand something to feel it. By the time the mind is able to comprehend what has happened, the wounds of the heart are already too deep.

—Spanish novelist Carlos Ruiz Zafón

The room was stark and bare: white carpet, white curtains, white walls, and no furniture except for a white crib. For more than a year, a baby girl lived there, cared for by a ragtag assortment of babysitters—mainly out-of-work actors or acquaintances, working shifts at three dollars an hour around the clock.

The child rarely knew if the person putting her to bed was the one who would dress and feed her in the morning. There were days at a stretch when her mother, who lived in an apartment three stories below, would not visit her. When the mother sometimes came upstairs for coffee, she would sit there with the babysitter, crying and lamenting her lot. "It just broke my heart," one of those babysitters, Krisann Morel, told me more than thirty years later. "It upsets me now. I really felt for that kid."

The room was nicknamed "the Ivory Tower" and the baby seen as some kind of infant Rapunzel, out of the Grimm Brothers fairy tale about a young girl locked in a tower.

During this time the child's mother never read to her, never put her to bed or took her to the park, and for a long time she resisted suggestions to have the walls of her child's bedroom painted in bright colors to give the toddler some stimulation. Only reluctantly did she give her a few toys to play with.

That baby girl was Angelina Jolie. She was sent to live in the Ivory Tower after her father, Jon Voight, left her mother, Marcheline Bertrand.

When Krisann told Marcheline that her daughter needed more time and attention from her, Marcheline responded, "Angie reminds me so much of Jon right now that I cannot be around her. It's just too painful."

Angelina's earliest childhood memory is of lying in her crib looking out the window toward the sky. Without knowing the circumstances, Angie would later see that experience as a metaphor for her life. "I've just been staring out a window all my life . . . thinking there was somewhere I could finally be grounded and happy."

ONE

There was a day after moving to Beverly Hills when I truly realized that I could actually marry someone famous.

—MARCHELINE BERTRAND

When Marcia Lynne Bertrand and her family moved to the Hollywood she and her mother had always dreamed about, neighbors in their hometown of Riverdale, Illinois, were more skeptical than jealous. "We couldn't believe someone we knew was actually moving to Beverly Hills," recalls Marianne Follis Angarola, a classmate of Raleigh "Rollie" Bertrand's. "There was some taunting of Rollie, because the idea of moving to Beverly Hills surely had to be a lie!"

Not only was it true, but the family, which shipped out of Riverdale in September 1966, was moving in some style. They had bought a new, four-bedroom, ranch-style home on an exclusive private estate in the hills above Sunset Boulevard, which was developed by Paul Trousdale in the late 1950s. While the parents would have been impressed by the acres of marble floor and the full-height windows that looked over the pool and on to downtown Los Angeles in the distance, as well as by the spacious backyard at 515 Arkell Drive, the Bertrand children were thrilled to be able to write to their friends back home that they lived on the same estate as Groucho Marx, Dean Martin, and Elvis Presley. Of course, no one in Riverdale believed them. Local legend has it that Debbie Bertrand even mailed her former school friends some loose change she had taken from the actor Don Adams—then the star of the TV hit *Get Smart*—to "prove" that she babysat for his children.

Marcia Lynne's younger brother, Rollie, quickly embraced the Hollywood lifestyle. For his fifteenth birthday his parents, aware of his ambition to be a Formula One racing driver, gave him a red Ferrari sports car—even though he was too young to drive. That little inconvenience did not put the brakes on the young roustabout. When he went on a date with Gina Martin, a daughter of Dean Martin's, he asked his friend Peter Martini to take the wheel. He clearly enjoyed life in the fast lane. As his friend Randy Alpert, the son of jazz musician Herb Alpert, recalls: "Raleigh was a great guy and a good friend. We had a million fun times in Beverly Hills. Girls, cars, girls, cameras, Wild Turkey, girls, Rainbow Bar and Grill, racing, girls, Martini House, parties, and very often some girls." A far cry from life in Riverdale.

In her own way, Marcia Lynne was at least as starry-eyed, if not more so, as the rest of her family. Like her mother, she avidly read the tabloids, soaking up the stories about the stars. There was a vicarious thrill about living in the midst of so many celebrities.

Nevertheless, her exciting new life had its social costs. Marcia Lynne was careful to conceal her family's unglamorous origins from her classmates at Beverly Hills High School, talking vaguely about one day living in New York. Fellow student Adriane Neri remembers Marcia Lynne as "quiet, inconspicuous, one of those artsy people on the edge of things."

It didn't take long for Marcia Lynne to absorb the overarching dictum of life in Hollywood: You can be anyone you want to be. After graduating from Beverly Hills High in 1969, she joined the Lee Strasberg Theatre and Film Institute and signed with the William Morris Agency to pursue modeling and acting work. She began to affect a more exotic persona, calling herself Marcheline, which she explained was the way her French-Canadian grandmother, Marie-Louise Angelina, pronounced her name. Her family still called her Marcia.

She took to drinking French vanilla instant coffee and collecting French crockery and other artifacts. Just to add an exotic frisson, the family believed that there was a dash of Iroquois Indian in the bloodline, dating back to their French-Canadian settler roots. Certainly with her swooping dresses, embroidered headbands, and long hair, she was a poster child for the hippie generation. As she left her teenage years behind, something changed inside her. She later told a close friend: "There was a day after moving to Beverly Hills when I truly realized that I could actually marry someone famous."

Marcia Lynne was born on May 9, 1950, to Lois and Rolland Bertrand. Roland had just been named manager of his father-in-law's bowling alley in Riverdale, Illinois. "Bowling was a heck of a business at the time," observes local historian Carl Durnavich. "Everybody bowled. You couldn't get a lane sometimes. People either played baseball or they bowled."

The nearby industrial town of Harvey was the largest manufacturing base in the country at the time; jobs were plentiful, crime was unheard-of, and everybody knew everyone else in the town of four thousand people. The Riverdale where Lois was raised was straight out of a Norman Rockwell painting, complete with white picket fences and roses around the door. Durnavich compares it to the setting of the movie *Pleasantville,* the story of a saccharine-sweet small town where uncomfortable and unruly thoughts and ideas were shuffled under the sidewalk.

Life in Riverdale was comfortable, secure, and recognizable—if a tad dull. Lois June Gouwens dreamed of getting out, of becoming a star on the silver screen. The highlight of her week was when the glossy movie magazines arrived at the grocery store across the street from the tavern her parents owned. The moment the magazines were unloaded, she would dart to the grocery, reaching up to the rack on the front counter for the latest issue of *Movie Mirror* and *Motion Picture.* Then she would curl up in a chair in the family's apartment above the bar and pore over the photographs of Betty Grable, Rita Hayworth, Ginger Rogers, and other Hollywood stars of the day.

Lois's father, Roy Gouwens, had earned his wealth the hard way, working as a cement laborer to save up for the down payment on a mom-and-pop alehouse that he and his wife, Virginia, known by everyone as Jean, called the Gouwens Tavern. In the community they had a reputation as straight dealers, honest, hardworking, and dependable. In 1941 they sold the tavern to Jean's sister and her husband, a deal that enabled Roy and a partner to open the ten-lane Parkview Bowling Alley just as the craze for the sport was taking off.

An only child indulged by doting parents, Lois had a dressing table in her bedroom decked out with a halo of lightbulbs just like in the magazine pictures she had seen of a typical Hollywood star's dressing room. At night she would spend hours in front of the mirror, carefully pinning her dark hair for the following morning's cascade of curls, as was the fashion of the day. As she pinned and brushed, brushed and pinned, she made her plans and dreamed her dreams. "One day I'm going to be a movie star," she told anyone who would listen, including her cousin Don Peters.

After she finished high school in 1946, just after the end of World War II, her parents paid for her to enroll at a modeling school in downtown Chicago run by Patricia Stevens. As she waited for the call from a Hollywood agent or pictured herself on the cover of *Vogue,* Lois worked in the typing pool of the upmarket Chicago department store Marshall Field. Even the commute into the big city provided an ersatz glamour and a cosmopolitan appeal when contrasted with the familiar faces and unchanging rhythms of her home village. Lois had been born and raised in Riverdale, like her parents, grandparents, and great-grandparents, her ancestors having sailed for America from Holland during the early nineteenth century.

As a big fish in a small pond, Lois was quite the catch, her family being long established and well-to-do, the nearest thing to aristocrats in a town like Riverdale, where hard work and decorum went hand in hand.

So it was perhaps no surprise when Lois started stepping out with bona fide war hero Rolland "Rollie" Bertrand. It didn't hurt that he was cute, too, short but with huge, expressive blue eyes. One of three sons of local farmer George and Marie-Louise Angelina, who were descended from the first French settlers in Quebec, Canada, Rolland had served with distinction during World War II, fighting with the First Army in the bloody combat through France and Germany. In November 1944 he was wounded in both legs during the advance on the Rhine and was taken to a military hospital in France.

On returning to Riverdale, he got a job in the bowling alley and soon afterward started dating Lois, their courtship helped by their mutual love of bowling and shared memories of Thornton Township High School in Harvey. When the couple married at St. Mary's Catholic Church on June 4, 1949, Lois was twenty-one, Rollie four years her senior. For Riverdale society, it is no exaggeration to say that this was the wedding of the year.

After the make-do and mend and rationing of the war years and beyond, the fact that the bride's Colonial-style satin gown was trimmed with

Chantilly lace and had a three-yard train was worthy of note, as was the fact that there were no fewer than seven bridesmaids and seven grooms-men, along with a ring bearer and a flower girl. That her father was able to afford a reception for six hundred at the Steel Workers Club in nearby Harvey, as well as a wedding dinner and breakfast at Fred's Diner, was a sign that bowling equaled big bucks—with social ambition to match. Even Lois's wedding shower was attended by more than a hundred local ladies, and the festivities were enlivened by an accordion recital by Hank Slorek. While not quite the Busby Berkeley production Lois might have dreamed of, it certainly made headlines in the local press.

It was not long after the couple's monthlong honeymoon touring Florida and Canada that Lois became pregnant. For a time after Marcia Lynne was born in May of the following year, they lived with Lois's parents, Roy and Jean, Rollie learning the ins and outs of the family business. In short order they were able to buy a home of their own, a modest white clap-board house on South Edbrooke Avenue typical for this lower-middle-class community.

If Lois's dream of becoming a model had been put on hold with mar-riage and motherhood, it was all but forgotten the following year, when her father, the driving force behind the Gouwens fortune, died suddenly. He was only forty-five. From then on his widow, Jean, was vice president of the family business concerns. Rollie ran the bowling alley, with Lois an active player in the ladies' league, although her second pregnancy, which brought them another daughter, Debbie, in 1952, hampered her bowling technique for a time. They completed their family in February 1955 with the arrival of their only son, Raleigh.

Around then the expanding Bertrand family moved from their wooden property to a sprawling brick home at 13840 South Wabash Avenue—on the right side of the tracks—that occupied two forty-by-ninety-foot plots. Even in a neighborhood in which no two houses were alike, their new home was a standout because of its size. Lois had had her eye on the five-bedroom mansion since she was a girl. At the same time, their new home was only four blocks from their bowling alley, close to Lo-is's extended family and, most important, large enough to house her mother, Jean, who came to live with the family when she was diagnosed with cancer. Lois, who is remembered as a devoted daughter, shouldered much of the nursing burden. The family business was expanding, too; in 1958 Rollie opened another bowling alley, on South Halsted Street in Chicago, where he played host to a national bowling tournament.

As for Lois's modeling ambitions, from time to time she did make an appearance on the catwalk at local charity events. At one ladies' luncheon in the summer of 1959, she joined nine other models in a fashion show in aid of the Knights of Columbus. Guests were advised that hats were by Beverly Hats and hairstyles by Ye Olde Haag Beauty Shop. Like many other mothers, however, she was content to channel her thwarted ambition through her daughters, particularly her older girl, Marcia Lynne.

While Marcia Lynne's father is remembered as "easygoing," a warm and generous man who liked a drink, Lois was the driving force in the family, an astute businesswoman and an ambitious mother. She wore the trousers in the partnership, brooking no opposition at home or at work. Her husband, passive and unassertive, did not command the respect from his children that was customary in the era of *Father Knows Best*. Nor did Lois's behavior toward her husband encourage deference to the patriarch. "Lois was very aggressive and goal-oriented," recalls her cousin Don Peters. "She had what we call in business a type A personality." She could chill with a look and knew how to hold a grudge. It was a quality known in the family as the "Bertrand freeze."

Although Lois was determined that one of her children would make it in the theater or in movies, only Marcia Lynne was as keen as her mother; her younger sister, Debbie, always wanted to be a nurse. Every Saturday morning Marcia Lynne and her mother would catch the electric tram into Chicago for acting, singing, and dancing lessons, and shopping trips to fashionable downtown stores. In time Marcia Lynne signed with modeling agencies. When the Drury Lane Theatre opened in Evergreen Park in 1958, Marcia became a member of the troupe of youngsters.

With her long dark hair and big, wistful blue eyes, Marcia Lynne was seen by many—not just her doting mother—as a naturally pretty young girl. "She was the beauty of St. Mary's," recalls Denise Horner-Halupka, who attended the local Catholic school with her. Remembered by her fellow pupils as quiet, unassuming, and pretty, but otherwise undistinguished, Marcia Lynne glided through elementary school and junior high, leaving barely a trace before moving up to Elizabeth Seton High School in South

Holland. There is a tinge of envy in the recollections of her classmates, several recalling that she lived in a large house on the right side of the tracks. Friendly but not forward, Marcia Lynne kept any dreams she had to herself.

As the sixties dawned, the Bertrands seemed destined to remain a well-to-do, influential local family whose every social event, from New Year's Eve dinners to recreational outings to places like Paw Paw Lake, was worthy of note in the local press. They were particularly remembered for their charitable efforts. For example, in August 1959 Rollie took a group of young local bowlers to watch the Yankees play the Chicago White Sox in the company of Hall of Famer Ray Schalk. As a friend of the family explained, it was something of a trade-off: The Bertrands were well aware that they were wealthier than most of the neighborhood but did not wish to appear aloof; they wanted to give back to the community that had made their fortune.

The death of Rollie's father, George, on September 18, 1962, and Lois's mother, Jean, just five days later seems to have jolted the family out of their routine. Perhaps there was talk around the family dinner table of new pastures. Certainly when Rollie flew to Oakland, California, in 1964 for a bowling tournament, the wonders of life out West gained a new intensity. It was not long before the Bertrands were California dreamin'. They went on vacation to the Golden State—and liked what they saw.

Of course, they were not the only ones. Thousands of young men who had enlisted during World War II and later the Korean War had enjoyed a taste of paradise out West at the military camps. So many had left the area that there were annual Harvey Day celebrations in various California towns. Several members of Jean's family—the Kashas—had moved to Arizona. As the thermometer touched thirty below outside, inside the bars and drinking joints of Harvey and Riverdale the talk often turned to how different life could be in California, a fabled place of endless sunshine, the Beach Boys, beach blondes, and peaches ripening by the roadside. More than that, the Golden State was somewhere to make a fresh start, to reinvent your life, to live your dream.

For the great majority it remained just that, a pipe dream. The death of Lois's mother gave the Bertrands the opportunity to live that dream. In her will, Jean Gouwens left all her properties, bowling alleys, and other commercial ventures to her only daughter. As the family discussed, idly at first and then with greater focus, the possibility of selling up and moving west, the voice of fifteen-year-old Marcia Lynne was pivotal. In school she kept thoughts of modeling to herself, probably worried about being teased by her contemporaries. In family lore it was now accepted, much to her mother's satisfaction, that Marcia Lynne wanted to pursue an acting and modeling career.

After high school she said she wanted to attend the Theater Arts School (now the School of Theater, Film and Television) at UCLA on Sunset Boulevard in Hollywood. It was a seductive vision; Lois could imagine her own dream of showbiz success being fulfilled through her daughter.

Opportunity came knocking when a consortium made a substantial offer for the family bowling business. While Rollie and Lois eventually planned to retire, it helped crystallize this momentous decision—and augment their finances—when Rollie secured a managerial job at the Century Plaza hotel in Los Angeles. So the Bertrands decided to move to Hollywood. As Lois's cousin Chuck Kasha recalls: "They wanted to get out of the business. They had worked hard and wanted to live the American dream."

When Jon Voight dreamed, he dreamed big. When he was just three years old, he saw himself becoming a great painter. It helped that his parents, Elmer and Barbara, dreamed big, too. On the eve of America's entrance into the First World War in 1917, the sports-crazy eight-year-old Elmer had gathered up all his youthful courage, marched into a golf club in Yonkers, just north of New York City, and asked for work as a caddie. He happened to be in the right place at the right time. Yonkers was the site of the first golf course in the United States—in 1888 Scottish immigrant John Reid had founded the Saint Andrews golf club—and in 1913, the local Jewish community had joined together to open their own course, which they named Sunningdale, after the historic course outside of London.

Not only was Elmer, the son of a Slovakian miner, given work as a caddie, but members also took the personable youngster under their wing, teaching him correct English and the proper use of a knife and fork, as well as the mysteries of the great game itself. Elmer—universally known as "Whitey"—flourished, and but for a back injury would have been, according to Jon Voight, "one of the greats." Instead he ended up as the club pro, a dapper, ebullient man, always ready with a funny story or a gag. The woman he married in 1936, Barbara Kamp, the daughter of a German immigrant, was also a keen golfer who knew how to enjoy life. At some point she founded the You're a Nut Like Me society, dedicated to overcoming everyday stresses through humor and imagination. "She was the most fun-loving person I ever knew in my life," recalled her longtime friend Susan Krak.

With three boys born in five years—Barry in 1937, Jon on December 29, 1938, and finally James in 1942—Barbara had to run a strict household, ruling her boisterous brood with a touch of Prussian discipline. Every Sunday she took the three boys to the local Catholic church, but at times it was like herding cats. As Jon's kid brother, James, recalls: "We were usually the last ones there. We would have to go and sit up by the altar."

Just as well. As Jon recalls, "As a kid I was always up to no good." When he was not dreaming of becoming a great artist, he spent his days climbing the highest trees he could find.

The real world of the imagination began at bedtime when Elmer arrived home. For a time he convinced his sons that he was an undercover FBI agent rather than a golf pro. As they sat on their bunk beds in their home off Lockwood Avenue, the curtain would go up on their father's nightly theatrical performance, Elmer spinning endless tales that he would make up on the spot.

"My father was a wonderful storyteller," recalls Jon Voight. "Those were magical experiences. I still have vivid memories of those times. And I think those experiences had a lasting influence on me. He would tell us stories about the Mississippi River and the riverboats. I think that's why I became an actor, to be like my dad. I was so thrilled to listen to him tell these tales." His father's imagination and his mother's chutzpah opened up a world of possibilities for their sons. As James recalls, "My dad would wake me and my brothers up in the morning and say: 'Boys, the world is your oyster.' Mom and Dad were encouraging us to hop our own fences." By the time he was six, Jon had already hopped one fence, having swapped thoughts of painting professionally for those of a career in the movies. Later, he dallied with the notion of becoming a professional comedian.

Whatever the future held for Jon and his brothers, in the Voight household there was one overriding passion: golf. All three boys took up the sport, Jon and James excelling. Indeed, James's later stage name, Chip Taylor, came about because for several Sundays in a row he had holed out from off the green. On one occasion Jon and Gene Borek, the assistant pro at Sunningdale, played in a national caddie tournament in Columbus, Ohio. It was not a successful venture. "When we got home on the train in Grand Central," recalled Gene, who later enjoyed fleeting fame as the club pro who scored a sixty-five at Oakmont, "we had eleven cents between us. I had the penny." While he never turned pro, Jon credits his father for instilling in him the balance and grace a good golfer needs—a point that Elmer never tired of making to his pupils. "The trouble with the average woman golfer is that she is too lazy; the trouble with the average male golfer is that he is too tense," was his stern mantra.

In addition to their love for golf, Elmer and Barbara were also keen movie- and theatergoers, Elmer finding inspiration for some of his bedtime yarns from films they saw at the local Roxy. Jon was not the only one who was inspired by his parents' love of the arts: James vividly remembers "the chill factor"—the sense of joy in performance—he experienced as a youngster. In the late 1940s, when he was seven, his parents took him to see the musical *My Wild Irish Rose,* about the life of New York Irish tenor Chauncey Olcott. He had been so reluctant to go that his parents had brought him along only because they couldn't find a babysitter. Looking back, he is glad they did. "I fought them the whole way," he now recalls. "But I'm sitting in the theater, the music comes on, and my body was, like, on fire. At the end of the performance I didn't want to talk to my parents. I just wanted to hold on to that wonderful feeling." The chill factor was the inspiration that eventually took him into a highly successful career as a lyricist.

As for Jon, he got the chill factor designing and painting sets for his school's theater productions. Though he did also take to the stage—his mother, a part-time teacher, was his first director, when he was in sixth grade—at that time he had no thoughts of taking up the profession.

Like his brothers, Jon attended the Archbishop Stepinac High School in White Plains, New York, and in between classes was an enthusiastic and talented stage designer. "We were in a real safe place to be creative, experiment," he recalls. It was the school's longtime drama teacher, the Reverend Bernard McMahon, now retired, who convinced a baby-faced Voight to move from stage design to playing the comedy lead of Count Pepi Le Loup in the school's annual musical, *Song of Norway,* an operetta about the life of composer Edvard Grieg. In his senior class the next year, Voight took the part of the valet Lutz in *The Student Prince.* The 1956 yearbook raved: "Complete with German accent and whiskers, Jon surpassed his amazing triumph of last year with a masterful handling of the play's main comic role." His leading lady was Barbara Locke, a student at the all-girls Good Counsel Academy High School in White Plains. "Oh, he was talented and charismatic," recalls Locke, who still gets the occasional surprise telephone call from her onetime leading man. "He was charming and always a nice-looking young man. The girls were crazy about him."

He was equally crazy about the stage and would pore over English theater critic Kenneth Tynan's reviews of West End plays. The work of actor Laurence Olivier held a particular fascination. "I would read these sections over and over—much before I ever made a decision about being an actor—fascinated by Olivier's ability to design these great roles so that they would come alive for modern audiences. It was intriguing how he set the performance for a beginning, a middle, and a climactic ending."

Yet even when Jon went off to college, he remained ambivalent about pursuing a career in acting. In 1957, after his freshman year at Catholic University in Washington, D.C., he changed his major from speech and drama to art while continuing to do stage design. Voight, who played college basketball, designed the cardinal that adorned the center of the basketball court, a section of flooring that is now on display in the school's Pryzbyla University Center. Serious-minded, ascetic, and thoughtful, he entertained thoughts of becoming a priest, but that ambition soon evaporated. "I couldn't have taken it," he explains frankly. "I loved gals too much." During his four years at the university, Voight, blond, blue-eyed, and touching six foot four inches, was sufficiently popular with both sexes to be elected president of the student body.

After completing his degree in 1960, he seems to have had yet another change of heart and returned to New York to try his hand at acting rather than art. With the political baton about to be passed from Eisenhower to Kennedy, the theater scene in downtown Manhattan reflected the rapidly changing cultural climate. Young actors saw themselves as artists and idealists, agents of change. The idea of chasing fame and celebrity was treated with disdain by the new breed of downtown thespians, among them

Al Pacino, Dustin Hoffman, Gene Hackman, and Jon Voight. Their hero was Marlon Brando, who, after performing in Tennessee Williams's *A Streetcar Named Desire* onstage in New York, boarded a plane to Hollywood to make a movie and declared that he would return to his first love, the theater, the instant filming was finished. These young tyros may have been idealistic, but they were also as competitive as any Wall Street trader. As Hoffman later recalled, "Actors are like women. Women check each other out in a way that men don't. They look at the breasts, they look at the legs . . . because they are in competition with each other. Actors check each other out in a not dissimilar way."

Voight enrolled with the legendary acting coach Sanford Meisner, who taught Method acting at the Neighborhood Playhouse. Along with contemporaries who included James Caan and Robert Duvall, he absorbed Meisner's dictum that "acting is the ability to live truthfully under imaginary circumstances."

Voight's off-Broadway debut in the long-forgotten *O Oysters* revue at the Village Gate nightclub on Bleecker Street in Greenwich Village was less than impressive. According to one critic—Voight remembers he was from Vermont—he could "neither walk nor talk." Nevertheless, he persevered. Voight and his roommate James Bateman, whom he had met at Catholic University, developed a comedy double act featuring two naïve hillbilly characters, Harold and Henry Gibson, the latter a derivative of playwright Henrik Ibsen's name. Bateman took Henry Gibson as his stage name, later finding fame as the flower-holding poet in the TV show *Rowan & Martin's Laugh-In.*

For his next effort, in 1961, Voight returned to the musical, a medium in which he had excelled in high school. He appeared as a temporary replacement for the Welsh actor Brian Davies in the role of Rolf Gruber, a Nazi who introduced the song "Sixteen Going on Seventeen" in the original Broadway production of the Rodgers and Hammerstein smash *The Sound of Music.*

Although he was with the show for only a short time, he made an impression on Detroit-born actress Lauri Peters, who played Liesl, the eldest Von Trapp daughter. Just sixteen when Richard Rodgers cast her in 1959, by the time she met Voight, Lauri was already a stage veteran and had been nominated for a prestigious Tony Award for her performance. They started dating, Voight struggling to find work while his girlfriend was trying to fit film roles around her nightly Broadway appearances. The blonde actress with the girl-next-door looks starred with teen heartthrob Fabian, the star of *American Bandstand,* and Hollywood veteran James Stewart in the family comedy *Mr. Hobbs Takes a Vacation.* Although it was inevitable that she would be romantically linked with Fabian, it was Voight who won her heart.

Lauri Peters was only nineteen going on twenty when she married Jon Voight in 1962. That year she starred alongside singer Cliff Richard in the classic British feel-good film *Summer Holiday,* released the following year, while her husband won his first TV role, a bit part in the long-running *Gunsmoke.* When the curtain finally came down on *The Sound of Music* in June 1963, Peters took on the role of Louisette in the play *A Murderer Among Us,* directed by Sam Wanamaker, which closed after its opening night in March 1964.

After other small TV walk-ons in *Naked City* and *The Defenders,* Voight snagged his first film role as the eponymous Fearless Frank, a dim-witted hayseed with matinee idol good looks who heads to the big city and is murdered and resurrected as a kind of comic-book hero. He was more successful on the stage, getting his first big break in an acclaimed off-Broadway revival of the 1955 Arthur Miller drama *A View From the Bridge* in January 1965, working opposite Robert Duvall and getting to know Dustin Hoffman, who was the show's assistant director and stage manager. Voight and Hoffman were both young, idealistic, and passionate about their craft, artistic purity held in far higher esteem than any siren call from Hollywood.

Then it was Voight who was making waves—if not money. After his success off-Broadway, he was invited to San Diego, where he was the star in the 1966 National Shakespeare Festival at the Old Globe Theatre. Significantly, in the downtime between rehearsal and performance, he was gripped by James Leo Herlihy's novel *Midnight Cowboy,* about the unlikely friendship between New York hustler Ratso Rizzo and a naïve Texas dishwasher who comes to the Big Apple to earn a living servicing sex-starved women. The oddball love story, published in 1965, rapidly attained cult status.

He put the book aside and continued his steady progress in off-Broadway theater, in March 1967 winning a Theatre World Award for his performance opposite Greek actress Irene Papas in the Frank D. Gilroy play *That Summer—That Fall.* He was not the only Voight boy to be making a name for himself: His elder brother, Barry, was on his way to becoming a world-renowned volcanologist, while his kid brother, Chip, had penned the song "Wild Thing," first performed by the Troggs, which became the summer anthem of 1966. As Jon Voight recalls: "I was one of the first people that he played it for, and I remember falling down on the floor laughing, and coming up saying, 'It's a hit! It's a hit! People won't be able to get it off their tongues!' It's a fun song."

His five-year marriage, however, was no laughing matter. An ambitious actor, tall, rangy, with soulful blue eyes and a ready smile, he attracted women like moths to a flame. "My God, the girls loved him. They would come backstage," recalls Dustin Hoffman. "They wanted to marry him and to mother him. He was a matinee idol off-Broadway."

Unsurprisingly, Peters and Voight decided to part company, their youth, time spent apart, and the temptations of success all playing a part in their decision to divorce in 1967. As Voight later recalled of that period in his life, "If you come out of nowhere, then suddenly everyone wants a piece of you, you get an inflated view of yourself. I always wanted to do the right things, responsible pieces and charity work, but in terms of the personal attention I got from gals, well, success is the greatest aphrodisiac of all."

Still, that same year he found himself eclipsed by his friend and rival Dustin Hoffman, whose performance in *The Graduate* rocketed him to stardom. By contrast, while Voight was gaining a degree of critical respect on the boards, he had done little on the big screen. "Jon had been the rising star in the theater, but after *The Graduate* it was Dustin who was the star," recalls photographer Michael Childers. "They were very competitive, but it wasn't bitchy. Everyone was trying to do their best work."

When Voight heard that the legendary director John Schlesinger had agreed to film *Midnight Cowboy,* the novel he had read the previous summer, he was desperate for a part, especially when Dustin Hoffman snagged the plum role of Ratso Rizzo. At the time, he and Hoffman were working together on the U.S. premiere of Harold Pinter's play *The Dwarfs* at David Wheeler's Theatre Company of Boston. "The way I saw my industry in the sixties was that the movies weren't about anything," Voight now recalls. "We didn't have the equivalent of a Kurosawa or a Bergman or a Fellini. Schlesinger was the answer for me."

Unfortunately, Voight was not the obvious answer for the English director. After screen-testing several actors for the role of Joe Buck, he settled on Michael Sarrazin, complaining that Voight looked too much like a Dutch boy. For Voight it came as a body blow, all the doubts and fears about himself and his career bubbling to the surface. He was approaching thirty, and what did he have to show for it—a crummy downtown apartment, a failed marriage, and a film career going nowhere? His father's testy fears that he was too much of a dreamer to make a living in the real world seemed to be coming uncomfortably true. "I felt sick to my stomach," he recalls. "I walked around like a wounded animal for a week." He bumped into Hoffman backstage in Boston and, swallowing his pride, asked him to put in a good word with Schlesinger.

Days later, he heard that Schlesinger might want to talk again after reviewing the audition tapes; the fact was that Sarrazin's agent had asked for too high a fee. As he waited for the verdict, Voight went out for groceries to kill time. On his way home in the rain he ran into a boxer who lived rough in the neighborhood. On impulse, he bought him a bottle of Scotch, took him back to his apartment, and made him a tuna fish sandwich. As they talked, he told the homeless boxer that he was waiting for a phone call that could change his life. "It took the pressure off me," he now recalls. "This guy had it a lot worse than me, so I felt more at ease." When the call came and Schlesinger offered him the role, the young actor and the old pugilist did a victory dance in his apartment. So excited he couldn't sit still, Voight gave the boxer his coat and then ran out into the teeming rain to really soak up the news. For his ticket to stardom, he was paid $17,500—a little over $100,000 in today's money. Hoffman had graduated to a much higher salary, earning $150,000, which would be close to a million dollars today.

While he might not have approved of the gamey subject matter (neither did the luminaries at Voight's Catholic high school, for that matter), at least Elmer Voight had the satisfaction of knowing that his son finally seemed to be making a living. Hoffman bought himself a $700 desk from his earnings, while Voight was filled with love and peace, literally dipping into his pocket and giving his friend Al Pacino money to fund an intriguing Heathcote Williams play, *The Local Stigmatic,* at the Actors Studio in New York.

Artistically Voight had hit the jackpot, working on a script with meat and meaning, with actors he admired and a director he respected. Filming, which began in April 1968, took place against a background of social unrest and rioting in Paris, London, Washington, and other major cities as dissatisfaction with the old order spilled out onto the streets. For two off-Broadway actors, the film somehow symbolized the changing mood. They realized that they were working on an edgy project at a risky time and gave it their all.

During filming Jon Voight moved in with his lover, Jennifer Salt, daughter of the movie's screenwriter, Waldo Salt, but it was the on-screen marriage of Hoffman and Voight that created the real buzz and excitement. Looking back, Hoffman describes their collaboration as like a boxing match. "It wasn't a case of upstaging one another, but it was let's see who can really act better in this scene," recalls Hoffman. At times it was a tad too authentic. There was a moment during shooting when Hoffman put so much energy into his character's tubercular cough that he vomited all over his costar's cowboy boots. "There's no way I can upstage vomit," Voight commented laconically.

What an increasingly anxious Schlesinger referred to during the shoot as "a pile of shit"—the mounting cans of uncut dailies—was edited into a film that would garner seven Oscar nominations. At the moment of Schlesinger's greatest fears about the yet-to-be-released movie, Voight took him by the shoulders and told him: "John, we will live the rest of our artistic lives in the shadow of this great masterpiece." Voight might have been gazing into the future at his own career.

In spite of Schlesinger's doubts and the censors' giving it an X rating, *Midnight Cowboy,* which was released in May 1969, the year of Woodstock, Altamont, the Manson murders, and mounting protest over the Vietnam War, scored a cultural bull's-eye with the audience and most critics, the right movie at the right time with the right message. Ironically, its surface modernity, sexual frankness, and cynicism masked the fact that the film was, in the words of Hoffman's biographer Ronald Bergan, "an old-fashioned movie about an innocent coming from the sticks to the big city and not finding the sidewalks paved with gold."

Now that he was a hot property in his own right, Voight remained true to his counterculture roots, eschewing films that merely exploited his good looks. He flew to London to star as the leader of a radical student organization in *The Revolutionary,* Voight sincerely believing that his medium held the message for change. As his girlfriend Jennifer Salt recalls: "Jon had that kind of 'I'd like to save the world with my work' attitude."

He seemed a natural choice to be included in the starry cast of *Catch-22,* director Mike Nichols's adaptation of Joseph Heller's classic black comedy, which skewered the cruel absurdity of modern warfare. While Gene Wilder claimed that he was the first choice for the role of the fast-talking, self-promoting black marketer Milo Minderbinder, Voight more than held his own in a cast that included Alan Arkin, Orson Welles, Bob Newhart, Art Garfunkel, and Martin Sheen. Like *The Revolutionary,* the film was neither a critical nor a commercial success, Voight's two choices post–*Midnight Cowboy* failing to capitalize on his initial triumph.

The Academy Awards in the spring of 1970 seemed to encapsulate the changing social and cultural landscape. As Voight told writer Peter Biskind: "When I went to the Academy Awards there was a split down the middle. Frank Sinatra, John Wayne and Bob Hope, I'd grown up with them, I admired them, but I was also of the new breed that wanted to see something changed. We were the sons of Brando." When he prepared to present one of the awards for Best Writing, he and the legendary Fred Astaire exchanged courtesies backstage. It symbolized to Voight the meeting of two generations, a civilized passing of the cultural baton.

That night, however, Voight handed an award to screenwriter Waldo Salt, while John Schlesinger won the statuette for Best Director, and *Midnight Cowboy* came away with Best Picture. Both Voight and Hoffman had been nominated for Best Actor in a Leading Role, but the challenge of the new generation was beaten off by the old guard when John Wayne won for his performance in *True Grit.*

Hoffman, who was paying a thousand dollars a week for daily psychotherapy sessions to cope with the pressures of his success, was so devastated by the result that he fled Hollywood and spent three months in Europe licking his wounds. His costar was deep into his role in another ill-fated film, Charles Eastman's *The All-American Boy,* playing a small-town boxer who refuses to acknowledge his talent and squanders his many opportunities, when John Boorman approached him about appearing in the movie version of James Dickey's book *Deliverance*. At the dark heart of this story about four middle-class city dwellers who find much more than they bargained for when they go on a canoeing trip down a wild river was the unsettling rape of the city men by mountain men, which served as a metaphor for the rape of America and nature by mankind.

For the artistically adventurous Voight, this should have been an enticing prospect. At this critical round in his career he considered himself out for the count. He had already turned down the lead in *Love Story*, arguing that he would have made the role "too complicated"—even though he was offered a share of the profits, which eventually rolled out at $50 million. As Boorman recalled in his autobiography, *Adventures of a Suburban Boy:* "He was in despair about his career. I wooed him. He resisted. He was too exhausted to do another picture. He felt he was too young for the role. He was too distraught to make decisions." In short, he had lost his nerve. They met, and Voight had good ideas for the role of Ed, the comfortable advertising copywriter, but he refused to commit.

Although Boorman didn't know it, he had an unseen ally. Voight's career might have been floundering, but one of the happy by-products of being a Hollywood heartthrob was that he got the girl, on or off the screen. Though he was still living with Jennifer Salt, he was very much in demand with the opposite sex. At that time, "free love" was not just a catchphrase, it was a movement, with sex as much a political statement as an act.

Jon Voight first met Marcia Lynne—now calling herself Marcheline—Bertrand in the spring of 1971 after an agent at William Morris proudly showed him a picture of his girlfriend, an in-demand model who had recently snagged a part in the TV drama *Ironside*. The agent made a big mistake. Jon liked the look of Marcheline and called her up out of the blue, subsequently inviting her for tea at the five-star Beverly Hills Hotel. Over strawberries, scones, and small talk, the thirty-two-year-old actor blurted out that he wanted to have two children with the young woman about to celebrate her twenty-first birthday. "The words just came out of my mouth," he later explained. "But she didn't blink, and neither did I."

Their second date, a week later, was hardly the stuff of romance, but it was critical in terms of Voight's conflicted career. As he later recalled, "I said, 'Marcheline, I'm reading this script tonight. You wanna come over and I'll read it out loud?' She said: 'I'd love to.' So I read through the rape scene and she didn't blink. I kept reading to the end and she said: 'Oh, it's a fantastic story! You should do this.'"

While Voight's recollection is that he called Boorman the following day to accept the role, Boorman tells a slightly different version of that phone call. Boorman says he telephoned Voight to report that he had snagged Burt Reynolds, Ned Beatty, and Ronny Cox for the picture. After an hour on the phone wooing the still-reluctant Voight, Boorman said that if he didn't decide in thirty seconds he was going to hang up. He did, and his brinkmanship worked. Voight called straight back and accepted the part.

Significantly, at a pivotal time in his life, Voight credited Marcheline, the cool, willowy beauty with the languid eyes and soothing manner, with settling his nerves and giving him the courage to take on a challenging masculine drama. This snapshot of a sweet, nurturing helpmate was one he now held dear, insisting that Marcheline join him on the set in Clayton, Georgia. That he was living with another woman, Jennifer Salt, when they first met did not seem to trouble Marcheline unduly. She could be quietly fierce, however, when the tables were turned, having learned the Bertrand freeze from her mother in full measure. When she discovered, for example, that her teenage boyfriend had had a one-night stand with one of her girlfriends, he was history. Even thirty years later, the girl's name could not be mentioned in her presence. She never forgot, nor could she ever forgive.

On the set, she swatted aside the amorous attentions of Burt Reynolds as easily as she did the Georgia midges. Indeed, Reynolds's increasing irritation with Jon Voight's uncertainty, his desire to analyze every gesture, grunt, and groan in a scene, may have stemmed more from thwarted romantic desire than from the daily acting duel.

As filming progressed in the treacherous rapids of the Chattooga River, Voight became more assured and confident. "He is the real thing: intelligent and intensely intuitive, skillful, yet with that mysterious something that great actors have, the ability to transcend acting, the ability to *become*," observes Boorman. The film, remembered as much for the dueling banjos refrain and the powerful male rape scene as for the themes of man at odds with nature, resurrected Voight's talent. It was his artistic deliverance. As Boorman recalls, "He says I saved his life by persuading him to do the picture, then did my best to kill him while making it."

Meanwhile, Marcheline was wrestling with her own romantic deliverance. At the time, she was in love with two men: Jon Voight and his friend Al Pacino. So when Jon asked her to marry him, she had to look deep into her heart. Shy and self-effacing, Pacino was not the type to try to steal a friend's girlfriend, particularly as Voight had been so generous with money for his theater group. It is a sign of how deeply he had fallen for Marcheline that Pacino pleaded with her not to marry Voight unless she was sure. As she struggled with her emotions, the decisive voice was that of her mother, Lois, who encouraged her to marry the Oscar-nominated Jon, who was then much more successful than his rival. Marcheline followed her mother's wishes and chose Jon Voight. But in her heart, Pacino would remain the great unrequited love of her life.

Jon and Marcheline married just before Christmas, on December 12, at Jon's home on Hanover Street in Brentwood, Los Angeles, which he was renting from TV director John Newland. John Boorman's son Charley, who played Voight's son in the movie, was ring bearer. Unlike the wedding of Marcheline's parents, this was a modest affair, with only fifty guests in attendance. As he was marrying for the second time, Voight would not have been able to marry in a Catholic church even if he had wished to do so. In keeping with the relaxed, informal vibe, Marcheline, who was increasingly known as Marche (pronounced Marcia), made her wedding dress from one of her shawls, Elton John's "Your Song" played, and the couple took their vows in the presence of Superior Court judge Marvin Freeman. Karen Ziff, an assistant TV producer, was one of the witnesses.

Amid the confetti of congratulations, their age difference, their short courtship, Marcheline's inner turmoil, and her husband's easy sexual magnetism were all forgotten. The Bertrands were living the American dream, rubbing shoulders with Hollywood royalty. Certainly it was a fairy tale come to life for Marche's mother, the fantasies she contemplated as she combed her hair in front of the mirror all those years ago becoming a glamorous reality. Any doubts Marche might have had about the match she kept to herself. As a close friend of hers commented later, "Her family all believed in the fairy tale and pushed their daughter into a marriage she didn't really want in her heart."

A couple of years later, one of Marche's friends was in turmoil about her own wedding plans. She wanted to marry hippie style, in bare feet with flowers in her hair in the local park. Her mother-in-law craved a church wedding. Marche's advice was clear and to the point. "You don't marry for yourself but your family," she told her friend.

TWO

This has been my burden for thirty-three years. I saw what happened to Angelina Jolie, and it haunts me to this day.

—KRISANN MOREL

After their wedding, the Voights moved into a one-bedroom apartment on the second floor of a modest six-story building fringed by palm trees at 468 South Roxbury Drive, overlooking Roxbury Park, one of the few public spaces in Beverly Hills. While the casual observer would be impressed by the Beverly Hills address, it was, as far as locals were concerned, on the wrong side of the tracks, the tracks meaning anything south of Olympic Boulevard. Hollywood movie stars are thin on the ground in what is jocularly known as the "Slums of Beverly Hills."

Marcheline soon discovered that she was pregnant. They planned to call the baby Haven, but sadly she suffered a miscarriage. As much as they both wanted children, it clearly wasn't time to start a family.

The apartment had a den and a small galley kitchen, which was fine as neither of them cooked. Occasionally Marche would buy a bottle of red wine and throw a steak on the grill, but that was about the extent of her culinary expertise. Apart from a wooden hutch containing a few knick-knacks and a photo montage of Marche in various modeling poses—head shots, in a long dress, in a bikini—the apartment was bare and spare. As one early visitor recalls, "When I opened the door I was struck by the simplicity of the way they lived. In a way it was comforting to know that a big movie star lived like this." The only sense of abundance was in the closet that ran the length of the hallway. It was filled with Marche's clothes, many with the tags from Bonwit Teller, her favorite Beverly Hills department store, still attached. "She was the kind of person who if she liked one thing would buy it in every color," recalls a friend. "She was very generous and gave me lots of hand-me-downs."

In a kitchen cupboard was Marche's guilty secret, a stack of tabloid magazines she kept hidden from her husband. Like her mother, she loved to read about the lives of the rich and famous. It gave her an illicit thrill, a glimpse into a world that continued to elude her. For while the William Morris Agency could get her modeling assignments, acting work was hard to come by, Marche still a regular at the Lee Strasberg studio run by his wife, Anna. If he had ever discovered her secret fascination with the stars, Jon would have been baffled. It was not part of his psyche. While he basked in acting glory and success, he, like Dustin Hoffman and others of his era, was indifferent to fame. He rarely gave interviews, nor was he interested in personal publicity. As an artist he wanted to do good work, to express himself onstage or on camera.

In July 1972, a few weeks after the Watergate break-in that would eventually lead to the resignation of President Richard Nixon, *Deliverance* was released. It was make-or-break not only for the director but also for his star actor. The omens did not look good. When he screened a first cut for Voight and other members of the cast in Beverly Hills, Boorman recalls, the movie was met with "utter silence and people hurrying out, avoiding my eye." The studio complained that there had never been a hit movie in the history of Hollywood without a woman in it.

They need not have worried. The movie captured the popular imagination, both commercially and culturally—to the extent that tragically thirty-one people died the following year while trying to paddle the same stretch of the Chattooga River portrayed in the movie. Not only did the film go on to be nominated for Academy Awards for Best Picture, Best Director, and Best Film Editing, it marked the rebirth of Voight's career; and symbolically, a few weeks after the film's release, Marche discovered she was pregnant once more.

Deliverance transformed Voight from a one-hit wonder to a genuine Hollywood heavyweight. He could be a contender. It was perhaps ironic that he and his friend Al Pacino were up against Marlon Brando for a

Golden Globe that year. Voight remained on the canvas; at the awards ceremony in January 1973 it was Brando who walked away with the prize for his role in *The Godfather*.

Brando's shadow loomed large that year. To celebrate the twenty-fifth anniversary of Tennessee Williams's sultry melodrama *A Streetcar Named Desire*, Jon Voight was asked to take on the role of Stanley Kowalski, the part made famous by the young Brando. It was not a successful revival. With Faye Dunaway as Blanche, the play, staged in April 1973 at the Ahmanson Theatre in Los Angeles, opened to lukewarm reviews. Critics felt that Voight underplayed the role in an attempt to offer a "non-Brando" interpretation. "He even throws dishes politely," noted *New York Times* critic Stephen Farber.

Voight had every right to be distracted. Both his sister-in-law Debbie and Marche were expecting. Jon even designed and drew a baby shower invitation for the sisters. On May 11, two days after her twenty-third birthday, Marche gave birth to their first child, a boy they named James Haven Voight. Taking a leaf out of her mother's manual for parental ambition, she deliberately gave her son a middle name that could be used for his future stage or film career. Life was repeating itself; just as her mother had lived through her daughter, so Marcheline planned, from the moment her child was born, to live through him.

The couple's joy was short-lived. Just a few weeks after James's birth, Jon's father, Elmer Voight, was killed in a traffic accident. At least the family had the consolation of knowing that Elmer had seen his grandson before he died. As Jon and his mother and two brothers mourned their loss, Jon reflected that his sixty-three-year-old father had lived long enough to watch his children mature—and succeed. That year Jon's brother Chip, whose song "Angel of the Morning" became an instant standard, released what *Rolling Stone* magazine described as one of the best country albums of the year.

At the time of his father's death, Jon was filming *Conrack,* based on Pat Conroy's book about his experiences as an idealistic young teacher instructing a class of semiliterate black children on St. Simons Island in Georgia. The project was very dear to his heart, not only because of the powerful themes of racism, poverty, and civil rights, but also as a tribute to his adored father. As the *New York Times* critic astutely observed, "His performance has a conviction that suggests that the theme of the movie matters a great deal to him." (In typical fashion, Voight treated the youngsters like members of his extended family, organizing several reunions in the coming years.)

During a break in the filming, he and Marche went for a drive in the countryside. They ended up following a church bus with the words "Shiloh Baptist" painted on the back. Jon suggested that Shiloh would be a good name for their next child. In fact, he wanted to go whole hog and call their second baby Shiloh Baptist. Marche demurred, saying that the name was too Hebrew. In time she would reconsider her view, though not for her own children.

Only months later, on November 1, the couple suffered another grievous loss when Marche's mother, Lois Bertrand, died of cancer. She was only forty-five. Her daughter, nursing six-month-old Jamie, was devastated. "She grieved hard and she grieved long," recalls a girlfriend. "Marche idolized her mother." As she mourned, she fondly remembered the fairy tales her mother had read to her at night, the advice she dispensed when Marche was a teenager. On the day of the funeral at St. Mary's Catholic Church in Riverdale, where Lois and Rolland were married, Jon was in Buffalo, on tour with *A Streetcar Named Desire*. In true showbiz style, he hired a private plane to take him from upstate New York to Chicago for the service. A limousine waited discreetly nearby to whisk him back to O'Hare airport so he could perform that night. The family was impressed by his modesty and concern. "As a big movie star we didn't know what to expect," recalls Lois's aunt, Esther Kasha, now ninety-three. "But he was really down-to-earth."

As a lasting memorial to Lois, the couple donated an altar cross to the church. It was a generous but somewhat ironic gesture: While Marche was very much a practicing Catholic, Jon had all but renounced his faith and was embarking on a lifelong search to find a god or gods who spoke to him. Describing himself as "totally nondenominational," he said around that time: "I don't know what the hell I am, but I'm on my way to finding out." It was to be a journey of some pain and loneliness. As his friend Dustin Hoffman noted: "Jon is a strict lapsed Catholic boy who has to pay for his sins in guilt."

He had little time for reflection, taking Marche and baby James to Munich, Germany, and to Austria to film *The Odessa File,* the movie version of Frederick Forsyth's thriller about a journalist who infiltrates a sinister group of former Nazis. He played opposite Maximilian Schell, who invited him to star in a film he planned to direct, *The End of the Game,* a sophisticated thriller about the cat-and-mouse game between a cop and a crook. Once again his family came along for the filming, which took place in Bern, Switzerland, in the summer of 1974 and featured English actor Robert Shaw, Jacqueline Bisset, and Donald Sutherland. Marcheline shocked the English contingent by breast-feeding James, now a toddler, in public. "We thought Marche was lovely—just an eccentric, a real hippie," noted a more European member of the acting fraternity.

Marcheline became friendly with Jacqueline Bisset and Maximilian Schell, enjoying the company of a celebrated troupe of actors, magazine images made flesh. Her father, Rolland, came along, too, not only for company after the loss of his wife but also to visit some of the battlefields he had seen during the Second World War. During the trip he met and fell for Elke, a German barmaid. After a whirlwind courtship, Elke, down-to-earth, hardworking, and frugal, became the second Mrs. Bertrand, moving into the Bertrand home in Trousdale with her teenage daughter, Gabriella. Rollie's older daughter did not approve, feeling that it was far too soon after her mother's death. As a consequence there was always friction between Marche and her stepmother, a coolness that time did not diminish. A sign of their strained relations was that when Marche organized parties for her friends and acquaintances she told—rather than asked—her father and stepmother that their home was the chosen venue.

In spite of these familial undercurrents, this was probably the happiest time in Jon and Marcheline's marriage. Not only was Jon productive, artistically and commercially, but Marche was pregnant again that fall. To their friends and family they seemed like a couple utterly devoted to each other. "They were very loving and tender," recalls Krisann Morel, who babysat regularly for James. "He was the total gentleman, always polite, opening doors for her, making sure she was comfortable. It was sweet to see."

Krisann was equally enchanted by their eighteen-month-old son, Jamie. "He was adorable," she recalls. "Supersmart, sensitive, and loving. Just a wonderful child." With some of the money Jon was now earning, Marche bought herself a Mercedes 450SL sports car with her son's name as the license plate: JHAVEN.

During Marche's pregnancy, they hired an out-of-work actress to cook for them, asking her to make "back East" food for the Yonkers-born Voight, who was missing his New York life. Meatballs, spaghetti, and veal cutlets were now all on the menu at apartment 206. "Marche looked so beautiful; we were enchanted by her," recalls their part-time cook, now an established character actress. "They were beyond in love, but maybe I was oblivious to what was going on."

That Christmas Jon headed back to the Big Apple, not only to see his family but also to coproduce a Broadway play, *The Hashish Club,* the story of five men on a drug trip written by Lance Larsen, which lasted for only eleven performances at the Bijou Theatre. The play was about as far away from regular Hollywood fare as could be imagined, but Voight had the ability to straddle the fringe and the mainstream.

At the Academy Awards in April 1975 he and the buxom Raquel Welch enjoyed a back-and-forth about peaks and valleys, Voight deliberately leering at her embonpoint before handing over the Oscar for Best Cinematography to the makers of *The Towering Inferno.* For Marcheline, not yet twenty-five and heavily pregnant, meeting an endless array of movie stars made it a night to remember. The high point for both of them was their conversation with Hollywood legend Fred Astaire, who was nominated for his supporting role in *The Towering Inferno.* When they returned to their modest apartment, Marcheline was glowing with the excitement of the evening. "She was thrilled to be mixing in this company," recalls Krisann, who babysat for James that night. "This girl from Illinois was simply starstruck— and who can blame her? It was so cute and sweet. She was in seventh heaven."

That same month the couple enjoyed another happy event when Jon was best man and Marche maid of honor at the wedding of their good friends Carlo and Lauren Stogel at the Beverly Hills Hotel. "During the ceremony they were looking at each other like they were renewing their vows," recalls Lauren, who first met Jon and Marche the previous Christmas, an encounter that Marche later said was "destined." What turned out to be an intimate thirty-year friendship came about thanks to Carlo's father, Syd Stogel, a producer for Columbia Pictures, who had taken a shine to Jon during the filming of *The Odessa File* in Munich. His wife, Angelina, adored Marche and baby James. When the Voight family later visited Rome, his son Carlo showed them around the city. They got on so well that Jon and Carlo discussed starting a film production company when Lauren and Carlo decided to move to Beverly Hills to start a new life.

On June 4, 1975, Marche and Jon celebrated the latest little star to join the family when Marche gave birth to a baby girl at the Cedars-Sinai hospital in Beverly Hills. They named her Angelina after Marche's Quebec-born grandmother, Marie-Louise Angelina, and Angelina Stogel. A further omen was the fact that Marche's favorite band, the Rolling Stones, had recently had a huge number-one hit, "Angie," which meant an awful lot to her. Along with Angelina, Marche gave her daughter the middle name of Jolie so that, like her brother, she could drop her surname when she went into show business.

As a Gemini, the child was destined to have a dual personality, the forces of good and evil, darkness and light, male and female, wrestling in her psyche. She would be at once adaptable, versatile, witty, and intellectual and nervous, tense, cunning, and inconsistent. Those who came to know her in the coming years would repeatedly attest to the fact that she was a true Gemini. In Jon's eyes she was perfect. He saw Krisann a couple of days after Angelina's birth and waxed lyrical about his "blue-eyed, beautiful daughter."

Years later, in a radio interview during which Angelina was in a different studio in another city, her father spoke movingly of the special moment when he first met her. "The last public conversation we had was when you were born. You don't remember it, but when you emerged from your mother's womb, I picked you up, held you in my hand, and looked at your face. You had your finger by the side of your cheek and you looked very, very wise, like my best old friend. I started to tell you how your mom and I were so happy to finally have you there and that we were going to take great care of you and watch for all those signs of who you were and how we could help you achieve all that wonderful potential God gave you. Your mom and I made that pledge, and everyone in the room started crying. But we [Jon and Angelina] weren't crying. We were enraptured in each other's gaze."

Even though Jon was no longer a true believer, Angelina was christened a couple of months later, with Maximilian Schell and Jacqueline Bisset, who had met the couple during the filming of *The End of the Game,* serving as godparents.

That fall Jon was invited by the theater department at the University of California in Northridge, north of Los Angeles, to be artist in residence for a semester and take the lead role in Shakespeare's *Hamlet*. The prospect appealed to him: Not only is *Hamlet* a rite of passage for any serious actor, but the production would also combine the talents of students and professionals. With his own father's death still fresh—he and his two brothers scaled a Montana peak to install a plaque in Elmer's memory—he saw the play as a way of exploring the father-son relationship.

He opened an office on campus and began recruiting his friends and colleagues, sending notes that began: "Do some Shakespeare, man; it will clear your head." The young off-Broadway producer Jon Avnet, who later went to produce Tom Cruise's breakout film, *Risky Business,* was brought in as the money man; Jerome Guardino, who directed Voight in *A Streetcar Named Desire* in Buffalo, agreed to direct; while Lance Larsen, Jon's close friend who appeared in *The Hashish Club,* was cast in the role of Horatio. His *Deliverance* costar Ned Beatty also agreed to take part but later dropped out. The cover of the program featured a sketch of Voight by the noted portrait artist Don Bachardy, lifelong lover of English novelist Christopher Isherwood.

As Jon began casting, the campus was abuzz with excitement. Such was the clamor among female students to appear onstage with a bona fide Hollywood heartthrob that more than twenty girls went out for the role of Hamlet's doomed lover, Ophelia. They all auditioned, but not one seemed to work in the part. As a standby Jon penciled in Lory Kochheim, who went on to appear in numerous TV shows, including *Mulligan's Stew.* Somewhat incongruously, while Voight was learning his lines, he would have baby Angie with him. Cast member Jeff Austin found himself dandling the six-month-old infant on his knee on several occasions during the production. At the same time, Jon was frequently on the telephone to John Boorman, who wanted him to star in his next movie, *Exorcist II: The Heretic.* After endless back-and-forth, Voight turned down the *Deliverance* director. Instead the role was played by Richard Burton.

Meanwhile, Jon went to see another play on campus, *Lysistrata,* a lewd and raunchy battle of the sexes by ancient Greek playwright Aristophanes, directed by the theater veteran Vincent Dowling. The plot concerns the decision by the women of Athens to withhold sexual favors until the men end the war they are fighting. When the men agree to their partners' demands, the figure of "Reconciliation" appears onstage. In Dowling's production the role was played by a beautiful student named Stacey Pickren, who walked onstage in a "nude-look" costume with a mass of flaming red hair. Voight was mesmerized, utterly entranced by the vision before him. "That is the woman I am going to spend the rest of my life with," muttered the thirty-seven-year-old actor, a comment that signaled the death knell of his four-year marriage. It was almost a carbon copy of the romantic impulsiveness that characterized his courtship with his wife.

Within a matter of days, theater student Stacey Pickren, who had not even auditioned for Voight's *Hamlet,* was cast in the role of Ophelia—much to the chagrin of Lory Kochheim, who was considered by her peers to be a much better actress. "The dynamic between Lory and Stacey was not good," recalls Jeff Austin, now an established actor. "Stacey felt threatened by her."

Jon and Stacey embarked on a wild and passionate affair that very soon became the talk of campus, with Stacey painted as an exotic and highly sexual young woman. It was later reported that Stacey, the daughter of a wealthy doctor, was a member of the Children of God sect, a free-love movement that practiced what the founder, David Berg, called "Flirty Fishing," in which female members were encouraged to show God's love by engaging in sexual activity with potential converts. Jon had reportedly shown his devotion to his new lover by wearing a "yoke" necklace designed and sold by the cult. "It was the Scandal of Northridge," recalls a member of the faculty. In time the lurid gossip ended up in print. For example, in his biography of Angelina Jolie, Brandon Hurst stated that when Marche was pregnant with Angelina, she came downstairs in their apartment and saw Jon kissing Stacey. She went upstairs, according to Hurst, "and began shaking with shock and, as she thought she would have a miscarriage, called an ambulance." Actually, the apartment was only on one floor, but the story stuck.

In fact, it was months after Angie was born that Jon first met Stacey, and certainly when Marcheline and their friends went to see the play in March 1976, she never suspected that the woman onstage was her husband's lover. One day he announced that he was going to tour with *Hamlet* and that Stacey Pickren was coming along. "Oh, are you having an affair with her?" Marche asked him innocently. It was said almost as a joke. After all, they were trying for their third child and had even gone away recently for a romantic weekend when his mother, Barbara, came to babysit. Everything seemed just peachy in their world, Al Pacino now a distant memory, a moment that had passed. "She hadn't a clue what was going on; not a clue," recalls her best friend, Lauren Taines, formerly Stogel.

It would have been easy for Jon to lie and make light of the matter. At that time he had absolutely no intention of leaving Marche and the children and making a life with Stacey. She was a wild and secret fling, who had taught him as much, if not more, as he had taught her. Instead, consumed by a mixture of Catholic guilt and natural honesty, he said yes. It was probably the worst decision he ever made, changing not only his life but also the lives of his children forever.

At that moment Marche's world fell apart. As much as she loved Jon, in her eyes infidelity was unforgivable. They went for marriage counseling, but it did little to salve the hurt; indeed, Marche felt angry that the therapist seemed to be siding with her husband because he was a movie star. Even though they were still sleeping together and went away for another romantic weekend to try to rekindle their love, it was a losing proposition. In time Marche closed the door to her heart and gave Jon the "Bertrand freeze," placing him in cold storage for life. As an intimate of the couple observed: "She learned the freeze from her mother. It is permanent. There is no recourse. It will hurt you in places you never knew could hurt. This is at the very heart of her tragedy, like nothing else."

While Jon was repentant, he was now unforgiven. As he wrestled with a domestic situation that had spiraled out of control, Stacey was the entrée to a life he could not resist: drugs and imaginative sex. He moved out of the apartment on Roxbury Drive and rented a place with Stacey, leaving behind a scene of emotional devastation. "Marche was so distraught about the breakup," recalls Krisann Morel, who became more a counselor than a babysitter. "Jon was the absolute love of her life. Every morning she would pour her heart out. 'What am I going to do, what am I going to do?' Marche would say. She was baffled, absolutely *tormented,* by his affair. She couldn't get her head around why he would leave her for another woman."

While Jon admits that the rift between them was "very severe," in the beginning they were civil to each other, a part of Marche hoping that he would return to his family and that she would awaken from what seemed like a bad dream. For a time Jon treated his estranged wife almost like a mother confessor, revealing intimate details of his relationship with Stacey. He was almost too honest about his new life, telling Marche about his drug use and bedroom antics. Krisann recalls: "She would say things like, 'They go to the bathroom in front of each other!' She was horrified. I told her that if she wanted to win Jon back, she was going to have to step up her sexual game. She was very straitlaced and conventional when it came to sex. At that time, Jon was a very sexy man. He walked into a room and he turned heads.

"I can tell you that Angie does not get her sexuality from her mother, that's for damn sure. It comes from her father. Marche was graceful, sweet, and kind, but she became a bitter, scorned woman and she never let that anger out of her heart. She never moved on when she lost her role as Mrs. Jon Voight, and made sure she clung to that fame for as long as possible. Don't get me wrong—I loved and adored Marche. But she never let go of her anger. Jon took away her fairy tale, and she felt bereft. I felt sorry for her."

After he moved out, Jon rented an apartment on the fifth floor of the same building on Roxbury where he had lived with Marcheline. It was a white, unfurnished room that he planned to use as a business address to which his mail, film scripts, and other work-related materials could be delivered.

Shortly afterward, Marche had Angie's white crib taken to Jon's fifth-floor apartment. This was the "Ivory Tower" where Angie lived for more than a year, with a random assortment of babysitters looking after her twenty-four hours a day. Marche's brother, Raleigh, would often recruit out-of-work actors or acquaintances to work in shifts at three dollars an hour.

Meanwhile, Angie's older brother, Jamie, stayed with his mother on the second floor. For a long time Jamie and Angie remained apart, except for occasional outings together to Roxbury Park. Randy Alpert, a friend of Marche's brother Raleigh, helped out for a time, making both Angie and James breakfast and taking them to the park. "I loved working for them," he recalls. "Marche was so gorgeous and sweet and kind. Truly an angel."

When I interviewed Krisann Morel for this book, she painted a rather different portrait of the household. Two years younger than Marche and a part-time model herself, at first she was confident, in control, chatting amiably about her days working at the Rainbow Bar and Grill on Sunset, remembering the night John Lennon was thrown out by overenthusiastic bouncers.

Nestled deep in her story lay a dark secret she had struggled to keep for more than half a lifetime. Now was time for confession. First, though, she wanted to set the scene. So she talked about Jon Voight; his blooming wife, Marche; the birth of Angie.

Her voice, so strong and firm, began to crack as, in her mind's eye, she journeyed back in time to what she called the Ivory Tower, the white room with the white carpet, the white doors, the white drapes, the white walls, and the white crib. And the baby girl, helpless and alone.

Remembering those days, Krisann twisted her wedding ring, and her face contorted in an effort to suppress the welling emotion. "This has been my burden for thirty-three years. I saw what happened to Angelina Jolie, and it haunts me to this day. As much as I wanted to help, I couldn't fix the hurt. I loved Marche, and I think she really loved her daughter, but the truth is the truth.

"Marche took her pain out on that child. She separated herself from that child because she looked a lot like Jon. She was fair like him and had his eyes."

Not surprisingly, Angie was very different from her brother, who enjoyed a close relationship with his mother. She learned to talk late, never crawled but walked at ten months, did not play with dolls or stuffed animals, and was rather aloof. "She now says that she doesn't like to be hugged. I can understand why," says Krisann. "You could hold her, but I could feel her pain. I was not the mother holding her. Angie had happy moments, but for the first two years of her life she was not a happy child. I hate to say it, but it's the truth. I can understand if Angie has abandonment issues, because she was abandoned as a child. Even she doesn't know why."

Certainly the way Angie was raised in the early months of her life raises red flags among clinical psychologists and psychoanalysts. The key to understanding this issue is the fact that babies are born without the capacity to differentiate or articulate their feelings and needs. They are in what is termed a "global undifferentiated state," their emotions, if not met, lurching from anxiety to panic and finally disassociation. It is the attention and response of the mother or other consistent caregiver that allows infants to develop basic trust, the capacity to regulate their emotional state. In short, a mother turns distress into comfort.

Babies who do not get this kind of response often develop self-destructive coping mechanisms for the intolerable emotion they feel. This means that a child who has not had a relationship with a mother or an adequate substitute remains in a global undifferentiated state, living without the words, ideas, or capacity to relate to his or her own experience. In later life this angst can be manifested in alcoholism, drug abuse, cutting, and suicidal tendencies.

As contemporary psychoanalyst Dr. Franziska De George, who has practiced in Beverly Hills for nearly twenty years and never treated Angelina or her family, says: "The child whose mother abandons them at six months not only has severe trauma, but beyond that the child is lacking a relationship with itself. The basic emotional building blocks are missing. It is a house, or personality, built on shifting sands. While the rest of the house may be working beautifully, the emotional part is missing. In later life this is even more confusing."

Marche's own depression and trauma would have communicated themselves to her daughter, further exacerbating the infant's feelings of alienation. Psychologist and author Iris Martin, who has specialized in working with chief executives and their families for the last twenty-five years but also never treated Angelina or her family, observes: "Angelina Jolie will have experienced profound abandonment, anxiety, and may have experienced depression. Early experience is based on two things: structure and trust. So her early attachment was fragmented, full of painful emotions. Her foundation of who she is is a mess."

At some point Marche agreed that her children could start to play with each other rather than be looked after on separate floors of the apartment building by different sets of babysitters. It was an economic as much as an emotional argument that won the day, Marche agreeing to pay her babysitters five dollars an hour to watch both children rather than hire two babysitters at three dollars each. The children played well together, and eventually James kept some of his toys, such as an electric car, in Angie's room on the fifth floor. As Iris Martin observes: "Jamie was probably a buffer for her. He comforted her. She was not getting human contact from anyone but the babysitters."

At the same time, Jamie was always the favored child, the one who was the focus of attention, the one expected to succeed in life. He was the monarch of the family, as the beautifully hand-drawn and hand-painted fourth birthday card saying "King James" showed. For that same birthday, Krisann embroidered a number four on his denim dungarees, while Jon's friend film director Charles Eastman came over to take pictures. Eastman later recalled that Angie was "kind of in the background that day. All eyes were on her brother." Angie's birthdays were much more low-key affairs.

Marche's anger and depression manifested itself not only in her distracted behavior toward her daughter, but also in the frenzied way she lived her life. Outwardly all smiles, generous and loving, adored by everyone, Marche, still only twenty-six, was nursing a wound so deep that nothing could really mend her broken heart. She became obsessed with her acting career, spending most days as a student at the Lee Strasberg school while a team of babysitters looked after her children. When she was not focusing on her craft, she was shopping for clothes—there was an ocean liner chest filled with unworn antique French baby clothes for Angelina—or buying expensive antiques, mainly country French style, from high-end stores in Beverly Hills.

The apartment, once so spare, was soon bursting at the seams, to the point that she held a couple of garage sales to dispose of some of her goodies. Expensive crockery and objets d'art went for bargain-basement prices. Although consumed with guilt over his behavior, Jon was infuriated with his estranged wife when he discovered that total strangers were wandering around his apartment picking and choosing mainly new and unused goods that he had paid for. Marche's stepmother, Elke, a frugal woman, was also perplexed and somewhat irritated by Marche's penchant for buying everything, even the children's underwear, from fancy stores like Saks Fifth Avenue. "She became a *huge* shopaholic," recalls Krisann. "The idea that she didn't have any money is nonsense."

Marche was naïve and rather careless about cash. Having always had money, she never felt the need to worry, especially as all the bills went straight to her husband's accountant for payment. On one occasion, for example, she signed an entire checkbook, leaving the amounts blank. It was a clear security risk, especially given the constant ebb and flow of transient babysitters, actors, and others at the apartment.

As in most separations, money soon became an issue. While Jon was concerned about Marche's outlays for babysitters, clothes, and furniture, Marche's blood boiled if she sensed that he was spending money on his mistress. On at least one occasion she was driven to fury when she saw a credit-card statement containing details about clothes from a store she did not frequent. "Look. He's out buying clothes for that tramp, his whore," she proclaimed.

Yet far from walking out on his wife and children and never returning, Jon Voight spent as much time as he could with Jamie and Angie. He was a constant presence at the apartment building, even taking Marche house-hunting, though she found nothing that suited her. It was a time of anguish, passion, and soul-searching. He alluded to that period in a later interview: " 'Free love'—what a poison that was. Free love, the destruction of family life and loyalties and the responsibilities of parents, and I've gone through that." In his defense he argues that in the morality of the times, what he did was not "so unusual or pernicious."

As much as he now rejected his Catholic faith, he could never escape the nostrums and beliefs stamped on his soul since childhood. When he visited the children, the struggle between the primal, lusty lover and the caring father was transparent. "Here is Jon Voight having a roll in the hay like he's never had before," recalls Krisann. "He has that exuberance you have when you are enjoying wonderful sex. And then he plays the role of dad. And quite honestly, I never saw any father who loved and cared for his children as he did. When he was not working, he came over all the time, if only for an hour." He regularly took the children to the park to play ball, and on several occasions Krisann was mistaken for his wife. As a change from Roxbury Park, Krisann would suggest that they all go "topless in Miranda," her nickname for her convertible sports car, and she, Jon, James, and Angie would head off to Venice Beach. (It suited Krisann, as she loved watching the bodybuilders work out in the open-air gym.) During one parental visit James and Angie performed their first "show." They were blacked up by Krisann and learned the words and gestures to the song "Mammy." Then Angie, two, and James, four, peformed their routine for their somewhat bemused father. "James was into it, Angie a bit confused," recalls Krisann.

While Jon got into debt—and therapy—in time Marche began to get her own love life back on track. She and several other recently separated or divorced women were members of an informal "First Wives' Club" of Beverly Hills, meeting over lunch or dinner. She and fellow acting student Jade Dixon regularly went out on the town, joining another acting student, Barbi Benton, then the lover of *Playboy* publisher Hugh Hefner, at the Playboy mansion. "We double-dated and shared all the secrets best friends share," recalls Jade.

As the estranged wife of aspiring Hollywood royalty—as well as a beauty in her own right—it was not long before Marche was being courted by any number of suitors. She enjoyed a flirtation early on with a then-unknown muscleman, Austrian bodybuilder Arnold Schwarzenegger, who was, like Marche, trying to break into Hollywood. When Marche told Jon about her encounter, he dismissed Schwarzenegger's ambitions, saying that his accent was too thick for him ever to get a speaking part in a movie.

Then there was Burt Reynolds, Voight's costar in *Deliverance,* whom she dated for a time and sent gifts to for his forty-first birthday in February 1977. He in turn sent oversize stuffed animals for James and Angie. Angie's godfather, Maximilian Schell, was another admirer who visited Marche at home, on one occasion giving Angie an expensive porcelain doll, one of her first-ever presents. Of course, no self-respecting young actress at that time could avoid an encounter with the legendary lothario Warren Beatty, who has had, according to his biographer Peter Biskind, around 12,775 lovers. Marche considered Beatty to be worthy of his reputation. One Christmas she bought him an expensive gift and had it delivered to his penthouse apartment at the Beverly Wilshire hotel.

What about Al Pacino, the man who had tried to dissuade her from marrying Jon Voight? They circled around each other for a while, Marche joining in with his weekend games of softball in a local park. "They had a mutual-admiration society," recalls Lauren Taines. The moment, though, had passed; they were both too quiet and passive to rekindle a romance. In addition, Pacino felt guilty about the prospect of dating his friend's wife. In her vivid imagination, Marcheline's dalliance with Pacino assumed a greater significance than perhaps it warranted. She would later tell her daughter that she had deliberately chosen the names of her children—Angelina and James—as anagrams or copies of Pacino's full name, Alfredo James Pacino.

It is difficult to know what to make of this story. Those who knew the Voights early in their relationship are adamant that Marche was absolutely devoted to Jon. In any case, Pacino's name is only a partial anagram of her children's names. Perhaps her assertion was a way of diminishing Jon's impact on her life, an attempt to redress the emotional balance. As a friend notes: "She had all these major players after her, and if she had gone with any of those guys, the war between her and Jon would have been over, since she would no longer have needed to rely on him for money."

A few months after the split, Marche decided that her career would be best served if she went to New York more often for auditions. She felt she had a better chance of finding work away from Jon's Hollywood shadow. Certainly there was no indication, as her daughter has since maintained, that she gave up her career for the sake of her children. Marche and an artist friend, who was on the babysitting rota, now regularly flew to the Big Apple, where Marche tried out for various roles. During one visit she met businessman Allan Mezo—sniffily described by one friend as a pots and pans salesman—in a New York nightclub. She enjoyed a short romance with the New York–based trader, and while he was never going to inspire her acting career, he helped her rebuild her self-esteem and cope with the rejection she felt from her husband. The thirty-one-year-old was a comforting shoulder for her to lean on—and to cry on. As he later told the *New York Post:* "She told me that Jon had not treated her well, and I think there were other women involved. She found it so painful, and it made it hard for her to trust another man." They met at the wrong time, Marche explaining as much in a letter she sent Mezo more than a decade later. "Perhaps I was just in too much emotional pain back then to appreciate you. The truth is, I never would have made it through that difficult time without you."

From time to time her excursions to New York coincided with Jon's work, leaving the children solely in the care of babysitters. Late at night on one of these occasions, Angie woke up screaming with a burning fever. Krisann, who was caring for her, bathed her in cool water to reduce her temperature. Frantically she tried to find Jon or Marche, but neither answered her calls. The next day Krisann took the sick toddler to a doctor in Beverly Hills. He was furious and told Krisann in no uncertain terms that he had no legal right to examine or medicate Angie without parental permission. He diagnosed an ear infection and reluctantly agreed to prescribe antibiotics. "It was a really frightening situation," recalled Krisann.

While Marche was looking for a break in New York, in the summer of 1976 Jon reprised the role of Hamlet at the Levin Theater at Rutgers University in New Jersey. The prize he really coveted, though, was a lead in a new Hal Ashby movie, *Coming Home,* about the unlikely romance between a serving soldier's wife and a paralyzed war veteran. Actor and vociferous antiwar activist Jane Fonda—known as "Hanoi Jane" following her visit to North Vietnam—was the driving force behind the movie. The idea had come to her after an inspirational meeting with wheelchair-bound Ron Kovic, whose painful memoir, *Born on the Fourth of July,* described his own injuries suffered during the Vietnam War.

While Fonda was to play the role of Sally Hyde, the frustrated wife of a U.S. Army captain serving in Vietnam, the film's producers were looking for a big-name actor like Sylvester Stallone, Al Pacino—now riding high on the success of *Serpico* and *The Godfather*—or Jack Nicholson to take on the part of the paraplegic, Luke Martin. Although Bruce Dern and Jon Voight were short-listed for the role of Sally's husband, Voight told Ashby he would much sooner have the role of Luke. Ashby was impressed with his early commitment. Not only was Voight a known antiwar campaigner, but even before he snagged the part of Luke, he started talking to vets to get a sense of their lives and experiences. This cut no ice with the producers. Ironically, given his torrid domestic life, Voight was dismissed as having "no sex appeal." Ashby stuck to his guns, and Voight took the lead role, with Bruce Dern cast as the hawkish husband. As a further sweetener, Stacey Pickren won the small part of Sophie.

Once he was cast, Voight bought himself a wheelchair, joined the Long Beach Raiders wheelchair team, and, in the fall of 1976, spent six weeks at the Rancho Los Amigos rehabilitation center in Downey, California, going home only to see his children. He immersed himself in the life of a paraplegic so completely that if one of his feet fell off the wheelchair, he would reach down and put it back on with his hands. A number of wheelchair-bound veterans came to Jon's house to join him and Hal Ashby in filmed sessions where they talked about their families, their friends, their chances of work, even their sex lives.

After the Christmas holidays, which Jon, Marche, and the children spent with her father and Elke, filming began in earnest. As much as he believed in the movie, Voight did not believe in himself. His acting nerve had gone, as it had before he agreed to make *Deliverance*. "I quit. I'm not good enough to do this part," he told Ashby. "Get Al Pacino or somebody." Like John Boorman, Ashby was able to gentle his troubled star and convince him to carry on even as he continued to fluff his lines.

From time to time family members came to watch the filming. On one occasion Jon brought his daughter along for the day. As he didn't have a portable crib, he used the drawer from a chest in his new apartment as a makeshift bed when she had her nap. While he was shooting a scene, Bruce Dern's ten-year-old daughter, Laura, acted as babysitter, in time regularly babysitting the toddler.

The set was closed, though, for the climax of Luke and Sally's romance, when they make love for the first time. While Ashby wanted to portray penetrative sex, Fonda was keen to show that their lovemaking was oral. She triumphed by the simple tactic of refusing to move her position on the bed. Ashby stormed off the set, but in the end his editing implied that Luke gave Sally orgasmic oral sex. One critic wrote that a crippled Jon Voight had "projected more potency than any other actor for quite some time." The film made such a strong case for the sensitivity and sexual prowess of "sensuous paras" that at the cast dance—attended by dozens of wheelchair-bound veterans who had served as extras—Jon said "No way" when one of the paraplegics invited Stacey for a wheelchair dance. "If you want to become a better lover," Jon noted, "you should hang around with them."

He was not the only one to have his macho hang-ups challenged. Later in the year, Ashby gathered actors and crew together to watch a rough cut. While the film was moving, most remembered the comment of Jane Fonda's husband, politician Tom Hayden. After the two-hour-and-forty-minute screening, he walked past Jon Voight and said: "Nice try." As Ashby's biographer Nick Dawson observes: "Hayden's cutting comment was possibly due to his anger at Fonda's sex scene with Voight." Her father, Henry Fonda, was even more upset, demanding that the scene be cut entirely.

The scene remained. On February 15, 1978, there were lines around the block for the movie's first New York screening, a testament to the public appetite for films that would address contemporary concerns and issues. Two days earlier, Jon and Marche Voight had formally agreed to separate, the petition duly signed and filed in Los Angeles Superior Court. The star of *Coming Home* had officially left home.

THREE

When I grow up, I'm going to be an actress. A big actress.
—ANGELINA JOLIE, SHORTLY BEFORE HER FIFTH BIRTHDAY

In the summer of 1978, Marche played a journalist in *Borderline,* a student film by UCLA graduate Ramon Menendez. He brought in his friend Bill Day to help with the lighting on the set in an apartment building in Hancock Park. As Bill adjusted the lights, he looked down and saw Marche discussing her role. "She was beautiful and sensuous and a total ten," he recalls. "I couldn't keep my eyes off her." The feeling was mutual. During a break in the filming, Marche invited the twenty-six-year-old student to her home to take pictures of the children. At least that was the excuse.

A few weeks later, Bill drove over to Roxbury Park on his Honda 450cc motorcycle—and fell headlong into the emotional vortex that was the unresolved relationship between Marche and Jon. When Marche introduced him to the children, James was wary of the interloper, while Angie was, as Bill recalls, a "bundle of exuberance and joy. One big pair of happy lips on a small body." Marche's actress friend Jade Dixon was also around to give Bill the once-over.

Suddenly Marche announced that Jon was coming to pick up the children. As Jon drew close, Angie started jumping up and down and clapping her hands. Instead of yelling "Daddy," she shouted, "Bill's here, Bill's here." Jon was not amused, saying, "Oh yeah? What's so great about Bill?" That first uncomfortable meeting in the park gave Bill a glimpse into the marital dynamics between Marche and Jon. "Marcheline suddenly became really cold. It was like another person. There was a bad blood in the water . . . real bad blood."

First Jon took Angie to the swings while James stayed with his mother. Then Jon tried to take Angie to his car so that she could spend the afternoon with him. Her squeals of glee quickly turned to tears, and Marcheline eventually convinced Jon to leave without the children. Clearly angry, he went without saying goodbye. It was a scenario that served as a template for the tumult between estranged husband and wife that would play out in front of their children again and again.

The romance between Marche and Bill blossomed, the film student occasionally staying over at her home. Her choice of boyfriend provoked different reactions inside the family. Even though he was now living with Stacey and squiring her around town, it was clear that Jon still carried a torch for Marche. The fact that Bill was a penniless student—rather than a big Hollywood swinging dick—gave him power and hope. Jon's mother, Barbara, and Marche's father, Rolland, were of different minds. Their message to Bill, roughly translated, was "Keep your hands off our girl." Marche's father would berate her in front of Bill as if he weren't there, telling Marche that Bill was only using her for his own ambitions. If she wasn't careful, she would lose her looks and Jon would never take her back. In their eyes Stacey and Bill did not exist; the only dynamic that mattered was the poisoned relationship between Jon and Marche.

In spite of parental disapproval—in time Rollie did come to respect and admire Bill—the film student found himself invited to stay with Marche and the children in the Roxbury apartment. By the fall of 1978 Angie's exile on the fifth floor was seemingly over. She shared the bedroom on the second floor with her older brother, while Bill and Marche spent their nights in the den.

Even though the grandparents—and Jon—might have not been happy when Bill moved in, the children felt comfortable with the new status quo. Angie started calling him "Daddy," which made Marche giggle. Bill was not so happy, thinking that if the redoubtable Barbara Voight ever heard Angie speak to him like this, she might hire a hit man to dispatch the interloper. Instead he suggested she call him "Daddy-O," and for a long time she addressed birthday and Christmas cards to "Daddy-O." On the other hand, James always called him Bill, endlessly amused by his full name, Bill Day.

His new role as Daddy-O did have its mishaps. When they went shopping at Ralphs on Olympic Boulevard, Bill and the children would wait outside while Marche quickly bought the week's groceries. To keep the children entertained, Bill devised a game called "Runaway Shopping Cart," where he would put the children in the cart, let it run down a steep ramp, and catch it just before it hit a wall. Angie and James loved the game, yelling with excitement as the cart hurtled toward the concrete wall. On one occasion Marche came out of the supermarket to see her children speeding down the path with, it seemed to her, no Bill in sight. She started to scream, which distracted Bill, who then lost control of the cart. The runaway trolley hit the concrete wall at full tilt, flipping over on top of the terrified children. They were uninjured, but that was the end of the game.

It was not Marche but the Beverly Hills cops who put an end to another childhood thrill. A regular after-dinner treat was Bill taking the children for a spin on his motorbike. Angie and James would take turns perching on the gas tank while he roared along Olympic Boulevard. One evening Bill and a helmetless three-year-old Angie were pulled over by a squad car. The uniformed police were so angry at his reckless behavior that he thought they were going to beat him up. After giving him a stern lecture, they followed him home—and then yelled at Marcheline, accusing her of being a bad mother.

Although the children called their mother "Marche Mallow" (she called Angie "Bunny," while Jon called his daughter "Jelly Bean"), there was nothing soft and squishy about her. She was a matriarch like her mother, Lois, and while she would defer to Bill—and Jon—on creative or business matters, she ran the household her way. She had few, if any, boundaries for the children, but that was the way she wanted it. Woe betide Bill if he tried to impose a little discipline on the daily routine—such as getting the kids out of bed and to day care on time. It led to numerous power struggles, and as often as not Bill ended up sleeping on a couch in the office they had rented in the seedy Palmer Building on Hollywood Boulevard. They decided to rent the $125-a-month office in the fall of 1978 after Marche consulted Warren Beatty about advancing her acting career. Not only did she want to fulfill her creative ambitions, but she also wanted financial independence from her estranged husband. Beatty agreed that she needed a professional show reel, and chipped in some cash for the office and for film equipment. The editor was Bill, who agreed to cut and splice Ramon Menendez's film *Borderline* into a demo. (The finished reel can be viewed at http://www.youtube.com/user/marchelinebertrand.)

It was a slow process; the equipment was primitive, and Bill had his student papers to research and write. It was, though, a "blissful" time in their relationship. "She was a very, very generous person," he recalls. "She would buy me clothes and wrap them up as gifts, made sure I was well fed and even made me a lunch bag—covered in sexual poetry—for when I went to the office." He took the children to kindergarten in the morning and either Jon or Marche picked them up in the early afternoon. This arrangement suited the rhythm of their relationship, as Marche liked to have what she called "alone" time, during which she sat in her bedroom writing poetry, reading favorite authors like Anaïs Nin, and indulging her passion for astrology. She had a personal astrologer and spent a lot of time studying the planetary influences on her life.

The stars were certainly out when Jon took his mother, Barbara, and girlfriend, Stacey Pickren, along the red carpet for the Fifty-first Academy Awards in April 1979. That night, while Bill worked late in the office putting the finishing touches on Marche's demo tape, Jon was receiving an Oscar from Diana Ross and Ginger Rogers for his performance as the romantic paraplegic in *Coming Home.* His was not the only triumph; his costar Jane Fonda walked away with the award for Best Actress, and Waldo Salt and colleagues took the Oscar for Best Original Screenplay. It is not hard to imagine Marche's feelings that night, the girl from Riverdale with dreams of stardom watching the father of her children bask in the limelight. Angie has since said that she has never watched *Coming Home* because the film also features Stacey Pickren, the woman she blames for the breakup of her parents' marriage. "I remember just growing up and thinking, 'God, what a tough night that would've been for [my mother] in her sweatpants with her two babies.'"

Angie did sit in her father's lap a few weeks later and watch his latest film, *The Champ,* which was released at the same time as the Oscar ceremony. The heart-wrenching story, about a father who returns to the boxing ring to justify his son's belief in him and ends up dying in his arms, had

Angie in floods of tears. The youngster truly believed that the man cuddling her that night was going to die. She was inconsolable at the thought of losing her dad. "Don't worry, darling; it's only a movie," Jon assured her.

It was Angie's mother who was in tears, this time of blind fury, at the way her demo tape was treated by Jon and his agency, William Morris. As her tape neared completion, Marche asked Jon to introduce her to an agent. He put her in touch with a young gun, Steven Reuther, now a big-time producer, who took her and Bill out for dinner a couple of times to discuss her career. Bill smelled a rat, believing that Reuther was under orders from Jon to placate Marche rather than find her work. To test his theory, he gave a tape to Reuther, telling him that it was Marche's new demo when it was just a blank tape. Reluctantly Marche went along with the ruse. A few days later, Reuther called Marche and waxed lyrical about her "terrific" performance and requested a further ten tapes to send to various Hollywood producers.

She kept her cool during the call, but erupted angrily as soon as she put down the phone. At that moment, Jon arrived to pick up the children for the evening. "Hey, Billy, how's it going?" he asked as Day exited stage left.

"Don't worry, Jonny, you'll find out," he replied.

After facing the verbal lash from Marche, a chastened Jon Voight and Steve Reuther promised to help her out. They were as good as their word. Jon was working on a project called *Lookin' to Get Out,* based on a script by Al Schwartz, the manager of Jon's brother Chip. Jon promised to give her a role in the movie, about the comic misadventures of two New York gamblers in Las Vegas, if he ever got the project off the ground. That said, he was also cowriting another script, *The Shore,* with troubled troubadour Dory Previn, so Marche's movie role was more of a possibility than a probability.

Reuther quickly earned his agent's chops, placing Marche in a Revlon commercial due to be filmed in New York in July. As a thank-you for all his help, she asked Bill to come with her, the couple staying at the St. Moritz hotel on Central Park. That commercial was one of the high points, if not the apex, of her career. Certainly Marche was never happier, posing by the Plaza hotel surrounded by an attentive film crew, finally the star of the show. At that moment it was her mother's dream come true. During a break in filming, she came over and hugged Bill. "I really think I should move here. I don't know why, I just think I have a future here."

She was serious, making plans for another trip to the Big Apple as soon as they returned to Beverly Hills. In the end, Marche, Bill, and the children spent Christmas and New Year's at the St. Moritz, enjoying a "wild" vacation in the snow. They treated the children to carriage rides in Central Park, went ice-skating at Rockefeller Center, and took in Broadway shows. The craziest moment was midnight on New Year's Eve, when the four of them threw clothes out of their hotel window in celebration. "We had a lot of fun," recalls Bill. "Marche was at her happiest, filled with hope, spontaneous, and open to all kinds of crazy ideas."

By contrast, her Oscar-winning husband was in crisis, about his career, his faith, and his future. It was not the first time, nor would it be the last, that Jon Voight would enter the dark night of the soul. In a classic Hollywood moment, Jon took a stroll along the beach at Malibu ruminating about love, life, and the whole damn thing. As he muttered to himself, "I don't know what I'm doing with myself; I don't know if I can do this much longer," he bumped into his friend Al Pacino. Voight poured out his heart. Pacino listened intently, then said, in that raspy voice of his, "You are *such* a great actor." Crisis over. At least for the night. "It's nice when you have pals who believe in you," recalled Voight, who nonetheless remained hugely conflicted.

While he enjoyed what he called an "open-door" relationship with Stacey, he admitted that he was consumed by jealousy, which caused considerable difficulty in their six-year partnership. "She's free to do what she wants, and I am free to do what I want. There are no rules," he confessed to writer Will Tusher. Then he added, "I can't handle the pain. I don't want Othello [the tragic Shakespearean character maddened by jealousy] taking over my personality." So it is not hard to imagine how Jon felt when Stacey later snagged a role as a hooker in *The Border* and flew to Mexico to film alongside three notorious womanizers, Jack Nicholson, Harvey Keitel, and Warren Oates.

A strange encounter at the now-fashionable Chateau Marmont hotel on Sunset Boulevard with his good friend director John Boorman symbolized the yin and yang that is Jon Voight. The English director arrived after a ten-hour flight from London to find Jon waiting for him, a script in hand. It was a story about two brothers, one a good-looking Beverly Hills doctor who took drugs and enjoyed wild sex with raunchy women, the other a dutiful family man who loved his wife and children. As Boorman soon realized, the script essentially described Voight's dual personality. Jon was so eager to hear Boorman's verdict that he wanted him to read the script immediately. His director friend said it would have to wait, as he was tired after a long flight. He went to his room, showered, and was glancing through the script when there was a knock on the door. It was a very angry Stacey Pickren. "That's my fucking life and I want it back," she screamed, grabbing the script and stalking out of the room. Needless to say, the project came to naught.

Voight's conflicted heart was vividly exposed on Valentine's Day 1980. Even as his lawyers worked on the divorce settlement, he sent a huge bouquet of flowers and a tender love note to his estranged wife. Unfortunately for him, Bill Day was home. He scooped up the bouquet and drove thirty minutes to Jon's house in Hollywood and hurled the expensive floral arrangement at his front door.

Just seven weeks later, on March 24, 1980, the divorce was finalized, Jon agreeing to a generous settlement. While California divorce legislation limits the time period for paying alimony, Jon, who was still paying support to his first wife, Lauri Peters, promised to give Marche $3,500 a month for life. In addition, he agreed to pay the same amount every month in child support.

The divorce did little to stem the undertow of rivalry that had started the moment Bill and Jon met. In the verbal arm-wrestling that characterized their relationship, they addressed each other as "Billy" and "Jonny," knowing that it got on the other's nerves. When James and Angie were enrolled in K–12 soccer, Jon and Bill took turns driving them to practice and were usually at the games—on opposite sides of the field.

An incident on Angie's fifth birthday, in June 1980, symbolized their uneasy relationship. In typical Marche style, the apartment was brimming with balloons and overflowing with food, presents, and excited children. An absolute perfectionist, Marche had spent hours hand-engraving invitations, carefully wrapping presents, and writing special notes. No one could ever match the care she took—a trait that would have unforseen implications for her scruffy tomboy daughter. Taking pride of place was a dainty tea service, a birthday gift Angie had carefully set out in a corner of the room. The birthday girl ordered her parents and Bill to join her for tea.

Once everyone was seated, she decreed, "No eating or drinking until we have said grace." Marche, who was becoming ever more devout, smiled and said, "That is so sweet, Angie." At that point Jon said they should all hold hands. There was no chance of Bill's holding hands with his rival, so instead he grabbed a tiny plate as if he wanted to eat straightaway. This piece of playacting didn't work, and again Jon tried to hold his hand. In the end Bill pulled away, saying, "I'm sorry, you and I are not holding hands." Increasingly angry, Jon made another grab for Bill's hand. Eventually they ended up praying rather than holding hands, Angie's prayer including a wish that the adults in her life could stop acting like children. The incident is a window into Angie's interior world: Raised in chaos and uncertainty, here was a little girl who was trying, in her own fashion, to find a safe place. Making peace between the people who dominated her life and provided that security was a start.

The other takeaway from this domestic quarrel was how precocious, independent, and self-aware five-year-old Angie was. She had a talent for the dramatic, too. As her father recalls: "Since she was a baby she wouldn't let you help her even with her ABC's. She'd say: 'No, I do it. I do it.' That's the way she is." Being brought up in a household with few, if any, boundaries, and a mother who practiced the Lee Strasberg method of parenting—always asking Angie how she felt when she was upset—encouraged Angie to express herself to the fullest. At kindergarten she formed a group called "the Kissy Girls," who went around kissing all the boys and giving them love bites. Some of the boys got so carried away, according to Angie, that they took their clothes off. "I got into a lot of trouble," she later told James Lipton, the host of *Inside the Actors Studio.* "I was pretty sexual at kindergarten and my mom often got calls."

From an early age she was confident in front of the camera, hardly surprising as film student Bill Day constantly had a video camera at hand. An early performance was when they visited Papa and Elke, who had moved to Las Vegas and opened a Little King delicatessen, and Angie stood in front of the camera selling the delights of her grandfather's restaurant. She told the pretend customers to eat at Little King or she would "punch [them] in the mouth." When Bill stopped rolling, James would try his hand with the video, Angie always the star of his productions. One of her first memories is James shouting, "Come on, give us a show." While James was an utterly beautiful boy, it was his sister who was the more photogenic, her face coming alive in front of the camera in a way that James could never match. So it seemed inevitable that he would follow his dreams behind the camera, while Angie remained up front and center.

Angie knew what she wanted—as she made clear to a former babysitter turned actress whom she and her mother encountered on San Vicente Boulevard in Beverly Hills shortly before her fifth birthday. "When I grow up I'm going to be an actress," Angie told her firmly. "A big actress."

A few weeks after this meeting, she made her film debut in *Lookin' to Get Out,* a film her father had carefully nursed into life but which only limped into movie theaters two years later to lamentable reviews. It was an intriguing family affair; Angie, her mother, and Stacey Pickren all had parts in the comedy, about two hapless gamblers who go to Las Vegas in an attempt to win back money they owe a New York gangster. Directed by Hal Ashby and filmed on location in the summer and fall of 1980, the wafer-thin story was most interesting for some of its parallels to the lives of the actors and director. One of the opening scenes features Jon Voight, all cocky swagger as compulsive gambler Alex Kovac, trying to chat up a pretty girl in a Jeep as he waits at a traffic light in his white Rolls-Royce. Jon flirtatiously asks the girl, played by the newly divorced Marcheline Bertrand, if she will marry him. She replies, with a knowing smile, "Not a chance." In a later scene, cut from the original movie, he watches, with benign indifference, when his partner takes the hotel hooker, played by Stacey Pickren, into their suite for sex. It was almost as if Jon Voight were gambling with his own heart, acknowledging the desire and jealousy he had for both the women in his life.

Perhaps the most autobiographical scene, though, involved Jon and his daughter. Voight's character has a child by Ann-Margret's character, who's now involved with the casino owner, but he doesn't realize until the end of the movie that he is the girl's biological father. When they meet, he feigns cursory interest. The girl is cute in her floral dress and straw hat, but he is in a hurry and not especially touched by the joy of fatherhood. In the original script, the child was a boy called Josh, and James, the Voight child deemed to have star potential, was penciled in to play the part. At the last minute Hal Ashby decided it should be a girl called Tosh. In fact, it was so last-minute that on the morning the scene was due to be shot, Angie had to fly from Las Vegas to Los Angeles in a private jet in order to be presented to the appropriate authorities so that she could obtain a minor's work permit.

What no one knew at the time was that Hal Ashby had a daughter named Leigh, whom he had never been able to bring himself to meet, even though she had tried to contact him on numerous occasions. Now the scene where Alex meets Tosh is interpreted as Ashby's attempt to vicariously experience the moment of reconciliation with his long-lost daughter. At an emotional viewing of the movie, a tearful Leigh, who never met her father before he died, commented, "I always thought that message in the film was there for me. I always knew he was my father. In Angelina he recognized me at the end of the movie and I knew how sad he was and how sorry he was." In later years that scene between father and daughter would take on further emotional resonance.

The filming of *Lookin' to Get Out* coincided with a rapprochement between Bill Day and Jon Voight. After prompting by Marche, Jon took the trouble to look over a screenplay Bill and his writing partner, Dan Ackerman, had produced for a course at UCLA. He liked what he read, as did his assistant, Kathleen, who passed it on to *Lookin' to Get Out* producer Robert Schaffel. Schaffel paid Day and Ackerman $5,000 for an option. "You have a little bit of talent there," Jon grudgingly told Bill Day.

In the seesaw of this emotional triangle, as mutual respect was entering the lexicon of Bill and Jon's relationship, Bill's romance with Marche was hitting the skids. Day sensed that now that she was hitting her thirties she was looking at the horizon and thinking about some of the big Hollywood names she could have had. A particular bone of contention was when Angie's godfather, Maximilian Schell, decided to visit when Bill was not around. Mostly, however, their arguments centered around his family. She refused to attend his brother's wedding, his grandfather's funeral, or any other family gatherings, this reticence leading Bill's two sisters to conclude that Marche just wasn't that into the man in her life.

Bill put those thoughts aside when he announced that he was blowing his option money on a vacation with Marche and the children in Hawaii. Their break, in early 1981, was a week of bliss, the children enjoying the surf, the sun, and the sand. Every morning white doves flew onto their hotel balcony—much to Angie's delight. She scoured the room for every morsel of bread and called them over: "Yeah, that's it, baby. . . . Eat, babies. . . .

There you go." While the episode revealed her mothering instincts, it also pointed out the contrast between her and her older brother.

As a youngster she loved animals, though they did not survive long under her casual ministrations. She dyed a mouse blue, which caused its imminent demise; a rabbit she called Tweety Pie (her brother nabbed the name Bugs Bunny for his own rabbit) died when she accidentally dropped the cage on it; a pet hamster she took into the shower died of pneumonia; and her lizard, Vladimir, was fried in the heat when a friend left him caged in the sun.

By contrast, James, who identified with Linus, of the blue blanket, from the "Peanuts" cartoon, was so passionate about inanimate objects that from an early age he got upset if he saw a condemned or ruined building. In time he would be one of the first in his class to have a personal computer, an Apple Mac. The young computer geek loved poring over manuals and talking about apps. His sister couldn't have cared less, being not remotely interested in "boy toys." She was, however, a tomboy, climbing trees in the expensive white French smocks her mother liked to dress her in—much to Marche's despair—or sliding down mud banks. She was mischievous, too. On a visit to her father and Stacey Pickren, she emptied a bottle of Mountain Dew and then peed in the plastic bottle. After letting it cool in the fridge, she offered the "drink" to her father's girlfriend. She was the only one who thought it was amusing. While Angie was reckless, adventurous, and willful—"always busy, busy, busy, just like her grandma Barbara," recalls Lauren Taines—James was much more considered, placid, and dutiful. She was a garrulous handful; he was quietly obedient. In short, Angie was a Voight, James a Bertrand.

Most weekends in Beverly Hills, Bill, James, and Angie would ride their bikes up and down the ramps at Century City shopping mall or go to a movie. Afterward, they would eat at a diner on Wilshire Boulevard, where as often as not Bill challenged the youngsters to a dare, such as eating all the butter on the plate or mixing ketchup and mustard in the water glass and drinking it. "Angie would always take the dare without question," recalls Bill. "James, on the other hand, would always try and negotiate a higher price." Marche never did work out why they regularly arrived home with tummy aches.

Shortly after the Hawaii trip, Marche upset the family balance when she told Bill that she was moving to New York with the children. Since the Revlon commercial, her career seemed to be going nowhere, even though she had enrolled in more acting classes and made a fresh video with a classmate. She loved New York, felt its energy would kick-start her career, and anyway, Jon promised to lend her money to enable her to buy a house there. In her mind this offer was translated into his buying her a house as part of the divorce settlement, which was not the case. As Bill Day still had to finish graduate school in Los Angeles, it seemed that Marche would be making the move on her own; and as Bill gradually realized, the offer of a house came with strings attached. It seems that Jon insisted that he was not paying for a place for Bill Day to hang his hat.

Unbeknownst to both men, there was another subplot in play. Before she flew to New York, Marche consulted her erstwhile suitor Al Pacino, who had a place in Snedens Landing on the banks of the Hudson River north of New York City. He recommended a suitable real-estate agent, and after looking at properties in Connecticut, Marche picked out a beautiful secluded wooden home on Woods Road at Snedens Landing, a few minutes' walk from Pacino's pile. Known locally as Hollywood on the Hudson, Snedens Landing was quite the artists' colony, home to dancer Mikhail Baryshnikov and actors Bill Murray, William Hurt, and Jessica Lange as well as Pacino. While Bill Day feared that Marche would become further enmeshed with the Voight family—Barbara Voight lived across the river in White Plains—it seems that Marcheline was also considering her options with regard to Pacino.

She was firm in her resolve, leaving for New York in the summer of 1981. In typical Marche style, she gave Bill Day her Datsun station wagon in return for a ride to the airport.

While Bill, numb and shell-shocked, retreated to live in the seedy office on Hollywood Boulevard, Marche, Angie, and James settled into life in their hidden house in the country. The children roamed through the woods and played in the streams, enjoying a very different life from that in the urban world of Roxbury Park. As predicted, Barbara Voight—who kept her distance from Jon and Stacey in deference to her daughter-in-law—was a constant presence, helping Marche to settle in. Marche later joked that she was being turned into a "Voight Wife," a reference to the movie *The Step-ford Wives,* about a small community where the women pander to their husbands' every whim.

As for the men in her life, Jon Voight visited her more frequently than she was comfortable with, ostensibly to see the children but as often as not staying the night. More intriguing, that summer she regularly took the children to the home of her neighbor Al Pacino. Whether her move to New York was in part motivated by dreams of reigniting her romance with the Bronx-born actor is unclear, but "whatever was going on there, it didn't work out," recalls Bill Day.

Ironically, Marche was instrumental in introducing Pacino to her friend Jan Tarrant, a New York acting coach with whom he had a daugh-ter, Julie Marie, in 1989. While Marche was initially surprised at the rela-tionship—at the time Pacino was dating Diane Keaton—when the baby was born, in characteristic style, she showered the couple with presents and later became Julie Marie's godmother.

Whatever hidden agenda lay behind her move to New York, in early November she called Bill Day after learning that he had been taken seri-ously ill with hepatitis A. It was an emotional conversation, the nervous small talk soon giving way to mutual tears and declarations of love, Marche saying over and over again: "I'm sorry, I'm sorry. I must have been crazy." Over the next few days the rapprochement continued apace, and Marche eventually asked him to join her and the children in New York.

It was more complicated than that, as Bill was still too weak to leave the apartment unaided. On impulse, Marche flew to Los Angeles, rented a car, picked him up, and took him to Woods Road in time for Thanksgiving.

Within days, Marche was talking of a new project. Now approaching thirty-two, she reluctantly acknowledged that her chances of getting an act-ing break were rapidly receding. Instead she wanted to start a production company with Bill. She had already spoken to her Beverly Hills–based fi-nancial advisor, Charles Silverberg, who saw Woods Road Productions as a tax-efficient project. Over the next couple of years Bill made a number of short films that not only fulfilled his course requirements but also turned in a modest profit. Thanks to Silverberg's colleague Marc Graboff, now a big wheel at NBC, all of Bill's films, *Holiday, Out of Order,* and *The Healer,* snagged licensing deals with HBO, Showtime, and others.

Marche and Bill were now a business team, and before long they were talking about marriage and having more children to finally cement the renewed relationship. In fact, Marche did get pregnant again but had a miscarriage early on. They felt their loss keenly, helping each other cope with a family tragedy.

At first Jon was unhappy that Bill was back, phoning him to express his displeasure at the changed domestic arrangements. In a heart-to-heart exchange, Bill explained that he and Jon's ex-wife were a partnership and that it was time for Jon to move on. Given the fact that Jon was still living off and on with Stacey Pickren, this seemed a sensible view. For once Jon accepted the revised status quo, reducing his visits to Woods Road and staying with his mother in White Plains, twenty-five minutes' drive away, when he was in New York. He even started to warm to Bill, becoming enthusiastic about a comedy idea he and his writing partner, Dan Ackerman, were working on called *Pulsar and Sullivan*. It was a take-off on the Bob Hope and Bing Crosby movies—but set in outer space. Jon was keen to play Sullivan. Unfortunately, the gap from story conference to commission was never bridged.

In fact, the fractious relationship between Bill and Jon became the basis of Voight's next film, *Table for Five*. In an increasingly autobiographical career, this movie, filmed during 1982, was perhaps his most personal work to date, dealing with the relationships among a divorced father, his family, and the new man in his ex-wife's life. Voight, who coproduced, played a business schemer and womanizer whose ex-wife moved from Los Angeles to New York and found a new man whom his children adored. He readily acknowledged the clear parallels with his own life, telling writer Jim Jerome: "There are male egos involved and there is friction—the whole territorial thing. We don't necessarily sync, but we each give ground. [Bill Day is] crazy about Marche and really loves the kids. That discomfort—balance of power—is similar to what's in the film."

He realized that he was tapping into a deeper well of unarticulated grief at a tearful lunchtime script conference at the Warner Brothers cafeteria in Burbank. Every man present—director Robert Lieberman, producer Robert Schaffel, scriptwriter David Seltzer, and Voight himself—ended up crying their hearts out as the group, all divorced or separated, talked about the pain of enforced separation from their children. As Lieberman, now one of Voight's close friends, recalls: "The film laments love lost, a family lost, and a decision to step up and be a good father. Jon was a very pained guy. A generous man, a loving man, but feeling really bad about Angie and James."

In spite of the sentimental theme—moviemakers Joel and Ethan Coen consider it their favorite tearjerker—Voight ensured that filming, which mainly took place on a cruise ship sailing the Mediterranean, had a family feel. He brought his mother, Barbara, on board as a cruise extra (along with an unknown Kevin Costner) and flew the children to Rome to watch the filming. In an elliptical reference to his own father, Elmer, Voight's character was a former golf pro who he acknowledged was a lot like his dad; charming, frequently out of town, and in need of constant approval.

While Voight, now forty-three, was at an age to recognize, if not correct, his mistakes, he thrashed himself publicly about the possible psychological damage he had caused his young children by his romantic choices. When the film was released in February 1983 to generally favorable reviews, he spoke more presciently than he could have imagined. "The kids are aware of the deep disruption that went on early in their lives. The guilt, anger and confusion made their way into their subconscious and I don't know what dues we'll pay later on."

For good measure, the former Catholic flagellated himself about the high price Stacey Pickren had paid for being by his side. He believed that being Jon Voight's girlfriend had cursed her career—though that didn't prevent her from getting a part in that year's summer smash, *Flashdance*. At the same time, he recognized that his possessive streak had ruined their six-year relationship. "There's really been quite a lot of pain," he said.

Amid this emotional angst, on the surface Angie and James seemed like ordinary kids. Even with their Beverly Hills background and famous father, they coped reasonably well with the other children at William O. Schaefer Elementary School in nearby Tappan. James was increasingly intrigued by Bill's world of cameras and filmmaking gear, while Angie, like her father, had an artist's eye; Bill proudly displayed some of her early drawings in the local diner. During school breaks they shuttled to California to spend time with their father or to Florida to join granny Barbara at her vacation home in Palm Beach.

Around this time Angie and James learned a lesson that lasted rather longer than the average New York minute. Within her circle of friends and family, Marche had a reputation for outlandish generosity, planning birthdays and other celebrations in lavish detail and always taking a bag of goodies when she visited friends. Ever the perfectionist, as her daughter recalls, "She would write four drafts to get the right birthday card ready." Sometimes she went way over the top, as when Bill had to hire a U-Haul trailer to carry the Christmas presents when they stayed at Papa Bertrand's home in Las Vegas.

Another feature of her benevolence was the way she "adopted" families of modest means and bestowed her love and generosity on them. She regularly visited blue-collar cousins of her brother-in-law Ron Martin's in Van Nuys in San Fernando Valley, California, giving them furniture and baby and children's clothes, and even making a video using pictures from their old family albums. Other distant Bertrand relatives would receive first-class airplane tickets to Hawaii and an endless array of gifts.

When they lived at Woods Road, that pattern continued, Marche focusing her largesse on the family of her African-American handyman, Thomas. For the first time, she got Angie and James involved, asking them to pick out some of their clothes to wrap up as gifts for the family. They were not overly interested, squabbling over the wrapping paper, but, with bad grace, they finally wrapped the chosen clothes.

Then they drove to the ramshackle two-story wooden house near the small town of Piedmont, where Thomas's grandparents, parents, and assorted other relatives lived. Marche was very comfortable in their company, and after a suitable period of small talk, she asked Angie and James to hand over their presents. At first they were uncomfortable, but as soon as they saw the smiles on the faces of the recipients, their mood changed. "Something just clicked in them," recalls Bill Day, who believes that encounter was a seminal episode in their lives. "They got it and seemed very pleased with themselves. It looked like they had discovered the joy of giving and wanted to know when they could do it again."

These visits were the exception rather than the norm for Marche. Naturally shy and reserved, she found it hard to make friends in the new community and missed her tight-knit Beverly Hills circle. She was at her happiest visiting the Malibu home of longtime friend Belinha Beatty, the ex-wife of *Deliverance* star Ned Beatty, and her two children, Johnny and Blossom, or seeing friends like the actresses Geneviève Bujold and Jacqueline Bisset.

Even though she was raised in the Midwest, she and the rest of the family found the East Coast winters hard to bear. With its huge windows and timber frame, their two-story house on Woods Road was constantly cold, especially with the winter chill off the Hudson. Most winter weekends were spent chopping wood and weekdays keeping the open fire going. Before too long Marche was looking to get back to the "Slums of Beverly Hills."

When her father, Rolland, was diagnosed with cancer in 1984 and began chemotherapy, it seemed a clear sign that she should be nearer to him. The children were shipped back to Los Angeles to spend the summer with their father, while Marche and Bill packed up the house. On August 25, the day before they were due to close up the unsold house and drive across country, their real-estate agent arrived with an elderly couple, Cass Canfield, president of the publishing house Harper & Row, and his wife, Joan H. King. After a cursory viewing, Canfield sat down and wrote them a check for a down payment on the $500,000 asking price, a number Bill made up on the spot.

Destiny, it seemed, was guiding the family back to Beverly Hills.

FOUR

*Angie puts on the tough kid act, but underneath she is very sensi-
tive. It's a cover-up.*

—MARCHELINE BERTRAND

In 1984, when she was nine, Angelina won an Olympic medal. It was for
English, probably for a report she wrote on President Hoover when she
was at El Rodeo School in Beverly Hills. Though English was not as yet a
recognized Olympic discipline, Los Angeles was hosting the games that
year, and the school held its own competition, in which every pupil was
awarded a medal, whether for the arts, math, or, of course, sports.

It was not, however, an entirely winning return for Angelina to her
hometown. As she enrolled midway through grade school, she was playing
catch-up, in class and on the playground. With her skinny body, braces,
and outsize lips, it was not long before her fellow pupils nicknamed her
"Nigger Lips" and "Catfish." She gave as good as she got, endlessly teasing a
Taiwanese deaf boy, Windsor Lai, with the rhyme: "Chinese, Japanese . . ."
One day he couldn't take it anymore and hit her, and a teacher forced him
to apologize for his behavior. Despite what must have seemed, at the time,
a terrible injustice, they eventually became friendly, Angie seeing Windsor
as an outsider like herself: a misfit among the wealthy and pretty children of
privilege and money.

Quiet and self-contained, Angie was a clever student and eventually
blended in. She was always busy, taking ballet lessons, learning the piano,
joining the soccer team, and becoming involved in school drama. Her interest did not surprise her father, who recalls: "She was dramatic when she
was a young girl, and she was always dressing up and designing little things,

skits for her friends and so on. I thought maybe this gal would become an actress."

Her parents and brother were always in the audience, as was Bill Day, who lovingly videoed those first efforts on the stage. For much of 1984, however, Bill had been occupied with filming the vicious Sandinistra/ Contra war in Nicaragua, the graduate film student finding it a struggle to switch from "fire fights, death counts, wild parties, and meetings with Werner Herzog" to domestic routine in Beverly Hills. He had always been a stabilizing influence, though, a fun, avuncular figure; and the children, especially Jamie, who shared his love of working behind the camera, were glad to have him around. It is no coincidence that James today exhibits many of Bill's mannerisms: He is fast-talking, quick-witted, and a brilliant mimic, especially of his father.

Bill's arrival home from the war did change the family dynamic, however, reigniting the rivalry between him and Angie's father. Jon Voight was a constant if largely unwanted presence for Marche and Bill, especially since he was now on his own, Stacey Pickren having left him for another woman, a hairstylist with whom she lived for several years. It caused endless friction that led to shouting matches and arguments that often ended with Bill storming out and spending the night in the office. "I don't know how Bill weathered the whole thing," recalls Lauren Taines.

All too often Marche seemed to be playing Bill off against Jon, and vice versa, happy to be Mrs. Jon Voight at social events one minute, wanting Bill by her side the next. Just as her mother, Lois, had brought up her children to love her more than their father, so, too, did Marche treat Bill and Jon as children, their protests and complaints summarily dismissed by the head of the household. James and Angie were constantly buffeted by this atmosphere of reproach and acrimony. It was as confusing as it was unstable.

That year the family, who first stayed in an apartment on Spalding Avenue before moving to a spacious duplex a few buildings north on Roxbury Drive, regularly drove to Las Vegas to spend time with Marche's sister and her ailing father. In a last-ditch bid to curb his cancer, Rolland Bertrand checked into a clinic in New Mexico, where he was injected with massive doses of vitamin A. It was not a success, and on April 8, 1985, he succumbed to the curse of the family. He was only sixty-one.

A gentle soul who utterly adored his children and grandchildren, Rolland Bertrand was much missed. Young Angie, then nine, was deeply affected by his funeral, intrigued not only by the physical process of death itself but also by how the occasion allowed individuals to reach out and connect. She found solace in a religious ritual invested with centuries of tradition and significance. It was comforting in its predictability, making her feel in control, less lost. In her imagination she dreamed of one day becoming a funeral director.

Her love of ritual also found expression in a fascination with knives and swords. She enjoyed not only their cold, unforgiving beauty and the intriguing stories they suggested, but also the thrill of holding, spinning, and throwing them. Knives, often decorated with ornate symbolism, stained with honor and battle, excited and inspired the collector in her. They spoke, too, to a deeper, unfulfilled need. As contemporary psychoanalyst Dr. Franziska De George explains: "Collecting—and perhaps ritual—is an attempt to soothe the emptiness where the connection to the self is missing. You become attached to things rather than people. You realize early on it is a bad thing to collect people, so you collect things. You cannot control people, but you can control things."

Angie was beginning to search for ways to understand and reconcile her inner turmoil. When she was just ten years old, she recalls playing a game with a friend, but no longer being able to conjure up the necessary fantasy world. From that time, life "started not to be fun."

It was an unsettling and unhappy time not just for Angie but for the whole family. Naturally her grieving mother, now thirty-five, was deeply affected by her father's passing, and her thoughts turned once more to marriage. Now it was Bill Day who was hesitant, not only because even after a relationship lasting eight years, Marche still refused to engage with his family, but also because of Jon Voight's constant presence.

For Angie, her father's increasingly eccentric behavior added a further layer of uncertainty in her life. On the surface, Jon was the perfect divorced dad, always around to help in the day-to-day lives of the children. He was not only the assistant soccer coach for the team both his children played on at El Rodeo, but he also regularly took James for baseball and basketball practice. Jon and Marche were always together for their children's open houses and parent-teacher conferences. "I don't think any parent was more known by the teachers," Jon recalls proudly.

Nevertheless, from 1985 on, the constant dad was drifting, physically present but engrossed in a tortuous and often tortured journey of the soul. He drifted farther and farther from the shores of his own family as he embraced different causes, religions, and, most hurtful, another family. In the narrative of Angie's life, the father who had abandoned her as an infant was once again abandoning his daughter.

The changes in her father were visible to all, the famously attractive Jon Voight beginning to resemble Nick Nolte's unkempt character from *Down and Out in Beverly Hills*. For a *People* profile in 1985, writer John Stark described him as he shuffled around his kitchen making an unappetizing bowl of oatmeal: "His tousled hair is in need of a trim. His plaid shirt looks as if he had slept in it and his jeans have food stains. His face is thin and pasty." He was a far cry from the strong, assured, didactic dad that Angie was used to. Jon took to quoting from the book of meditations and prayers by Mother Teresa, surrounded by portraits on his living-room wall of his spiritual guides: Gandhi, Martin Luther King, Jr., rabbi and philosopher Abraham Joshua Heschel, John and Bobby Kennedy, Helen Keller, and Hindu teacher Paramahansa Yogandanda.

Producer Richard Fischoff worked with Jon in 1985 on *Desert Bloom*, in which Jon played a troubled World War II veteran. "It was after the filming that he went on macrobiotics and lost a lot of weight and seemed to have found God, spiritualism, and mysticism. I got the feeling that he had been through rough times." This spiritual struggle was also apparent in his performance that same year in *Runaway Train*, the story of two escaped convicts whose destiny and doom is to hide from their sadistic prison pursuers on an out-of-control freight train in the bleakest of Alaskan winters. The final scene portrays their wild, almost messianic hunger for freedom as Voight's character, Manny, stands atop the thundering train, arms outstretched like an ice-bound Christ, headed toward the embrace of a certain death. The spirituality of the role spoke so strongly to Jon that costar Rebecca De Mornay pointed out that it was *her* character who was supposed to connect with God rather than his.

Always a seeker of life's mysteries, he now seemed absorbed in this pursuit to the near exclusion of everything else, including his interest in the quotidian details of his children's lives. He did, however, win a Golden

Globe in January 1986 for his performance in *Runaway Train,* giving an acceptance speech that owed more to the pulpit than to the teleprompter. "I am so thankful that I can portray suffering souls, that you may see in some form or other a small light of God," he told a rather bemused audience. Before he left to celebrate with his mother, Barbara, and Stacey Pickren, who no longer shared his life but had a role in the movie, Voight remarked that his receiving the award had been ordained by God.

Perhaps appropriately, he took to the red carpet again in March for the Academy Awards with an ersatz angel by his side. Angelina, uncomfortably dressed in a white, frothy outfit chosen by her mother, even gave her first red carpet interview, all of four words. She confirmed that it was her first time at the Academy Awards, thanked the interviewer for complimenting her on her dress, and said she was "sort of" nervous for her father. She, James, and granny Barbara were in the audience as their father lost out to William Hurt for the award for Best Actor in a Leading Role. "I remember having to pee" was her abiding memory of the glittering evening.

It was her father's choice of his next movie, an ostensibly high-minded story called *Eternity* about a journalist's attempt to expose government corruption, that was to affect her life. Or, more accurately, his decision to work with an obscure filmmaking family, the Pauls. It was baffling. Their approach to movies, treating them as just another commodity, seemed diametrically opposed to everything the Oscar-winning activist held dear. As family patriarch Hank Paul made clear: "It's very similar to financial sales—putting together a presentation, having a product or service, packaging it, and approaching people." In business since 1978, Paul Entertainment had produced two low-budget movies, costs kept to a minimum partly because this close-knit family did virtually everything themselves: Hank's wife, Dorothy, had a casting agency; his son Steven, a child star from the 1970s, was company president; his son Stuart wrote scripts and directed; and his daughter, Bonnie, was a country singer and an actor. Bonnie first met Jon when she was working in a hip Beverly Hills restaurant, the Old World, but she got to know him best through Stacey Pickren, who took acting classes with her. As his relationship with Stacey unraveled, he was drawn closer to the Paul family.

Voight was blind to any criticism of the Pauls or their work. While he basked in the critical afterglow for his bravura performance in *Runaway Train,* the Pauls' concurrent effort, *Never Too Young to Die,* about a hermaphrodite rock star's attempt to pollute the Los Angeles water supply, was described by the *Los Angeles Times* as "not just bad . . . aggressively bad: bad with a vengeance." Undaunted, Voight agreed to work with the film's scriptwriter, Stuart Paul, inscribing on a napkin that he and the Jewish family had a "spiritual contract" to "love, respect, and protect each other's psyches." Friends and family saw instead a gullible, lonely, and rather naïve artist taking a dangerous path, financially and creatively.

The storm clouds were not immediately apparent. After the Oscars, Bill Day gallantly treated Marcheline, Angie, and James to another vacation in Hawaii, though the struggling documentary producer had to be financially bailed out by Marche. It was a favorite place for all of them, and the vacation was a happy time, a break from their quarreling—and a chance to get away from the pervasive presence of Jon Voight. Shortly afterward, in March 1986, Bill and Marche joined Debbie, Ron, and their children in Las Vegas to spend more family time together as well as to deal with Rolland's estate. In his will, Papa Bertrand left his second wife, Elke, the bulk of his fortune, while his three children, Marcheline, Debbie, and Raleigh, shared what was left from the bowling alley business. There was a dispute with Elke over the disposal of the family chattels, namely, silverware, china, and Rolland's collection of antique grandfather clocks, all earmarked for the grandchildren, which led to a family argument and an expensive court case in August 1986. Marcheline was so angry with Elke, with whom she had always had an uncomfortable relationship, that she made sure James and Angie never saw her again. Her decision broke their step-grandmother's heart. "She loved those kids, but Marche wouldn't allow her to see them," recalls Krisann Morel, who met with Elke some years later. Marche's righteous indignation was an all-too-familiar feature of her complex character. The Bertrand freeze, an unwillingness to forgive and move on, was a quality that blighted the rest of her life.

Although Angie lost a step-grandmother and gained a grandfather clock in this legal battle, it was her father's financial decisions that had an impact on her life. Significantly, Jon transferred his financial affairs from his longtime advisor Charles Silverberg, who had kept Marche and Bill's Woods Road company afloat, to the Paul family, who remain his representatives to this day. Jon had given the Pauls a loan to fund their film projects, the money taken from the sale of the Snedens Landing house and from cashing in his pension early—and taking the tax hit. His son, James, was present when he offered the Pauls the cash, describing how they first turned down the money and then grudgingly accepted it as though they were doing him a favor.

It was a decision that had far-reaching consequences, ultimately souring relations between father and daughter, among others. Even after he had given his savings to the Paul family, Marcheline still believed that as part of the divorce agreement, he owed her a house as well as alimony and child support. While this was not legally accurate, she had a strong case. He had offered to buy her a house when they separated and had handed Stacey the deed to the house they had lived in after they split. He was morally if not legally obligated to support the mother of his children. As the years ticked by and, as Marche understood it, the money loaned to the Pauls was not returned, she became increasingly agitated.

Jon continued on his self-appointed mission to help the Pauls, who portrayed themselves as plucky independent filmmakers taking on the might of Hollywood. With their encouragement, he began to explore Judaism more closely, contributing to Jewish charities like Chabad and in time, according to his friend John Boorman, even considering converting to Judaism. "He was always giving his money away to various causes," Boorman says. "Now it was Jewish charities."

When Boorman and Jon met, their discussions ranged far and wide. Now Boorman noticed that Jon would pepper his language with intemperate phrases like "Christianity is the heresy of Judaism." It was a new mind-set that seemed to reflect the certainty of the zealot rather than the seeker after enlightenment. In a quest to deny the existence of Christ—an intellectual flip-flop even from his speech at the Golden Globes—he took to calling friends in the early hours of the morning and reading passages from the Bible in support of his contention. In Boorman's view the Paul family now "controlled" his friend.

Indeed, such was the concern that Marcheline discussed with family friends the possibility of staging an intervention, a procedure used to save individuals from drugs or cults. In truth, Jon Voight needed saving from himself, not from the Paul family. As another friend of the Bertrand family observed bluntly: "All was well through *Runaway Train,* and then he literally came off the rails."

Jon agreed to be godfather to Skyler Shuster, the daughter of Bonnie Paul and Beverly Hills cigar bar owner Stanley Shuster, who was born in October 1986, the year Angie was eleven. Indeed, it often seemed that he was able to forge a better connection with other kids than with his own, mentoring and advising numerous youngsters over the years. That said, Angie later became very close to Sharon Shuster, Skyler's older cousin.

As Jon's friend director Rob Lieberman explained: "He is a lonely man. Very tortured. At the core of him is the search for a family and for a god. That has taken him down a number of different roads. The Pauls are a pious, close-knit Jewish family, and Jon found that very appealing. They welcomed him in, and I often saw him in restaurants with the entire Paul family. Not occasionally but regularly. It's a trade-off. He got a family, a religion, and a goddaughter; they used his name to gain access and funding."

Most weekends he took Angie and James along to gatherings with the Paul family. While James mastered a wicked impersonation of Steven Paul, Angie, now aged twelve and going through puberty, loathed these lunches and dinners. For all her subsequent behavior, she was a naïve and rather gangly girl who felt awkward when she was the subject of attention. She was uncomfortable when Steven Paul, then twenty-seven, looked her up and down, and was embarrassed, too, by the life-size portraits of *Playboy* centerfolds on the walls. The girl who already had an acute sense of being out of step with the world didn't feel able to discuss the issue with her parents, not even her mother. Nothing happened but she talked to a family friend, who recalls: "She didn't understand it. She said the guy was creepy and looking at her funny. She was just a kid and upset."

Angie was interested in boys but still coming to terms with the hormones racing through her skinny body. When Lauren Taines took her and a friend camping on the beach at Carpinteria on Memorial Day weekend in 1987, for example, Angie and her pal behaved like classic pubescent girls: giggling together and watching the boys walk by their tent, their gaze shielded by huge sunglasses. "They were adorable," recalls Lauren. At a friend's twelfth birthday party, held at the Closet Stars karaoke bar in Burbank, she and her friends took to the stage in a variety of outfits, ranging from outsize plastic ears for a tuneless version of "Stand by Me" to a nun's habit for an equally discordant if funny rendition of "New York, New York" and what can only be described as a black angel's outfit for a shambolic sing-along to Prince's "Purple Rain." They were silly, giggly, and having fun. The adults in Angie's world saw her rather dramatic fascination with death and knives as no more than a passing juvenile fancy, like stamp collecting.

If anything, she was behaving more like a grown-up than her parents, who were forever squabbling, the ugly dance among Jon, Marche, and Bill endlessly upsetting and unsettling. A showbiz party at the Beverly Hills home of producer and agent Edgar Gross one Saturday in 1987 was typical. Marche wanted to attend the social event with Jon rather than with Bill Day. There was commercial logic behind the decision—she wanted to buttonhole director John Boorman about the latest Woods Road project, a fresh take on the Robin Hood story. After a ten-year relationship, this was a breaking point for Bill Day, who was no longer prepared to take part in a "freak show." Meanwhile, there was another shouting match in front of the children, more nights in the office, and another messy compromise.

Eventually Bill and Marche spoke briefly to John Boorman and his then wife, costume designer Christel. Chain-smoking, sharp, and funny, Christel was a theatrical grand dame with little time for Hollywood froth. Ever since meeting Marche during the filming of *Deliverance,* she had kept a parental eye on her, sympathizing with her and encouraging her during the ups and downs of her relationships with Jon and Bill. They agreed to meet the next day to discuss the Robin Hood project, as well as Jon Voight, the Pauls, and Marcheline's financial concerns.

For once Marche got much more than she bargained for—and for once Bill got his due. Before listening to their pitch for Robin Hood, Marche's surrogate mother gave her a verbal dressing-down. "I'm really disappointed in you," Christel told her. "You have let Jon Voight ruin your life. And now you are letting him threaten your relationship with Bill." As much as she adored Marche, Christel had seen through her ploy of playing "Mrs. Jon Voight" in public, careless of the hurt it caused Bill and the resulting damage to her relationship, not to mention the confusion it sowed in the minds of her children.

At the same time, Jon Boorman promised to use his good offices to find a top lawyer to help Marcheline recover what she considered to be her money. Knowing how passive Marche was, he made the offer with the proviso that she should only contact the lawyer once she had decided to go ahead with the case. She never made the call. Instead she started going to church and lighting candles in the hope that her prayers would be answered.

Nonetheless, the issue of the money ate away at Marcheline, adding to her abiding sense of betrayal and bitterness. Marche conveyed her grievances, however unfounded, to her children, leaving Angie and James wondering why their father had favored another family above his own.

It didn't help that while Jon labored long and hard over the script for *Eternity,* he was no longer working. Unlike Marcheline, who was quite materialistic, Jon was utterly careless of possessions, living a simple, almost monastic life. Apart from a tuxedo and a couple of silk scarves, his wardrobe was threadbare. His wants were simple; he was reputedly so concerned about the environment that when he wrote a script he looked at the length and worried about the number of trees to be cut down.

"I don't believe in using money to make investments to make more money" was his mantra. By the late 1980s, he literally had none, and for a time his phone and electricity were cut off. "It was one of the toughest times of my life," he later recalled. "I just didn't feel good about myself. I was doing some much-needed soul-searching, but it played havoc with my career."

It played havoc with his children, too. As James and Angie moved into adolescence, a time in life when keeping up with one's peers is hugely important, they felt the lack of money acutely. James, who moved in with his father, later recalled that one of the "saddest" events in his life was having to do without a car when he reached sixteen. He told writer Sharon Feinstein: "Try to imagine. You go to Beverly Hills High, one of the wealthiest high schools in the nation. Even the cheapest car that anyone has is brand-new. All my friends are well-off. I have a movie-star father and no car. It was debilitating." He didn't even attend his high-school prom because of the shame of having to be driven by his father. "The significant years of dating and getting to know yourself, I didn't experience any of that," he complained, though he failed to mention that he'd never bothered to get a driver's license because he was nervous about driving.

His sister, who is as unworldly and nonmaterialistic as her father, has recalled shopping for clothes in thrift stores while her friends went to posh stores like Fred Segal. She remembers moving into apartments that got "smaller and smaller" because her father was not focused on Hollywood and work. Yet the roomy duplex apartment they had on Roxbury Drive was much bigger than the one they'd had before they left for New York. And they didn't move from it once they got there.

One story of deprivation that Angie tells is of protesting to a teacher that she couldn't type her papers on a computer because she didn't own one and having her teacher respond, "Have your father buy you one." As her brother was one of the first kids to own a much-coveted Mac, this is a surprising assertion. Certainly she had enough pocket money to amass an extensive and expensive collection of knives and swords. In truth, she may have had no interest in computers and preferred writing with a pencil.

Whether or not she and James wanted to admit it, their father's humanitarian missions on behalf of Vietnam vets, American Indians, the homeless, and many other causes deeply imprinted itself on their social conscience. As bombastic as he could be in an argument, Angie learned to give as she got, enjoying the back-and-forth of debate with her father.

Like Jon Voight, Bill Day experienced his own conversion as Angie reached adolescence. In 1988 he became heavily involved in environmental activism, with activists from Greenpeace and the Rainforest Action Network as well as committed celebrities like actor Dennis Weaver and producer Bonnie Bruckheimer gathering at the Roxbury apartment.

Somewhat incongruously, Angie got a vivid taste of the world beyond Beverly Hills thanks to her passion for collecting knives. She and her parents were regulars at a store in Santa Monica that sold African artifacts, including masks, shields, and drums as well as spears, knives, and swords. It was run and owned by an outsize character, Jean-Pierre Hallet, who had survived nineteen brushes with death in his dedicated struggle to save the Efe pygmy tribe in the African Congo. Bearded, brave, and eternally optimistic, Hallet gave her a taste of what it is to be passionate about a cause and to work hard to protect a people who were misunderstood and vulnerable. Angie found him utterly mesmerizing, Hallet regaling the twelve-year-old with hair-raising stories about his adventures in the heart of Africa, perhaps recounting how he killed a charging lion with a spear to win initiation into the fierce Masai tribe or the time deadly poison from a pygmy dart was leached from his wound, saving his life in the nick of time. "She would have been left with a lasting humanitarian impression from someone deeply connected with primitive people," observes his son Bernard. "He was an inspiration to many and described his concern about the survival of the Efe pygmies with passion and fervor." This charismatic explorer, who died at age seventy-six in 2004, had a deep impact on Angie, possibly inspiring her own future concern about the world's forgotten. She later talked of him with affection, saying how she would have liked to have had the opportunity to photograph him.

Angie, though, was now on her own adventure, exploring the untamed but gloomy jungle of her adolescence, wrestling with her emerging sexuality, her feelings of worthlessness, and a restless need to discover who she was.

Her transformation was stark. Gone forever were the giddy girly clothes, games of dress up, and silly sparkly sequins. For the morbid and maudlin teenager, black was indeed the new black. She swapped her pink ballet ensemble for that of a modern-day, vampire-fascinated goth: lace-up Doc Martens boots, T-shirts, jeans, dog collars, lipstick, eye shadow, and nail polish in every shade—as long as it was black. For a change the punky goth did wear red—in the form of a dog collar, mimicking the clothes Michael Jackson wore for the *Thriller* album.

Angie's appearances at the Oscar ceremonies of 1986 and 1988 seemed to symbolize the transformation from white to black, light to dark. The first time she walked down the red carpet, Angie, then ten, suitably shy and bashful, wore a white net fairy-princess dress that looked as if it had been chosen by a well-meaning mother who didn't quite get the fact that her daughter was no longer in kindergarten. For her second appearance, just before her thirteenth birthday, Angie, unsmiling and ill at ease, was all in black. While it seems she had chosen the outfit herself, she looked as though she would rather have been anywhere than on the red carpet with her father. Asked if she aspired to follow in his footsteps and become an actor, she replied coolly: "Not really." In later years she had no recollection of attending the event.

Teased because she was so skinny as well as for her punk getups—at that time common teenage attire in London or New York but not in sunny Beverly Hills—she hung out with a small clique of like-minded outsiders in Roxbury Park or at Westwood Arcade, which was a short bus ride away. In those days Westwood Arcade was the place where kids went to experiment with drugs (magic mushrooms were popular) and where rival gangs of surfers, skateboarders, and graffiti artists tested their mettle—and muscle. "Angie was a rebel ahead of her time," recalls a classmate. "If someone was going to get into trouble, it would be her."

Budding artist Windsor Lai, socially excluded and bullied because of his hearing disability, remembers seeing Angie and her gang in Westwood Arcade, where he smoked his first cigarette, a Marlboro, thanks to her. "As a person she was very quiet and just blended in," he recalls, "but then she did all kinds of mad things. Sometimes she would act spaced-out like a drug addict or seem wasted. Then she would grab you unexpectedly and start silly dancing like a mad waltz."

Her circle included Evelyn Ungvari, whose sister Natalie later became inadvertently embroiled in the White House scandal involving her friend and fellow Beverly Hills High alumna Monica Lewinsky; Elan Atias, who became a reggae singer; child actor Keith Coogan; and Chris Landon, son of *Little House on the Prairie* star Michael Landon. During this time Landon and Angie were "inseparable," united by the fact that both were cursed with famous fathers, and both felt they were misunderstood outsiders.

She affected a brittle, intimidating presence, chilly and unapproachable, with the edgy "don't mess with me" attitude of the outcast. Doodles on her school notebook give an insight into her adolescent mind-set. There are drawings of the devil and of swords, knives, and other weapons, and phrases like "Death: extinction of life, hell, suicide, mental suffering," and "Autopsy: examination of a corpse."

As macabre as her musings seem, there was a practical and personal purpose behind them. She had an ambition to be a funeral director, and even sent away for the Funeral Service Institute handbook, which she still has, and completed the multiple-choice test. In her eyes, the role of a funeral director was life-affirming, helping people come to terms with their grief and celebrating the life of the loved one they had lost. At the same time, she had a dawning awareness that longevity was not a Bertrand family characteristic. "Death never scared me," she later observed. "Death is always something I wanted to understand."

Her friendship with Chris Landon accelerated this sense of the macabre, as well as her fascination with the mechanics of death. He and his director father would spend their Saturday evenings watching horror movies, a genre that inspired Chris's future career as a scriptwriter. Not only was it a way of bonding with his dad, but his escape into movie horror also helped dull the constant bullying he suffered at school because he was effeminate and gay.

For a time he couldn't sleep without the comforting sounds of a horror movie playing in the background. "I would go to bed and fall asleep to the sound of Mia Farrow screaming," he says. "[*Rosemary's Baby* is] one of the most flawless horror movies ever." Closer to home, when Michael Landon contracted pancreatic cancer, Angie would have seen or heard about the stages of his decline—he died in 1991—firsthand.

With the shadow of death came thoughts of suicide, the thirteen-year-old feeling "low about living" and thinking about "not being around." "It was when the reality of life set in, the reality of surviving," she says.

Psychologist Iris Martin sees her black moods differently. "Her suicidal thoughts came about because she has no sense of self. She had internalized all that abandonment as a baby and that was expressed as feeling that she was invisible and worthless. Any time she felt valuable she would have to punish herself."

Angie's first response was to withdraw. There was a central numbness in her soul; she was a teenage girl super-saturated with a life of drama who could no longer bring herself to connect. All this swirl of emotion became too much to cope with. She had lived through the uncertain vortex that was her parents' on-and-off, up-and-down, too-close, too-distant, ultimately enigmatic codependent relationship, watched her father turn from a swaggering Hollywood star to a pitiable and impoverished seeker, and witnessed the drama of life between Bill and her mother, the shouting matches and the slamming doors on the way to another night in office exile. But her feelings were much more primal, rooted in those days in a crib in the Ivory Tower, anxious, terrified, and often alone. From this sense of abandonment, although she was not aware of it, all else flowed. She later recalled, "I had that problem early on when I couldn't feel a bond with another human being. Mostly it was all about trying to connect." One day she announced that she no longer wanted to be hugged, and even today friends know to welcome her not with a hug but with a handshake. She decided that tears, too, were a waste of emotion; unable to cry herself, she felt disdain when others did.

It is interesting that, at her mother's urging, she enrolled at the Lee Strasberg acting school but dropped out after only a short time, saying she didn't have the "memories" to undertake the emotionally challenging course. When her mother took her to acting auditions, she deliberately wore the wrong clothes or refused to read the lines and act out the scene. Her aggravation seemed aimed as much at her mother, who was only repeating her own mother's maternal ambition, as at these auditions, Angie seeming to resent being pushed in this direction. Undaunted, Marcheline also took her to modeling cattle calls, but, self-conscious and nervous, Angie couldn't bear being looked at like a piece of meat. In the end she told her mother that she just couldn't do it.

On some level, she was simply revolted by herself. "I was always that punk in school," Angie told writer Nancy Jo Sales years later. "I didn't feel clean, and, like, pretty. And I always felt interesting or odd or dark maybe, uh, you know, could feel sexy." While the language is very awkward and inarticulate, it is revealing about her juvenile mind-set. The word "clean"—a word that crops up time and again—is a curious choice to describe her feelings in the context of her sexual desires. When most adults look back on their teenage angst, they find themselves reaching for words like "gawky," "shy," and "awkward." Angie was feeling sexual at an age when she believed she ought to be feeling clean and innocent, suggesting that she was too immature to cope with her own precocious desires and needs.

Moreover, she had few, if any, adult boundaries to rein her in. Certainly the word "no" did not figure in her mother's lexicon, Marcheline reasoning that if she was her daughter's friend Angie would tell her everything. Whereas James was a biddable son, Angie was wild and adventurous, sneaking out of the house at night and going to Westwood to join her gang.

She tried every drug going, developing a particular taste for cocaine. On at least one occasion she or her friends called Marcheline to pick up Angie when she collapsed, freaking out and out of control, after taking a psychedelic drug.

"I was raised by my mom and everything was emotional, and even if I would do something crazy, if I would be out all night and would come back, you know, at thirteen, and be doing stuff, she'd cry and then I'd feel like the worst person in the world because I hurt my friend, my girlfriend."

Her mother's reaction is instructive. While most parents, worried about their children's safety, would angrily chastise their young daughter for staying out all night, Marche not only accepted her behavior but also made it about her own pain. Her mother, as Angie said, was not her mother but a girlfriend, moreover a girlfriend who was asking her daughter to manage her hurt—in effect, to mother her.

Marche's odd response was critical at a time when her daughter was entering puberty and experiencing the classic teenage hormone rush. The days when Angie had a crush on Mr. Spock from *Star Trek*—also Jon's favorite TV show—were long gone, although she did, through her father, get to meet *Platoon* star Willem Dafoe, who she thought was "hot." "I wanted to be promiscuous and was starting to be sexual," she recalled.

Shortly after moving from El Rodeo to Beverly Hills High School in September 1989, Angie was dating—and losing her virginity to—her first boyfriend, a distinctively attired teenager called Anton with a big fat silver chain that started from his belt, fell to the back of his knee, and then climbed up to his back pocket, where it was attached to his empty wallet.

At her mother's suggestion, the fourteen-year-old Angie and her boyfriend started living together at her home on Roxbury Drive. Young Anton, whose family had moved away to Encino, stayed with Angie, her mother, and, at times, her brother—at least on school nights. To make the young couple more comfortable, Marcheline gave up the master bedroom with its huge Chinese wedding bed and moved into a smaller bedroom. While she thought her liberal behavior meant that she would be able to keep an eye on them, the proximity of the master bedroom to the street made it easy for them to sneak out at night, which they did regularly. By all accounts Angie's live-in boyfriend was polite, quiet, but something of a handful. "If Anton wasn't a nice boy beneath the punk gear, Marche wouldn't have let him in," argues Lauren Taines.

Angie herself says that she lived with Anton for two years from the age of fourteen, though her family and friends remember that the young punk was only around for six months or so. Her mother's logic was that Angie was going to have sex anyway, so best to encourage her to stay at home, where Marcheline could exercise some control. "She pushed Angie into living with him so she could keep an eye on them," said Lauren Taines. Not that Angie found her first experience of sex particularly fulfilling—especially with her mother sleeping next door.

With hindsight, Angie believes her mother's indulgence was a "very smart thing." She told James Lipton: "I wasn't sneaking around. I had my home, my base, so I was safe." This rationalization obscures the fact that the absence of boundaries encouraged her to behave like a wild child bride, whether she wanted to or not. Psychoanalyst Dr. Franziska De George observes: "This behavior seems like an attempt at avoiding conflict on the part of the mother, rather than thinking of the developmental needs of the child, who may be too young to deal with the feelings of a live-in relationship and premature sexuality."

Certainly it didn't make sense to Jon Voight, either, when he found out what was going on, or to Bill Day, when he arrived back in Beverly Hills after a trip to the Amazon. Their objections were brushed aside, Marcheline explaining that she didn't want her daughter having sex in the back of a car. On domestic matters, Marche's word was law. (There is no word about how the boy's parents felt.)

Nonetheless, Jon Voight confronted his sullen daughter about her live-in boyfriend, her drug abuse, and other issues, voicing his disapproval in "a big fight" with her. The irony is that while Angie viewed her father as a stern disciplinarian, he believes that, because of his abiding guilt over the divorce, he failed to challenge her enough.

Voight later told CNN's Paula Zahn that he was "very upset" about Angie's experimentation with drugs during high school. "This was the beginning of her retaliation against me for the anger she felt when I left her mother. It was very difficult for me to scold or reprimand her. I backed down partially because I felt some guilt about the divorce and partially because I was hoping that things would go away. It was a big mistake."

Voight would have been even more horrified if he had known what was actually going on in the master bedroom. As time went on, Angie felt there was too little connection between her and her boyfriend when they had sex. She could not "feel," that is to say, enjoy an orgasm. One drunken night, she grabbed one of her knives and cut her boyfriend, and he cut her back; they were both covered in blood. It was a moment, as she saw it, of primitive honesty, giving her a sense of being both dangerous and alive. By cutting she felt she had broken free of her emotional bonds.

She later described the consequences of that evening: Her jugular vein narrowly missed being severed, and after going to the local hospital she was patched up with gauze bandages covering her wounds. As she tells it, the worst moment of this night of honesty was lying to her mother the morning after about how her injuries had come about. While she was certainly cutting, there is a degree of dramatic hyperbole in this story. Even Marche would have noticed something as obvious as a bandage on her neck.

There was an incident, less physically serious, which considerably alarmed her mother. One morning Angie emerged after cutting some of her hair with a knife, in the process of which she had also cut her neck behind her ear. As Marche discussed this incident at length with her circle of friends, it's hard to imagine that they wouldn't have heard about it if indeed her daughter had nearly cut her throat.

This is not to downplay Angie's behavior, which exposes a deeply troubled psyche. That the first time she experienced the act of cutting gave Angie such a sense of honesty, of being alive, is typical of those who ultimately become "cutters," addicted to slicing their own flesh. Most people have the ability to self-regulate internal pressure and conflict. However, those in what Dr. De George describes as a "global undifferentiated state," emotionally unformed because of their childhood trauma, are not able to manage their feelings. So for cutters, the physical pain is a welcome release, a kind of melting inside, and an escape from unmanageable emotional torment. Paradoxically, after a cutting episode, which normal people would find distressing, cutters feel a sense of control. Once again the world makes sense— the bleeding rationalizes the emotional distress. But it is only a temporary solution, the sense of relief attended by shame and confusion. So the pain starts coming back. When the darkness becomes overwhelming, cutting is once again the release.

Even at the time, Angie realized that this was not a healthy relationship, particularly for her boyfriend, who was not by nature aggressive. "My first boyfriend cried a lot and it was a load of high drama that I could do without." Those pesky "feelings" again.

Nonetheless, the demons roiled within. Angie continued to cut herself for several more years, the act of self-mutilation soothing her troubled psyche, releasing emotional pain and inner rage. "It was somehow therapeutic to me," she later told CNN, acknowledging the effect but not understanding the cause underlying her cutting behavior. Those who saw her naked noted that the cuts were deep and almost entirely related to sexual anatomy—her breasts and inner thighs—as though she was revolted by her own sexuality, perhaps reflecting her sense of not being "clean." "The cuts go deep. She was really hard on herself," noted a friend.

While Anton was on the scene, of most concern to her family was her dramatic weight loss; Angie was clearly suffering from an eating disorder. Her anorexia nervosa was literally fed by her cocaine use, the drug dulling her shaky appetite. She was taken to a psychologist, who told her that she had a choice: either start eating or be admitted to the hospital. Angie started eating. Current wisdom suggests that the origin of most eating disorders lies in the complex relationship between parent and child and the desire for control. So perhaps it was Marcheline's trifecta of setting no real boundaries, her quiet yet relentless ambition for her daughter, and her own perfectionism that sent Angie into a tailspin of seeking to control something, anything, in her own life. No one, certainly not the messy Angie, could live up to Marche's standards. She controlled her daughter in a way that Angie couldn't fight. So she fought herself, controlling her eating habits, the one aspect of her life she alone was in charge of in a fractured and scattered world.

"Angie couldn't risk expressing that primal rage against her mother, so the rage was directed against the self," says psychologist Iris Martin. "What comes with that is suicidal thoughts and self-mutilation, as well as eating disorders like anorexia and bulimia. They are all assaults on the self."

For most of her life Angie had been defined by her mother's vision of femininity, which simply wasn't hers: the beautiful Victorian smock dresses that she deliberately ruined by climbing trees, the inappropriate white angel outfit she wore for the Oscars, the modeling cattle calls that the gawky teenager with a mouthful of braces found excruciatingly embarrassing, and the acting classes she was too young to cope with. Her mother was living through her daughter, just as her own mother had lived through her. For a sensitive, intelligent young girl, the pressure of needing to be successful to avoid her mother's disappointment and the dread of being abandoned again if she failed must have been overwhelming.

As her mother rightly observed, beneath the bravado was a susceptible little girl. Marche once said: "Angie puts on the tough kid act, but underneath she is very sensitive. It's a cover-up." And that sensitive little girl couldn't handle what she had gotten herself into. So she retreated by going back into childhood, her anorexia a way of desexualizing herself. The last thing she needed was to be living with a teenage boy when she was just four-teen. She needed to hear the word no. As Angie struggled with anorexia, Marcheline decided it would be best if Anton left the family home. His de-parture effectively ended their relationship.

As tough as Angie may have appeared to be on the outside, her inability to cope with the young woman she was becoming—or was expected to become—affected her day-to-day life. Her schoolwork suffered, and she moved to Moreno High (Continuation), the "alternative" school-within-a-school at Beverly Hills High that specialized in providing flexible study for students with behavioral problems such as substance abuse and chronic truancy. It was also a fast track for bright pupils like Angie who wanted to graduate early so they could focus on a career in the entertainment indus-try. As part of the program, she underwent regular counseling, now joking that only at Beverly Hills High School could students gain credits for ther-apy sessions.

Naturally, her counselor focused on the damaging impact on her life of her parents' breakup. She now recalls, with typical bravado: "The doctor was probably going on about my father and mother while I was doing acid on the weekends and bleeding underneath my clothes." As dismissive as she was about this focus—describing the process as "manipulative"—her coun-selor was at least trying to address the root cause of her problems. Angie's drug use, eating disorder, and cutting were clearly symptoms, a way of dull-ing or avoiding her emotional pain. In the presenting narrative of her life, she had been abandoned by her father, and sustained by her mother, who had given up her career to raise her. Black and white, dark and light, devil and angel. While the story she told herself contained an element of truth, it was not the whole story. It was *her* true story, not *the* true story.

Her father sensed the way the wind was blowing when he drove her to a friend's house after picking her up from school one day. When he asked about the people she was seeing, her reply was both disturbing and bemus-ing. "We're all alike; we're kids whose fathers aren't there for them." At that moment he realized she was speaking from a script prepared, at least in part, by her mother. As he later told TV host Pat O'Brien: "There was this programming of the kids, obviously from the terrible hurt and anger that her mother had. It was passed on to the kids and I was working against that continuously to let everybody know of my love." Often feeling excluded from his daughter's life, he now started writing letters to Angie in an attempt to connect with her.

The glowering resentment between father and children was obvious to all. For a couple of years, gawky teenager Brian Evans, who first met Jon Voight in 1989 at a Beverly Hills charity event in aid of the homeless, got a ringside seat to this endless boxing match. The Oscar winner took a shine to the seventeen-year-old, who was trying to make it in comedy improv, introducing him to James and suggesting that he take Angie out "sometime"—presumably to wean her away from her live-in boyfriend, who soon found himself out of her life anyway.

Brian Evans was only too happy to comply, and he took Angie on a few innocuous dates. Even though he was two years older than Angie, Evans felt like an "awkward nerd" in her presence, daunted by her sheen of self-contained sophistication. "She was quite introverted but knew how to stand up for herself," he recalls. "She struck me as being very much in control of herself. Not a lost soul in any way."

When she was with her father, the distance between them was immediately apparent. "I could feel her sadness," Evans recalls. "She was not a happy person, and she was very unhappy with her dad. She just didn't like him much and gave him one-word answers to his questions like she was only there because she had to be."

Her brother, James, was constantly locking horns with his dad. Even though he was now living mainly with his father at his home, Evans noticed that he still sided with his mother in family arguments.

Over the next few months, Evans came to see Voight as a surrogate dad. Coming from a checkered background himself, Evans rather objects to the hostility James and Angie displayed toward their father. "He was such a cool guy who did all the dad things. They didn't want for anything, didn't have to struggle, and yet resented their father."

Just as his children wanted to be independent of Jon Voight, so, too, did Marcheline and Bill Day. They were convinced that their film production company was the avenue to financial freedom; all they needed was to snag a big deal. When they heard of the true story of an environmental David facing a corporate Goliath in the Amazon, they thought they had struck gold. The concept, which they called *Amazonia,* attracted Hollywood heavyweights of the caliber of Ridley and Tony Scott. Their joy, though, was short-lived; the project languished throughout 1989 in the eternal damnation of development hell.

The disappointment was crushing, the collapse of their joint project effectively marking the end of Woods Road Productions and the beginning of the end of Bill and Marche's eleven-year relationship. One night after dinner at Moonshadows, a beachfront restaurant in Malibu, they walked on the shore, acknowledging that the tide had gone out on their relationship. Marche, now approaching forty, turned her attention instead to the potential of her children and their future. Bill was intent on building his own film career. Shortly afterward, he left to film another ecological documentary in Ecuador.

Like her mother before her, Marcheline was now living her own dreams vicariously through her children. She expected great things of them.

Nor was she the only one. One summer's day Windsor Lai, who had a growing reputation as an artist within the Beverly Hills High School community, came over to chat with Angie. She was sitting on the grass with her friend Evelyn Ungvari, quietly reading a book about Andy Warhol. Evelyn looked up and said to him: "You should draw her. One day she is going to be famous."

FIVE

Here she was seventeen and naked in front of a camera, watched by a bunch of strange guys. I couldn't understand why she did it, but I felt that this was a girl who knew what her goals were.

—Cyborg 2 actress Karen Sheperd

Like father, like daughter. As much as it may have irked her to admit it, Angie was as ambivalent about her future career as the teenage Jon Voight had been. With her unsatisfactory experience at the Lee Strasberg theater studio still fresh in her mind and with her mother's guidance, Angie was leaning toward modeling. Not that she embraced that path with any special enthusiasm; she was doing it to please her mother.

Modeling versus acting, her father versus her mother, life versus death: The yin and yang of her adolescent Gemini soul was on mawkish display when she agreed to accompany her father, who was guest of honor, to the Yubari International Fantastic Film Festival in February 1990. She claimed to be disinterested in her father and in the film industry, but here she was flying halfway around the world to a Japanese mining town.

Not that she proved especially effusive company. Her father was shocked at her withdrawn manner and wraithlike appearance. "She was almost like a ghost. I found out later about the cutting, the self-mutilation," he recalled. During the five-day visit to the land of symbolism and imagery, Angie got her first tattoo. Appropriately, it was the word *"kanji,"* Japanese for "death."

Her absorption with death did not stop her from following her mother into that most ephemeral and superficial of professions, modeling. It was her second attempt at this career path, Angie having been too self-conscious when her mother first took her to auditions at the age of ten. Now fourteen and struggling with anorexia, somewhat perversely she made the grade. In the fashion world, skinny is good; skinnier is better. With her bee-stung lips, flawless skin, and aura of reluctant, somewhat sullen, sexuality, the schoolgirl was soon in demand, at least in the European market. Back home, American magazine editors wanted models with girl-next-door appeal. It was not long before Angie was flown to shoots in London and New York, accompanied by her mother.

As with many models, the focus on her looks made her more critical of herself. "I always thought I looked like that blonde Muppet Janice with a big mouth and hair parted in the middle," she told writer Jane Rusoff. "When I was starting out I just wanted to be like a regular kind of pretty and not have 'different' features." It became a refrain; her desire to be "the other girl." At the same time, she dressed like a punk and identified with outsiders like the hero of *Edward Scissorhands,* the cult movie released in December 1990 that was a must-see for every goth worth her black mascara. Angie was smitten with actor Johnny Depp, who played Edward, an isolated figure with scissors for hands who lives in an attic and falls for the teenage daughter of a suburban family who cares for him. The movie's themes of alienation and self-discovery, as well as the disheveled figure of Edward Scissorhands, spoke to the angst-ridden Angie.

She may have been uncertain about herself and her looks, but modeling agencies soon recognized her potential. During 1990 she signed with Elite Model Management, home of supermodels Linda Evangelista, Naomi Campbell, and Cindy Crawford. It was at the height of the agency's influence; that same year Evangelista uttered the immortal quote about her profession: "We don't wake up for less than ten thousand dollars a day." While not quite in that league, Angie, still only fifteen and in her final year at school, was earning rather more than pin money, doing catalog work for stores like JCPenney and featuring in a Ben & Jerry's ice cream commercial.

At this time she showed little ambition to go into acting. Certainly that was her reaction when aspiring singer Brian Evans asked if she wanted to go into films. "I *don't* want to be in the entertainment industry like my dad," she told him emphatically as they sat in a limousine on the way to the October 1990 premiere of *Book of Love,* a gaudy rite-of-passage movie set in the 1950s. Perhaps it was just as well. During his fleeting if memorable appearance as a Boy Scout with a candle sticking out of his rear end, Evans glanced over at the daughter of an Oscar winner. She smiled and shook her head in disbelief. "Thankfully she did not ask me if I was a Method actor," he says ruefully. "At least she was not in the same business at the time."

Her antipathy toward acting had more to do with her father than with the profession. Anything she was going to achieve in life, she told herself, she was going to do without her father's help. She made this sentiment plain the moment she walked through the door of Robert Kim's photography studio in Los Angeles in early 1991. Even though her father had given her a ride there, she pleaded with makeup artist Rita Montanez: "Please don't tell Robert who my dad is." Rita was as good as her word, and throughout the four-hour shoot the portrait photographer had no clue about Angie's famous father. Rita recalls: "She was very self-contained and never wanted anyone to help. She wanted to do it all herself. It was very important for her to achieve her goals without her father's help." Indeed, Angie insisted that he stay in his car rather than come into the studio to pick her up. It was only later, when Rita was working on another of Angie's jobs, at the Photo Studio in Sherman Oaks, that she realized there might be another reason why Angie was so keen to keep her father in the background. Though it was early in the morning, Jon was disheveled, hadn't slept, and seemed disoriented. "Angie never gave anything away about her father. When I saw him, I understood why."

Meanwhile, the photographer, Kim, himself a former child actor, thought Angie had made the right choice to focus on modeling rather than acting. During the shoot the bespectacled schoolgirl never said a word. "She was a skinny teenager wet behind the ears and was so quiet that I could not possibly see her emoting in a movie." Yet the camera loved her; Angie came alive under the lights. "She had an edgy kind of energy," he recalls.

During a phone conversation, Marche told Kim that Angie's sultry yet youthful look had come to the attention of French *Vogue*. Magazine executives had frequently phoned mother and daughter in an attempt to lure her to Europe, telling them that within two years Angie would become a star. Angie was not interested. "She's a big girl; I can't force her to do anything," Marche told the photographer. Whether this was an accurate reflection of Angie's career or Marche's overactive imagination at work, Kim had his own opinion about what she should do next. At the end of the shoot, he took Angie aside: "Go to Paris for a couple of years and come back rich and famous," he counseled. She shook her head in disagreement. "I want to make it just like my daddy made it—through hard work and talent," she told him.

Yet just weeks after posing for head shots at Kim's studio, she was telling quite another story. In the spring of 1991 Jon Voight, remembering that *Peter Pan* had been Angie's favorite story, arranged for her and James to visit his friend Dustin Hoffman, who was playing Captain Hook in Steven Spielberg's continuation of J. M. Barrie's classic children's novel. As thoughtful as his gesture was, it seemed to reflect how Angie's father was always several steps behind her development. By the time she was ten, she had realized that she could no longer live in her imagination like a child, and yet here she was, almost six years later, watching the making of a movie about a child who never grows up. For the brooding teenager, her age of wonder had long gone.

Nor was Hoffman overly impressed when he met her on set, describing Angie as a "tall, thin, gawky-looking girl with a mouth full of braces." When he casually asked what James and Angie planned to do with their lives, he was surprised at Angie's certainty. "She gave me a laserlike look of intensity and she says, 'I'm going to be an actress.' And I went home to my wife and I said, 'I don't think this kid has any idea what a tough road she's got.'"

It was a road made all the tougher by her gradual estrangement from her father. In their complex relationship, her adolescent contempt and disdain, fueled by an underlying competitive drive, warred with an almost maternal concern for his well-being.

Around the time they visited Dustin Hoffman on the set of a fairy tale, her father was involved in a personal tragedy that could only exacerbate parental concerns about Angie's flirtation with death and suicide. Jon had let a young woman, Julie "Cindy" Jones, take temporary occupancy of an apartment he was renting near his home in Hollywood. Vivacious, glamorous, and fun, the thirty-three-year-old had a dark side, and had twice attempted suicide. One weekend early in March 1991, Julie and a girlfriend went skiing at the Lake Arrowhead resort in California. They arrived back late, Julie's friend noticing Jon Voight walking his dog as she dropped Julie off. While Julie, who was troubled by a bitter divorce battle, had frequently been distraught during the ski trip, she seemed to have calmed down.

As police records would later show, a few minutes after arriving home, Voight spoke with Julie on the telephone. Shortly after that one A.M. phone call, Julie put a .25-caliber Beretta handgun to her chest and shot herself through the heart. At seven o'clock on the morning of March 11, Jon Voight went to see her and found Julie dead in a pool of blood on the living room floor. She was dressed entirely in white—even down to a pair of white socks and white shoes, as though she were a bride about to meet her maker. The autopsy stated the cause of death as "gunshot wound," and noted that there was a great deal of alcohol in her system.

After her funeral in Sacramento, Voight organized the cleaning of her blood-spattered apartment as well as a ceremony of remembrance at his home involving Native American chanting for her departed soul. At the time, he was filming *The Last of His Tribe,* a TV movie about Ishi, the last survivor of the Yahi Indians of California, which earned him a Golden Globe nomination.

Julie's death—and the circumstances surrounding it—affected him deeply. That he was the last person to speak to her ignited incredible guilt. Voight wondered if he could have done more to save her—and if his daughter, emaciated, hostile, and prone to suicidal thoughts, could end up the same way. The trauma of finding Julie Jones's body shaped and heightened his concerns about Angie, Voight never forgetting the blood and the horror of that terrible day.

In the summer of 1991, after earning a California High School certificate— the equivalent of graduating—from Moreno High (Continuation), Angie again enrolled in her mother's alma mater, the Lee Strasberg studio, and later joined the Met Theatre Company, where her first role was as a talking salamander. As much as she might have fought against it, her father was in the audience for her first public workshop performance, in an adaptation of the 1930s slapstick comedy *Room Service,* made famous by the Marx Brothers. He was surprised at what he saw. Angie played the part of Gregory Wagner, a fat, balding German, as a female dominatrix. "I was a little shocked," Jon later recalled. "But the shock came from the realization that, oh my God, she's just like me. She'll take these crazy parts and be thrilled that she can make people chuckle or whatever." Whether she liked it or not, she was closely following in her father's footsteps. Later, her reading of

Catherine in Arthur Miller's *A View From the Bridge* would move Jon Voight to tears, no doubt in part as it reminded him of his early success on Broadway in the same play nearly thirty years before.

To prove her commitment to her new career, Angie took her collection of punk and ska CDs, as well as books by European philosophers and authors like Dostoyevsky and Nietzsche, and moved out of her mother's roomy duplex and into a studio apartment above a garage just a few blocks away. The move also enabled her to demonstrate to casting agents and others in the industry that she was "emancipated," that is to say, independent of her parents and no longer affected by child labor laws. Her mother had for once put her foot down, telling her that she would help her achieve her goals only if she focused on her chosen path, be it acting or modeling or a combination of both. Even Marche was not prepared to take her on another round of sullen auditions.

This period of her life marked a genuine sea change, Angie giving up the aimless days hanging out at Westwood Arcade and the nights taking drugs, watching movies, and socializing. As for Anton, he was now history. She actually gave acting her all, determined to make it without her father's help. Among all the pleasures of living on her own, perhaps the greatest thrill was that she got to use her own phone. Normally it is teenagers who spend their lives on the phone, but at Roxbury Drive it was Marche, leaving Angie frustrated and irritated that she couldn't speak to her friends.

If acting was a competitive sport, then it was a competition Angie was determined to win. She got herself in shape by learning to box at Bodies in Motion gym in Santa Monica. "I don't get in the ring, as I don't want to get my teeth knocked out. But it's great for self-defense," she told Rita Montanez.

Already fascinated with knives and swords, she took up fencing at the Westside Fencing Center under the watchful eye of an instructor who doubled as a movie stuntwoman. After the sessions, she and friends practiced the moves she had learned, using wooden brooms as swords.

For a time the young, black-garbed goth learned the waltz and the tango at the Arthur Murray Dance Studio in Beverly Hills. (Like her father, she suffers from curvature of the spine, which is why when people meet her they are impressed more by her ramrod straight posture, which she learned in order to correct the defect, than by her "pillow" lips.) Teacher Kent Sterling, who has been instructing for thirty years, recalls: "She was a fast learner but did not stick with it long enough to really become a dancer." Still, with her lean good looks and an upright natural grace, the school was keen for her to help sell lessons to potential clients.

Jon Voight was impressed. "It was like she put herself through the Royal Academy of Los Angeles," he recalled. "She took acting classes, voice lessons, fencing lessons, boxing—whatever she thought she needed as an actress."

It was her mother, however, who provided day-to-day guidance as Angie went through the daunting process of Method acting, learning, for example, to feel "in orange."

"I used to work with my mom," Angie recalled. "She was the most amazing support for an actor. She used to write letters to my characters. She always read the script, made a bunch of notes, and wrote these letters. She was a great person to talk to about things, and she loved the process so much." Rather like Lee Strasberg himself, who was a better teacher than he was an actor, Marcheline, who never had the sense of timing necessary to make it in movies, proved herself to be an excellent manager and coach for her daughter.

There was an extra dimension that propelled Angie onward. Beneath her public persona of an unnervingly quiet, self-contained, well-mannered, and seemingly docile girl, albeit dressed like a punk, was a young woman desperate to use acting as a vehicle to express and explore her inner turmoil. She placed her passion for acting on a par with her need to cut herself, as a way of communicating her feelings. As she later told James Lipton, "There's something inside of us that we want to reach out, we want to talk to each other, we want to throw our emotions and our feelings out and hope that we make some sense and we get an answer. The best way to do that is emote and hope that there would be a response."

As for many young actors, that response was the sound of silence. Dustin Hoffman had been right in predicting it was going to be a tough road. According to Angie's reckoning, she and her mother attended at least a hundred auditions. At first she went for girlfriend roles or the girl at high school, but she was always rejected. "I was just never that girl," she says. As far as casting agents were concerned, she was not regular or conventional-looking enough; they told her that she was too dark or too ethnic. "It was clear that my career was going to be full of very bizarre, strange women—which ended up being the ones I liked anyway," she recalls, her later bravado masking her intense disappointment at a time when she almost gave up hope of getting a break.

Ironically, when Angie snagged her first gig, in a music video of "It's About Time" by the Lemonheads, she played "the other girl," a love-struck schoolgirl. She got the part because she could "tear up" on command.

If casting agents were still to be convinced by her on-screen persona, rock star Lenny Kravitz was certainly intrigued when she appeared in his video. After the shoot, he asked her "stage mother," Lauren Taines, who she was. "She's going to be a big star," said Lauren coolly. "Yeah, I know, but who is she?" Kravitz persisted. "You take one step near her and I'll cut your hands off," Lauren replied.

It was easy to understand why Kravitz was fascinated. Angie's next performance, as an elusive yet beguiling teenage temptress in Antonello Venditti's steamy music video of "Alta Marea (Don't Dream It's Over)," shot on Venice Beach, anticipated her slinky sexuality. After the shoot Angie and her family went to the Redondo Beach home of Chip Taylor's son Christian to celebrate her minor success.

Although the music videos were a stepping-stone, she had yet to land a speaking part in an actual movie. Though her film career seemed stalled, her modeling work continued apace. In April 1992, shortly before her seventeenth birthday, she faced the toughest choice of her fledgling career.

A swimwear company wanted a fresh face to replace supermodel Cindy Crawford, whose celebrity meant that she was better known than the line. After spending hours looking through books of models, photographer Sean McCall was going cross-eyed searching for the right girl. It was only when Rita Montanez, who had now worked with Angie on several shoots, showed him Angie's Elite card that he realized he had found her. "She was the obvious choice," he recalls.

While at five feet, seven inches she was short for a top model—though that never stopped Kate Moss—she had the exotic European look he was searching for. With her long limbs, perfect skin—her only blemishes a few scratches on her hand from the cat—and a certain elusive sexual poise, she seemed ideal. There seemed to be no obvious sign of cutting.

As she changed into various swimsuits for the shoot in McCall's cramped condo in Brentwood, she was upbeat and self-confident, a real natural. "For her age she was the most natural girl in front of a camera I had ever seen," recalls McCall. "She was unself-conscious, whereas many teenage girls are like deer in headlights." At one point she complained about the hot studio lights, and McCall told her that compared to movie lights, these were like candles. "I would go through that for a movie," she said nonchalantly.

Certainly she was a shoo-in to be the face of the brand. The swimwear executives loved what they saw and arranged for a full-scale shoot on location in the State Park at Malibu, the home of the TV show *Baywatch*. Shortly before she was due to take over from supermodel Cindy Crawford, however, Angie decided against going on the shoot, saying that she had decided to focus on acting. "If that doesn't work, I will go back to modeling," she explained. In the end, Californian blonde Caprice Bourret got the gig, going on to become best known as a lingerie model and a favorite of British men's magazines.

Angie's decision was risky. If she had gone into modeling full-time, she would quickly have made a name for herself, whereas in the world of acting she was still a nobody. Within a matter of weeks, however, the gamble paid off. Angie had the chance to test McCall's theory about studio lights when she auditioned for a big-budget sci-fi film initially titled *Glass Shadow*. Then the producers slashed the budget from $40 million to B-movie proportions and changed the title to *Cyborg 2*—making it the sequel to the 1989 original starring muscleman Jean-Claude Van Damme. In spite of the film's vastly reduced scope, there were still three actresses—*Legends of the Fall* star Karina Lombard, martial-arts expert Cynthia Rothrock, and a model named Blueberry—vying for the role of Casella "Cash" Reese, an "almost human" cyborg designed to seduce and destroy. While Angie had a modest show reel (her modeling shoots augmented by five student shorts made by her brother while he attended USC film school), the moment she walked into the casting suite, she nailed the gig. "She sucked the air out of the room, she was so gorgeous," recalls director Michael Schroeder. "She was special from the get-go, so talented she is a force of nature. She seemed to have the acting chops in her genes. I had a good feeling about this girl."

Not everyone on the set was so impressed. Her costar Elias Koteas had reservations about a girl just seventeen being cast as his love interest, given their age difference—he was thirty-two at the time. Since it was a tight twenty-nine-day shoot and she had to appear nude in a love scene, it was important that she was emanicipated and therefore exempt from child labor laws.

While Michael Schroeder soothed the concerns of his leading man, others were equally doubtful about his choice of leading lady. Former world judo champion Karen Sheperd, who was playing an evil cyborg, was asked to give Angie some basic instruction in martial arts. When her mother dropped Angie off at a North Hollywood dojo—a garage turned into a karate studio—Karen, like the rest of the cast, was well aware that this was Jon Voight's daughter. "She was skinny as a bird, arms like twigs, and she was so young and so brittle I had real doubts and thought, 'Here we go, Hollywood nepotism.' I was afraid I was going to hurt her."

Angie told her that she had "dabbled" in boxing, which Karen took as a way of saying she'd done nothing before. So she expected little from the two-hour session, teaching Angie how to punch without breaking her wrist as well as kicks, blocks, spins, and the basics of holding her body in a fighting stance. "She was lacking coordination and not that agile but really focused." As well as learning her lines, she was instructed to spend the next few days doing her fighting homework—punching in front of a mirror.

When shooting began on September 28, 1992, Angie quickly impressed her fellow actors with her dedication, her supple grace, and a willingness to work hard and take instruction. While the $2,500-a-week paycheck came in very handy, the experience mattered more to Angie. "She was an old soul," recalls Karen Sheperd. "Not a flippant girl but mature beyond her years. I've worked with up-and-coming actors like Angie and they are punks. They throw tantrums and think that the whole world revolves around them. She wasn't like that; she was self-controlled but open-minded to ideas on set no matter where they came from."

Angie had only one rule—her father's name was not to be mentioned. Even though she used her middle name, Jolie, which her mother had presciently chosen when she was born, Voight's shadow was ever present. Fellow actor Ric Young had just finished a charity telethon with Jon to raise funds for Chabad, while Michael Schroeder had worked with him on a film about the Chernobyl nuclear accident a couple of years before. Young takes an artistically matter-of-fact view of Angie's inner turmoil concerning her father. "Every actor has a scar, some conflict," he observes. "They are always at war with somebody. If you have a wonderful childhood, there is no conflict. But acting doesn't work that way; a person has to go through a lot."

As much as Angie might have disapproved, Jon visited the set a couple of times, pleased that his daughter was in the hands of a "caring" director. At the time, he was rehearsing for his first stage role since playing the title role in *Hamlet,* the play that had cost him his marriage sixteen years before. In November 1992 he starred alongside Ethan Hawke in Chekhov's *The Seagull* at New York's Lyceum Theatre. It was a move that was to have bizarre consequences for his tenuous relationship with his daughter.

Notwithstanding her famous father, Angie came to be seen by cast and crew as quiet but not aloof, serious about making a good job of her first movie role. She normally kept to her trailer, resting, smoking, or learning her scenes. One break from the exhausting routine came when legendary Hollywood star Jack Palance arrived on set for a couple of days to film his scenes. Other actors, including Angie, gathered in his trailer to listen to the actor, who is of Ukrainian descent, declaim Russian poetry. For the most part, though, Angie was focused on the work, knowing that this was her movie and her break, and she had to make the best of it. "She was really responsive to direction and could make changes without hesitation," recalls Michael Schroeder. "Being brought up in the business, she understood instinctively how movies are made."

Her nude scene with Elias Koteas, which was filmed on a closed set toward the end of the shoot, did give her pause. Michael Schroeder made it as easy as possible. As the cameras rolled, he played a seductive aria from Erich Korngold's 1920 opera, *The Dead City.* While her nude scene was tasteful and relatively tame, other cast members were concerned. "I felt sorry for her," recalls Ric Young, appreciating that young actors can be "cursed by beauty," like Marilyn Monroe was. "Everyone wants a piece of you, yet you have to be ruthless about keeping yourself to yourself. Angie has that inner toughness."

It was a toughness that might have been helped, or honed, by what psychoanalyst Franziska De George describes as Angie's ability to dissociate, which was related to the impulse that caused her to cut herself. If it was awkward to do a scene naked, she simply removed herself emotionally, switched gears, as cutting switched her pain from emotional to physical. Finally, her troubled background could serve an even better purpose than supplying a well of chaotic feelings to draw upon as an actress. It could give her the means to do what she had to, suffer what she had to, in order to succeed as an artist.

After the scene, Karen Sheperd, who had become a mother figure during filming, took her aside and asked if she was okay. "She said that she was glad that it was behind her. Here she was seventeen and naked in front of a camera, watched by a bunch of strange guys. I couldn't understand why she did it, but I felt that this was a girl who knew what her goals were. She could see the big picture. She knew that she had the looks, the connections, and that if she stayed focused and absorbed it all, this film was going to be her stepping-stone."

While she may have given that impression then, that was not the way Angie saw herself when she first viewed the completed movie. "When I saw it I threw up for three days" is her now-famous account of her movie debut. "My brother held me and I went back to school and didn't want to work again." Indeed, she says that it was a year before she summoned the courage to go for another audition.

Given the fact that she had left school, perhaps it wasn't surprising that the film's director remembers the incident rather differently. She came over to his house in Hollywood for dinner and a viewing. Understandably apprehensive, she sat with Schroeder, and when the movie ended, she told him that she had to be by herself and drove off into the night. The next day she called him to apologize. "Sorry, I was blown away by the movie and had to leave," she told him. She called again a couple of days later to tell him how much she liked the film. That night he took her to a bar in West Hollywood and bought Angie her first martini. "I love the movie and I love you; it's all great," she told her director. As he says, "A lot of actors won't go to the movies they are in. When she came out with me she was fine." She had once again moved past her own feelings.

Such was her enthusiasm that she immediately agreed to reprise her role of Cash for the sequel due to be filmed in 1993. She had already started prepping the script when the film's new star, Zach Galligan, then riding high after *Gremlins*, insisted that a "name" actress be cast in Angie's part. When the new producers chose Emmy Award–winning TV actor

Khrystyne Haje, director Michael Schroeder was so angry that he quit the movie and returned only when he was threatened with legal action. "When I told Angie that they had decided to go with someone else, she was so gracious," he says, describing his time making *Cyborg 3* as the worst experience of his career.

It was almost as bad for Angie. She had pinned her hopes on having a breakthrough with this movie. As it turned out, she hardly worked for more than a year. During this hiatus, Marche did an "amazing" job with her daughter, encouraging her to work hard at modeling so that she would have a lot of material for her acting show reel.

Marche had other, more ethereal plans to help Angie snag a foothold on the acting ladder. They met with Marche's regular psychic, who also helps the San Francisco police on unsolved cases, and she would take an object Angie was wearing and "see" her destiny through the vibrations she felt. Her mother also pinned her hopes on a subject that had fascinated her for years: astrology. Mother and daughter would read the runes, or rather the stars, seeking a pathway for Angie's acting journey.

Marcheline even bought an astrology computer program to pick out the signposts in the stars that would guide Angie's career. Unfortunately, she did not like the astrological map that the computer spat out: Angie's chart specifically pinpointed a "controlling mother" who could make or break her career. Marche refused to let Angie see this chart, insisting that her friend Lauren Taines alter the actual computer program so that it was wiped from the memory. It was a telling incident.

In general, however, Marche and Lauren were so pleased with the program that they decided to set up their own company, Open Sky, to advise clients about their astrological charts. Unfortunately, the perfectionist in Marche ensured that the project was stillborn. She spent so long worrying about the punctuation and grammar for the company brochure that the venture never got off the ground—or, more appropriately, came to earth.

While Marche was poring over syntax, Angie enjoyed some consolation for losing *Cyborg 3* when she beat hundreds of other young hopefuls to become the face of *Young Miss* magazine. The resulting commercial, made in the summer of 1993 by *Se7en* and *Fight Club* director David Fincher, showed a sultry Angelina walking down a dark and dirty New York street as cars marked with words like "sex," "drugs," and "career" careened into one another. As the face of *Young Miss,* she was the knowing go-to girl to guide other teenagers through these hazards. The voice-over said, "It's her world, you just live in it," a phrase that could serve as a metaphor for her life—at least outwardly.

It was that knowing, self-possessed, somewhat enigmatic quality that attracted the attention of cameraman Mark Gordon, a recent graduate of the American Film Institute, who was producing a couple of surreal "haiku-style" short films for his portfolio. He hired Steven Shainberg, who would later direct *Secretary,* to write and direct them. When they were considering actors, Gordon's stylist friend Brad Bowman raved about a beautiful new model he had seen at an agency. It was Angelina Jolie. They arranged to see her and hired her for one spot, *Angela and Viril.* Filmed in black and white in June 1993, the short film depicted Angie sitting on a bed in the lotus position, meditating, while Viril typed rhythmically the numbers one through one thousand on an old typewriter. Just eighteen, she was, according to Gordon, "extraordinarily beautiful and exotic." As he observes: "She appeared shy but also had a reserved confidence with the shooting process." Gordon and Shainberg liked Angie so much that they hired her for the second short, *Alice and Viril.* This time, Viril meets Alice at a convention for lawn products. She asks him to hold his head underwater for three minutes, so he plunges his head into a fish tank while Angie's character lounges nonchalantly.

As surreal as this no-budget movie was, it paled in comparison to Angie's real life. During his Broadway run in *The Seagull,* her father had met Laura Pels, a wealthy French-born theatrical producer who agreed to finance a filmmaking company, Jon Voight Productions. Pels invested $4 million, and the Paul family agreed to produce a slate of movies, including *Double Russian Roulette, Reverse Heaven,* and a trio of films based on Hans Christian Andersen fairy tales. A few months later, in late 1993, Pels first became suspicious of the Paul family after receiving, as she later told the *New York Post,* an anonymous letter detailing lawsuits involving the family. While the sender of the letter has never come forward, the result was that Pels decided to sue Steven Paul as well as Stuart and Dorothy Paul and their companies for fraud and embezzlement.

That same year, Jon Voight's manager, Steven Paul, moved into a palatial mansion in Coldwater Canyon. This rankled with Marcheline, who was still waiting for her ex-husband to get his money back and buy her a house. Not only had he given Stacey Pickren the deed to the home they lived in when they parted, but now his manager was moving into an exclusive area, while Voight struggled to pay his bills.

What to do? Marche could buy a home only if Jon gave her the money she felt she was due—which couldn't happen until the Paul family had repaid the loan. According to her, they had told Jon that they couldn't afford to give him the money. So, she reasoned, what if she showed Jon financial paperwork to prove that they had ample cash to pay him back?

That was the logic behind a madcap scheme cooked up by Marche, Angie, and a couple of close friends to find the proof: They would take the trash from the street outside Steven Paul's house, go through it in search of financial documents, and present them to Jon, who would see the light and demand his money. If that didn't work, they would bundle up any incriminating papers and pass them on to the FBI.

The first part of the plan went off without a hitch. One night shortly after the Los Angeles earthquake in January 1994, Marche's girlfriend and her friend's boyfriend (brought in for "muscle") quietly drove to Steven Paul's home and filled the backseat of their Mustang convertible with large trash bags that were awaiting collection. Then they drove to Marche's apartment and poured the trash on the kitchen table, and Angie and her mother, wearing rubber gloves, went to work sorting through the garbage. Angie and Marche uncovered a thick file of documents relating to expensive office furniture and other fittings, various film production companies, and other paperwork that suggested, certainly in Marche's mind, that the Pauls had much to answer for. "Angie loved playing detective; she found the whole thing very amusing," admits a coconspirator.

Part two of the operation—confronting Jon Voight and passing on the information to the FBI—never came off, however. Marcheline lost her nerve not only about approaching her ex-husband but also about compiling a dossier that the authorities would take seriously. There is no evidence of any actual wrongdoing on behalf of the Pauls, and Jon remains closely affiliated with them.

The saga had several more plot twists. In the summer of 1994 Voight filed a countersuit against Pels, accusing the sixty-three-year-old of treating him like a "sex object," and claiming that Pels withdrew financing for his projects when he rebuffed her advances. She responded by describing his lawsuit as "inane," a smoke screen to distract attention from her $4 million lawsuit against his manager and the rest of the Paul family. (After further legal maneuvers, he retracted his allegations in September 1994, apologizing for the pain he had caused Pels and her family, and Pels's lawsuit against the Pauls was subsequently settled and dismissed.)

In the meantime, Angie was not finished playing detective. At her mother's urging, she visited her father's home in Hollywood to snoop around for more financial paperwork linking her father to the Pauls. Marche was concerned that he had signed legal papers that would make him liable for any lawsuits or costs associated with the Pauls' financial schemes. Angie was able to report back that he was not involved as a partner, nor was he financially liable. "It was a great relief for Marche," recalls a friend with intimate knowledge of the matter. "A huge weight was lifted from her shoulders."

Still, Angie continued to poke her nose into her father's financial affairs. On one occasion she met a woman movie executive at her father's home and, according to the story she told friends, advised her not to invest in any of her father's schemes. The executive took Angie's advice at face value and refused to invest.

While this made an amusing anecdote for Angie, the underlying story was rather tragic, exposing her utter lack of respect for her father. As entertaining as Angie may have found it to embarrass Jon Voight and interfere in his private financial dealings, she was ultimately a helpless pawn in the long-running war between her mother and father, usually siding, whether she wanted to or not, with her mother.

Ironically, during this family detective drama, she landed another film role, that of a witness to a murder who refuses to give evidence in court. She played a street junkie, Jodie Swearingen, in the conspiracy thriller *Without Evidence,* based on the true story of the unsolved murder of Michael Francke, the head of Corrections for the State of Oregon, who was thought to have uncovered a drug ring shortly before his death. The movie was filmed in Salem, Oregon, during May and June 1994, and Angie's performance was described as "heartbreakingly touching" by *Variety* when the low-budget independent was released two years later.

A few weeks after that film wrapped, she enjoyed a complete change of pace, appearing in *Love Is All There Is,* a romantic comedy loosely based on *Romeo and Juliet* that was filmed in the Bronx and at Greentree Country Club in New Rochelle, New York. She played a girl who falls in love with the son of a rival Italian catering family. Once again Angie found herself having sex on camera, except this time her star-crossed lover, played by Nathaniel Marston, was a month younger than Angie, and their love scene was played for laughs, Marston's character's parents walking in as they got hot and heavy beneath the sheets. When the comedy was finally released in May 1996 to generally lukewarm reviews—"woefully unfunny," said the *Hollywood Reporter*—it was notable for the way Angie handled an Italian accent.

Life was decidedly unfunny for Angie, too. After the shoot she experienced the typical depression associated with the ending of a collegial venture such as making a movie. In Angie's case, though, it was compounded by her feelings of worthlessness and alienation. She didn't want to return to Hollywood, where she would be prey to her parents' interminable skirmishing, so she stayed in a New York hotel room, contemplating life. Or rather, contemplating taking her life. "I didn't know if I wanted to live because I just didn't know what I was living for," she later told *Rolling Stone*. She decided to take sleeping tablets and cut her wrists with one of her knives. She didn't have enough pills, however, and she asked her mother, once again her passive if innocent enabler, to mail her more. Then she wrote a note for the hotel's housekeeping staff asking them to call the police so that no one would have the distress of finding her body. She spent the rest of the day wandering the streets of New York, at one point looking at a kimono. Angie hesitated about buying it, realizing how absurd such a purchase would be given her immediate intent.

As she considered her decision, she appreciated that her mother would feel guilty for providing the sleeping pills. At some point, lying on the bed, she came to a conclusion of sorts: "You might as well live a lot, really hard, and not give a shit, because you can always walk through that door. So I started to live as if I could die any day." The next day, she went back and bought the kimono.

For a girl who pondered suicide on numerous occasions, her next purchase suggested an underlying will to live. Her last two movies, together with her modeling work and an appearance that year in a Meatloaf rock video, enabled this unconventional girl to behave in a very conventional way. Just nineteen, she had enough money to put a down payment on an apartment in West Hollywood. She had seen her mother have to rely on the intermittent largesse of her father, and that life was not for her. Even as she triumphantly asserted her independence, her father still acted as guarantor for the loan.

Once again, though, she felt a profound depression afterward, spiraling into a mood of anger, sadness, and hopelessness. As much as she embraced life, burning faster and running harder than her contemporaries, so did she reject life, as she rejected herself. It was almost as if she felt she didn't really deserve a home of her own.

Once she got the keys to the apartment, she found herself sitting on the floor sobbing because she had to pick out a carpet color and didn't think she would live long enough to see the carpet installed. Having a nice home of her own, it turned out, didn't resolve her inner torment. And now she was truly lost: If a home didn't provide the feeling of being finally "home," what would?

But Angie is a survivor. As writer Chris Heath laconically observed, "Crying over the pointlessness of home decoration in an impermanent and unreliable world, she eventually did the smart thing and chose a carpet anyway."

"Dark gray," she recalls. "I didn't get that happy. It was a very, very dark gray."

SIX

*She knew about needles and tattoos and heroin and she had an
innate wild sexuality. That is what the camera captured. It filmed
her courage and her chutzpah.*

—*PLAYING GOD* DIRECTOR ANDY WILSON

After more than two years of focusing on her acting career, Angelina
had no social life to speak of and no boyfriend since Anton had been
sent packing. Her life was a relentless round of acting classes, occasional
auditions, and rejection after rejection. The couple of small roles she had
snagged in low-budget films after *Cyborg 2* were not going to make a Hollywood director or producer sit up and take notice. By the fall of 1994 she
was depressed and frustrated; the name Angelina Jolie was just not opening any doors.

Seeing her despair, her mother, who was now her manager, broke the
cardinal rule of Angie's professional life, her refusal to piggyback on her
father's name. Without breathing a word to Angie, her mother called her
agent, Hollywood veteran Richard Bauman of Bauman-Hiller, and told
him that he could start to tell casting agents that Angie was indeed Jon
Voight's daughter. As the name Voight was rather better known than Jolie,
very soon doors started creaking open. To this day Angie doesn't know that
it was her father's name that helped her get her first big break.

In any event, she needed more than her father's name to win her first
mainstream role; dumb luck played a starring role, too. When fifteen-year-
old actress Katherine Heigl, who had earned plaudits from French actor
Gérard Depardieu for her role in his latest film, *My Father the Hero*, decided
to drop out of a teen cyber-thriller, *Hackers*, Angie was invited to audition.
Even though Angie impressed director Iain Softley, she was up against

formidable competition, including Hilary Swank, Heather Graham, and Liv Tyler, for the role of computer whiz kid Kate "Acid Burn" Libby.

Given Angie's antipathy toward modern technology, it was rather ironic that the English director eventually chose her. Unlike her computer geek brother, she prided herself on using only a pencil. "I hate computers," she would say during interviews to promote the film. She was not the only one. Her costar Jonny Lee Miller also had a love-hate relationship with the world of technology. "I'm not someone who needs to talk to someone in Russia at four A.M. on the Internet or store lots of information," he later explained. It was but the first connection on the road to romance.

At first glance, Jonny Lee Miller neatly fitted the template of the rather fey young men who had drifted through her life. Good-looking, quietly charming yet diffident to the point of shyness, Miller, known as "Jonny Leave Me Alone" by his friend actor Robert Carlyle, seemed the antithesis of a strong, macho male. For Angie, an alpha female, he fitted the mold established by her friendship with the openly gay Chris Landon, her sobbing live-in lover, the "nerdy" Brian Evans, and of course her brother, the favored son endlessly waiting for his father to give his career a kick-start rather than relying on his own chops as his sister was doing.

Yet, as she was soon to discover, Miller was much wilder than his meek and mild persona suggested. For once the intensely competitive Miss Jolie found herself uncomfortably lagging behind. Like Angie, Miller was from a theatrical family—his grandfather Bernard Lee played "M" in the first twelve James Bond films—and Miller had appeared onstage and on TV since he was nine. A member of the National Youth Music Theatre, during the summer vacations he and his best friend, actor Jude Law, regularly performed at the Edinburgh International Festival. Before joining the cast of *Hackers,* he had held his own playing opposite the redoubtable Helen Mirren, the hardboiled detective in the TV drama *Prime Suspect.*

Initially, his pleasantly hypnotic English accent proved Angie's undoing. "Englishmen appear to be so reserved, but underneath they're expressive, perverse, and wild," she says. She soon discovered that Miller, a serious runner, skydiver, and martial-arts fan, was as fascinated by tattoos as his new girlfriend. Two years older than Angie, he had a rat and a snake on his arm, courtesy of his "crazy" youth. Together they would explore the world of the needle much more intensely.

In the early days, though, the tomboy in her tried, and usually failed, to best her costar on Rollerblades, the couple bonding as they prepped for their roles as cool computer hackers. When they reported for work in September 1994, they spent several hours a days padded up and learning to Rollerblade in Battery Park in New York City and another four hours a day under the tutelage of a computer expert learning how to type and understand the intricacies of cyberspace. "Racing Jonny on Rollerblades was a big part of our relationship," Angie recalls. "We had read a lot about computers and met computer hackers. With a lot of lines, I didn't know what I was talking about."

For his part, as much as Miller professed to be a Luddite, he spent hours playing computer games, one of his favorites the adventures of a buxom action heroine, Lara Croft. Angie, on the other hand, to the bemusement of other cast members, found a scene in which she had to rummage through garbage in an alleyway endlessly amusing. "I thought of you when I was doing it," she told a fellow conspirator in the real-life garbage run on Steven Paul's house.

Perhaps appropriately, given the juvenile nature of the movie, her love affair with Jonny evolved in the schoolyard, much of the filming taking place in November and December 1994 at Stuyvesant High School in the TriBeCa neighborhood of Manhattan. "I always fall in love while I'm working on a film. It's such an intense thing," she recalls. At the end of a passionate and at times exhilarating experience came the inevitable feeling of deflation and depression as the bonds forged in the intensity of the moment were casually cut. In spite of their closeness, when filming ended, Angie, once again sad and despondent, asked Miller to forget about her and move on. She returned to Los Angeles, but they nonetheless kept in touch, developing a long-distance relationship.

Angie had work to do. In many ways her role as the edgy but brilliant tomboy "Acid Burn" anticipated her next character, a charismatic drifter named Legs Sadovsky in *Foxfire,* based on Joyce Carol Oates's novel set in the 1950s. It's the story of a group of high school girls who are inspired to confront a sexually abusive teacher when a mysterious female James Dean–like character appears out of nowhere to urge them to take on authority and explore their true natures, including their dawning sexuality. The opening shot establishes the mythic mood, the leather-clad Legs dramatically arriving at the school gate in the middle of a thunderstorm. "I saw Legs as being androgynous but sexual in a very animal sort of way; free, fascinating, intriguing and touchy," Angie told writer Gary Dretzka.

Before filming began in Portland, Oregon, in March 1995, she was reminded that for all the exploration of character, the search for essence, she was involved in a game for overgrown children. She remembers being in her father's bedroom excitedly showing him the butterfly knife she was going to carry and the leather pants she was going to wear for the *Foxfire* shoot. He then showed her the hair extensions, bracelets, and rings he would be using in the Los Angeles–based crime drama *Heat*. "It was just like two kids playing dress up," she recalls. For all her issues with her father, there remained a residual bedrock of understanding. "Now it's great because we can talk on a level few people can talk to their parents on," she told *Empire* magazine. "Not only can we talk about our work, but our work is about our emotion, our lives, the games we play, what goes through our heads." The good news, too, was that he was back working, doing what he did best. As much as she railed against him, he was her dad and she cared about him. Watching a man she admired, albeit grudgingly, spiral out of control had been a painful experience.

For Angie there was no boundary between a role and real life. As she noted, she absorbed the character, becoming that person and living through the role. On set, she was Legs Sadovsky even when the cameras stopped rolling. She was not the only one. Fellow actress Hedy Burress was as granola offscreen as on, enjoying hiking and communing with nature; Sarah Rosenberg was the token grunge; while Calvin Klein model Jenny Shimizu was a contradictory presence: A crop-haired motorbike dyke, she gave off a butch vibe but was actually sweet, demure, and easily dominated. Both onscreen and off, Angie was an intimidating presence, her dark, brooding charisma terrifying and attracting.

Actress Michelle Brookhurst, who played the class bitch, Cindy, vividly describes having to shout, "Who the fuck are you?" in a potentially violent face-off with Angie's Legs. The problem was that Michelle, then sixteen, was wary of Angie. It didn't help her self-possession that, in Method acting style, Angie would yell and scream and continuously clear her throat in preparation for the scene.

"Even at nineteen, Angie was the most formidable person I have ever met," recalls Michelle, now a stylist. "Everyone was slightly terrified of her, not because she was mean or unkind. She was not like that at all. It was like meeting a serial killer or a member of the Mafia. There was something dark there that scared me. She had that unsettling presence. Watching her was like watching a snake uncurling. She is inaccessible, like a force of nature, as if she was from a different planet."

The screen "scent" left by Angie was sniffed out by film critic Robert Butler. He noted perceptively: "If *Foxfire* is remembered for anything it will be as one of the earliest screen appearances of Angelina Jolie, who has a face the camera loves and seems a likely candidate for fully fledged stardom."

Certainly, Angie was by far the most experienced actor in the group of teenage girls sequestered in a luxury hotel in Portland's Pioneer Square with an acting coach. Shimizu struggled with her role as a troubled drug addict and needed particular attention. For first-time director Annette Haywood-Carter, this was a baptism of fire. During filming virtually all members of the camera crew were fired, and the girls were endlessly indulged—filming halted for hours, for example, so that Hedy Burress could enjoy her "moment" alone on an empty bridge that served as a metaphor for personal growth. Editorially there was indecision about whether this was a liberating revenge fantasy or a rite-of-passage movie, as Maddy, a conventional young woman played by Burress, has her sexuality awakened by Angie's Legs. Every night the girls were handed new pages of dialogue to learn, reflecting the indecision at the top. In the end, Haywood-Carter filmed two endings, one with Legs and Maddy kissing, the other with Maddy holding back.

While the kiss ended up on the cutting-room floor, another quasi-erotic sequence did make it to the big screen. In a long scene shot in an empty house, Legs tattoos the breast of each of her teenage disciples. "I loved doing it; it was sensual and fun," she later told James Lipton. "It was a very lovely time between women."

While there was sexual hesitancy on film, among the actors and crew there was no such inhibition, the eight-week shoot turning into one long and decadent sorority party. On one occasion all the girls went to a strip club, a bespectacled blonde lap dancing for Angie and her "wasted" crew. For the first few weeks Jenny's girlfriend visited from New York, bringing small presents. Angie bided her time. Although she was still developing her long-distance relationship with Jonny Lee Miller, she admitted that she fell in love with Shimizu the moment she saw her audition for the movie.

At first Angie thought the dark-haired model was a rival for her role of Legs, but she relaxed when she realized Shimizu was up for Goldie, the troubled addict. "I noticed her sweater and the way her pants fitted and I thought: 'My God!' I was getting incredibly strong sexual feelings," she told the London *Sunday Mirror*. For the first two weeks the girls just lay on a hotel bed chatting. Eventually Jenny, then twenty-four, made the first move and undressed her costar. "She was very sexual and very comfortable and very domineering. I could tell she wasn't a normal teenager," Jenny later told Sky TV, acknowledging Angie's precocious behavior. "I've never kissed anyone with a bigger mouth than Angelina Jolie. I always thought I had huge lips, but when I met her it was like two big water beds." Much of their passion lay in resisting temptation before wildly embracing each other, Jenny describing this masochist element of their love affair as being acted out in their minds rather than in bed. "It's not like we dressed in leather and hung each other up in chains or anything like that," she said.

When Miller, who was under the impression that he was Angie's boyfriend, visited the set, Angie took the English actor and Shimizu out for dinner and explained that she cared for them both and that she and her costar were sleeping together. "She was honest—that's how she's been her whole life," Jenny recalled. After this heart-to-heart, the three went back to the local strip club. "I don't really do threesomes," Jenny explained later. "It was a good friendship for all of us to have. There wasn't much conversation with Jonny. I think he was very threatened by me. Who wouldn't be?"

In the peripatetic world of acting, Angie returned to Los Angeles after filming ended in April, while Miller bleached his hair and flew to Scotland to appear in *Trainspotting*, Danny Boyle's movie based on Irvine Welsh's tawdry tale of drugs and low life among a motley crew of Edinburgh youths.

Around this time another man came into her life who would have a profound influence on her career. Her brother James's graduation from USC took place during the filming of *Foxfire*, and she had wanted a clause in the contract to allow her leave to attend the ceremony. For some reason it was omitted. Angie was furious, and went to the graduation anyway—a fraught family event that saw the permanent estrangement of her mother and her mother's sister, Debbie, over the trivial matter of the allocation of tickets. As a result of this contractual mix-up, Angie decided to move to a bigger agency, William Morris. As she was low on the agency totem pole—at the time, Billy Bob Thornton was riding high with *Sling Blade,* Quentin Tarantino had a hit with *Pulp Fiction,* and Sean Penn and Bruce Willis were hot—she was relegated to an agent's assistant, Geyer Kosinski.

Inside the William Morris offices, Kosinski, an exuberant if rather arrogant party animal, enthusiastically championed her cause, even when others questioned his judgment. She was seen as a wild card, a starlet who had done little of note—apart from attract the wrong sort of publicity. "He believed in her absolutely," recalls a WMA colleague. "He told everyone that she was going to be a great movie star." In time his home would become a shrine to Angie, every room dominated by pictures of his client. While she thought it was "creepy," he soon had her in his thrall. Tough, thick-skinned, and driven, Kosinski was the classic hard-boiled agent who went everywhere with several cell phones—even on a date.

Although Angie liked his focus, her mother was not so impressed. As Angie's manager, Marcheline had effectively guided her career to date, keeping an eye on contracts and accounts while helping with scripts. Now all that changed, with Kosinski driving the editorial side of her career and Marcheline taking over the finances—for a reduced percentage of Angie's fees. While this arrangement could charitably be described as creative tension, there was little affection between mother and agent over the coming months and years. At some point Marche was delighted when she discovered a $15,000 payment discrepancy, and thereafter she watched Angie's accounts like a hawk. For his part, Kosinski frequently undermined Marche's attempts to develop film and TV projects for herself and her children.

Over time Angie and Geyer developed a dysfunctional father/daughter relationship. While Angie felt she had the final say over her career, Kosinski was the one who pulled the strings. Eventually their relationship evolved into the Hollywood equivalent of a royal court, Marche and Kosinski intriguing against each other. Ultimately, though, it was Kosinski who came to control Queen Angie. A family friend who watched this dance observed: "Angie is a typical Gemini and split the responsibilities. Marche didn't trust Kosinski, and while Angie loved her mother, she pitted them against each other. It was checks and balances. There was no love lost there."

Nor was there any love lost between Jonny Lee Miller and Jenny Shimizu. As much as he might have considered himself Angie's boyfriend, it was clear that her relationship with Jenny was no passing fancy. The two women continued to see each other in Hollywood, their ideal night spent cruising strip clubs with Angelina in hot pants and a matching skintight vest. "I even took her to dominatrix joints, and she loved them," Jenny told writer Georgina Dickinson. "The naughtier the better. Then we'd go back to wherever we were staying, desperate to rip each other's clothes off and act out the moves we had seen. They were amazing nights."

Even though she was younger and less sexually experienced than Jenny, it was Angie who was the dominant in their relationship, reflecting her long-held desire to "be one of the boys." "If a strap-on was involved, she would wear it," joked another friend from this sexually experimental period in her life. "She would be the one to tell you to suck her cock."

While her friend, speaking on condition of anonymity, was heterosexual and in a relationship, when Angie first met her she invited her and her boyfriend for a threesome. The girl declined, but nonetheless her friendship with Angie flourished, and she came to know Angie well over the next few years. Marche was thrilled about this friendship, observing that she was the first girlfriend Angie had ever had that she was not sleeping with. As this platonic girlfriend recalls: "I'd never met a true bisexual before Angie and wasn't sure if they even really existed. To quote my little sister: 'Bisexuals are just greedy.' But I feel Angie is a true bisexual. She lusted after women, just as she did with men. It definitely was not an act. She is mega-sexual. When it comes to men, she is interested in those in the spotlight. When it comes to women, they are her true love. She is attracted to women she is friends with."

Psychologist Iris Martin sees more in Angie's behavior than adolescent experimentation, tracing it back to her early months left alone in her crib, her life an unconscious search for a mother. "Most women have women friends and they are like your sisters. You don't want to fuck them. If you are starved of intimacy, if you have been abandoned, you feel like nothing inside. If you have an attraction to a woman, it is going to end up sexual.

108

The slightest reaction to intimacy is completely overblown, as it taps into her well of neediness."

Psychoanalyst Dr. Franziska De George also focuses on Angie's scattered childhood, her disassociation from herself. "Bisexuality is part of being lost; it is a way of expressing yourself. If you don't understand yourself and what you need, you are going to experiment."

There was, too, a darker motive behind Angie's sexual experimentation and willing embrace of bisexuality—revenge. On one occasion she and Jenny Shimizu went to a photo booth near the beach at Santa Monica and made out for the camera, Angie licking and French-kissing her lover. When she next saw her father, she asked him if he wanted to see some pictures, pulling out the lewd set of her and Jenny. She knew full well that Stacey Pickren had left him for another woman, and teasing and humiliating him was her payback for the fact that he had left her mother. "I think a lot of her dabbling with other women was to take a stab at her father," observes Lauren Taines.

Whatever the motivation behind her on-and-off relationship with Jenny, she was reunited with Jonny Lee Miller that September to publicize *Hackers*. Their first experience of a mainstream release was not entirely enjoyable. The reviews were lukewarm to hostile and, in spite of all her efforts, in the round of media interviews, the chief interest in Angie was about her famous father. The focus was as much on why she no longer used her last name as on her role in the movie. "I don't want to be hired because of my name," was her patient refrain. "I'm not ashamed of my background. I'm very proud of my father and the work he's done. But I don't want anyone to be expecting me to be him." Little did she know the unwitting part her father had played in her snagging her first decent role.

There was no chance of anyone's expecting her to be like Jon Voight for her next movie, *Mojave Moon*. Publicity for *Hackers* over, in October 1995 she headed out to the desert in Palmdale, California, where she was soon sensuously licking an ice-cold beer bottle in a roadside diner in a blatant attempt to lure middle-aged Danny Aiello into giving her a ride. The comedy thriller perfectly showcased her sexual presence; critic Rod Dreher described her as "so sinuously sexy she makes contemporaries Liv Tyler and Drew Barrymore look like church ladies."

Throughout the shoot, she was nursing a secret sadness: Her grandmother Barbara Voight was in the final stages of bone cancer, and on December 3, just days after filming wrapped, the eighty-five-year-old matriarch passed away in Palm Beach, Florida. During her illness, Barbara, an indomitable crackerjack of a woman whose personality reminded friends of Angelina's, had displayed her customary cheery disregard for age and infirmity, her son Jon deliberately choosing film roles that would give him the chance to take her to parts of the world she had never seen. It was for this filial purpose that he took the part of agent Jim Phelps in *Mission: Impossible*, which starred Tom Cruise. His mother had always wanted to see Prague, where the blockbuster was filmed. "She loved it," Voight recalls, describing how he pushed his mother around the castle district in her wheelchair. "In the last year of her life we had that wonderful experience." A fighter to the end and filled with a life force, his mother soon began asking: "Where are we going next?"

As it happened, two big screen projects presented themselves. In *Rosewood* Voight was offered the role of a white storekeeper who saves black neighbors during a vicious race attack, and in *Anaconda* he was due to travel to the Amazon to be eaten by a giant snake. His mother had no hesitation. "I've never been to the Amazon," she said. She passed away before she could make that trip, but not before her illness had encouraged her youngest son, Chip, to give up his addiction to gambling and go back to songwriting.

It was Jon who took on the responsibility of speaking for the family at her funeral. He wrote a lot of notes the day before—he is always careful to prepare his speeches—but after a restless night was struggling to find the right tone with which to speak about his beloved mother. In the morning, when he told Angie about the trouble he was having, he remembers that she spoke to him like a director to an actor. "You'll do great, Dad. Just speak from your heart; you've got it all." Her encouragement helped him capture his mother's irrepressible spirit in his tribute. "There's something about Angie that knows how to handle things," he observes.

For a girl intrigued by funerals, even Angie was taken aback by her grandmother's bizarre final requests. At the open-casket visitation before the funeral, Marcheline was one of the first mourners to go forward and pay her final respects to her mother-in-law. When she returned to the pew, she was ashen-faced. "Angie, I want you to be really prepared when you go up there," she told her. Angie asked what was wrong with her grandmother. Marche would not explain, saying, "You will have to see for yourself." When Angie went to say goodbye, the matriarch of the Voight family was laid out according to her last wishes: dressed in a red bikini with a set of golf clubs by her side. She died as she lived—one of life's great enjoyers who could raise a smile, or a rictus grin, even in the face of death.

From being one of the congregation, Angie was once again just a face in the crowd when she watched her boyfriend enjoy his moment of triumph a few weeks later. She flew to Glasgow, Scotland, in February 1996 to join Jonny and the rest of the cast at the premiere of *Trainspotting*. Described as "Jonny Lee Miller's girlfriend," she was such an unknown at the after-party that she was not even mentioned in media reports of the list of attending celebrities.

This was her boyfriend's chance to bask in the limelight as critics heaped praise on a film that, despite the gruesome scenes of drug abuse and violence, was described as "a true original movie which everyone should see." Danny Boyle's film went on to win an Oscar nomination as well as British and European awards. The scene in which Jonny's character, Sick Boy, meditated on the cultural significance of Sean Connery was singled out as matching any sequence dreamed up by cult hero Quentin Tarantino. This was Scotland's answer to *Pulp Fiction*.

Six weeks later, on March 28, 1996, Jonny and Angie were married in an intimate, almost apologetically small civil ceremony in Los Angeles. Only her mother and Jonny's best friend, Jude Law, were witnesses. Absent were her brother and her father, who had previously met Jonny on the set of *Hackers* but was still filming *Mission: Impossible*. Also missing was Jonny's family—parents Alan and Anne and his journalist sister, Joanna. They had called him in Los Angeles in some agitation when they had read about their future daughter-in-law's very public discussion of her lesbian lover as well as her drug issues. They wanted to know what their son was getting himself into. Little did he know.

"SICK BOY" WEDS FORMER ADDICT was the dismissive headline in the London *Daily Mirror*, Angie confessing: "I have done just about every drug possible, cocaine, ecstasy, LSD and, my favorite, heroin. Although I have been through a lot of dark days, Jonny has helped me see the light."

Though it wasn't her first walk on the conservative side, it seemed an impetuously conventional decision to marry at all. After all, Angie was still seeing Jenny, still attracted to other women and exploring her sexuality. In marriage she was, once again, the sidekick and not the star. As a child, she had lived in the shadow of the favored son, James, who was always seen as the one most likely to succeed. At school and as she took her first steps on Hollywood's greasy ladder, she had parried questions about her famous father, constantly measuring herself against his luminous and intriguing life's work. Now she had hitched her wagon to a man whose career seemed about to take off. *Trainspotting* was his breakout movie, a chance for stardom that his colleagues, notably Ewan McGregor, seized with both hands.

Enough about them, Angie's fragile ego protested, what about *me*? It was only days after she had said "I do" that she was having second and third thoughts. As a family friend notes: "She was wild, impetuous, and adventurous. At that time in her life she didn't see marriage as lasting forever; she saw it as an adventure." In other ways, marriage was a sanctuary, a haven of independence from her mother. With no Bill Day on the scene, Marcheline's total attention was on her daughter. They spoke every day on the phone, her mother learning all Angie's secrets. It was as claustrophobic as it was affirming. Her husband, though he didn't know it, was a buffer of sorts, a lightning rod and a useful way to get out of things Marcheline wanted but Angie didn't. Soon, though, it was clear to Angie that what she wanted to get out of was the marriage.

On what was effectively their honeymoon—a European junket in May to promote *Hackers*—she realized that all the media questions concerned her father and her husband. No one seemed interested in her. It became so irritating that she said on Spanish TV that she was not even related to Jon Voight. "It was weird to immediately be married and then you kind of lose your identity," she told *The New York Times* with a wide-eyed wonder that was as naïve as it was instructive. "You're suddenly somebody's wife and you are like: 'Oh, I'm half a couple now. I've lost me.'"

A morning TV show where the happy couple were showered with rice and given a toaster as a wedding present was a turning point. "I need to get myself back," she thought. Whoever that was—she herself admitted that she spent so much time living the lives of her movie characters that she didn't have "much of a personal life" of her own.

What was intriguing was that in a matter of weeks, her private and very intimate civil ceremony was the most talked-about wedding of the year. She told journalists that she had had a large cross tattooed on her stomach the day before the wedding as a tribute to her beloved. It covered a little dragon with a blue tongue that she had had done in Amsterdam during a riotous trip that involved games on a water bed. "No longer appropriate," she explained.

She revealed, too, that their union hadn't been a big white wedding but "a small black wedding." As intimate as it was, she made sure the world knew all about it, telling the media that the groom wore black leather, while she wore black rubber trousers and a white shirt with his name written on the back in blood carefully extracted from her body with a clean surgical needle. "It's your husband; you're about to marry him. You can sacrifice a little to make it really special," she explained, her own love of ritual overlaying the existing marriage rites. Not so much the blushing bride as the bloody bride, especially as the groom had a long name. Fourteen letters, to be precise. A lot of blood, but more ink spilled all over the celebrity magazines as the media became increasingly intrigued by this bizarre and highly photogenic actress. Sexy *and* dark; it was an explosive media combination.

While Angie ruminated on what she had gotten herself into, it was Jonny's mother, Anne, who inadvertently put a spoke in their romantic wheel. She worked in the production department at the BBC in London and had been contacted by her friend Johanna Ray, a casting agent and the ex-wife of tough-guy actor Aldo Ray, about the latest movie she was casting, *Playing God*. The surreal tale of drugs, gangsters, and a good doctor gone bad was the breakout movie for *X-Files* star David Duchovny. The actor had such an influence over the $24 million production that he even chose the director, former circus impresario Andy Wilson, because he liked his work on the British cop series *Cracker*.

Even before the filming of *Playing God*, scheduled for August 1996, began, the production was a mess. There were almighty arguments about the script, originally by Mark Haskell Smith but rewritten by Larry Gross, and deemed by Andy Wilson to be "unfilmable." Not only was the script unfinished, but the editorial team was having hell's own job finding a leading lady. After talking with Anne Miller, Johanna Ray watched *Hackers* and liked what she saw of Angelina Jolie. When she discussed her name with the *Playing God* producers, however, they were against even calling her in for an audition.

They originally wanted the gangster's moll, Claire, to be a big name and a blonde, penciling in Charlize Theron, Cameron Diaz, and *Species* star Natasha Henstridge for the part. By contrast, Andy Wilson, directing his first Hollywood feature, saw the bloody thriller as a "weird, slightly surreal" homage to maverick director Nicolas Roeg, who made the iconic movies *Performance, Walkabout,* and *Don't Look Now.* He felt the lover of the ruthless crook played by Timothy Hutton should be dark-haired, with an enigmatic European quality. Dutch actress Famke Janssen, star of *GoldenEye;* Jennifer Tilly, from *Bound;* and actors from *Twin Peaks* all auditioned, but no one was deemed suitable. As Andy Wilson explained, "Casting is 90 percent of the filmmaking. It is being an alchemist, working out if the actors fit together. A director is like a sorcerer. Anyone can make a film. It's all in the prep; that's where you exhaust yourself."

Unfortunately, these sorcerers could not find a female apprentice who would have the right chemistry with David Duchovny, who played a blacklisted doctor with a drug problem, and the devilish hoodlum, Academy Award winner Timothy Hutton. Angie Jolie was literally the last actor to come in for casting. Such was the frantic nature of their search that Wilson used a handheld camera to film Angie in his office as Duchovny watched from the side. "She came in and hardly looked at any of us," recalls Wilson. "She read for a scene around a bonfire in the desert and she was electrifying. She had a great understanding of what she was doing." Both he and David Duchovny knew this was the girl for them, but the producers had other ideas, continuing to insist on a blonde "name" to help carry the movie. After increasingly acrimonious discussions, the director and his leading man finally won out, and Angie found herself being fitted for costumes—clothes by designers like Dolce and Gabbana, Richard Tyler, and Mark Wong Nark—mere days before preproduction began. It was quite a transformation from her personal wardrobe of leather pants and tank tops. "Angelina had to look like an expensive sports car—sleek and streamlined," said costume designer Mary Zophres.

During filming, coproducer Melanie Greene said graciously of the female lead: "She has the wisdom of an old soul . . . the grace and style of an older woman. You want to peel away the layers when you meet her."

The casting of Angelina was such a coup for her ambitious young agent, Geyer Kosinski, that even though he had broken bones in a boating accident in late May, he rose Lazarus-like from his sickbed to call *Variety*, the Hollywood trade journal, and personally confirm their story that Angie was the female lead for *Playing God*. In doing so he ensured that he, not Marcheline, was linked with the up-and-coming young actress.

At long last David Duchovny had got the girl. Or rather, he thought he had got the girl. His rival Timothy Hutton had other ideas. It greatly amused the director and other members of the cast and crew to see Hutton and Duchovny, two legendary Hollywood swordsmen, vying for the attention of a woman fifteen years younger than either of them. That Hutton was reportedly dating Uma Thurman, and Duchovny, who years later entered a rehab center to confront his sex addiction, was seeing actress Téa Leoni did not seem to matter as the duo dueled for the affections of the "newly married but still dating" Mrs. Miller.

As for the director, he was thrilled with the offscreen shenanigans. "Angie was only twenty-one but as sexy as all hell. She enjoyed the company of all the guys," recalls Andy Wilson. "During the preproduction and filming she was splitting up with Jonny, and for some reason it gave her great energy, which was fabulous for the movie. Then Tim and Angie started their affair on set. Tim was *besotted* with her, *besotted*. Actually, David was rather jealous."

There were many consolations for the dejected star. When filming began in August, virtually every day carloads and sometimes coachloads of young girls, all *X-Files* fans, would appear at the location, some even throwing their panties at Duchovny. As Hutton and Angie made merry, Duchovny, according to Andy Wilson, began an affair with a crew member.

Although Hutton pursued and won the girl in real life, Duchovny, in Wilson's view, enjoyed one of two of the "sexiest sex scenes never seen by a cinema audience." Filmed by Anthony Richmond, whose bedroom scene between Donald Sutherland and Julie Christie in Roeg's *Don't Look Now* is widely credited as the most erotic sex scene in cinema history, Duchovny made love to a naked Angie as music from Massive Attack played in the background.

In the end, Disney and Touchstone, who were funding the movie, axed the scene, arguing that it was too erotic and romantic and detracted from the gangster plotline. By contrast, an equally sexy scene shot between Hutton and Angie in the back of his Jaguar as fellow gangster Gary Dourdan looked on was deemed by the producers to be too much of a celebration of the criminal classes. For the public, who will never see the uncut version, Wilson attests that the scenes were "fucking horny."

As for Angie's husband, cuckolded after four months of marriage, Jonny Lee Miller spent his days mooning about the Hollywood home of Roger Taylor, from the rock band Queen, which the actor was renting for the duration of his now-estranged wife's shoot. During what Andy Wilson described as Miller's "cry fest," he would pour his heart out to English actor Andy Tiernan, who played one of Hutton's heavies and, like Miller, had cut his teeth on the TV crime drama *Prime Suspect*. Kept apart from his wife, Miller would ask Tiernan how Angie was coping on set, using his friend as a shoulder to cry on. As Andy Wilson saw it, Angie and Miller "were just too young to marry." He recalled: "I had to treat all actors equally, so I tried not to get too involved in what was going on."

Eventually Jonny did the decent thing—and went off with another woman. Or two other women, to be precise, if only on the screen. He flew to Montreal, where, thanks to the recommendation of Keith Carradine, he had been cast in *Afterglow,* a four-handed romantic comedy directed by Alan Rudolph. He played a buttoned-up young executive who does not want to have children with his sexy wife, Lara Flynn Boyle. When she has an affair with a local handyman, he enjoys a fling with the handyman's wife, played by Julie Christie, in her heyday one of the world's most desirable women. Doubtless the irony of the situation was not lost on Miller.

While her husband might not have wanted to hear it, Mrs. Miller was coping remarkably well on set, coolly and calmly embracing an unusual filming process. With the director deeming the script "garbage," Angie and her fellow actors would spend much of each day improvising their dialogue before the cameras rolled. It was a test of character and ability, and, according to Wilson, she "pitched in like a rock-and-roll star."

As Angie became more and more comfortable with improvisation, Wilson could sense that "an extraordinary actress" was emerging from the creative chrysalis. "When you film people, you don't film technique or talent, you film the eyes," he says. "What is going on in there will be captured by the camera. With Angie there was an enormous amount going on. She knew about needles and tattoos and heroin and she had an innate wild sexuality. That is what the camera captured. It filmed her courage and her chutzpah. As with all great actors, you never focus on technique, you film their spirit."

Taking a page from her mother's book, she was the only member of the cast who bought the director a gift when filming ended. "It was perfectly chosen and very touching," he says. Indeed, at the end of every film Angie was punctilious about buying presents for cast and crew. She was aware that the big-name actors who earned the most were invariably given the most handsome and lavish gifts, so she ensured that no one was left out.

Work was now flowing for Angie, who flew from Los Angeles to central Texas to immerse herself in *True Women,* a sweeping historical saga spanning five decades, from the Texas Revolution through the Civil War. For once she kept her clothes on, which was just as well, as the TV movie, filmed on location in October and November, attracted the attention of a former and a future First Lady and a future president. The then governor of Texas, George W. Bush, and his wife, Laura, as well as Lady Bird Johnson, were among the spectators watching the reenactment of the stormy scenes surrounding the Reconstruction Convention of 1868. They looked on as Angie's character, Georgie Lawshe Woods, a spoiled and self-centered Southern belle who goes through a humbling epiphany when she discovers that she is part Cherokee Indian, delivered a retort to the body of male politicians who rejected the idea of female suffrage.

It was a powerful moment in a vivid, if overly earnest, historical drama that attempted to capture the hardships and triumphs of three women in one extended family whose lives were evoked by their descendant Janice Woods Windle in her best-selling 1994 novel. As director Karen Arthur, who corralled a largely female cast, observed: "Growing up in our country we never find out about the women, the normal women. These women are heroes to everybody whose lives touch theirs, but they were unsung."

To prepare for their roles, the three leads, Angelina, Annabeth Gish, and Dana Delany, visited many of the real locations, met with their characters' descendants, and communed with their spirits in Texas graveyards. During filming the author was on hand every day to answer questions about their characters. Dana Delany, who was the first of the trio to sign up for the movie, said of her character, frontierswoman Sarah Ashby McClure: "I thought of Sarah doing everything that John Wayne does, but she did it pregnant." It was a test of a different kind for Angie, whose performance easily measured up against those of her more experienced costars. When the movie was screened the following May, Angie was praised for making her character the most interesting, if least noble, of the three.

Angie was still immersed in the feisty character of Georgie Lawshe Woods when, during the filming of *True Women,* she went for an audition that very nearly proved her undoing. It was for another period piece, a TV biopic about the controversial governor of Alabama George Wallace. She was reading for the part of Cornelia, his outrageous and sexy second wife, in front of veteran director John Frankenheimer, helmsman of *The Manchurian Candidate, The Train, Birdman of Alcatraz,* and many other films. Wearing bright red lipstick and a black dress, she nervously did her reading. Then Frankenheimer, in an attempt to calm her nerves and break the ice, casually mentioned, "So Jon's your father. How's he doing and what's he up to these days?"

For Angie, not to mention the willful Georgie, this was a familiar and maddening refrain. As she later told *Back Stage* magazine: "My heart just sank and I thought: 'He didn't pay attention to anything I just did.'" She found herself suggesting that Frankenheimer call her father himself if he was so interested in his health, and stalked out of the audition.

Within minutes Geyer Kosinski was on the telephone, berating her for storming out and for "dressing like a geisha girl." As far as Angie was concerned, the elderly director had been rude and hadn't paid attention to what she was saying. "He didn't even care about me as an individual," she complained.

Kosinski convinced her to wipe the lipstick off, calm down, and return to the audition for a second try. It was a triumph, and she landed the part that would change her life. Very soon everyone would be talking about her, rather than about the men in her life.

SEVEN

I can't fucking see. I can't fucking dance and I can't fucking sing.
What the fuck am I doing here?

—ANGELINA JOLIE ON THE SET OF THE ROLLING STONES
VIDEO "ANYBODY SEEN MY BABY?"

In the half-light and on a good day, curly-haired Franklin Meyer likes to think he bears a passing resemblance to Bob Dylan. But when the craggy-faced New Yorker has an ever-present cigarillo clamped between his yellowing teeth, think more Warren Oates from Sam Peckinpah's *The Wild Bunch.* Frank has a lived-in face, though his blue eyes, which have seen more than their fair share of debauchery and decadence, still twinkle. Now sixty-four, he is old-school New York, fondly remembering the days when downtown Manhattan was bad, mad, and dangerous to know. A friend of Andy Warhol's—"as much as anyone ever was a friend of his"—he learned filmmaking from that first master of the "reality" genre. As a young actor, Meyer appeared in one of Warhol's Factory epics alongside drag queen Candy Darling. When he asked the great man for direction, Warhol replied: "Do whatever you feel like doing."

So he did. For the next twenty-five years he worked as a cabinetmaker before discovering, somewhat late in life, that dealing drugs was easier on the hands and knees. He took over from an "inept" pothead at the legendary Hotel Chelsea, home to actors, artists, and musicians, including Mr. Dylan himself. Meyer offered what he proudly called a "full-service, one-stop shop" for everything from heroin to ecstasy, quaaludes to cocaine. His ninth-floor apartment was, he insists, never a "shooting gallery" but a modern-day salon where conversations ranged far and wide as the somewhat rich and relatively famous sniffed, snorted, and smoked.

Like the desk of the late TV talk-show host Johnny Carson, Meyer's dealing desk was higher than the rest of the room so that he could look down on his seated clients. It also hid the shotgun as well as the 9mm and 32mm handguns that he loved to handle, admiring the mechanism of the weapons just as he loved to tinker with his collection of antique watches. He insists he never used the guns in anger. It was all part of the daily theater played out for his well-heeled or artsy clientele.

At some point during his new career as a dealer he took a line, so to speak, from Warhol's playbook and decided to film the goings-on behind the locked door of apartment 921. He called his attempt at cinéma vérité *Hand Job Files,* after the time he and another cameraman, a well-known New York director, were filming a lesbian S&M dominatrix being whipped and the second cameraman got a touch carried away. Over the months and then years, he filmed forty-odd hours of footage ranging from the banal to the plain weird: designer Marc Jacobs, in coat and scarf, chasing a line, or a beautiful, half-naked girl freebasing. Others were filmed but not doing drugs, including a black rapper talking about his brother's breaking into the home of his fiancée's parents; a client's girlfriend performing desultory oral sex; director Abel Ferrara growling around the apartment; and the irrepressible singer Chaka Khan being Chaka. While he has yet to find a suitable distributor, he proudly shows visitors, including the author, his uncut documentary.

Central to the casting for his reality TV show was the sometimes blonde, sometimes dark-haired figure of Angelina Jolie. She first appeared at his door in February 1997, when she was filming *Hell's Kitchen* in New York while also working with John Frankenheimer in Los Angeles on the biopic of George Wallace. Directed by Tony Cinciripini, *Hell's Kitchen* was a down and dirty story of revenge, drugs, and sleazy sex; Angie played a vengeful girlfriend wanting blood atonement for the death of her brother. When she first arrived at Meyer's apartment, she was accompanied by her screen lover, fellow actor Johnny Whitworth, who played Patty, a young punk who accidentally shot her brother and later had rough, drug-fueled sex with Angie's addict mother, played by Rosanna Arquette.

Like her movie character, Angie was bleary-eyed, and her left hand was bandaged after an accident on set. Even though it was the first time Angie had met her new dealer, she was so careless of her image that she allowed

Shortly before her seventeenth
birthday, Angelina was in
contention to replace supermodel
Cindy Crawford as the face and
body of a swimwear brand. While
the camera loved her, she decided to
focus on her acting career instead.

Sean McCall

The wedding of Angelina's maternal grandparents, Rolland and Lois Bertrand, in 1949 was an elaborate affair with seven bridesmaids and groomsmen. Lois dreamed of making it in the movies or as a model, passing on her ambition to her eldest daughter, Marcia Lynne. *Courtesy of Don Peters*

Every Saturday, Angelina's grandmother Lois took young Marcia Lynne from the small community of Riverdale, Illinois, into Chicago for dance, singing, and acting classes. It was her mother's ambition to see her daughter's name up in lights. *Courtesy of Carl Durnavich*

When she left Beverly Hills High School in 1969, Marcia Lynne, who called herself Marcheline as an adult, pursued a career in modeling. *Beverly Hills High School Yearbook*

Jon Voight and a heavily-pregnant Marcheline Bertrand seem the picture of mutual adoration and happiness after she watched him perform in a Los Angeles stage production of *A Streetcar Named Desire* in April 1973. A few weeks later she gave birth to their first son, James Haven Voight.

Peter C. Borsari

Angelina Jolie Voight was born in Beverly Hills on June 4, 1975. Her far-seeing mother gave her a distinctive middle name so that she would have her own stage identity should she wish to pursue a career in acting.

Lauren Taines

Shortly after Angelina was born, Jon Voight was asked to organize a student production of *Hamlet* at the University of California, Northridge. During rehearsals he spent as much time as he could with the new arrival. Here he is at home on Roxbury Drive, wrestling with his lines and cradling baby Angelina in his arm as family friend Lauren Taines looks on. Visitors were always struck by how simply this Hollywood star lived. The decoration is plain except for a Tiffany lamp and an antique trunk bought by Marcheline.

Courtesy of Lauren Taines

The building on Roxbury Drive in Beverly Hills that provided an unconventional home life for Angelina. For a time after the breakup of her parents' marriage, Angelina lived apart from her mother and brother, cared for by various babysitters. This episode provides many clues to Angelina's future behavior. *Author's collection*

Jon Voight's passionate affair with college student Stacey Pickren ended his marriage, with dramatic consequences for his family, particularly infant Angelina. He met the budding actress when she played Ophelia to his Hamlet. Their wild affair is still referred to as "The Scandal of Northridge." *Peter C. Borsari*

Jon Voight and Stacey Pickren enjoy a joke with Dustin Hoffman. Both he and Hoffman were nominated for Oscars for their performances in *Midnight Cowboy*, the first X-rated movie to win an Academy Award. Stacey was by Voight's side when he won an Oscar for *Coming Home* in 1979. Marcheline, who used to love going to the Oscars with her husband, watched the ceremony on television. Her daughter has never seen the movie because of the painful family associations. *Peter C. Borsari*

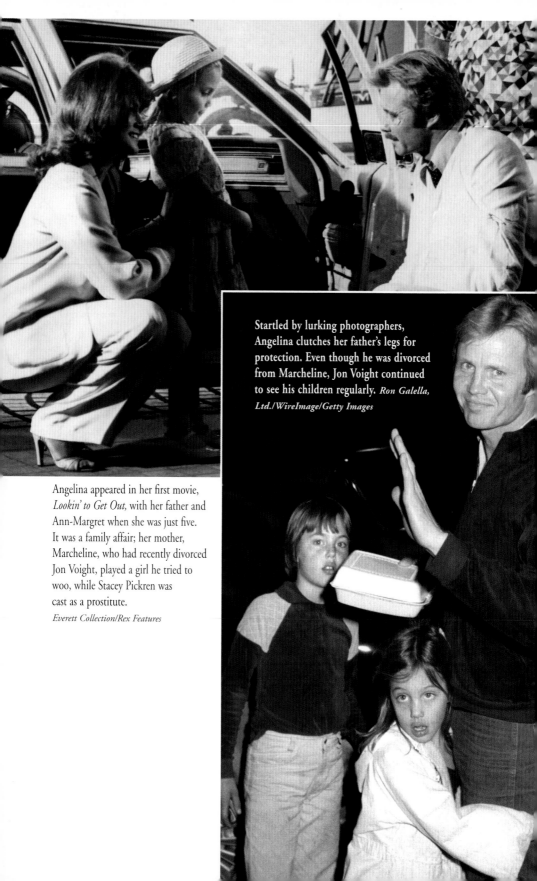

Angelina appeared in her first movie, *Lookin' to Get Out*, with her father and Ann-Margret when she was just five. It was a family affair; her mother, Marcheline, who had recently divorced Jon Voight, played a girl he tried to woo, while Stacey Pickren was cast as a prostitute.

Angelina's mother loved to buy her expensively embroidered or delicate antique dresses. Her daughter loved to climb trees and slide down mud banks. Shortly after this picture was taken, in June 1980, Angelina was climbing a nearby tree. It was the beginning of the end for her long dress. *Lauren Taines*

Angelina was always protective of and maternal toward younger children. She took a special shine to Sean Stogel, then three, teaching him how to blow bubbles and, in later life, how to ditch his girlfriends. *Lauren Taines*

Bill Day, who was Marcheline's partner for eleven years, Marcheline, and young Angelina, aged six, celebrate Easter 1982 on the grounds of the Beverly Hills Hotel by dressing in Hawaiian regalia, in celebration of the family holiday they had enjoyed on the island. *Courtesy of Bill Day*

Jon Voight watches his son, James, practice hoops. Besides basketball training, Voight helped coach James and Angelina for the school soccer team. *Ken Regan/Camera 5*

Angelina, known as Angie as she grew older, with her mother at their apartment on Roxbury Drive in Beverly Hills in December 1987. Marcheline was an absolute perfectionist, spending hours carefully decorating the Christmas tree to her satisfaction. *Lauren Taines*

Angie and her friend Chris Landon, the son of *Little House on the Prairie* star Michael Landon, were voted the couple with the best legs by their fellow classmates at El Rodeo School in Beverly Hills. For a time the couple were inseparable friends, united in part by the fact that both had famous fathers. *El Rodeo School Yearbook*

Best Legs
Angie Voight - Chris Landon

Windsor Lai '89

During her final year at El Rodeo School, Angie was reluctantly taking acting classes, mainly to please her mother. Although she was not much interested in the profession at the time, it seems her friends believed in her. Her friend Evelyn Ungvari suggested to budding artist Windsor Lai that he sketch her. "One day she is going to be famous," she told him.

El Rodeo School Yearbook

When she was ten, Angie enjoyed her first walk down the red carpet, for the 1986 Oscars, where her father was nominated for his starring role in *Runaway Train.* Her startling white angel dress was clearly chosen by a mother who still thought she was in kindergarten. *Rex Features*

Two years later, Angie was wearing her favorite color, black, the twelve-year-old just entering her punk phase. She has no memory of the night she joined her father and brother at the 1988 Oscar awards ceremony.
Eugene Adebari/Rex Features

In her first starring role in the sci-fi drama *Cyborg 2,* Angie, then seventeen, was trained in martial arts by Karen Sheperd, who played an evil mutant. When she first met her, Karen thought Angie was too skinny and weak for the part, believing that "Hollywood nepotism" had triumphed over talent. By the end of the shoot she admired Angie for her quiet ambition and raw ability. *Karen Sheperd*

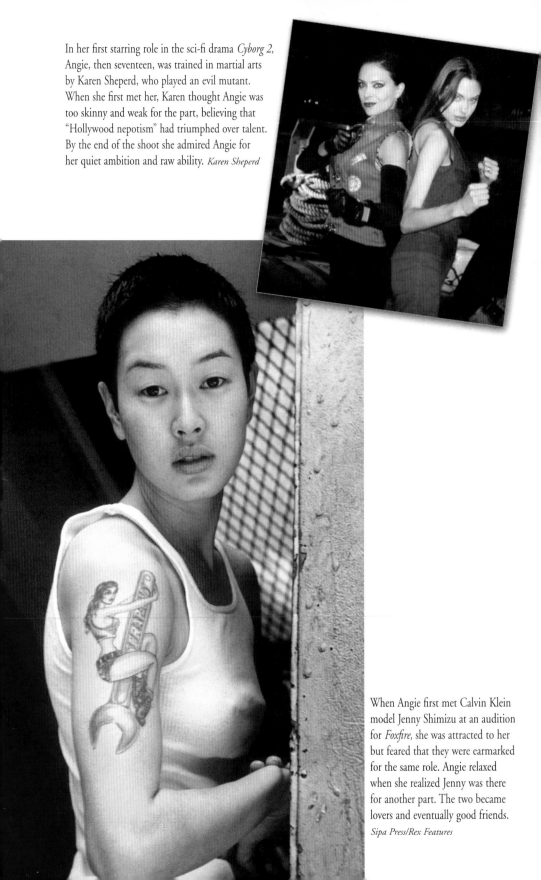

When Angie first met Calvin Klein model Jenny Shimizu at an audition for *Foxfire,* she was attracted to her but feared that they were earmarked for the same role. Angie relaxed when she realized Jenny was there for another part. The two became lovers and eventually good friends. *Sipa Press/Rex Features*

...et English actor Jonny Lee Miller during the making of the high-tech thriller *Hackers* in the fall of 1994.
...competitive, with a mutual love of tattoos, the couple enjoyed a long-distance romance, eventually
...an intimate ceremony, with actor Jude Law and Marcheline Bertrand as witnesses, on March 28, 1996.
...he occasion Angie wrote his name in her blood on the back of her white wedding shirt.

Within months of her marriage, Angie began an affair with Timothy Hutton, her costar in *Playing God*. "He was besotted with her. Besotted," remembers director Andy Wilson.
Ron Galella, Ltd./WireImage/ Getty Images

Angie relaxes with other members of the cast between takes on the set of *Playing God*. Director Andy Wilson, far right, recalls: "She was only twenty-one but sexy as all hell." *Andy Wilson*

Joey's favorite student, Angelina Jolie

Emotionally exhausted and depressed after filming *Gia*, Angie learned to play the drums in order to relax and in hopes of playing in Tim Hutton's garage band. She was taught by Jefferson Airplane drummer Joey Covington, who believes the exhilarating exercise helped save her life. *Courtesy of Joey Covington*

Bleary-eyed and out of sorts, Angie, who cut her hand during the filming of *Hell's Kitchen* in 1997, meets her drug dealer Franklin Meyer for the first time at his apartment in the infamous Chelsea Hotel. She was accompanied by actor Johnny Whitworth, but there is no suggestion that he was buying or using drugs. After that first conversation, she left with sixty dollars' worth of heroin and cocaine. "She never bought or did a lot," Meyer recalls.

Franklin Meyer

Angie talking to her father from her new apartment on New York's Upper West Side. She let herself be filmed by Franklin Meyer for a grungy documentary he called *Hand Job Files*.

Franklin Meyer

With her unruly mane of golden hair covering her face, this is an unusual shot of Angie framing her famous lips. Her dealer Franklin Meyer, who took the shot, discussed setting up an artists' colony in upstate New York with the actress, who wanted to learn how to make masks and casts, particularly of women's breasts. *Franklin Meyer*

Meyer to take her picture for his collection. Then she scored sixty dollars' worth of cocaine and heroin.

For the next three years "Frank from the Chelsea" was her dealer, supplying her from time to time with her drugs of choice, heroin and cocaine. The odd couple soon became friends, shopping, dining out, and even visiting his elderly father, Howard. Angie and Frank, whose mother, Sylvette Engel, was a talented artist, even talked of buying land and forming an artists' colony in upstate New York. Angie wanted to learn to paint and sculpt. Her true passion, though, was for making masks and casts, on several occasions using plaster of paris to make molds of her own breasts. She was as intrigued by the beauty of women who had suffered partial or full mastectomies as she was by the use of hot candle wax and nipple clamps during lesbian S&M sessions. "It has to come from a real place," she told the camera.

The star of *Hand Job Files* was as witty as she was uninhibited. During a filmed chat about childhood pets, she joked that Frank's girlfriend, Danielle, should sue Warner Brothers, the makers of Bugs Bunny cartoons, after Danielle revealed that when she fed lettuce to her pet rabbit it died. (Actually, Bugs Bunny's staple diet was carrots, but it got a laugh.) Angie confessed that when she was growing up she was equally unlucky with her own pets, recounting the countless small tragedies under her stewardship.

As happy as she was to chat endlessly on camera, her visits to Frank's salon were not merely social. She was there to score. Frank, though, is reticent about Angie's drug use, seeing her more as a friend than an addict. "She never bought or did a lot," he recalls. "She was not a serious career drug addict. I never remember her spending much more than a hundred dollars at a time." Still, he cautions: "Whether you smoke, shoot, or snort heroin, in the end you end up at the same place. It's the same game no matter how you do it."

Most of the time she preferred to smoke, finding comfort in the lonely ritual of "chasing the dragon." This elusive pursuit of the ultimate high involved heating her heroin on a piece of aluminum foil and carefully ensuring that the liquid did not coalesce into an unmanageable mass before inhaling the smoke through a second, rolled-up piece of aluminum foil.

Her behavior caused sufficient alarm on set for the wife of a producer, who was also her driver, to call a close friend of her mother's and outline what was going on. Marcheline's reaction was instructive. Passive as ever, she proposed doing nothing, arguing that Angelina was a twenty-one-year-old adult who was responsible for her own behavior. "But she's your daughter," said her friend, horrified at Marche's willingness to accommodate her daughter's self-destruction. In the end Marcheline agreed to go to New York and confront Angie. Over lunch she held her daughter's hand and, in her wispy, ethereal way, tentatively asked, "Now, Angie, tell me the truth. Are you doing drugs?" Angie looked her in the eye and said, "No, Mommy, I am not," and then proceeded to eat a whole hamburger and fries to show her mother that her appetite was healthy. The encounter was very Marcheline, who always wanted to be her daughter's best friend rather than her mother.

As ever, her father learned about her drug use some time later and from sources other than his ex-wife. He got on a plane and tracked Angie down. As he later told TV host Pat O'Brien, he could see what he called "real psychic pain" etched on her face, a torment she seemed to relieve with drugs. "You can't help me! You can't help my pain!" she screamed at her father, pleading with him to let her deal with her situation on her own and asking him to give her the night to recover. Reluctantly, he bowed to her will, leaving her to her own devices. It was a decision he later came to regret. However well-meaning, his one-man intervention had little chance of success without the full support of the rest of the family and the involvement of a qualified expert on drugs.

As dramatic and emotionally draining as this encounter was, it gave only a partial portrait of the complex relationship between father and daughter. Like her father, Angie was and is a savior by nature, wanting to save everyone she can. Just as her father was trying to save her from herself, so did she want to save him from himself. A twenty-one-minute telephone conversation with him filmed by Franklin Meyer is revealing. At times she sounds like his mother, admonishing him for spending too much time punishing himself rather than enjoying his money and his life. "I want you to teach me things," she told him, adding, "Making yourself happy makes us happy." At the same time, as she began to appreciate the business she was in, she could see more clearly how he had squandered his talent. He took roles way beneath his ability and stature, while rejecting parts that might enhance his career. One example around this time was the Tom Cruise–

produced movie *Without Limits,* about the famous 1970s Olympic runner Steve Prefontaine and his legendary coach, Bill Bowerman. Both Angie and James thought Jon was perfect for the part of Bowerman, but he turned it down. The role went to Donald Sutherland, who received accolades for his performance.

She took a similarly maternal interest in her brother's career. In spite of subsequent events, they had never been especially close. As a kid, James was the typical elder brother, telling his sister to "scram" on the rare occasions she wanted to play with him. They had different interests and outlooks on the world, typified by the fact that James loved being behind the camera, Angie in front. When he was at college he would not speak to or see his sister for months on end. He seemed destined for a career as a director, especially as he showed genuine talent, at USC winning the George Lucas prize. Friends recall that when he was making his student movies, which starred his sister, he affected the guise of a French New Wave director, wearing a beret and a striped shirt. During one film in which Angie appeared half naked, he announced portentously that it was a "closed set."

When James graduated, however, he was so painfully shy that he couldn't bring himself to attend interviews, even when he was on a short list of one. It was a surprise when he suddenly switched gears, deciding, somewhat belatedly, to follow his sister into acting. Unlike Angie, he had never had an acting lesson or shown any interest in that branch of the business, yet his father dutifully introduced him to all the casting agents in town so that they would remember his face. Angie pitched in, too, helping him snag his first screen role, as a bartender in *Hell's Kitchen.* She reported back to her father that she was thrilled to see how much her rather diffident brother had grown in confidence during the shoot.

It was James who took her to the emergency room of the local hospital when she cut her hand. As she later recalled: "James was just great. I saw how he would be as a dad or a husband. He was so cool under pressure, held my other hand, and got me a lollipop and kept making jokes." Whatever concerns Marche and Jon had about their daughter's drug use might well have been soothed by the fact that her brother was on hand to keep an eye on her. But it was not quite as simple as that; Angie was very private about her drug use.

Moreover, she was bouncing back and forth between New York and

Los Angeles. The *Hell's Kitchen* shoot in New York was organized around her commuting schedule to Los Angeles, where she played Cornelia in *George Wallace*. It was a meaty role, the ballsy character of Cornelia straight out of the Barbara Voight school of life. A crack shot, record-holding fisherwoman, onetime rodeo performer, and professional water-skier, she was a woman who loved adventure, driving the 100-mph pace car at the opening of the Indianapolis 500 and riding in a National Guard Phantom jet. "I wanted to be the first woman on the moon," Cornelia Wallace once recalled. "I was never wild, but I was daresome. I'd try most anything one time."

During her research into Cornelia's character, Angie discovered that she was also a classical pianist, saxophonist, and organist, and wrote and performed folk songs with the likes of the "king of country," Roy Acuff. Angie made the mistake of mentioning Cornelia's singing career to director John Frankenheimer, who suggested that Angie, who cheerfully declares that she cannot carry a tune in a bucket, strum the guitar and sing Acuff's signature song, "The Wabash Cannonball," at an election rally. Angie was being way too modest. Like her father, who sang on Broadway in *The Sound of Music,* Angie has a pleasing singing voice.

As colorful and accomplished as she was, Cornelia was forever captured in the public imagination the moment on May 15, 1972, when Governor Wallace was shot five times by would-be assassin Arthur Bremen during the presidential campaign and she threw herself on her husband's body. She was pictured cradling her husband's head, his blood soaking her yellow suit jacket, using her own body to shield him from further attack. As Angie tried to uncover the soul of Cornelia Wallace, she carefully studied the *Time* cover photograph of that moment, an image that spoke to her of not only Cornelia's courage, but also her love and her loyalty. "She loved him and cared for him," observed Angie. "She could have been shot herself." Cornelia is much more matter-of-fact about the famous magazine cover: "Fortunately, I'd just been to the hairdresser. Women think of things like that."

Wallace, played by Gary Sinise, was left paralyzed from the waist down, his injury giving added poignancy to the film's opening scene, in which Cornelia and Governor Wallace enjoy a breakfast cuddle on top of their hotel bed before hitting the campaign trail. The three-hour TV biopic charted Wallace's transformation from a racist governor and political opportunist who stood in front of Foster Auditorium at the University of Alabama in 1963, temporarily blocking the entrance of two black students and proclaiming "Segregation now, segregation tomorrow, segregation forever," to a man who, after he was shot, deliberately brought a large number of African-Americans into his administration. In a dramatic and true scene, he arrived in his wheelchair at a black church in Montgomery where Martin Luther King Jr. once preached, and begged the congregation for forgiveness for his past misdeeds. "I have learned what suffering means. I know I contributed to that pain [of the black community], and I can only ask for your forgiveness," he told them.

The allegorical nature of Wallace's transformation—his Faustian pact to win power and his downfall and subsequent contrition—was what drew Frankenheimer, a lifelong liberal and a friend of Bobby Kennedy's, to the film in the first place. When the cameras stopped rolling, the veteran director of nearly fifty TV and feature films declared that it was his best movie ever. While neither the ailing subject nor Cornelia agreed with his judgment—"They depicted me incorrectly," she complained—the critics were largely on the director's side, and the TV movie went on to be nominated for nine Emmy Awards.

The experience of being involved in a historically provocative drama—such was Wallace's continuing influence that Frankenheimer was not able to film in Alabama—had a powerful impact on Angie. "For the first time I saw the grand scale of what you can attempt and what you can achieve," she remarked, sentiments that echoed those of her father thirty years before when he starred in the hugely controversial *Midnight Cowboy*.

She had enjoyed, too, a grand, if unrequited, passion during filming. Angie, like other actors, admits that she falls in love with her costars, and she fell hard for her screen husband, Gary Sinise. That she was still married, and that Sinise, twenty years her senior, was married with three young children, mattered not. She was besotted. For once her mother, who listened to her daily reports from the set, pleaded with her not to pursue him. The infatuation soon passed, Sinise oblivious to his potential romantic jeopardy.

As ever, her father was out of the loop. While his dream was to "share the screen with [his] kids," Angie was ambivalent about working with her father, wondering if she would be able to take direction from him. Their edgy, rather wary relationship was symbolized by the fact that when they recorded a joint interview in June 1997, shortly after filming for *George Wallace* wrapped, he was in a Toronto studio, while she was in New York completing *Hell's Kitchen*.

When Voight mentioned Angie's husband, Jonny Lee Miller, and their friends Jude Law and Ewan McGregor, the nascent competition that characterized all of Angie's relationships bubbled to the surface. She complained that she expended a lot of energy just keeping her clothes on and steering clear of girlfriend roles, but felt that her husband had been "blessed with some great projects that don't need to be fixed." Not that her husband necessarily would have agreed. While she was working in the California sunshine on one of John Frankenheimer's finest films, he was lying in a freezing muddy field in Scotland surrounded by disembodied corpses. In *Regeneration*, based on Pat Barker's novel, he played a British officer rendered mute by the horrors he witnessed during the Somme offensive in World War I, where thousands of soldiers were slaughtered in a matter of minutes. Although the corpses were artificial, the bitter cold, the clinging mud, and the stagnant water were all too authentic. Miller could have been forgiven for thinking that the lady doth protest too much.

In May, Miller joined twenty other up-and-coming British thespians at the Cannes Film Festival to celebrate the "extraordinary renaissance" of the U.K. film industry. Miller was very much a part of that dynamism. He and a group of like-minded colleagues, including his pals Jude Law, Ewan McGregor, Sean Pertwee, and Sadie Frost, had taken control of their own destiny and formed a production company, Natural Nylon. That summer they were in serious talks to promote a raft of projects that included *The Hellfire Club,* about a group of eighteenth-century libertines, and *Psychoville,* a satirical thriller. It didn't hurt their cause that *Afterglow,* starring Miller and Julie Christie, was released that month to rave reviews. "Serious and comic, frivolous and substantial, giddy and lyrical all at the same time," wrote critic Emanuel Levy.

Levy's silky sentence could have served as a partial description of the brief and somewhat unusual marriage of Angie and Jonny. The word "ironic" would have been apt as well: For example, while Angie was seeing her dealer in New York, her husband was playing in a charity soccer match in Glasgow to raise money for a drug rehabilitation program.

While the peripatetic life of an actor meant that they spent much of their union apart, on the infrequent occasions when they were together, few would have realized that they were thinking of formally separating. In a pattern she would follow for some years, Angie and her husband, at least in public, were passionate to the point of flagrant exhibitionism. When they went out with their friends to a restaurant in Los Angeles, they would make out in front of them and the other customers. "Quite frankly I found it tiresome going out with her when she spent all her time sucking her lover's face off," recalled one girlfriend. When they visited the homes of their friends, Angie would often ask to borrow the host's bedroom for twenty minutes so that she and Jonny could have a "quickie." "She was an exhibitionist; she liked the effect her sexuality had on people, how it discomfited them," noted one of the witnesses to her sexy performances.

With Timothy Hutton lurking quietly in the background, Jenny Shimizu was often the third wheel in Angie and Jonny's relationship. As Angie once admitted: "I probably would have married Jenny if I hadn't already married Jonny. I'm quite free with my sexuality." That summer her girlfriend became part of TV history when, in May 1997, she was one of a host of celebrities, including Demi Moore, Billy Bob Thornton, and Oprah Winfrey, who appeared on an *Ellen* special in which the show's star, Ellen DeGeneres, acknowledged that she was a lesbian. Although that appearance enhanced Jenny's celebrity, others were not so fortunate. Angie's former babysitter, actor Laura Dern, played Ellen's love interest in the celebrity-packed show and found herself struggling to find work for a year or so afterward.

During this period Jenny was staying with a girlfriend in the Hollywood Hills. One night Jenny invited Angie and her husband over for a kind of double date. As Jonny and Jenny's girlfriend chatted inside, Angie and Jenny stripped and slid into the open-air swimming pool. "It seems like hours we caressed each other under the surface, again and again," Jenny later breathlessly told a British tabloid. "It was one of our horniest nights ever. The fact that Jonny or my other lover [whom she later described as a "no-nonsense knockout"] could have caught us at any moment just made it more thrilling."

I'm alone; I'm dying; I'm gay; I'm not going to be able to see you for weeks," Angie told her husband in July 1997 as she closed the curtains on her hotel windows in downtown Los Angeles and began to absorb the essence of tragic cover girl Gia Carangi, a notorious heroin addict who, in the mid-1980s, became the first celebrity model to die of AIDS, at the age of just twenty-six.

With this dramatic sentence, Angie effectively closed the door on her year-old marriage. Jonny returned to his old life in London, but the couple perversely remained the best of friends. There was further collateral damage. Her carelessness with her pets continued. The couple had already dispatched Vlad the iguana to reptile heaven through the good offices of the local vet. Now it was the turn of their pet snake, Harry Dean Stanton. When they couldn't find anyone to kill the mice that Harry needed, another visit to the vet ensued. As this was the second time Angie had sentenced a pet to death, the vet agreed to find Harry another home—as long as Angie promised never to get another animal. "I realized that being with me was not the best thing for a pet," she wryly observed.

It was perhaps as well that she left behind everything that touched her life as she embarked on a potentially dangerous and challenging emotional journey. As an actor who "became" her characters, she realized early on that in Gia she was absorbing an uncomfortable second skin, a body double whom she feared she might one day become. Angie observed: "Gia has enough similarities to me that I figured this would either be a purge of all my demons or it was gonna really mess with me."

It was a scary prospect, and understandably she was hesitant about taking on such a physically and emotionally demanding leading role. She had already enrolled in a part-time film studies course at NYU, and it was only Geyer Kosinski's wheedling intervention that convinced her to consider the role in the first place. Part of the bargain was a walk-on role for her brother. When she met first-time director Michael Cristofer, who had already seen two hundred actresses audition, he, too, shared her doubts about her strength and willingness to embrace the demanding part. "Although she's extremely striking, it was not easy to see how beautiful she was. Her presentation of herself was pretty rough. I think having to parade around and call herself beautiful was an issue for her," he recalled.

While there had been some talk about casting supermodel Cindy Crawford, who was known as "Baby Gia" early in her career, it was Angie who clearly captured the essence of the doomed model, whose brief life was a postmodern fairy tale—there was no happy ending. "Angelina is probably as adventurous a person as Gia in many ways, even if she didn't act on all those impulses," observed Cristofer, who added that she shared Gia's "pervasive innocence and vulnerability." A five-hour meeting between Cristofer and his potential leading lady cleared up any remaining doubts in her mind. He took her carefully through the script, explaining that while it described the drug-fueled modeling world, Gia's aggressive lesbianism, and her fragile love affair with makeup artist Linda, played by Elizabeth Mitchell, the heart of the story was the desperate search by a tortured soul to find love after Gia's mother, played by Oscar winner Mercedes Ruehl, abandoned her when she was only eleven.

Gia's profound sense of rejection; her bond with her mentor and surrogate mother, model agency head Wilhelmina Cooper, played by Faye Dunaway; her love affair with Linda; and her mother's tentative attempts at reconciliation formed the emotional spine in the brief life of a young woman who, less than two years after starting modeling, was on the covers of *Vogue* and *Cosmopolitan,* and featured in a major fashion campaign for Versace (his own funeral took place in Milan during filming in July 1997). All too soon came the fall, a downward spiral of pills, cocaine, and mainlining heroin. Shortly before her death, the model known as "Sister Morphine" was reduced to living on the streets and selling jeans to buy food.

In her earlier work, notably *Hackers* and *Foxfire,* Angie had demonstrated that she could play the feral punk chick with a switchblade and a wild attitude to match. With *Gia* she also had to show vulnerability, convincing audiences that behind the artificial swagger was an insecure little girl desperately looking for love. This was her challenge, as her fellow *Foxfire* actor Michelle Brookhurst observed: "In our film there was a level of fearlessness about her; she was emotionally untouchable. But where is the vulnerability in Angie as Gia? To make her sympathetic we have got to understand why we root for her."

In exploring the mother-daughter relationship she was tackling new territory. Now that she was joined at the hip with her own mother, how far did the imprinting experience of abandonment when she was in the cradle, those first memories of looking out at the sky—an open window on her back was one of her first tattoos—inform her screen performance, even at the edge of her creative consciousness? Her screen mother, Mercedes Ruehl, perceptively touched on Gia's psychic scar, telling writer Alanna Nash: "Drugs are a manifestation of the problem, but the real problem is the wound. In the screenplay we have a mother with a narcissistic wound and a daughter who is narcissistically wounded herself, from a kind of heartbreaking neglect. They're both having to get through the day with massive tricks of denial."

The overriding theme of Gia's life was an emptiness in her soul forged by fears of abandonment, subject matter that was closer to Angie's own life than she perhaps realized. Ironically, she touched on her empathy for Gia's experience of parental loss, understanding the model's feelings by comparison with her own life. "If I didn't have her, if she left [when I was] eleven," Angie said to the *Toronto Sun* about Marcheline, "I would have been looking for that my whole life, that kind of love and comfort." Family friends believe that though she never acknowledged it publicly, Angie did realize that she was, obliquely, confronting her own relationship with her mother.

As she began to explore the "dark places" in Gia's—and hence her own—psyche, the first thing she did was watch Gia's infamous *20/20* interview, in which she affected an English accent and dreamily explained that she no longer took drugs. Initially Angie "hated" her new screen persona, but her feelings turned to warmth, even love, as she read Gia's private journals and jottings and talked to those who knew her. One scene encapsulated her explosively vulnerable character: Gia stalking out of a modeling shoot dressed in full Japanese regalia and climbing on the back of a Harley motorbike, ridden by stuntman and actor Chuck Zito, to zoom off into Manhattan in search of drugs.

Even though Zito appeared only briefly in the movie, he, like many others, was captivated by Angie. After filming finished, Zito, founder and onetime president of the New York chapter of Hells Angels, promised to take her for a ride on the back of his Harley. He was as good as his word, the besotted ex-con making a special trip to California to take the actress, twenty-odd years his junior, for a long, slow, comfortable ride on what is known as the "love ride." In her naïveté she had thought she was going for a ride on the back of his Harley; he thought he was traveling three thousand miles for rather more. An acrimonious argument ensued, and Zito returned to New York.

Angie's impulsive acceptance of Zito's invitation was very much in

Gia's mercurial character. However outrageous her behavior, everyone ended up liking her—even a photographer she pulled a knife on. Like Angie, Gia was the "other girl"; with her dark hair, volcanic temper, and stormy eyes, she was very different from the "clean" girls, the fresh-scrubbed, all-American blondes who were then the norm in the modeling industry.

In the end Angie admitted that Gia was the kind of girl she would have liked to date and go to bed with. Describing Gia as a "perfect match" for her, Angie noted: "We represent the same role in life . . . outspoken, a bit tough, funny and out there, crazy, very opinionated and also soft and vulnerable." At one point in the movie, Wilhelmina, reviewing Gia's modeling pictures, says: "Tough, vulnerable, old, young, decadent, innocent, male, female." She could have been speaking of Angie.

Before the $8 million shoot finished in August 1997, Angie agreed to Cristofer's request to appear in his next movie, *Original Sin,* based on Cornell Woolrich's novel *Waltz into Darkness.* She also, reluctantly, indulged her mother. During filming she had turned down the chance to perform as a nightclub stripper in the latest Rolling Stones video, "Anybody Seen My Baby?" It was only endless pleading by Marcheline, who utterly idolized the band and knew all their lyrics by heart, that brought about an unwilling change of heart. "Please, darling; please do it for me," Marche begged.

When Angie arrived at the video shoot in Manhattan later in August, she was in a foul mood. As part of her stripper "look" she had been asked to wear colored contact lenses, but when she put them in everything was a blur. As the show had to go on, she stumbled into the fake concert hall, looking for the stage. "I can't fucking see," she announced to anyone in earshot. "I can't fucking dance and I can't fucking sing. What the fuck am I doing here?" Watching this vision in a gold corset and stockings swearing like a trucker were the Rolling Stones. Mick Jagger, just five years younger than her father, was instantly smitten.

As the cameras rolled, Angie danced onstage, all the while ogled by Jagger and the rest of the Stones. Tiring of the charade, Angie pulled off her blonde wig to reveal her bald head—shaved during the filming of *Gia*—and stalked out of the club into the Manhattan traffic, promptly followed by Mick Jagger. Afterward Angie observed that, for a girl with two left feet, she had been inspired by the spirit of Gia to strut her stuff onstage. "I just went for it," she said. "I think Gia would have loved it."

Mick Jagger clearly did. He might not have found his baby in the video, but he knew that he wanted to find out more about the sexy woman standing half naked before him. Much more. It was the beginning of a two-year quest that was as decadent and depraved as any event in the Stones' storied sexual lexicon—a magnificent if frustrating obsession as Jagger, at the time fifty-four and still married to Jerry Hall, then pregnant with the fourth of their children, pursued this erotic vision around the world.

Central to this unfolding romantic drama was Angie's mother, who now lived vicariously through her daughter. Angie was everything her quiet, reserved, passive earth mother could never be: wild, adventurous, sexy, a rock-and-roll chick. Enter into this mix Mick Jagger. Marche had adored him from afar since she was a teenager. As unhealthy as it was, it was perhaps understandable why she encouraged Angie's relationship with the rock-and-roll roué. For the next two years, unbeknownst to her daughter, she played cupid, encouraging Mick Jagger and advising him on how best to pursue his suit with Angie, eager for them to marry one day. She had controlled so much of Angie's life—her clothes, her boyfriends, her career—that choosing a husband for her was the logical next step. Perhaps it was just a coincidence, but from this time onward Marcheline frequently counseled that it would be for the best if Angie and her husband, Jonny Lee Miller, formally divorced.

Certainly it was not long before Marcheline was planning her daughter's wedding in France. She decided that Jon Voight was not going to be invited and that afterward she would live in an annex of her daughter's home with Jagger. "Marche loved Mick for Angie," recalls Lauren Taines. "She felt that he could teach her about fame and how to handle it. She wanted them to marry."

Marche was blind to any contradictions in pushing her daughter, then using heroin, into the arms of a married man of, to put it kindly, dubious repute, after complaining bitterly for years about her own philandering ex-husband. When Lauren posed this thorny question about her double standards, Marche was quiet for a long moment. "He's my idol," she said simply.

Marche's fantasy actually seemed within reach. Certainly Jagger's phone messages indicated that he was willing to give up everything for the object of his desire. He courted Angie assiduously, reduced to a "sniveling wretch" in the face of her seductive disregard. For once it was a case of the biter bit, as the man whose romantic Rolodex included Brigitte Bardot, Carla Bruni, Anita Pallenberg, Carly Simon, and Bianca Jagger left Angie endless telephone messages, pleading, beseeching, begging her to speak to him and then meet him. "Angelina, why aren't you calling me? Where are you? Please phone me," Mick, one of the world's great lotharios, implored.

Unfortunately, he left the messages on the wrong phone. During the video shoot he had asked Angie for her number. Such was her indifference that she gave him her mother's home number. When Marcheline first heard this voice on her answering machine, she was amazed that the man she worshipped was so infatuated with her daughter. She saved his messages and played them to friends. "It was literally astonishing," recalls Lauren Taines. "Here was Mick Jagger virtually sobbing down the phone."

When Mick finally managed to speak to Angie, he invited her to join him for the weekend in Palm Beach, Florida, while the band took a break from the *Bridges to Babylon* tour. Though she spent time with him, she refused to have sex, claiming that she was having her period. "She was messing with his head," recalls Lauren Taines.

Jagger's timing was all wrong. Not only was Angie coming out of the most emotionally draining movie of her fledgling career, but Mrs. Miller was juggling a ménage of her own. Angie recalled: "I was feeling emptier than ever. I was scared of going out like Gia."

She returned to New York to resume her studies at NYU—and to leach the ghost of Gia out of her psyche. It was her Greta Garbo moment. "I've chosen to be quite alone," she told writer James Endrst. "I knew it was going to take me a while to say goodbye to Gia, to put myself back together. I kind of died and I'm still feeling a bit of that pain Gia did." She even considered giving up acting, feeling that she had been eaten alive by Gia Carangi.

"Her commitment to a role does saturate her being," says *Gia* director Michael Cristofer, now a close friend. "I think she knows when she takes on a role it's going to permeate her self and how she lives and who she is."

Angie was plunged into one of her bleakest cycles of despair and gloom as she tried to say goodbye to the new love of her life. In perhaps the most melodramatic of her flirtations with suicide, she decided to hire a hit man to do the deed, paying him in a bizarre installment plan so that no one would notice the money going out of her bank accounts or feel guilty for causing her death. Angie says she was introduced to her killer by the friend of a friend. (While her gun-toting drug dealer Frank Meyer, who was in regular contact, would probably have been the go-to guy to arrange contact with the underworld, she never mentioned her scheme to him.)

In fact, her assassin turned out to be a character straight out of the "tart with the heart of gold" playbook. The would-be killer apparently told her to think about her plan for a month and then, if nothing changed in her life, to come back to him. "It's so weird and so complicated and . . . so like a fucking movie," she told *Rolling Stone* magazine. Quite.

Salvation of sorts came when she learned that she had been nominated for a Golden Globe Award for *George Wallace.* "Suddenly it seemed like people understood me. I thought my life was completely meaningless and that I would never be able to communicate anything and that there was nobody who understood . . . and then I realized I wasn't alone," Angie says of that time. "Somehow life changed."

Although her mother believed she was "overdramatizing," her frequent thoughts of suicide were entirely consistent with her "undifferentiated feeling state," her inability to connect with herself. As Dr. Franziska De George observes: "The ultimate dissociation is suicide. What better way to get rid of your feelings completely than by killing yourself? It's not so much a wish to die as it is a wish not to endure feeling tortured anymore, to feel so desperately lost."

Angie finally gave vent to the furies within when she tried to learn to play the drums. In early September, during one of her frequent visits to Hollywood, she contacted one of the world's best drummers, Joey Covington, formerly of Jefferson Airplane and Hot Tuna, and asked him to give her lessons. They ended up practicing at the Doheny Drive home of legendary composer Henry Mancini, of "Moon River" fame and a record seventy-two Grammy nominations, where his son Chris had a jamming studio. At first Angie was timid, then Covington said to her, "Okay, give me the names of the ten people you hate." Among the names were those of her father and her agent, Geyer Kosinski. Covington wrote the names on gaffer tape and attached them to different drums. Then Angie really let rip, the physical effort cathartic and exhausting. During one session she pulled a switchblade from her back pocket, explaining that she was a cutter. "I have low self-confidence and suicidal tendencies," she said with a directness that was as refreshing as it was unnerving. Several months later, Covington attempted suicide but was discovered by his partner. He subsequently discussed this episode with Angie, who wanted to know every nuance of the experience. It was clear that she had given considerable thought to the subject. Covington told her: "It was not fun, not fun at all. My advice is, don't do it."

After the six sessions, which continued off and on during the fall of 1997, Chris Mancini photographed her holding the drumsticks high above her head in exhilaration. "I sincerely believe the drums helped save her life," says Joey Covington. "They gave her a focus and a sense of achievement."

It is worth pointing out that for all the talk of suicide and self-harm, Angie was a thoughtful and nurturing young woman. During her drum sessions she befriended guitarist Bobby Ciarcia, who had just been diagnosed with multiple sclerosis, and she listened sympathetically as he talked about his constrained life. She even went—without any prompting from her parents—to a charity ball in aid of the illness.

Back in New York, a $1,500 electronic drum kit, on which she could practice using headphones without disturbing the neighbors, had pride of place—along with her knife and sword collection—in her new apartment on the fourteenth floor of the fabled Ansonia building on the Upper West Side. Angie blended right in with the sophistication and decadence of the baroque edifice. Over the course of its colorful history, live seals had cavorted in the fountain in the entrance lobby; chickens, cows, and a live bear had been housed on the roof; and a swingers' club, called Plato's Retreat, had only recently been evicted from its basement enclave.

There was an ulterior motive behind her drum lessons. She was quietly seeing Tim Hutton, who also had an apartment in New York, and wanted to join jam sessions with his garage band. "She quickly learned the basics of drumming so she could impress Tim and his friends," observed a girlfriend. She was not quite so passionate about his other hobby: renovating and restoring derelict apartments in New York and then selling them for a handsome profit.

Unlike Tim Hutton, who worked on only a film or two a year, Angie was constantly on the go, commuting between New York and Los Angeles. In between drumming lessons, she went parachuting over the California desert (presumably to match her husband in his daredevil antics) and

135

bike riding. She simply didn't have the time for her husband, Mick Jagger—or suicide.

Still the Rolling Stones singer persisted. Knowing that Angie was nominally married but dating, he cooked up a plan to snare her. Jagger's film production company, Jagged Films, approached Jonny Lee Miller about a film they were casting, *Enigma,* about World War II code breakers. While Miller was an excellent actor, eminently suited for the period British drama, Jagger had an ulterior motive. He assumed that as Miller and Angie were still good friends even though they were leading separate lives, she would visit him on the set. That would give him the opportunity to spend more time with her. Or so he thought.

In the meantime, Miller called Angie and innocently told her that he was being considered for a part in a Jagged Films production. Angie listened but never breathed a word to her husband about why she suspected he was being courted. When confronted, Jagger confirmed her suspicions. Angie was furious at his underhanded behavior, screaming that she never wanted to see or speak to him again. As convoluted casting-couch maneuvers go, it was in a class of its own.

Jagger paid a high emotional price, falling into a deep depression as a result of Angie's silence. He was now the recipient of the Bertrand freeze. "He was completely heartbroken by her," notes Lauren Taines. The freeze lasted for months, Angie given further pause about any future dalliance when Jerry Hall gave birth to her fourth child with Mick, Gabriel, in December 1997. Angie's heart thawed only after Stones drummer Charlie Watts called her and pleaded with her to call Jagger, as he was in utter despair. Reluctantly, she agreed to resume their relationship, and the love-struck rocker invited her to join him on tour in Brazil in April 1998.

The freeze in her relations with Jagger coincided with a further thaw between Angie and her husband. In October 1997, with rumors of a formal separation swirling, Angie stated the obvious—that she loved her husband but was no good at being married. "I wasn't even a good friend because I was just absent and . . . I'd go for drives and disappear or go film something and be in hotels forever and not do anything, not have friends, not visit, not hang out. I couldn't calm down and just live life."

For a few brief weeks before Christmas and over New Year's they tried to revive their marriage. They spent time in New York before Miller headed to the Czech Republic to make *Plunkett & Macleane,* a period drama about two highwaymen, with his friend from *Trainspotting* Robert Carlyle, then reunited in Scotland for the wedding of Carlyle and makeup artist Anastasia Shirley at the remote but utterly luxurious Skibo Castle on December 28. The candlelit midnight union was an irresistibly romantic affair, what with the skirl of pipes, the swirl of kilts, and a seemingly endless supply of the finest malt. It was the final hurrah for Jonny and Angie, who decided to go their separate ways. Days later, Angie explained to writer Chris Hutchins: "Right now I'm not living as a married woman. Now we're both busy growing up."

Significantly, she chose her father, rather than her mother, brother, or husband, to accompany her to the Fifty-fifth Golden Globe Awards at the Beverly Hills Hilton in January 1998. Although she felt as if she were crashing a party where she didn't belong—she even considered covering up her growing array of tattoos—this was very much her home turf. Angie had walked by the five-star hotel every day on her way to and from school.

When she won Best Supporting Actress for her role in *George Wallace,* that was a cue to party till dawn, her father wondering whether she really should be drinking tequila shots at five in the morning. She was joined in her late-night drinking by Leonardo DiCaprio, who had been nominated for Best Actor for his role in the unsinkable movie, *Titanic.* Their date was arranged by those unlikely Hollywood cupids, their agents, Geyer Kosinski and DiCaprio's reps Rick and Julie Yorn. Even though they left the party together, the *Titanic* star did not float Angie's boat; the actress told friends afterward that even though they shared a shower together in his hotel suite there was little sexual rapport. The most memorable event was Angie mislaying the pair of diamond earrings she had borrowed for the evening. Thankfully they were insured, Angie leaving her mother to fill in the insurance claim form.

When Angie finally got home and listened to her answering machine, among the many messages of congratulations there was one from her now-estranged husband and another from her lover, Timothy Hutton. Her response was jaded; she told friends that if she hadn't won, neither would have bothered to call. Her mother's answering machine was also working overtime. Photographer Robert Kim, who took her first head shots and advised Angie to take up modeling full-time, called Marche and said: "It's a good job your daughter didn't listen to us and never went to Paris!"

Now the world was listening to Angie. Days after the Golden Globe celebrations—*George Wallace* won the award for Best Miniseries or Television Film—she was center stage at the premiere of *Gia,* held at the Directors Guild in Hollywood. This time all her family was on parade, including her parents; her brother; her godmother, Jacqueline Bisset; and her husband. They heard HBO Pictures president John Matoian tell the celebrity audience: "If we hadn't found Angelina Jolie, we wouldn't be here tonight." Afterward her father said of her performance: "I'd like to act with her and I'd love to direct her. She's the real thing." Just as when she watched her first movie, *Cyborg 2,* she went home feeling sick, but she nonetheless embarked on a round of interviews to promote the movie.

She was frequently asked about the lesbian love scenes, her own drug use, and her modeling career. Her responses ranged from her trademark unflinching honesty to confusing evasion. She told *The Cable Guide* that she "loved" the sex scenes with costar Elizabeth Mitchell. "She hadn't done a love scene before and she hadn't been with a woman before. I was looking forward to kissing her and touching her and watching her discover that and hopefully, enjoy it. I think she did. I become more romantic with women. I love women."

She took a rather more equivocal approach when quizzed about her own use of drugs. "I hate heroin because I have been fascinated by it," she told *Entertainment Weekly.* "I'm not immune but I won't do it now, at all, because luckily I've found something that replaces that high, which is my work." She emphasized to *The New York Times:* "Knowing what I know now, I would not do heroin now." This was news to her dealer Frank Meyer, who confirms that he was supplying her with heroin throughout the filming of *Gia* and beyond.

Equally surprised was fashion photographer Sean McCall, who had picked her out as a future swimwear supermodel, when she told *The New York Times* and others that she had "failed miserably" in her attempts to be a model, recalling how she felt "terrible" when she was put into a swimsuit and measured all over, like a piece of meat. As Sean McCall recalls: "It's baffling that she would say that. We never measured her or even considered it. She was certainly no failure; as a model she was on the brink of great success. She could have out–Kate Mossed Kate Moss if she had stuck with it."

The dramatic license she took with her own life imbued her with the brio to take on an outsize character like Gia Carangi. Critics loved her outstanding performance, the doyenne of the film world, Pauline Kael, paying Jolie just about the biggest compliment she had to give: "This girl could play both the Brando and Maria Schneider roles in *Last Tango in Paris*! Where in the world did she come from?" Others were equally complimentary. The *Daily News*'s Will Cooper wrote: "Hers is the real art behind this artifice and her fire is what makes HBO's *Gia* burn so brightly." *Variety* described her performance as "a mesmerizing tour de force," while Lee Winfrey of *The Philadelphia Inquirer*, Gia's hometown paper, wrote: "If you like to see the birth of a star, watch *Gia*."

It was not only Angie who received plaudits; her screen mother, Mercedes Ruehl, was also singled out for expressing the complex relationship with her daughter. "Even more than Jolie, Ruehl puts character into the role of the self-destructing Gia, helping us to understand where the daughter's insecurities and fits of childish pique come from," observed *Newsday*. "Ruehl also manages to convey guilt over Gia's demise, even as she denies it."

Friends and acquaintances who had lost touch with the young Angelina Jolie were equally impressed by her performance, mainly because it reminded them of the girl they once knew. School friend Windsor Lai watched her on TV and said, rather innocently: "Oh my God, that girl acts just like a girl I knew in eighth grade." Only later did he realize he was responding to the girl he'd once sketched. For makeup artist Rita Montanez, the Angie she knew and Gia were interchangeable. "It was almost like she wasn't acting. But her dark side is a disguise that hides something else, the relationship inside the family. Nothing much makes sense about her."

Meanwhile, her mother was busy mapping out Angie's future. With Jonny Lee Miller out of the picture, she went to see her regular psychic to ask about the chances of Angie's marrying Mick Jagger. The psychic was blunt, telling her that she would marry an older man, but it was not going to be Mick Jagger. Marcheline was devastated—and determined to prove her wrong.

EIGHT

I feel like I am just a piece of luggage on an airport carousel waiting to be picked up. Please pick me, please pick me.

—TIM HUTTON TO ANGELINA JOLIE

It was not so much a stairway to heaven as an elevator ride to ecstasy. He told her he was going to buy a pair of pants. She was heading for the hotel lobby. As they stood in the elevator, both felt a shock of attraction. Then Billy Bob Thornton, actor, director, and musician, climbed into a chauffeur-driven van and embarked on his shopping trip in downtown Toronto. The word "pants" conjuring up all kinds of thoughts in her head, Angie sat on a wall by their hotel and tried not to faint or swallow her cigarette. Irresistible object meeting improbable subject. "What was that?" she later recalled of that first encounter with her latest "screen husband" in early 1998. "I didn't know what to do."

Even for Billy Bob, four times married and with three children to his name, this was a new experience. "I felt like I had been hit by a bolt of lightning" is the way he later described first seeing Angie, who played Mary Bell, the sexy, boozy wife to Billy Bob's air-traffic controller in *Pushing Tin*. Ever the artist, he later commemorated the moment his life changed by writing the song "Angelina."

Of course, it wasn't supposed to play out like that. In the Hollywood version of droit du seigneur, where the local nobleman enjoys the pick of fair maidens, Angie was the choice of the movie's leading man, John Cusack. He had already taken her out for dinner in Beverly Hills, ostensibly to discuss her role as the cheating wife who falls for Cusack on-screen, but also to give her the Cusack squeeze. She came away from that dinner thinking about romance—but not in the way that Cusack imagined. He had also invited his good friend Al Pacino to dine with them. Throughout the evening, all Pacino did was talk about Angie's mother. When she spoke with Marcheline the next day, Angie told her: "I could swear he was in love with you." Only then did Marcheline give her wide-eyed daughter a glimpse into her own secret past.

When Angie and John Cusack later sat in the hotel bar in Toronto shooting the breeze, the star of *High Fidelity* and *Grosse Pointe Blank* had the quiet confidence of a man who knew how his evening was going to end.

Cue the arrival of Billy Bob Thornton, old enough to be Angie's father and a decade older than Cusack. She would later tell girlfriends that the crestfallen look on Cusack's face when she left the bar with Billy was priceless. Angie's evening was about to get a whole lot more amusing. She enjoyed telling the story of their first bedroom encounter, during which she discovered the truth of Hollywood rumors about Billy Bob's prodigious talent. Before they consummated their passion, Billy, with faux embarrassment, apologized for what she was about to receive. "He told her that he was hung like a mosquito," recalls her New York dealer, Frank Meyer, with scarcely disguised glee. "Then he pulled out this knee knocker. That certainly put a smile on her face."

Understandably, she told a rather different version in public, assuring CNN's Larry King, among others, that while she was "tempted" to bed Billy Bob when they first met, it was another two years before her love was consummated. "I was happy to be his friend and that was good enough," she said. (It was a claim that would be repeated years later, about another man on another film.) Of course, at the time, she was quietly dating Timothy Hutton, while Billy Bob, according to the New York *Daily News,* became engaged to his live-in lover, Laura Dern—Angie's onetime babysitter—who flew in from Vancouver, where she was filming *The Baby Dance,* to celebrate.

Angie didn't just have competition for Billy Bob from Laura Dern, but also from another woman on the set who found a lasting place in Billy Bob's heart. Canadian air-traffic controller Sheila McCombe, who was training Cusack and Thornton for their roles, was Angie's worst nightmare—beautiful, smart, funny, athletic, and aggressively ambitious: the living, breathing embodiment of "the other girl." Certainly John Cusack and Billy Bob thought so, flirting outrageously with the blue-eyed blonde as she taught them the language and tricks of real-life air-traffic controllers. Director Mike Newell recalled: "John made for her like a hunter at the first set of the season." He had a serious rival in Billy Bob, who invited her to dinner with her friends at local Toronto restaurants and called her constantly. Sheila found their attentions amusing—and flattering—recalling how Cusack and Thornton tried to outdo each other. "They wanted to impress me by being the best," she recalls with some amusement. "I was very strict."

Billy Bob clearly enjoyed her company. "We'd hang out with Sheila and she was just like this girl we knew," he recalled. "Then she'd be on the set, like no nonsense, 'No, this is what you do.'" When the film was finished, Billy Bob kept in contact, romancing her under the radar. Her friends would later say that the friendship deepened in time and he asked her to marry him—even though he was still engaged to Laura Dern. Sheila shoots down the marriage talk, the fighter pilot's daughter stating: "He talks like that with everyone. He is a very talented man. We came close for a little bit."

So who was this rather unlikely object of desire for the talented and beautiful? Born on August 4, 1955, in Hot Springs, Arkansas, to a psychic mother and a basketball coach and history teacher father, Billy Bob had an upbringing that was genuinely hardscrabble, living in a shack without electricity or running water and often eating the game he caught in the woods. The only real choice he ever got was which switch his father would beat him with at night in his impotent rage at their financial plight.

As a teenager, Billy Bob formed his own rock band; later he would always consider himself a musician first, an actor second. He was the star pitcher on his school baseball team—he was good enough to win a tryout for the Kansas City Royals—but, like Angelina, he always thought himself an outsider, his extreme poverty setting him apart. "I was the bucktooth hillbilly who lived in the middle of nowhere," he recalled. In 1973, when Billy Bob was eighteen, his father died of lung cancer. Despite his father's past cruelties, Billy Bob was constantly at his bedside in his waning months, nursing him and reading to him. This quasi-religious experience taught him the transformative power of forgiveness, a quality that marked him as a man and informed his artistic journey. It would in time distinguish him from Angelina.

After his father's death Billy got into drink and drugs, dropping out of college, where he studied psychology, after a couple of semesters. Eventually he moved to Los Angeles to pursue a career as an actor and a musician, playing drums and singing with the South African band Jack Hammer. With few acting parts for someone with his background or thick Southern accent, he took on a variety of menial jobs to scrape together a living. Perhaps the lowest point was when he was admitted to the hospital with myocarditis, an inflammation of the heart.

A chance conversation with the legendary Billy Wilder at a film industry Christmas party where he was working as a waiter transformed his life. When Wilder suggested that he focus on writing if he wanted to find a niche in Hollywood, Thornton teamed up with an old friend, novelist Tom Epperson, to write scripts. After an assortment of small roles in TV and films, he brought his most enduring creation, the mentally handicapped but astutely simple killer Karl Childers, to the screen in *Sling Blade*. He was a character who for years had haunted Billy Bob, who first wrote a stage play about the simple yet morally complex Childers.

With *Sling Blade,* the "hillbilly" outsider was suddenly very much an insider, winning an Academy Award for Adapted Screenplay for the 1996 tour de force. But the tics and twitches Billy grew up with remained, his genuine talent often overshadowed by ribald discussions of his many idiosyncrasies, including an obsessive-compulsive disorder that left him with a morbid fear of flying and a hatred of harpsichords, silverware, and antiques, particularly French furniture. Born into poverty, he was literally terrified of putting a silver spoon in his mouth.

His romantic life was as complex as his many quirks. Though married and divorced four times, he was living with a member of Hollywood royalty, Laura Dern, when director Mike Newell cast the actor with a flying phobia as the Zen-like air-traffic controller Russell Bell. The daughter of well-respected and Oscar-nominated actors Bruce Dern and Diane Ladd, Laura Dern had first met Thornton during the filming of the celebrity-studded *Ellen* show in April 1997, when the star, Ellen DeGeneres, publicly outed herself as a lesbian.

At the time, Billy Bob was in the midst of an acrimonious divorce from his fourth wife, Pietra, who had angered him by claiming in court that he had physically abused her—an allegation he denied—and then, as a final insult, posed nude for *Playboy,* declaring that the spread was her version of an Oscar. For an old-fashioned Southern gentleman, polite but essentially chauvinistic, this was unacceptable behavior.

As was his wont, he quickly moved on, soon sharing the home Laura Dern was renting from comedian Dudley Moore. Even though it was a whirlwind romance, the omens seemed good, especially since Laura's mother, who fancied herself a sage and a psychic, had earlier read the runes and forecast her daughter's love match with this affable good old boy. Her prediction reinforced their feelings that they were indeed soul mates, destined to share the rest of their lives together.

Billy Bob was immediately welcomed into the bosom of the Dern family. Down-to-earth but with an offbeat sense of humor, he meshed well with Laura's father, Bruce, who was known for his funny if far-fetched stories, his love of gambling, and his life as a bon vivant. "Billy and Laura were stone cold in love," noted a close associate speaking on the condition of anonymity. "In the beginning it was Billy who made the running. Within a matter of weeks he convinced her that they should get married." It was such a wild and passionate affair that they took compromising pictures of each other, which despite their fame they had developed locally and kept under lock and key for their future perusal. "Theirs was a possessive and intense love," noted a friend from that time.

As was her pattern, Laura set about shaping herself to the new man in her life. When she was engaged to the lanky, urbane Jeff Goldblum, she neatly dovetailed into his lifestyle: driving a BMW, listening to jazz, collecting modern art, and eating and drinking only the finest foods and wines. After Billy breezed into her life, all that changed. When he planted a Confederate flag in the master bedroom, it was a cue for Laura to cast out her designer duds and her collection of French antiques and silverware, and buy herself a new wardrobe of checked shirts and cowboy boots. Out, too, went the BMW, and in came a Volvo station wagon to accommodate Billy Bob's boys from his marriage to Pietra, William and Harry.

Laura threw out her Chet Baker and Charlie Parker in favor of what Billy called "shit-kicking music" by the likes of Buck Owens, Dwight Yoakam (with whom he formed the film production company Cross River), and the bearded rock wizards ZZ Top. Indeed, when the band came to visit one day, their stretch limo was so long it couldn't get in the drive of

Laura and Billy Bob's Coldwater Canyon home. There were other changes. Laura, whose eyesight had been affected after she was bitten by a poisonous insect as a child, was careful with her diet and ensured that Billy started to look after himself, seeing to it that he consumed organic vegetables, tofu, and lots of herbal drinks. For good measure she quietly removed all the hard liquor in the house. The results were plain to see in his public appearances. Under Laura's care her boyfriend was looking healthier and fitter than he had in years.

He bought a $3.2 million home in Mandeville Canyon, near to luminaries such as Arnold Schwarzenegger, Tom Hanks, and Steven Spielberg; and the couple's remodeling plans, which included a nursery, were well under way by the time Billy arrived in Toronto. His life seemed settled—until that encounter in the elevator.

Fresh from filming the thriller *A Simple Plan* in Minnesota, he knew little about Angie before taking the gig as her screen husband. It was only when a friend pointed out that she was phenomenal in *Gia* that he watched the movie—and was suitably impressed. Even though their mutual agent, Geyer Kosinski, had once told Billy Bob that he and Angie would get along (as he also had told Angie and Leonardo DiCaprio), they had never met before. Angie later recalled that for some unknown reason she had deliberately avoided him at industry events in Hollywood.

Certainly if Laura had been concerned about a rival, it would not have been Angie but Billy Bob's assistant, Odessa Whitmire, a pretty blonde from North Carolina who worshipped her boss. She would sit in her pajamas chatting with him late into the night when he stayed at the Sunset Marquis hotel, his rock-and-roll home away from home, where he worked on lyrics and songs for his debut album, *Private Radio*. But Laura, it seems, trusted her man. "If Laura was worried about Odessa, she never showed it," notes an associate.

If anything, it was Angie's agitated state of mind rather than her sexual allure that perturbed Laura. Like many others, she was aware of rumors circulating around Hollywood about Angie's behavior on the set of *Hell's Kitchen* in New York. During the filming of *Pushing Tin,* she and Billy Bob shared what director Mike Newell described as "a low-key friendship." The English auteur was impressed by Angie's focus and offbeat talent: "She is someone who would have fit in during Paris in the 1920s," he recalled.

"Very, very unordinary." The only time Billy Bob's and Angie's behavior raised eyebrows was at the end of filming, in late April 1998, when they visited Daemon Rowanchilde's tattoo boutique, Urban Primitive, in downtown Toronto. Billy Bob had a couple of names covered up on his hip and arm with a new energy wave design, while Angie also received energy waves just below her navel. It was an intimate moment, physically and emotionally. Angie has not only linked tattoos with positive events in her life but has also confessed that she finds the physical act of tattooing sexually arousing, saying in particular that the heavy rattle of the needle turns her on. "It gives her a sexual buzz," notes a fellow aficionado. The effect is similar to that of cutting. When her skin was pierced she would enjoy an endorphin rush and feel spaced out, calm after the storm of emotions swirling inside her.

From the tattoo shop, they headed over to the Skydome and watched the Rolling Stones in concert, unaware of yet another scheme by the besotted Mick Jagger. Previously Jagger had invited Angie along to watch the show and party with him afterward. The way he had manipulated Jonny Lee Miller still fresh in her mind, she had graciously declined, saying that she had a busy filming schedule. He was not to be denied. Knowing Billy Bob of old, Jagger called him up and invited the entire cast and crew to the concert. Now Angie was obliged to go. At the time, Mick didn't know about Billy Bob and Angie, and vice versa. Before the concert, Jagger made sure he knew exactly where Angie was sitting. During a break, when he ceded the stage to Keith Richards and the others, a security man came up to Angie. "Mick Jagger would like you to go backstage and meet him," the guard intoned before leading her through the throng to where Jagger was waiting. Curiously, Jagger gave her a cashmere sweater, and they made out until he had to go back onstage, their public canoodling watched with openmouthed astonishment by actress Rebecca Broussard, then the partner of Hollywood legend Jack Nicholson. The following day Broussard called Marche and told her excitedly: "You'll never guess who is in love with Angie—*Mick Jagger*." Marche smiled at the news, knowing already how far and how fast the man she had idolized for three decades had fallen for her daughter.

After the concert, Billy Bob, Angie, John Cusack, and other cast members partied with the band, Billy Bob and Mick Jagger still completely in

146

the dark about each other—until his go-between, Marcheline, told Jagger about Billy Bob soon after.

In this heavyweight contest, Jonny Lee Miller was back in the ring as well. The week before the Stones concert, Angie had flown to London to attend the BAFTA Awards with her husband, and they had watched their friend Robert Carlyle win Best Performance by an Actor in a Leading Role for his performance as a male stripper in the classic British comedy *The Full Monty*. The estranged couple reunited again to attend a friend's wedding in May, but the distance between them was obvious. Jonny was in tears, wailing to fellow guests that he hoped he and Angie could still be friends. "Initially he charmed her with his English accent, but she became really strong and ate him alive," observed a friend who watched the breakup. Actually, the knockout blow was delivered the moment he heard that Angie had gone for a tattoo with another man.

As for Billy Bob Thornton, he was very low-key in his assessment of Angie when he returned from filming in Toronto. He had more plaudits for John Cusack than for his screen wife, referring to her often as "just a kid." In public he considered himself "her mentor," not daring to think that this exotic creature had fallen for his offbeat charm. It was entirely typical of the man. "He was unsure of himself," notes a former girlfriend. "At that time he wasn't the big stud he likes to think he is now." His insecurity was evident when Hollywood mogul Harvey Weinstein visited him at his Coldwater Canyon home. As Billy waited for the arrival of the Miramax boss, he paced up and down the driveway muttering to himself: "I'm a ditch digger. I'm not a director, I'm not an actor, I'm a ditch digger. I'm not worthy. I'm not worthy." When Weinstein carelessly flicked ash from his expensive cigar over Thornton's $25,000 rug, he never complained.

Angie returned to Hollywood uncharacteristically kittenish in her admiration for her latest costar. She had always wanted to be with an artist, a man who could do more than act; now she had fallen for a real live one. Still, neither felt entirely free to pursue their initial animal attraction: Billy Bob was engaged, and Angie was technically still married and was also stepping out with Tim Hutton, who accompanied her and a kilted Robert Carlyle to a wedding in New York in June.

Her art now imitating her life, Angie's latest movie, *Playing by Heart*, appropriately dealt with the convoluted and interconnected love lives of various couples in Los Angeles. "Talking about love is like dancing about architecture. But it ain't stopped me from trying," says Angie's character, Joan, a sassy but irredeemably romantic gold-trousered nightclubber. The optimist in Joan did not speak to Angie; the actor managed to connect to her only by conjuring childhood memories of "making people laugh and wearing glitter underwear." Angie observed, "I've always had a tough time focusing on love or asking for love or asking someone to hold me."

Filmed in her hometown during the summer of 1998, it was an ensemble movie with a high-octane cast including Sean Connery, Gena Rowlands, Gillian Anderson, and Angie's screen love interest, Ryan Phillippe. In a strange twist of fate, *Playing by Heart* was her fallback movie after *Pushing Tin.* She had taken time off during filming in Toronto to screen-test for the part of Marla Singer in David Fincher's *Fight Club,* a story of violence and strange romance that starred Ed Norton and Brad Pitt. At the time, Brad was furiously fending off rumors about a liaison with Jennifer Aniston after he and the *Friends* star had gone on a blind date organized by their respective agents. The role eventually went to English actress Helena Bonham Carter.

The shooting schedule on *Playing by Heart* was so tight—just forty-one days—that when her father offered to take her out for dinner to celebrate her twenty-third birthday, she said no because she had big scenes the next day. Instead he came to the set and read lines with her. As her usual practice was to actively discourage her father from visiting her on set, this change in attitude did not go unnoticed. "There was a moment when she said, 'Dad, you can come to the set; they know who I am now,'" recalled Jon Voight, who publicly voiced his ambition to make a movie with his talented daughter "before the end of the millennium."

Even though she felt the character of Joan bore little relation to the real Angie, she was thrilled when the "man who made her feel like a little girl," Sean Connery, phoned her and Ryan Phillippe to congratulate them on the intriguing romantic dynamic they had conveyed on-screen.

While Angie was involved in her latest movie love affair, Billy Bob and his fiancée were strolling hand in hand down the red carpet at the premiere of *Armageddon,* a big-budget science fiction thriller, held at the Kennedy Space Center in Florida. Thornton's gaunt appearance, which he ascribed to healthy living, and his public affection for his fiancée—she was "as tightly attached as his sinister tattoos," noted one commentator—were the talk of the evening. Afterward, they took off for Billy's home state of Arkansas, where they played a madly-in-love married couple who couldn't forgive or forget their respective romantic pasts. (Ironically, one iron rule in the Thornton household was never, ever to mention the name of Laura Dern's ex-fiancé, Jeff Goldblum.) The movie, *Daddy and Them,* which Billy Bob also directed, was a real Hollywood family affair: Laura's mother, Diane Ladd, and her friend Kelly Preston appeared in it, while Billy Bob's agent, Geyer Kosinski, produced. "It's about a family of white trash alcoholics," Thornton observed. "I got all my misfit friends together and we made a movie."

Angie was dealing with a rather more sinister misfit, desperate to snag a role in the grisly thriller *The Bone Collector,* about a serial killer. It meant working with one of her acting heroes, Denzel Washington, who plays a quadriplegic detective who teams up with a young but talented forensic detective, Amelia Donaghy, to track down the murderer. "I begged for the part of Amelia, I just wanted it so badly," she later told writer Anne Bergman. "I loved who she was. She was very street."

The real reasons behind her desire for the part may have been more complex. After two roles in which her character was led by her heart, she felt a need to return to a woman who was strong, cerebral, intuitive, and self-contained. She believed that this change of emotional pace completed her as a human being in some way, that portraying a kaleidoscope of screen characters would round out her own personality. This emotionally mechanistic approach, a kind of "painting by numbers" attempt to fill in the gaps in her character, implied that at the heart of Angie there was no "there" there. As a young actress she felt she was a blank canvas on which other characters played, and she got tattoos to literally mark the things about her life that were important to her, to show what she stood for. She saw herself as a cipher who only could evolve through her characters, who stained her soul long after filming finished. "I suspect she's happiest when she's not being Angelina Jolie" was the astute observation of director Phillip Noyce.

Even the daredevil in Angie had private doubts about this latest character; she was haunted by a script that at first reading, she admitted, had "scared her to death." Not only did she have to confront a corpse covered in rats, but she also had to jump fully clothed into New York's East River.

"I wasn't sure I could play her, but that was perfect because she's not sure she can do her job either," she observed.

Angie admitted that during her research, she threw up when reviewing pictures of brutal crime scenes. That did not prevent her from decorating a wall of her New York apartment with black-and-white and color photographs of mutilated bodies, car-crash victims, and murder scenes to get in character, the montage ghoulishly reminiscent of Warhol's early photographic work, particularly his Death and Disaster series.

If she was uncertain about her involvement in the project, so, too, were the suits at Universal Studios. In a now-familiar refrain, they made it clear that they wanted a star name to carry the big-budget movie. Even though she had won a Golden Globe for *George Wallace* and enjoyed the backing of director Phillip Noyce and veteran producer Martin Bregman, they won the duel with Universal only after taking a budget hit.

"They took a big risk," admitted Angie, whose most nerve-wracking moment in the casting process came when she had to get the once-over from Denzel Washington. Prudently, she covered her hair, which was spiked and dyed pink for *Playing by Heart,* with a head scarf, only to inadvertently pull it off halfway through dinner. She still got the gig, transferring the shyness and awe she felt toward Washington to her character when filming began in September 1998.

There were other anxieties. During filming she became so thin that she had to be padded beneath her clothing. There was concern among her family and friends that once again she was anorexic and that she was still taking drugs. Her mother spent time with her on set to monitor her. When the grueling four-month shoot was completed, Angie's performance was more than competent—it was compelling. "The focus groups couldn't stop raving about Angelina," recalled Noyce. "Finally Washington couldn't resist shouting out: 'And what about Denzel? Don't you think he was great?'"

Angie certainly thought so. Like Sean Connery, he was an alpha male, solid, dependable, and true. She could not say the same for the other big man in her life, her father. Fall 1998 marked a distinct plunge in the temperature of their stormy relationship. Indeed, the frost never really left.

In an interview on *The Howie Mandel Show,* Jon Voight spoke enthusiastically about his son and daughter and their differing acting ambitions, but his brief TV appearance set off a deadly round of family misunderstandings.

James's girlfriend, Leanne, a waitress in a pool hall, thought Jon had said on TV that James should not attempt acting as there were enough actors in the family. This upset James, who complained to his mother. Although a friend urged her to wait until they had seen a transcript of the show, Marcheline called Angie, who was incensed with her father for publicly humiliating her brother. Ever the savior, she pledged to employ James herself, Marche willingly agreeing to take a cut in her manager's percentage so that brother and sister could work together. Not that Angie's agent, Geyer Kosinski, showed much enthusiasm about a two-for-one deal. "He realized where the talent lay," noted a friend.

By the time Marcheline read the transcript from the Mandel show, which proved that Jon had spoken only well of his children, the die was cast. Marcheline simply shrugged and said: "Well, he's done plenty of other nasty things to me." By loosening their ties with their father, she drew her children closer into her orbit, just as her mother, Lois, had always encouraged her children to love her the most and treat their father with disdain. Unaware of what was actually said on the show, from now on both Angelina and her brother subscribed to the story that their father had failed to help James in his career. As angry as James and Angie were, and as often as they repeated the tale of woe to their circle of friends, neither of them raised the issue with their father. For all her bluster, Angie avoids direct confrontation. As a result, their father had no way of knowing why he was being treated so coolly.

Very soon he was threatened with being frozen out of the family forever. Once again it was the vexatious issue of Marcheline and her house. With Angie now living in New York, Marche's thoughts turned to settling back East. She planned to live in the same exclusive neighborhood in Connecticut as Rolling Stone Keith Richards, buy two dogs (which she was going to name Bowie and Jagger), and one day befriend Richards while she was out walking them. One property she liked, which was riddled with damp and woodworm, was on the market for $900,000. The drip feed of complaints against her ex-husband—it was now twenty years since they formally separated—was relentless. Finally Angie, once again in full savior mode, took matters into her own hands and called her father. She told him bluntly that unless he bought her mother a house she would never speak to him again. That Angie had become embroiled in an ancient feud between her parents shocked their friends, the feeling being that it was Marcheline's fight, not her daughter's. Nonetheless, her intervention broke the logjam. While he demurred at paying for a house in the $900,000 price range, he did write Marche a check for $500,000. Marche put it in the bank—and never bought a house on either coast.

During this time it was not so much her family's fortune but her own career that was consuming Angie. She was bouncing back and forth between New York and Los Angeles, deluged by requests for interviews, photo shoots, and film promotions. In December 1998, for example, she won the Breakthrough Performance by an Actress award from the National Board of Review for her role in *Playing by Heart,* made her first appearance on the *Late Show with David Letterman* (where she haltingly discussed the end of her marriage to Jonny Lee Miller), appeared on the cover of the now-defunct glossy *Mirabella* with the tag VENUS RISING— ANGELINA JOLIE IS THE NEXT SCREEN GODDESS, and enjoyed the deliciously thrilling sensation of seeing her name up in lights, almost crashing her pickup truck when she drove by a giant poster of her and Denzel Washington in Hollywood. While the movie received mixed reviews, it made a big splash worldwide, taking in $151 million at the box office.

Angie was making an even bigger splash, nominated for a second Golden Globe for her electrifying performance in *Gia.* The irony was not lost on her or Billy Bob that one of her rivals for the accolade was Laura Dern, the star of *The Baby Dance,* in which she played a white trash mother trying to sell one of her brood. Angie reserved her biggest splash for the awards ceremony at the Beverly Hills Hilton on January 24, 1999. As Laura Dern and her dapper black-suited fiancé applauded, Angie claimed her second Golden Globe and shortly afterward made good on her promise to jump fully clothed into the hotel pool.

She explained that it was a childhood dream, on hot summer days, yearning to dive into the pool. When she and her friends tried, they were thrown out by hotel security. This time no one was going to stop her— although she wasn't quite as reckless as she first seemed, quickly changing out of her glittering Randolph Duke gown into a bodysuit before taking the plunge.

Joining her in the pool were the black-tied trio of her estranged husband, Jonny Lee Miller; her agent, Geyer Kosinski; and her brother, James

Haven. It was an interesting tableau, captured by TV producer Jeremy Lou-werse and his camera crew. Clutching a bottle of Perrier-Jouët, Angie en-couraged others to join the party. Prudently, no one did so, in spite of her pleading. During her midnight swim, the hierarchy of her relationships was clearly apparent—as was her need to snag the limelight. Her agent kept a discreet distance from the star of the show, Angie far more relaxed with her brother, climbing on his back for a piggyback ride around the pool while leaving a space between herself and her husband, with whom she was friendly but rather tentative.

At some point she swam over to Louwerse and encouraged him to dive in. When he demurred, she grabbed his arm and pulled him, his bottle of Morgan's rum, Cohiba cigars, walkie-talkie, cell phone, and pager straight into the pool. "It was a very sexy thing to do," he now recalls, though at the time he was more concerned about his equipment than with snagging a date with the Golden Globe winner. After conducting a rather bizarre interview in the pool with a sound man holding a boom mike over their heads, he let her swim away. It was a moment that stuck with him not just because of his encounter with a clearly flirtatious and friendly Ms. Jolie but also for what it said about her career trajectory.

"That incident symbolized her transformation from unknown wild child to superstar publicity machine. She knew what she was doing when she jumped into the pool. At the same time, she showed her innocence and playfulness, which we didn't really see again in public. Even though she wasn't an innocent, it was the end of the age of innocence for her. You can see the transition right there, the wide-eyed excitement matched by a kind of knowingness, a girl who instinctively knew she was headed for great-ness."

Louwerse made his own media splash, receiving a standing ovation when he arrived at the office of *Access Hollywood* the following morning. His unusual and exclusive interview was broadcast on heavy rotation na-tionwide. There was a price to be paid, however, for a midnight swim with a future screen goddess. When he arrived home at three in the morning, smelling of booze and soaking wet, his irate girlfriend asked what the hell he had been doing. His reply, "Swimming with Angelina Jolie," was per-haps not the most judicious in the circumstances. With that she headed for bed, while he slept on the couch. The next day she moved out.

On the way out, too, was Jonny Lee Miller. The separation was made formal on February 3, ten days after the Golden Globes, the couple citing "irreconcilable differences" in papers filed in Los Angeles Superior Court. "Jonny and I are still crazy about each other, but we have the sense of needing to move on in different directions" was her somewhat disingenuous epitaph for the marriage.

For Angie it was a new beginning, which began with a dark journey into her tremulous soul. A few days earlier she had articulated a manifesto for the rest of her life: "I can never stand still. While I'm alive I'm going to move as quickly as possible and live as much as I can, and I won't consider if that is good or bad for my career."

Angie was as good as her word. She covered the walls of her trailer with porn, went to work in a mental hospital, and made a name for herself.

The character that propelled her firmly into the public consciousness as an actor of note was Angelina herself. Or at least a variation of her. Like a lioness hunting a gazelle, she pounced on the part of Lisa Rowe, the wild, rebellious sociopath in *Girl, Interrupted,* and devoured it with unconcealed relish. "I'm Lisa; I identify with her," she explained, arguing that after *The Bone Collector* she needed to play a less cerebral character. Angie had already bonded with the character of the sexy and coldly amoral young woman several years earlier, when she read Susanna Kaysen's searing 1993 memoir about her stay in McLean Hospital, a private psychiatric institute in Massachusetts, during the socially turbulent sixties.

Kaysen's seventeen-month sojourn in the upscale but secure institution, where previous patients included poet Sylvia Plath, singer Ray Charles, and balladeer James Taylor, who based his song "Fire and Rain" on his experiences, prompted a provocative meditation on the nature of sanity, teenage female sexuality, adolescent angst, and the glib medical link between nonconformity and the label of mental illness. During her stay, Kaysen, who was diagnosed with borderline personality disorder, shared camaraderie, occasionally friendship, with the troubled young women on her ward.

It was this latter theme that director James Mangold emphasized in the movie version of the book, whose title derives from a Vermeer painting, *Girl Interrupted at Her Music.* He and Winona Ryder, who played Susanna Kaysen, spent three years working on the project, Ryder viewing the movie as a "child of the heart." By the time the movie was released it was Ryder's heart that was broken, as Angie effortlessly walked away with all the honor and glory. From the moment she read for Mangold, she nailed the character of Lisa. Astonished by her portrayal, he stated, with characteristic Hollywood understatement, "God has given me a gift." As Mangold later recalled: "It was clear to me that day that I was watching someone who was not acting. There was someone speaking through her; it was a part of herself."

Her performance was more hell than heaven, with Angie proving that the devil had not only the best tunes but also the best lines. Innately competitive, she stole every scene in which she appeared, experienced actors like Vanessa Redgrave and Whoopi Goldberg expertly mugged by this feral force of nature. Even the animals were upstaged. In one scene, when she was faced with a hissing cat, instead of flinching or swiping it away, Jolie calmly gave it the once-over, stared it down, and then hissed right back. As for Winona Ryder, she unwittingly provided the palette for Angie, her shaded, introspective performance the perfect canvas for Angie's wild-eyed, ballsy inmate whose escapades, and frequent escapes from the hospital, gave the movie vibrant color and texture. Angie was the Hockney to Winona's Vermeer. Film critic Pauline Kael described Angie's picking off her feminine costars one by one like bits of sweater lint. "Those poor actresses," she told Allen Barra. "She's absolutely fearless in front of a camera. This girl would scare the crap out of Jack Nicholson in [*One Flew Over the*] *Cuckoo's Nest*."

Looking back, Winona is keen to emphasize that she fought hard for Angie to get the part of Lisa, feeling sorry that the two-time Golden Globe winner was not yet taken seriously as an actress. "I never really felt like I got the chance to know her," she blithely told *BlackBook* magazine of the three-month shoot, during which she was effectively incarcerated morning till night with Angie and her fellow actors in an unused building at a mental institution in Harrisburg, Pennsylvania, that was turned into a replica of 1960s McLean Hospital.

It was hardly surprising. In the movie the two eventually become enemies, and with both of them deep into Method acting, personal interaction was edgy and often hostile. Playing an openly aggressive, emotionally inert sociopath, Angie kept in character even when the cameras had stopped rolling. If Winona complained of a headache or tiredness, Angie would shrug indifferently, explaining that Lisa never felt anything. Winona wasn't the only one to feel Angie's social freeze. One evening actress Brittany Murphy, who played Daisy, a socialite who lived on a diet of chicken and laxatives and was bullied by Lisa, was talking to Angie off set. After a brief chat Angie told her baldly, "Wait a minute—what am I talking to you for?" Murphy replied, "Can't we take a break for a while?" Angie just laughed and moved away.

Angie cocooned herself in her trailer, plastering the walls with porn pictures because they made her "feel provocative, open, and sensual," and quietly smoking heroin, according to a close friend interviewed on the condition of anonymity. Her drug of choice helped her focus during the long hours of filming, but it also made her feel safe as she embarked on a high-risk, high-wire performance.

She also read the script notes and comments her mother had sent her. It was part of a familiar mother/daughter routine, Marche always on hand to talk through her roles. Her mother even gave her the glove puppet that she ended up using in the film. And the family connection didn't end there: "Angel of the Morning," a song written by her uncle Chip Taylor, became part of the sound track.

While Angie's coolness to Winona and her costars could be wrapped up in the Method acting explanation, the simple fact was that she didn't really bond with anyone on the set. "She couldn't stand Winona," observed a girlfriend. "Angie seemed to do much to undermine Winona in the name of acting." That Winona had been engaged to Johnny Depp, the object of Angie's teenage crush, may have added a further frisson. The leading lady was not the only one in her crosshairs. Angie argued with the director about the way he shot and eventually cut the movie, and publicly snubbed a production assistant, Andrea Mitchell, whom she had earlier befriended, at a party. Whether it was Angie staying in character as Lisa, or the first sign of diva behavior from a normally down-to-earth actor, her attitude irritated the hostess of the party, then a close friend of the actress's. "It was rude and so unnecessary," she observed. "She cut Andrea loose for some reason. When she tires of someone, she literally writes them out of her life."

Mick Jagger knew the feeling. During filming he invited her to the Stones concert in Philadelphia in March. While she had turned down his invitation to join him in Brazil, she did attend the gig but, much to Jagger's chagrin, did not hang out with him backstage. After the concert she drove back to the film set. More revealing than her teasing indifference toward Jagger was the dance of deception between Angie and her mother. She called Marcheline after the concert and told her that Jagger had asked her to marry him. Whether it was said in jest or to please her mother, Marcheline was understandably thrilled and excited—until she called Jagger to congratulate him. He was utterly bemused, complaining that Angie hadn't even bothered to see him after the show, let along accept a proposal of marriage.

While Jagger felt he was on the outside looking into Angie's life, Timothy Hutton was very much on the inside. She might have stayed in character in her dealings with Winona Ryder and other actors on the set of *Girl, Interrupted,* but when she wanted, Angie quickly became Angie. During breaks in shooting, she frequently visited Hutton at his Pennsylvania home, which was near the film set. Angie immediately struck up an affectionate friendship with his ex-wife, Debra Winger, who lived nearby, and she "adored" their son, Noah, now a documentary filmmaker, who was then aged twelve. Angie and Hutton, who met on the set of *Playing God,* first appeared publicly as a couple at the Oscars in March.

Angie could only look on as Billy Bob Thornton, nominated for Best Performance by an Actor in a Supporting Role for *A Simple Plan,* was passed over for the award in favor of James Coburn. Whatever the couple felt for each other, at that time their lives were going along different paths; while Angie was romancing Tim Hutton, Billy Bob and his fiancée, Laura Dern, were actively discussing starting a family. Laura Dern could barely contain her excitement, telling one visitor: "I've waited all my life to find the right man to have a baby with. It's like a dream come true. We are both getting older and we are just so ready." Her mother, Diane Ladd, was equally thrilled that her daughter had finally found "Mr. Right," telling friends that she couldn't wait to be a grandmother.

Laura, then thirty-two, wanted everything to be perfect, flying English feng shui expert Karen Kingston from her home in Bali to "space clear" the couple's new home in Mandeville Canyon. Kingston spent a day going through every room in the house, dispersing negative energy by putting special salt in the corners, strewing the floor with flower petals, ringing bells, and chanting in order to cast the demons out. She paid special attention to the windowless walk-in closet by the master bedroom that Laura and Billy Bob had chosen as the nursery. Laura's only concerns focused on the swimming pool—her sister, Diane, had drowned in a tragic accident at the age of eighteen months—and the hill rats that were occasional unwelcome visitors.

She was blissfully happy, indulging Billy Bob's frequent stays at the Sunset Marquis hotel in West Hollywood. The discreet hotel, a favorite hangout of the rock aristocracy, features numerous pictures of Thornton, including a larger-than-life head shot in the entrance foyer. Once inside, Billy Bob was king of all he surveyed, using the basement recording studios to make music till the early hours. A popular figure among the staff for his Southern courtesy, he liked to have what was known as his "harem," his assistants, including Odessa Whitmire, at his beck and call. She was with him when he directed *All the Pretty Horses,* based on the novel by Cormac McCarthy, in New Mexico. During the shoot, in March and April 1999, she met and eventually became engaged to actor Matt Damon.

It was perhaps just a coincidence that around this time Angie and Tim Hutton were seen making out at the hotel's open-air bar. Patrons, including a session musician and his partner, were mesmerized by their public display of affection, the consensus being that the couple should get themselves a room. Whether or not her behavior was aimed at making Billy Bob jealous, it certainly fit in with Angie's exhibitionist tendencies. In April, when *Pushing Tin* was released, the *New York Post* reported Angie and Tim in a "late-night liplock" at McAleer's Pub on Amsterdam Avenue in New York, while a married couple who went out for dinner with them found their company "boring" because they only had eyes—and lips, mouths, and teeth—for each other. The same month, when Tim introduced her to his friend musician Neil Young at his postconcert party at Madison Square Garden, reports again focused on the couple's public smooching.

Apart from the sexual attraction, Angie's decision to take up drumming to please Tim, and their discussions about renovation projects, which ultimately came to naught, showed an unusual degree of commitment. The couple was so enraptured by each other that rather than buy engagement rings, they discussed tattooing their ring fingers. When Angie had a runic "H" tattooed on the inside of her wrist, it was assumed it was a sign of devotion to her current squeeze. She later said it was "H" for Haven, her brother's surname.

As with much in Angie's life, nothing was quite as it seemed. Didactic in her film choices, she was equally compartmentalized in her personal life, particularly when it came to romance. Whether he liked it or not, Tim Hutton was just one suitor in the revolving door of her life. He sensed as much, coming to realize that, even though he was older, more experienced, and an accredited heartbreaker, he was simply a pawn being toyed with by a ruthless queen in a chess game he had no understanding of. "I feel like I am just a piece of luggage on an airport carousel waiting to be picked up," he whined. "Please pick me, please pick me."

Her wild ride during her twenties was simply Angie catching up after the adventures of her teenage years, when she focused on getting a hand-hold on Hollywood's greasy pole. As her stage mother, Lauren Taines, explains: "As a teenager Angie didn't date; she was entirely focused on her career. So all the wildness came out when she had made it as an actor. She was having the time of her life."

NINE

My brother and I are going to get married.

—ANGELINA JOLIE AT A FRIEND'S PARTY

It was the moment she had waited for her whole adult life. At last Marcheline Bertrand was about to meet her rock-and-roll idol, Mick Jagger. Although they had been talking on the phone for nearly two years, they had yet to see each other in the flesh. As the big day approached, Marcheline could hardly contain her nervous excitement. She flew to Las Vegas in mid-April 1999 for the show, heading backstage at the MGM Gardens to say hello before the band took the stage.

The first person she saw was Charlie Watts, who knew all about Jagger's crush on her daughter, having acted as go-between when Mick slumped into a depression after Angie refused to speak to him. He pointed out Mick's dressing room, which was down a long corridor. As she made that lonely walk, Marche could barely contain her sense of anticipation about meeting the man of her dreams. Her timing, however, could not have been worse. Suddenly Jagger emerged from his dressing room, a man in a hurry heading for the stage.

"Hi. I'm Marcheline," she said.

Mick smiled and said, "Oh, it's so good to meet you," but he was in a rush. "Look—I have to go onstage now. Can we talk after the show?" He gave her an airy wave and went to take his bow. Marcheline was completely devastated by what she considered a snub. Nothing could console her. She watched the concert, but never went to the after-party. Nor did she ever speak with him again. Though he didn't know it, Mick Jagger had fallen prey to the Bertrand freeze.

Marche put a brave face on her disappointment, telling friends she'd had the time of her life. She would later describe it as a "wild and magical" evening in which she partied until late. While Mick Jagger had fallen out of favor, he was in a perverse way responsible for saving her life. Days later she fell ill, at first thinking she had come down with pneumonia as a result of her brief flirtation with a rock-and-roll night out. After a series of tests over the next few weeks, her greatest fear was confirmed—she had cancer. The curse of the Bertrand family had struck again, this time taking the form of ovarian cancer. Thankfully it was discovered in the early stages, and under the care of the internationally recognized cancer surgeon Dr. Beth Karlan at Cedars-Sinai hospital in Beverly Hills, she went into remission. Marche felt that if she hadn't fallen ill right after the Stones concert, her cancer would have been discovered too late. "I never imagined they would play an important part in saving my life," she noted later.

During this very stressful period, Jon Voight was a constant visitor, spending hours at Cedars-Sinai as Marche recovered from the operation. Her younger sister, Debbie, had her bags packed, ready to visit and renew a relationship that had hit the rocks during James's college graduation in 1995. As Debbie was about to begin the drive from home, Marcheline said that she wasn't yet ready to meet her. She would never see her sister again.

As she gradually recovered, Marcheline asked her ex-husband if she could move in with him. As he only had a small two-bedroom rented apartment, he suggested that she move back into their first-ever apartment on Roxbury Drive. When he gave it the once-over, he could see that the landlord had neglected the one-bedroom apartment, so Voight spent around $30,000 on general maintenance, new carpets, furniture, and drapes. Ever the perfectionist, Marcheline complained that the curtains were half an inch too short. While his concern and generosity toward Marcheline earned Jon some brownie points with Angie, he had still racked up a large emotional debt. As a girlfriend who knew Angie well at this time remarked: "She didn't really want him around. She wanted to punish him for the way she believed he had treated his wife and children."

Angie articulated her own deep-seated fears about the family curse artistically, writing her first script, called *Skin*, about a girl (a thinly disguised Angie) with a terminally ill mother and a family history of cancer who discovers that she has cancer in one breast but decides to have both breasts removed. "It was very deep, very hard-core," said someone who read the script.

Ironically, while Marcheline had put Mick Jagger into the deep freeze, Angie was feeling much warmer toward him. Jagger, not known for his largesse, had sent Angie a pair of $5,000 diamond earrings that he bought for her in New York. In May 1999, before her mother's cancer was diagnosed, she was thinking of joining him in Brazil during the *No Security* tour. Her friends, not privy to this two-year samba of enticement and rejection, were astonished and alarmed. That same month he had fathered a child by his mistress, Brazilian model and TV host Luciana Gimenez—and yet Angie was going to Rio de Janeiro to meet with the singer. "I told her that she was out of her fucking mind to have anything to do with him," recalls a close friend. "She didn't take a blind bit of notice. It was all part of her great adventure."

That month another suitor joined the queue. In late May 1999 Angie began filming *Gone in Sixty Seconds,* the Jerry Bruckheimer remake of the 1974 cult classic by H. B. Halicki in which ninety-seven cars were wrecked in ninety-five minutes. Actor Nic Cage earned $20 million as the former car thief about to pull off the ultimate heist, Angie considerably less as his singer-songwriter lover. It was an amusing juxtaposition: Angie drove around Hollywood in a battered pickup truck and didn't think she could sing, whereas Cage was a classic car nut, in 1997 paying a world-record price at auction for a Lamborghini. While her financial rewards were not as considerable as those of her costar, her standing in this fickle trade was high enough that she was offered top billing along with Cage.

In an industry as byzantine and hierarchical as a medieval court, this was a signal honor. Perversely, she turned it down, choosing to be named alongside the other actors, who included Robert Duvall and Giovanni Ribisi. She made it clear that she enjoyed being treated as one of the boys, preferring the testosterone-fueled atmosphere to the estrogen energy of *Girl, Interrupted.* "I wanted to be around a lot of men," she explained. "I've been around women in a mental institution for way too long."

Certainly men wanted to be around her.

During the filming of *Gone in Sixty Seconds,* Nic Cage was constantly calling her apartment. She was amused rather than seduced by the preposterous spending of Nic, a Beverly Hills High School alumnus who lived in a faux castle on the edge of Los Angeles. One day she took Cage, then married to actress Patricia Arquette, on a trip to a discount store, Pick'n Save on Hollywood and Vine, to remind him how the other half still lived. It didn't have the desired effect; he subsequently ended up buying a handful of tropical islands with his movie earnings.

It was not only Nic Cage who was circling her; Tim Hutton, Billy Bob Thornton, Jonny Lee Miller, and a lovelorn Mick Jagger still had her cell phone number on speed dial. In time they would be joined by Australian actor Russell Crowe, whom she met during the promotion for *The Bone Collector.* She kept her stable of men in different compartments, never letting on that each was an interchangeable part of her posse.

Despite the pack of A-listers beating a path to her door, she wasn't particularly interested in the usual Hollywood gossip about who was dating whom. There were just two exceptions to her rule of studied indifference: Johnny Depp, whom she had adored since *Edward Scissorhands,* and golden boy Brad Pitt. For some reason Pitt intrigued her, and she closely quizzed a friend who had worked with him, eager to know what he was like. As a youngster, he had a reputation, rightly or wrongly, as a "stoner," observed actor Ric Young and others. He was a guy with a quirky sense of humor who only seemed to date A-list celebrities, which merely served to pique her interest. "She never took any notice of the Hollywood scene," recalls her friend, "so her interest in Brad was truly unusual."

Regardless of her interest, Angie had enough suitors to worry about without encouraging more. While her girlfriends were concerned that she would get hurt by one of these notorious players, Angie had the insouciant confidence of a woman above the fray, not caring or feeling enough to get her heart broken. The psychology seemed clear: As a youngster she had witnessed her mother's torment at her father's hand, and now she was making it one woman's mission to tame a team of top-class heartbreakers. Tame and break them she did, teasing them, tempting them, and then tossing them aside. She was also following the lead of her mother, who, after the split from Jon Voight, had been courted by the likes of Al Pacino, Burt Reynolds, and Warren Beatty. Both she and Angie clearly forgot the advice of actor Jacqueline Bisset, Marche's friend and Angie's godmother. As Jacqueline was fond of saying when one of her girlfriends dated a thespian: "Good God! Not him. He's an *actor*! Never go out with an actor."

Instead Angie quietly dated a rock star, keeping Mick Jagger on a string like the others, always wanting more. During this romantic dance, Angie's father was the unwitting wallflower, oblivious to what was really going on. One day he was shopping with Angie in Saks Fifth Avenue in New York when Charlie Watts spotted her and came over to say hi. After he had gone, Jon Voight whispered to Angie: "Dark side, dark side; these people are a bad influence." It was all Angie could do not to laugh. "Dad, if anybody is a bad influence on the Rolling Stones, I am."

Her father had no idea just how bad. One night Angie took her Jumpin' Jack Flash to a bondage club in New York, a venue complete with dungeons and rooms where guests played doctor, among other, darker games. During their visit, most likely to the Vault, a now-defunct club with a celebrity clientele, she told friends that they were all whipped. "That was Angie; wild and great fun to be with," said her friend. "She might have said that she had slept with only four men, but she is a total sexual deviant." Certainly Angie knew her way around the sadomasochist scene, later telling *Time* magazine's Jeffrey Ressner about the night she dragged an agent from the Creative Artists Agency on a tour of Manhattan's bondage clubs. "S and M focuses you on survival," she explained. "It's a weird cleansing of self."

The keen blade of a knife and the sharp bite of a skillfully wielded whip; it was all of a piece for a girl attempting to connect with herself, to dull the primal pain of abandonment. At the same time, the elaborate routines of sadomasochism appealed to her sense of ritual, her love of drama. As Dr. Franziska De George observes: "The ritual is a carefully orchestrated experience designed to invoke specific feelings, which can be stopped at any time. This is like being in complete control of your life. You design an experience, and during that time you know exactly what is coming and what to do. It's like predicting the future and handling it perfectly."

Angie was always raising the bar for violence, testing the limits of herself and others. One night, when she was having trouble with a movie executive who was a fellow guest at the Raffles L'Ermitage Hotel, where she and a friend were staying so that they could smoke heroin, she ratcheted up the level of aggression after the initial flirtation developed into him stalking her. During one exchange, the executive jammed his foot against the door to stop her from closing it. Instantly she whipped out a tiny penknife and stabbed at his foot. That ended the confrontation—her clear enjoyment of this violent dance giving the impression that it was part of a perverse game she both loved and knew how to play.

As far as her circle of intimates was concerned, Mick Jagger was a glamorous if aged sideshow to the main event, her "official" boyfriend, Tim Hutton. Even so, they were worried that Hutton, fifteen years older than Angie and a notorious heartbreaker, would leave her as so much romantic roadkill should she actually succumb and fall for him. They need not have troubled themselves. While Hutton was clearly besotted with her, Angie's heart, or more accurately her desires, lay elsewhere.

She made it clear that it was the name "Billy Bob Thornton" that she wanted tattooed way below her bikini line. As *Gone in Sixty Seconds* wrapped in early September, she began jonesing about it to tattoo artist Friday Jones, who had tattooed Angie a couple of years before. Having seen the mess Angie had made of her body by her self-inflicted, prison-style tattoos, Friday was not keen, thinking Angie's decision would come back to haunt her. "I thought it was a crackpot idea," recalls Friday. She resisted Angie's entreaties for weeks but was finally worn down with her insistence. "You just don't say no to Angie."

On October 6, 1999, they arranged to meet at the Hollywood Hills home of a mutual friend, a married amateur photographer who regularly joined Angie to indulge in their craving to smoke heroin. While Friday reluctantly got to work, her friend took a series of black-and-white and color Polaroid pictures of Angie. As the needle cut into her skin, she lay on a couch languidly smoking a Marlboro cigarette, naked except for two black crosses made from electrical tape covering her nipples. Sensual rather than sexy, the pictures convey a sense of moody eroticism, reminiscent of Marianne Faithfull, the quintessential rock chick (and onetime love of Mick Jagger), in her decadent prime.

Initially Friday wanted to use a light, fluid script that would match the contours of Angie's body and could easily be removed or disguised. Angie was insistent on choosing the typescript Helvetica, a rigid and upright font, which was a very obvious, literally unavoidable statement. "I used a Japanese technique involving light gray ink in case she ever wanted to grow her pubic hair over the tattoo to disguise his name," recalls Friday, who was also struck by how deeply Angie had scarred her inner thighs. "In my experience, cutters are often girls with absent fathers. They take out the emotional pain on themselves; it gives them a sense of being." Friday's experience suggested that cutting could evolve into an addiction to tattoos, clearly the direction toward which Angie was moving.

Angie saw tattoos as celebrating and marking important events in her life. As she says: "Usually all my tattoos came at a good time. A tattoo is something permanent, when you've made a self-discovery or something you've come to a conclusion about." So the fact that she chose to mark her most intimate sexual area with Billy Bob's name speaks volumes about her feelings for him.

In fact, Angie found herself in a romantic dilemma much sooner than Friday could ever have anticipated. The next day Tim Hutton called Angie from London and asked her to marry him. It was not the first time he had asked, but this particular invitation caught her unaware. For once Angie was at a loss for words—or a suitable response. She called her photographer friend for urgent advice. "What should I do? What should I do?" Angie wailed.

Her friend's reply was matter-of-fact. "Buy yourself a pair of crotchless panties and keep the lights down low."

It seems that Hutton's offer was mere bravado, the last hurrah of a lover who knew he was on the way out. "She settled the score for all the women who had been hurt by him," notes a girlfriend. Within short order he was romancing children's book illustrator Aurore Giscard d'Estaing, niece of the former president of France, whom he married three months later, on January 21, 2000. Stories circulating in October that Angie broke down in tears over the breakup in front of director Penny Marshall while reading for her upcoming movie *Riding in Cars with Boys* were well wide of the mark.

Tears were alien terrain for Angie; the girl who disliked being hugged or touched only ever cried for the camera. Ironically, a couple of weeks later the dry-eyed girl who was turned on by testing limits and pushing buttons finally met her match: herself. The woman who could never go too far finally went too far—and fell off the emotional edge.

For the premiere of *The Bone Collector* in November 1999, Angie deliberately invited her lesbian girlfriend, Jenny Shimizu; her estranged husband but constant friend, Jonny Lee Miller; her brother, James Haven; and another friend, a fellow heroin user. To spice things up even more, she and her guests all shared the same hotel suite for the night. If she thought she was going to be the ringmaster in some weird interaction, she was in for a shock. During the night Jenny made a pass at Angie's addict friend, in part to make Angie jealous. The ploy worked, perhaps too well. It was more than Angie could handle, "freaking out" at the emotional menagerie—ex-husband, lover, fellow addict, and brother—that confronted her. "For once she went too far and it all ended in tears. Hers," noted her friend.

During this emotional carousel ride, there was one man in her life who refused to leave her alone: her father, even though their public displays of fond togetherness on the red carpet or in the media were largely a charade. When the cameras were pointed elsewhere, father and daughter maintained a hostile, sometimes belligerent, distance. In interviews they talked about working together—perhaps, suggested Angie, in a remake of the 1985 comedy *Clue,* based on the board game. Her father seemed taken with the thought, saying in another newspaper interview that it would be "great to play these really dopey characters, partially because we're both taken so seriously now." Angie even talked about the possibility of driving across the country in the Cannonball Run with her father.

In keeping with this mutual adoration society, she told *Entertainment Weekly* in November 1999: "We've found a great relationship now," while Jon Voight was hoping that the day would soon come when his daughter was more famous than he was. "Angie and I are great friends and that fact is one of the joys of my life," he told the *Toronto Sun.* As ever, Angie capped the love fest when she declared to a Scottish newspaper: "I actually hate Jolie. I would rather have been Voight."

The reality was very different. In the well-worn narrative of Angie's life, which she unveiled to anyone who cared to listen, her father could do no right, her mother no wrong. Her story, learned at her mother's knee, was that her louse of a father had abandoned his wife and children for another woman, never paid child support, and effectively left the family destitute. Tattooed on Angie's heart was this story of betrayal, neglect, and selfishness. One lurid tale, which she repeated often, was that shortly after her parents' separation, her mother had been waiting by an elevator, and when the doors opened she saw her husband's mistress on her knees performing oral sex. All the time Angie was growing up, she absorbed her mother's tale of woe wholesale as Marche spent hours on the phone complaining about her ex-husband.

For most of her teenage years, Angie had deliberately kept her father out of the loop regarding her life. Now, thanks to the various media interviews she had given about her drug use, her cutting, and her suicidal tendencies, his eyes had been opened. Her father was particularly worried about her heroin use, seeing for himself the physical changes the drug wrought on her slim frame. He was not the only one to notice, both inside and outside the family. On one occasion James Haven found her unconscious on the floor of an apartment. His initial concern turned to alarm when he couldn't wake her up. Eventually she revived, but it was a harsh insight into the unwholesome life she was leading.

Even casual observers could see she had problems. As *Time* magazine's Jeffrey Ressner noted in November 1999 around the release of *Girl, Interrupted:* "The girl could use an interruption of protein. Her skin seems pasty, her face is gaunt and barely made up, and her famously full, pouty lips appear in need of Blistex."

In arguably the most honest profile of her career, *Esquire* writer John H. Richardson described meeting her at the Museum of Modern Art in New York in November 1999 and, after two minutes of her undecipherable conversation, starting to look for track marks on her tattooed arms. "I feel very much like I'm dealing with a crazy person," he wrote. "Half of what she says I can't follow, it's in some private language. Her sentences are like sheets of mist that start to evaporate the second they hit the open air."

Many other celebrity profilers followed in Richardson's uncertain footsteps, losing themselves in a meaningless swirl of mangled syntax, undecipherable thoughts, and unfinished sentences.

Although her father was determined to confront Angie about her health, she ignored his phone calls, destroyed his letters, and stayed at the homes of her friends or checked into local hotels to elude him. It became a sad game of hide-and-seek, father bouncing around town looking for his errant daughter, Angie ensconced with a girlfriend getting high on heroin. His friends believed that in desperation, he hired a private eye to find out where she was and what she was doing. When he discovered where she was staying, he would buy stuffed animals and leave them in the lobby of the hotel. After the bellman brought them to her, she would deliberately feed what she considered pathetic peace offerings to her friend's eight-week-old pit bull, Bruno, who quickly chewed them to a pulp. It was symbolic. "You were never there for us growing up, so fuck you trying to have a relationship in our mid-twenties," she said.

One evening Angie and her friend were smoking heroin in a suite at the Raffles L'Ermitage in Beverly Hills when there was a knock at the door. As they had recently ordered steak and red wine, they assumed it was room service. When Angie opened the door, it was her father, who was standing there in a camel coat. "Get out, get out, get out! I don't want you here!" she screamed at him. He made a grab for her, but Angie pulled away. "Calm down, calm down," he told her. He then asked Angie's friend to leave so that he and Angie could have a confidential father/daughter conversation. She refused. "Don't you have a father?" he asked plaintively. As her own father had abandoned the family when she was a youngster, she had no sympathy for Jon Voight. She stayed where she was.

Voight was at a loss as to what to do next. Running through his mind was how actor Martin Sheen had turned his son Charlie in to the authorities after he violated the terms of his probation by using drugs again. Martin Sheen, himself a recovering alcoholic, voiced a sentiment that had profound resonance with Angie's father: "When a life is at stake and it's your child, you become fearless in a lot of ways. You just become a fanatic."

Finally Angie yelled: "Call security. Get him out of here." Instead they reached a compromise, phoning her brother, James, to come over. Once James arrived, her father and Angie's friend both left. "I knew she was safe, and I left," he later told TV host Pat O'Brien, "but I shouldn't have."

Her father's attempted interventions were mere distractions from the main pursuits in Angie's life at the time—chasing the dragon and then surfing the Internet, shopping for a foreign special-needs baby on various adoption agency Web sites. It seems she wanted the most deprived child she could imagine, a desire that perhaps echoed her own unarticulated feelings of abandonment and damage. "She felt that she didn't have a childhood and wanted to give a child the childhood she missed," observed Franklin Meyer, who discussed her desire to adopt with her on numerous occasions. She was inspired in part by reading and talking about the African-American entertainer Josephine Baker, who adopted twelve multi-ethnic orphans, whom she called her "rainbow tribe," as a protest against racism in America in the 1950s and '60s. Described by novelist Ernest Hemingway as "the most sensational woman anyone ever saw," Baker was much more than a celebrated singer and dancer who mesmerized audiences in Paris with her near nude performances at the Folies Bergère. During World War II she worked for the French resistance, her bravery rewarded with the Croix de Guerre. Married four times, with numerous women lovers, including the artist Frida Kahlo, such was her standing that following the assassination of Martin Luther King Jr. she was asked by his widow to lead the civil rights movement. She declined, worried about the safety of her rainbow nation. Her enthralling, vibrant, and committed life would form a template for Angie's own future direction.

Long before she started searching for a special-needs child, Angie excitedly told a "stunned" Mick Jagger that she planned to adopt a Native American baby, whom she would name after him as a celebration of their relationship. How serious she was remains an open question. "She was just teasing him and messing with his head," argues Lauren Taines. Angie did go along with Jagger when he invited her to the home of record producer Richard Perry to watch the Lennox Lewis–Evander Holyfield fight in November 1999, Angie amused and not a little jealous about the fact that whenever she left the room, actress Farrah Fawcett was "crawling all over" her date for the night.

With Angie immersed in moviemaking, her mother did much of the administrative spadework in the search for baby "Mick Jagger," although this was not her strong suit. Marche and Lauren attended a Native American awards ceremony in 1999 in the hope of making contacts with a suitable adoption agency. Thanks to the help of activist, musician, and poet John Trudell, whom Marche had met years earlier, she was introduced to comedian Charlie Hill, whose wife, Leonora, works with a Native American adoption agency. They arranged to meet at the Earth, Wind & Flour café in Santa Monica to talk through the mechanics of adoption, whereupon Marche realized that the process was complicated. If Angie wished to adopt a Native American child, she first would have to prove lineage linking the Bertrand or Voight family to an indigenous tribe. If she could not, she could only foster a child and even then would be obliged to raise the infant within Native traditions. As a devout Catholic, Marche eventually came to balk at these strictures and to gently discourage Angie from taking this route. For a time, however, Marche persevered, discovering, with John Trudell's help, that the Bertrand family, who descended from the original French settlers in Quebec, Canada, had slender links to the Haudenosaunee Iroquois tribe. By then the moment had passed and Angie was looking elsewhere.

As much as Angie might complain about her father in private, she was opinionated but not confrontational, playing the obedient daughter when they met socially. On these occasions she relied on her brother, James, to be her wingman, brother and sister giving each other support in dealing with their overbearing father. In spite of their differences, she had Christmas lunch with her father at his favorite Beverly Hills restaurant and even sent him a Christmas card of her wearing a cowboy hat. The black-and-white Polaroid picture was taken during the same session when she was tattooed with Billy Bob's name.

"Her bark was always worse than her bite," recalls a friend. It was not only with her father that she slid around awkward issues. After the Hollywood premiere of *The Talented Mr. Ripley* in December, the film's star Jude Law invited Angie and other friends, including model Kate Moss, to his hotel suite for drinks. Angie was furious that Kate Moss had been invited, knowing that she had recently had an affair with her ex-husband, Jonny Lee Miller, and had been engaged to Johnny Depp. Even though Angie had been "married but dating" during her time with Miller, Angie threatened to punch Kate if she dared to show her face in the hotel suite. The willowy model duly appeared in the company of Jude Law. Rather than confront her, Angie left the room.

While Angie preferred her brother to be by her side when she tackled their father, their relationship was complex, at once mutually dependent yet detached. Angie and her brother were welded forever as guardians of the story of their lives, reinforcing each other's memories. "They were always together; they hung out as a team," recalled their father. "Angie cared so much for Jamie, and Jamie was always taking care of her." While they had formed a profound and loving bond of support during their parents' difficult divorce, gradually the differing trajectories of their careers shifted the balance of power between them. When they were children, James was the one expected to be a star, Angie the neglected also-ran, always fighting for oxygen inside the family. When Jamie won the George Lucas award for his filmmaking as a student and Angie struggled as an actor, it seemed that they were running true to type. For all their much-vaunted closeness, while James was studying at the University of Southern California and Angie worked on her career they hardly spoke for three years. Like his mother, James was not a self-starter, always waiting for someone else, usually his father, to give him a helping hand. By the time he finished college, Angie was way up the ladder, and their roles were reversed. The young boy who identified with Linus now had his tough-minded, ambitious sister as his security blanket—and paymaster.

Smart but shy, James loved basking in the glow of his sister's stardom. In her own way she smothered him with kindness and concern, sometimes humiliating and belittling him along the way. For example, when they were at a party in the Hollywood Hills with numerous fellow actors, Angie loudly announced to the assembled throng: "My brother and I are going to get married." Her statement so shocked other partygoers that one actor, who had been on the set with James while he waited for his father to get him a role in the movie *Rosewood*, was moved to shout: "Are you out of your fucking mind? Don't say such ridiculous shit." Those in her circle were well aware of the "weird" interaction between brother and sister, seeing how James hung around his sister and was resentful of anyone else who talked to her. Yet when he had girlfriends, she was equally disapproving: She did not like that his waitress girlfriend, Leanne, for example, and felt that he should pay court to her. Of course, it was different when Angie was in a relationship, notably during her marriage to Jonny Lee Miller. Then she rarely if ever saw or spoke with her brother.

When she flew to Sydney, Australia, to promote *The Bone Collector* in November 1999, she took her brother and a few friends along for the ride. One night she went for dinner to actor Sam Neill's home, spending the evening with Tom Cruise and Nicole Kidman. When she returned to the hotel she said, tongue in cheek, "Do you know, if Tom Cruise and my brother came out as a couple, I think the public would embrace them." While her off-the-wall comments baffled her small group of friends, they were consistent with her impulse to provoke.

The first sign was at the Golden Globes ceremony in January 2000, where she won her third award in a row for her supporting role in *Girl, Interrupted*. As she clutched her statuette, her hair an odd shade of gray, she stood on the stage on the arm of her brother. "I had to bring my brother up here," she said in her acceptance speech. "He just had to see the view from up here." On the one hand, this could be seen as a kind, thoughtful gesture; in another light it was a professional humiliation, a tacit admission that big brother didn't have the acting chops to earn his own award.

In March she flew back from Mexico, where she was filming *Original Sin* (originally titled *Dancing in the Dark*) as part of her earlier agreement with *Gia* director Michael Cristofer, to attend the Academy Awards. When James Coburn announced that Angie had won the award for Best Actress in a Supporting Role for *Girl, Interrupted,* Angie, looking every inch the goth vampire of her youth with long black hair extensions and a Cruella De Vil black dress, was overwhelmed; she sincerely did not expect to win and had no victory speech prepared. She hugged her tearful brother, his own hair bleached blonde in what seemed to be a joint style statement, and kissed him on the mouth before making her way to the stage. "God, I'm so surprised no one's ever fainted up here," she told the audience at the Shrine Auditorium. "I'm in shock. And I'm so in love with my brother right now. He just held me and said he loved me. And I know he's so happy for me. . . . Winona, you're amazing. And Whoopi, everybody. My family for loving me. Geyer Kosinski, my mom, who's the most brave, beautiful woman I've ever known. And my dad, you're a great actor, but you're a better father. And Jamie, I have nothing without you. You're the most amazing man I've ever known, and I love you." For once she broke her no-crying rule before leaving the stage.

This was the expressive hors d'oeuvre before the sensational main course. After the ceremony the couple made their way hand in hand along the red carpet, James clutching his sister's award and proudly posing with it, looking as triumphant as if it were his own. Hollywood was left gasping for breath, as gossips pondered the possibility that Angie and her brother had an incestuous relationship. Original sin indeed, or as a New York tabloid put it, SMOOCHY JOLIE AND BRO TOO CLOSE FOR COMFORT. In another assessment, writer Chrissy Iley was struck less by the sexuality than by Angie's deeper cravings. "It's all about attention, calculated effect and wild abandon coming from the soul of the needy and the already abandoned." Unrepentant, they later enjoyed another swooning, openmouthed kiss at the *Vanity Fair* party.

Angie made an effort to douse the flames of the tabloid firestorm. "I didn't snog my brother," she said. "I wanted an Oscar my whole life—my father had one. Me and my brother had a very difficult upbringing. We both survived a lot together and it meant a lot that he supported me my whole life. And in that moment, you reach to kiss somebody and you end up kissing their mouth. Who cares? It wasn't like we had our mouths open, it wasn't some romantic kiss."

Members of her circle, who had witnessed the intense interaction between brother and sister, were rather more cynical, seeing the symbolism in Angie's stark black outfit. "It was the kiss of a vampire," observed a friend from that time. "She drained the blood out of any career James had. It was the kiss of death for his dreams of being an actor." Instead James was forever imprinted on the public imagination for this one titillating act. While neither brother nor sister would ever acknowledge it, a psychologist might well argue that her swooping kiss was an unconscious moment of revenge for the childhood years of living in her brother's shadow. The fact that he avoided his sister for some months after the incident perhaps reflects his annoyance and confusion.

In the immediate aftermath James was both irritated and coyly teasing with the media about what was really going on in his sister's life. Gossip-mongers were looking in all the obvious places, but had chosen the wrong target. Indeed, if they had gone to the Sunset Marquis hotel, where Angie went to celebrate her Oscar win, they would have seen her and the pajama-clad Billy Bob Thornton sitting outside amid the lush shrubbery talking and whatever until the early hours. Days after the ceremony, James Haven told writer Elizabeth Snead that Angie had a "special someone," which would leave those implying an incestuous relationship looking ridiculous. Just to confuse matters, though, James averred that he was shortly going to get his first tattoo. Naturally, it would be his sister's name.

As a sly coda to this episode, *Original Sin* director Michael Cristofer filmed a scene, deliberately or not, in which Angie, a beautiful seductress, is watching a play from a box in the theater. Onstage, Faust, played by her brother, looks over to her and says: "Who was it sent her to her ruin, I or you?"

When she transformed herself from vampire to vamp, returning to Mexico to resume filming the day after her Oscar win, Cristofer, probably Angie's most sensitive director, tried to ensure that she did not fall into the same psychological slump that had followed her previous successes, notably her suicidal drift after finishing *Gia*. Cristofer and Angie's costar Antonio Banderas assembled the cast and crew and, with the help of a mariachi band, serenaded her as she lay sleeping in her trailer. When she emerged bleary-eyed, the crowd of well-wishers each gave her a red rose to celebrate her victory. When all was said and done, Angie stood there with two hundred roses in her arms. "Everybody was emotional. It was kind of like I was their little girl," she later told *Premiere* magazine. "I felt like the little girl was going to survive this business."

It was not just her psychological state but her medical condition that Cristofer was monitoring closely. During the making of the movie, Angie and her Hollywood addict friend made a serious attempt to wean themselves off heroin. It was a painful, painstaking, and very difficult journey, her friend taking two years to get clean. Her friend even moved from Los Angeles to keep away from temptation. Angie did not have that luxury. Not only was she working on *Original Sin,* but she was also on a short list of one to play the lead in a big-budget action movie, *Lara Croft: Tomb Raider,* based on a favorite computer game of her ex-husband's. "Jonny used to play Tomb Raider all the time, and I used to compete with this woman," said Angie. "Taking on this part is a woman's revenge, isn't it?" The role appealed on a number of other levels, too; at last she would be playing the good girl, the clean girl, the posh girl. "When they called me I nearly fell over," she recalled. "It's like, 'Oh God, it's the woman we all compete with.'" Even better, Lara was the beloved daughter of a strong but doting father—a relationship that must have appealed to Angie. Equally important for the girl who took pleasure in kicking famous swordsmen to the curb, Lara Croft allowed her to beat men at their own games. She was destined to be Hollywood's first-ever big-box-office, all-action heroine. Even better than the movie's $7 million payday was the realization that she was now muscling in on territory traditionally patrolled by the likes of Bruce Willis, Arnold Schwarzenegger, and Jean-Claude Van Damme. Her drugs versus her ambition; the struggle was prolonged and difficult.

"Being addicted to heroin is not the same as being an addict where their compulsive behavior rules their life," observes Candy Finnegan, a professional interventionist. Angie seems to have been in the former category, a functioning heroin user.

The symptoms of heroin withdrawal are often compared to those of a bad case of flu, with watery eyes and nose, dilated pupils, muscle cramps, bone pain, and an aching body, together with diarrhea, vomiting, and loss of appetite. An addict suffers from acute cravings, especially at the three-day stage, and these are often accompanied by severe depression and suicidal behavior that can last for weeks. It is the psychological need that usually reels an addict back into using the drug again. Even taking heroin substitutes like methadone or OxyContin merely ameliorates the condition. Angie had some methadone in liquid form but, as her friend testifies, she really struggled to wean herself off heroin, some days staying clean and then sliding back. The only real solution for any addict, according to a Hollywood-based addiction specialist speaking on condition of anonymity, is to undergo medical treatment and to do "profound daily work" similar to the twelve-step program for alcoholics. There is no sign that Angie, not a joiner by nature, ever went down that path or needed to. "There is no such thing as 'was a heroin addict'; it does not exist in nature," argues the specialist. "A heroin addict has just three options: Continue, find a replacement, or undergo treatment and daily work."

Angie's father later told *Access Hollywood* that he made another intervention, flying to the film set in Mexico when he heard whispers on the Hollywood grapevine that she was in bad shape. When he arrived, he discovered that she was in the hospital with high blood pressure and that doctors feared she might have an aneurysm, a rupture of the artery going to the brain or the heart. Once her medical condition was stabilized and she was well enough to continue filming, her father was happy to learn that a doctor trained in psychiatry would oversee her detox program during her stay in Mexico.

It didn't help her equanimity that Angie, who played a seductress, literally, to die for, was romantically linked to her leading man, Antonio Banderas. That his wife, Melanie Griffith, and child were on set, too, did little to stem the gossip. Angie told Larry King that she found the accusations "ridiculous, insulting, awful, and disgusting. . . . It's probably one of the worst things I've ever felt accused of," she said, knowing whose name was tattooed below her bikini line. While Banderas may not have featured on her horizon, she was being somewhat economical with the truth when she told writer John Millar in March 2000 that romance was not a part of her life. "I'm not dating anybody and haven't been. I'm completely celibate and single. I don't know what a date really is. I have a lot of buddies but I haven't had anyone special since Jonny." Try telling that to Messrs Jagger, Hutton, and Thornton.

In the spring of 2000 Laura Dern and her fiancé finally moved into their remodeled home in Mandeville Canyon. Shortly after settling in, Laura invited some of her Hollywood friends, notably Jennifer Aniston, Lisa Kudrow, Courteney Cox, and a heavily pregnant Kelly Preston—she gave birth to Ella Bleu on April 3, 2000—to her new home for a painting party. Each woman had a canvas set up in the kitchen with paints and brushes. The idea was that they would all express themselves. When a hill rat started crawling down the kitchen range hood, the mood of creative self-improvement gave way to screams of terror, with Kelly Preston grabbing a broom and trying to push the rat back up the chimney. When the party ended in disarray, Laura Dern saw the unwelcome visitor as a dire omen. Nonetheless, she was desperately in love with Billy Bob, the couple seen out and about at numerous low-key social events in Hollywood.

At the end of March Laura was due to fly to Chicago to play a sexy siren who seduces a dentist played by Steve Martin in the comedy *Novocaine.* The problem was that Billy Bob, the inherently chauvinist Southern gentleman, didn't want her to do the movie, fearing that Laura, who had a tendency to follow the traditional Hollywood pattern of falling for her leading men, would end up romancing the then single comedian. He was jealous, plain and simple, his fears spilling over into bouts of anger and unfair jibes that she was simply a gold digger after his money. Dern was in a bind. She wanted to make the movie, yet was worried about Billy Bob and his jealous moods. Eventually she flew to Chicago in a state of some anxiety.

She had every reason to be nervous. Around this time a well-known TV host was arriving at the Raffles L'Ermitage and met Angie as she was coming out of the elevator. She was on the phone and in a hurry. After a brief exchange of pleasantries she said: "I'm trying to find this guy I kinda know because I'm kinda horny right now." And off she went into the night, looking for Billy Bob.

TEN

People like Angelina don't have attractions, they have addictions.
                                    —Psychologist Iris Martin

Just about the only thing staying level was her Greyhound cocktail, a potent mix of grapefruit juice and vodka, as Angelina Jolie swayed and sashayed her way through the lobby of the Sunset Marquis hotel. She was a woman on a manhunt, and her quarry was Billy Bob Thornton. She quickly proved herself to be an equal opportunity seductress, however. Now firmly in the role of Bonny Castle, the ruthless, amoral femme fatale in her latest movie, *Original Sin,* she was breathing alcohol fumes but oozing sex and seduction. Certainly Billy Bob's observation that actors' roles often reflect what is going on in their real lives was never more apt. Spotting Billy's spiritual healer and registered masseuse, Ingrid Earle, about to leave the hotel, Angelina asked if she knew where Billy was. Then Angie gave Ingrid the once-over and drawled that if she saw her giving Billy Bob a massage, she wouldn't be able to keep her hands to herself. She was clearly implying an invitation to a ménage. Ingrid smiled and explained that the only happy ending in her work was spiritual. "When she was coming on to me she was very insistent," she recalls.

Angie's pursuit of Billy Bob became increasingly frenzied during the winter of 2000. During breaks in her own filming in Mexico, Angie flew to Los Angeles or to Reno to be with her lover, who was filming the comedy *Waking Up in Reno,* about the redneck world of giant truck rallies, with Charlize Theron and Natasha Richardson. More often, though, she hung around the Sunset Marquis hotel, knowing that Billy Bob was making music in the studio basement. Sometimes, when his cell phone was switched off or he was unavailable for some reason, Angie frantically called anyone and everyone: the hotel concierge and manager, his business associates, friends, and even staff at his new home in Mandeville Canyon. Though Angie was obsessively jealous of his sometime assistant, Odessa Whitmire, who now mainly worked for actor Ben Affleck, she called her frequently to locate Billy Bob. Angie was perhaps right to be wary of the blonde beauty from South Carolina, who was heard ending phone calls to her boss with the words "I love you."

During this time Angie frequently stayed at the hotel—room 102 was her favorite—spending days in her suite. Such was her notoriety that on one occasion, even though she had requested privacy and housekeeping staff were ordered not to disturb her, the hotel management was worried enough to get in touch with her father after she had remained behind locked doors for several days straight without even contacting room service. When Voight arrived at the hotel, they unlocked the door to her ground-floor suite. Angie emerged disheveled and, according to one witness, "out of it," but otherwise unharmed.

Once again her emotional tumult and obsession had its roots in her early childhood, the profound unknown wound the emotional jet rockets that propelled her journey. As psychologist Iris Martin observes: "Abandonment makes people go nuts. It means that the minute you become close to someone and you start to have an attachment to them, you constantly think they are going to leave you. So you harass them with phone calls, you show up in the middle of the night, you confront them at work and talk to your friends incessantly about them."

At the same time, Angie deliberately courted disaster by hooking up with men like Jagger and Thornton, who could prove their devotion to her only by the act of betrayal, Jagger by cheating on Jerry Hall and Thornton by leaving Laura Dern. This was her version of Brecht's *Caucasian Chalk Circle,* the victors by definition losers. On some level, their behavior confirmed her preexisting contempt of men, "proving" them to be as unworthy of love and respect as her father.

Yet Billy Bob had one advantage over all her other suitors. As she confessed to her addict friend: "When I am with Billy, I don't need drugs." Swapping her desire for heroin for an infatuation for the actor-musician,

Angie saw him as her white knight, her savior. Entirely understandable, says Iris Martin. "People like Angelina don't have attractions, they have addictions."

In the midst of this emotional frenzy, Billy Bob was playing it very cool. After a while, though, his dismissive "she's just a kid" stance no longer fooled anyone. "Come on, buddy," remarked a girlfriend. "You know Angie is crazy about you. I'm not a lesbian, but I would sleep with her." Given his own insecurities, Billy Bob liked to be surrounded by a harem of female admirers. Not only was he living with Laura Dern, but he enjoyed the company of Odessa Whitmire, was in contact with air-traffic controller Sheila McCombe, and regularly made romantic overtures to other women.

He was now about to make Angie his harem of one, asking her to have his name tattooed where everyone could see it. She did so a few days after her triumph at the Oscars in March, albeit, according to her tattooist Friday Jones, with some reluctance.

For all her pursuit of Billy Bob, those in her circle insist that it was he who issued the ultimatum for her to marry him. Otherwise, he would go back to Laura Dern—who didn't yet realize that she had been ditched. It didn't take long for the news to leak, however, the New York *Daily News* reporting on April 7 that Billy Bob and Angelina were now an item, as evidenced by the tattoo on her arm.

Laura Dern's mother, Diane Ladd, responded with understandable shock. "Billy Bob Thornton is a real Dr. Jekyll and Mr. Hyde. Billy Bob told me he wants my daughter to be his wife and I know they've talked about having kids. I don't know how to make sense of it." Meanwhile, Laura's father, Bruce, was one of the stars of Billy Bob's latest movie, *All the Pretty Horses,* although he was not invited to the Los Angeles bowling alley where Matt Damon, Penélope Cruz, and other costars of the film joined Angie and Billy Bob in a celebration tournament in April.

Diane Ladd would have been even more confused if she had known that Angie and Billy Bob had decided to take a long road trip that echoed the road trip of *Daddy and Them,* the movie in which he and Laura Dern played a white trash couple with a booze problem. In late April, after Angie finished filming *Original Sin* in Mexico, they rented a Chevy Tahoe—they found the name endlessly amusing—and spent a few days driving two thousand miles, first to Las Vegas, then to Flagstaff, Arizona, then to

Billy Bob's home in Little Rock, Arkansas, before ending up in Nashville, where Billy Bob planned to lay down tracks for his debut album, *Private Radio*. "We had a really great time, stopping in motels along the road," she recalled, saying that the couple had enjoyed themselves so much they considered buying their own motel. During the weeklong road trip, Angie was in full trashy mode, feasting on junk food at roadside diners. "I'd insist on stopping at McDonald's every half an hour to get a Happy Meal," she was keen to point out, though both had, at some time, suffered from eating disorders. Their time together was as intense as it was illusory, a temporary escape from Hollywood and the real world.

As Angie was shortly going to be out of the country for six months, their romantic road trip effectively constituted not only their honeymoon but—though they didn't know it at the time—also one of the longest periods they would ever spend together. There was one problem. They weren't married. On April 24, while they were away, Angie's lawyer petitioned the court to finalize her divorce from Jonny Lee Miller. This left the coast clear for them to wed. When Angie left Billy Bob in his Nashville studio, they were planning to spend a couple of nights together when he hosted the Country Music Awards in Los Angeles on May 3. Before that moment madness lay.

While he was recording his album, she intended to return to Los Angeles. By now media speculation about the couple was rife. On April 28 *E!* entertainment correspondent Ted Casablanca, citing sources in the Jolie camp, announced that they had eloped. Hold your pretty horses, responded Billy Bob's folks. "They are not married and not engaged," said his spokesman, as Billy Bob threw himself into his music, his first love and best distraction. He says that his OCD is such that when he is recording he cannot take a break or stop until a track is as perfect as he imagined it. He does not take calls for anything or from anyone—apparently including his increasingly frantic new lover.

After the wild intensity of their road trip, his silence was deafening. Nor were his spokesman's public pronouncements reassuring. Endless fears assailed the actress: that he had cold feet, that he had gone back to Laura Dern, or even that he had died.

In her heightened state, struggling to stay off heroin and wrestling with her addiction to Billy Bob, Angie went to pieces. She was used to being in full control of a romantic script in which the voice on the other end of the phone pleaded with her to love him or at least to see him. Billy Bob's inaccessibility unnerved her. Where was her white knight when she needed him most?

Her account of the next few hours is contradictory, incoherent, and inexplicable. "I ended up going crazy because I thought I had actually lost him," she later told Larry King. In another version of the incident, however, she said that she had had a huge fight with a male friend—though not Billy Bob—and feared that this unnamed friend had been killed or injured as a result of their argument. Angie called her mother, who was alarmed by her daughter's hysterical mood, especially since she was stuttering for the first time in her life.

Angie flew from Nashville to Los Angeles, where Marcheline met her at the airport and they saw a doctor. At Angie's urging, they decided it would be best if she were admitted to the Neuropsychiatric Institute at the UCLA Medical Center for seventy-two hours so that she could be monitored. They knew about the place from drummer Joey Covington, who had spent time there following his suicide attempt. On reflection Angie now feels that she had some kind of nervous breakdown provoked by her grief over the possibility of losing Billy Bob. As Dr. Franziska De George observes: "With Billy Bob she must have felt the hope of finally being seen, of opening a door to look into herself and come out. Emotionally she is like a baby. When she couldn't access him, she was left locked in torment again." She considers Angie's decision to place herself under medical supervision rather than resort to her "tried and tested disassociative mechanisms"— taking drugs, cutting herself, and toying with suicide—to be a "tremendous progression, truly admirable."

In a surreal instance of life imitating art, Angie found herself in a ward with a group of troubled young girls, many of whom had seen her Oscar-winning performance in *Girl, Interrupted*. "In some weird way it's nice to know that everybody's insane," she recalled.

Angie's breakdown arose from her inability to "self-soothe" her fears in the way that most people are able to do. As Iris Martin observes: "We all self-soothe by going to the mother within, and she doesn't have that infra-structure. It is one of the reasons why she is a brilliant actor. Ordinary people don't lose themselves that easily in a person or a process."

Eventually Marcheline located Billy Bob and, against Angie's wishes, asked him to see her. In their first conversation on the phone, she was still barely able to speak and couldn't stop crying. They were reunited shortly before the Country Music Awards, her trauma further bonding the couple.

On May 5, 2000, within twenty-four hours of his arrival in Los Angeles, they had tied the knot in Las Vegas. For $189 they reportedly bought the Beginning package at the famous Little Church of the West wedding chapel, where six thousand quickie ceremonies take place each year. Billy Bob wore jeans and a baseball hat, Angelina a blue sleeveless sweater and jeans, walking down the aisle to the traditional strains of "Here Comes the Bride" and carrying a rose and carnation bouquet. Watched by the best man and witness, Billy Bob's cinematographer friend Harve Cook (curiously, her mother was not present), the bride promised to love and honor but not to obey her director boyfriend. The wedding ring that Billy Bob placed on Angie's finger was almost an afterthought, purchased for $29 from a woman selling jewelry in a bar. Duly betrothed, they walked down the aisle as man and wife to the sound of the Righteous Brothers singing "Unchained Melody." "The wedding was perfect for us," said Billy Bob later. "It was cheesy and beautiful and profound and intense and lighthearted and humorous. It was everything." For a wedding present he gave her a white rat called Fat Harry.

Soon the world knew what had been apparent to the cast and crew of *Original Sin*. As Antonio Banderas observed: "It was very obvious that this girl was in love. When somebody's in love, you don't hide it. I was very happy for her because actually I like Billy." The need for acknowledgment, for everyone's good wishes, was strong for the new bride, who was now stepmother to Billy Bob's sons, William and Harry. "We were becoming a family. We wanted everybody's blessings, [and] when I couldn't be near him I started to go nuts," she recalled. She said later that her "whole family" helped pack her bag the night before she went to Vegas. "They were so happy," she told *Us Weekly*.

Her brother, whom she called the minute she walked out of the chapel, wished her happiness and hoped that "this [was] it." A few weeks later, he described himself as Billy Bob's brother-in-law, "for now." Her father, typically, was blindsided, surprised that she had tied the knot with a man he hadn't met. When a writer for *Empire* magazine inquired if Billy Bob had asked for his daughter's hand in marriage, "a long, uncomfortable pause" ensued. Angie was more upbeat, telling writer Elizabeth Snead: "My dad likes him. My dad loves me so much he's never seen me so happy." When he finally met his son-in-law, Jon Voight gave him and Angie wedding presents of rings, poems, and a self-penned drawing of the couple, and he later helped them move into their new home.

If Voight was surprised, their friends were perplexed by their impulsive behavior. One of Billy Bob's friends, who heard the news on the radio, left him a message on his answering machine saying, "Dude, I told you to fuck her, not marry her!" Lauren Taines later discussed the union with Guns N' Roses guitarist Slash, predicting, "Trust me, this girl is going to break Billy Bob's heart." Billy Bob himself later told friends that he had never been so impulsive in his life. (Or, he vowed, would be again.) But no one's shock and misgivings could touch those of Billy Bob's fiancée.

L aura Dern has a reputation in Hollywood for crying ugly. Her face contorts into a grimace, and racking sobs convulse her body. What she did on-screen was nothing compared to the way she howled in pain as she absorbed the fact that Billy Bob had left her for Angie.

She was filming the comedy *Novocaine* in Chicago when she heard the news from a tabloid reporter. "I went to work one morning and he ran off and married Angelina Jolie," she told friends in disbelief. She had never for a moment seen it coming; their last conversations had been about starting a family together and her upcoming role in *The Gift,* the movie he had written with her firmly in mind. Their lives seemed just peachy, Billy Bob quoted in the May issue of *Men's Journal* as saying, "I'm now happily involved with someone who's my best friend." A month later he was singing a different tune in *Us Weekly:* "I want her to be happy. But it was over. That's all." The sorest part was that she had been left for the girl she regularly babysat for on Saturday nights. Sitting in her trailer in Chicago, she told friends: "How can I do a comedy when my whole life has been destroyed?"

As the enormity of his betrayal began to sink in, so, too, did the practical reality. Their house was in his name, so she could not live there. Her old rented home in Coldwater Canyon, which she had intended to buy before she met Billy Bob, was now sold. She was effectively homeless. For some time, too, the star of the kinky thriller *Blue Velvet* had experienced the creepy nightmare of being stalked, forcing her to engage the services of celebrity security expert Gavin de Becker. The breakup with Billy Bob left her in a bind; she wasn't a big moneymaking star and yet, because of the stalker, was not able to live in a regular, unprotected house.

While in Chicago she met Oprah Winfrey and poured out her tale of woe. The talk-show host was outraged and encouraged her to sue Billy Bob, even putting Laura in touch with the legal team that had represented her during her long fight with the Texas beef industry over remarks she made on her show about mad cow disease. Laura followed Oprah's advice and sued her former partner, eventually arriving at a confidential settlement that ensured that she could never mention him in interviews in return for a lump sum payment, estimated at around $800,000.

At the time, though, nothing could compensate her for the torment she was going through. It was a struggle trying to be funny on set. To make matters worse, she discovered that Billy Bob had ordered the security codes to be changed on the locks to their Mandeville Canyon home so that Laura could no longer gain access. While she had no wish to stay there—or, for that matter, to even see the place again—it contained all of her memorabilia, her prestigious movie awards, treasured photographs, and important business correspondence. The night before the locksmith was due to arrive, Laura Dern made urgent phone calls from Chicago to a handful of close friends, including *Friends* actress Courteney Cox and singer Sheryl Crow. In a late-night operation worthy of a Hollywood heist movie, they rolled up in their SUVs and proceeded to rifle through the house, taking everything Laura owned and cherished.

It was small consolation. When she returned to Beverly Hills in June, she was a changed woman. "She looked spent, like she had cried the life out of herself," observed a friend. "She was still in love with Billy Bob and not ready to move on." As she licked her wounds, she made sure that the tight-knit celebrity community knew that she was now homeless and living out of a suitcase, staying at the Four Seasons hotel, in Meg Ryan's guesthouse, or with Sheryl Crow. "She played the victim card to the hilt," recalled an associate.

A few weeks later, she was casually browsing through CDs at the now-defunct Tower Records on Sunset Boulevard when she had a bizarre spiritual experience. As she was looking at a Ben Harper CD, an angel appeared before her, hovering above the "A–M" aisle in the pop/rock section and telling Laura that the Californian musician was her true soul mate. "Call him, call him," the angel implored, before fading away. Laura did as she was bid, or rather, in the way of Hollywood, she asked her publicist to call his publicist.

Neither Laura Dern nor the bossy angel seemed any more troubled by the awkward fact that Harper was married, with two toddlers, than Angie or Billy Bob had been about his engagement to Laura. Dern and Harper duly hooked up, officially in the fall of 2000 when he was separated, and within weeks she was pregnant, giving birth to Ellery on August 21, 2001. It was doubtless a wild rumor that when Harper's wife, Joanna, discovered her husband's tryst with Laura, she stormed backstage at one of his concerts and punched him in the nose.

For her part, Laura was transformed by the new man in her life. "Something that one might have thought would destroy her made her stronger," said her friend singer Melissa Etheridge. "When she told me she was pregnant [with Ellery], she was very proud and very excited. She was saying, 'This is the next new chapter in my life.'"

No sooner had Angelina opened a new chapter in her life than she promptly closed it. She arrived in London in early May, days after her marriage. The carefree road trip was soon a distant memory, a rather dazed Billy Bob back again in his Nashville recording studio while Angie was instantly cocooned by the studio, the *Lara Croft* producers keen to protect their $100 million investment. Much was riding on a girl who was struggling to come off heroin, and who had been a patient in a mental hospital just a few days earlier. Nerves were not helped by the fact that the script was not yet finished and wouldn't be until June. Director Simon West, whose only previous writing experience had been for a Budweiser commercial, was frantically reshaping and rewriting three previous attempts by teams of scriptwriters. At least that left plenty of time for Angie to get in shape—and get in character.

Angie was met at Heathrow by the burly tattooed figure of Mickey Brett, the former bodyguard of Tom Cruise and Nicole Kidman, hired to protect the studio as much as the actress. He was under instructions to report any misdemeanors, as were all members of the new court surrounding Angie. As part of her contract, she was under an eleven o'clock curfew, a production executive explaining: "She's just not allowed to go out on a tear. She knows the score, but the curfew is just to protect everyone." Often movie underwriters insist that leading actors take drug tests and have physical exams before they will insure the production. While it is not clear whether this rule was invoked for *Lara Croft,* Angie had to be healthy and in top shape because she was doing most of her own stunts. She had her own one-woman boot camp, which included a nutritionist; a dresser; two personal trainers, including Josh Saltzman, who got Sarah, Duchess of York, into shape; three stunt doubles; a judo and boxing instructor; a body double; a makeup designer; and a dialect coach to round out her vowels so that she spoke just like Lara Croft, a sexy yet wholesome upper-class English archaeologist who lived in a mansion but could get down and dirty with the best.

Brilliant, tough, witty, and voluptuous, Lara Croft embodied the qualities of the "other girl" whom Angie had long aspired to be. For her new film role, she had to be positive, bright, focused, and confident. Edgy and wicked, too—but in a wholesome way. Even Lara's sexual appeal was strictly PG-13, focusing on her ample bosom and tight shorts. "She enjoys being a lady, but there's a side to her that just wants to get free and wild and dirty and do something dangerous," Angie said of her new persona. "There's a part of me that wants to be like Lara Croft. There's a part of me that is Lara Croft."

For the Method actor in Angie, this was her rehab role, the best chance she would ever have of getting clean. She was forced to enjoy a veritable feast of cold turkey. Not only had she given up heroin, but cigarettes, sugar, and booze were off-limits, too. Vitamins, kickboxing, and yoga were her new diet, with side dishes of bungee ballet, weight training, deep-sea diving, dogsledding, and gymnastics.

Original Sin director Michael Cristofer, who understands her psyche better than most, shrewdly observed: "When she did Lara Croft, she needed to find and explore and live inside that part of her personality that was strong and healthy and physically in extraordinary shape. I think she had come out of a really bad time and she was getting herself together in a very good way through the shoot of that film."

While she had clearly moved up in the world—the faux biography of Lara Croft included the fact that she was a boarder at the Scottish alma mater of Princes Charles, Andrew, and Edward—her heart belonged to Billy Bob and his down-home Arkansas world. For a girl who immerses herself completely in her roles, even when the cameras have stopped rolling, this was a first for Angie, the actress living as both the poised, independent, and cultured Lara Croft and as Billy Bob's outrageously sexy wife. The vivid contrasts at the heart of her Gemini character were now apparent, Angie the first to acknowledge this duality. "I like to collect knives but I also collect first-edition books." As Princess Diana's former astrologer, Penny Thornton, who has carefully studied Angie's birth chart, noted: "She is a natural iconoclast, a dominant strong personality who is bold and ballsy and refuses to be manipulated by anyone." Angie's chart indicates that during her marriage to Billy Bob she came closest to her true nature, while playing two roles at once: Mrs. Good Old Girl and the self-contained adventuress Lara Croft.

In early June 2000, just after her twenty-fifth birthday, Angie was back in down and dirty mode as she and her husband—Angie in black leather trousers and a gray T-shirt, Billy in a loud print shirt and a baseball hat—groped, kissed, and pawed their way along the red carpet for the Hollywood premiere of *Gone in Sixty Seconds*. "Hey Angie, give us a little Billy Bob action," yelled the photographers as the newlyweds smooched for the cameras. FORGET GLAMOUR—LET'S WATCH JOLIE AND THORNTON NECKING, headlined the *Chicago Tribune*.

The couple oozed sex, the tabloids enjoying a feeding frenzy as Billy Bob and Angie held court at the Sunset Marquis hotel and freely discussed every thrust of their rampant love lives. An indication of what a freak show they quickly became was that when Billy Bob ate papaya fruit for breakfast—his usual morning repast—it was said that he could only eat orange food because of his many and varied obsessions. Even though they had only spent a few days together as lovers and rather less as a married couple, they were as eager to dissect their sex lives as are juveniles who think they have discovered sex for the first time. They were so into the first flush of unbridled passion that each would have been hard pressed to say on which side of the bed the other preferred to sleep.

In a series of no-holds-barred interviews, they were so obviously into each other that *Us Weekly* declared, "Forget unconditional love. Thornton and Jolie have unbounded love, the kind of perpetually boiling body heat that inspired poets and pay-per-view programming." With this wall-to-bedroom coverage, *Gone in Sixty Seconds,* which was poorly received by the critics, earned more than $230 million worldwide.

During one typically overblown poolside chat at the Sunset Marquis, Angelina opined, "You know when you love someone so much you can almost kill them? I was nearly killed last night and it was the nicest thing anyone ever did for me." Billy Bob further explained: "I was looking at her sleep and I had to restrain myself from literally squeezing her to death." Angie added that in their new house they were going to install a padded room so that they could "go crazy."

During what was less an interview than a piece of performance art, Billy Bob marveled at the way Angie moved her wineglass—"That's almost sex," he mused—adding that they had known each other "since the dawn of time." For her part she got off on the way he said "football," stroking and nibbling him during one interview and pointing out that if one day they spontaneously combusted it would be from an overload of sex. Angie admitted that her nickname for her husband was "lunch," as in "lunch box," relating to his prodigious manhood.

When it came to specifics about anything other than their sex life, they were evasive, Angie saying that they first became "amazing friends" during the filming of *Pushing Tin:* "I just wanted to be near him all the time. And I missed being around him when work was over." Asked about her drug use, she waffled before Billy Bob interjected: "I like to say things that are true and say them hard. She does not take drugs."

Just so that everyone had gotten the message that they were head over heels in love—"Sex for us is almost too much," declared Billy Bob—they planned to weld their Oscars together (if Angie could find hers). As a final flourish, they gave each other necklaces with vials of their own blood. That they were later revealed to be lockets with a couple of drops of blood to remind each other of their passion and commitment was rather lost in the madness, as the stories about them became ever more lurid: Billy Bob was said to have hired a nurse to extract his blood so he could send it to Angie while she was filming in London, and they were rumored to keep a knife under the pillows to slash at each other with during wild sex sessions. Meanwhile, Angie confessed to *Talk* magazine that she had lived with a guy when she was just fourteen. Her "considerate" father had given the union his blessing, she said somewhat disingenuously. Little wonder that Jon Voight later described her behavior at this time as "exhibitionist."

When Angie appeared on *The Tonight Show*, it was her mother who was on her mind. She brandished a piece of paper in front of Jay Leno that contained the incest jokes he had made following Angie's notorious kiss with her brother at the Oscars. With a hooting, hollering audience on her side, she berated the comedian for his "stupid" wisecracks, saying that they had made Marcheline feel sick. Anyway, she continued, she and Billy Bob had better things to do than watch late-night TV. The audience got the hint, whooping their approval. Then she returned to her favorite subject, Billy Bob, describing him as "the sexiest creature that ever lived."

"I love him and you know that," she chided Leno. "We are perfect for each other."

In the sexual froth and foment, it was easy to forget that Billy Bob was an artist of quirky genius and Angie one of the most accomplished screen actors of her generation. Besides the primal sexual pull, it was one of the main things that attracted her to him, or the idea of him, in the first place. She wanted to live like an artist. Only later did she come to realize that living *like* an artist was not the same as living *with* an artist. Angie was not hardwired to be an artist's muse or helpmate.

In June, after four weeks of marriage, most of them spent apart from her husband, Angie was confident enough to tell *USA Today* that she felt "more content, safe, centered and alive." She had more surprises in store. Having previously been interested only in adoption, she shocked her circle when she told an Australian newspaper that she wanted to make her husband a dad again. "I would love having children with Billy," she said. "But I know that some people fall in love with their child so much that they don't put as much focus on their husband or wife, so right now I am getting to know my husband and his children. But if we had a child, it would be amazing."

When they were in Hollywood, the couple stayed at the Sunset Marquis, the Four Seasons, and the Peninsula, living a very ordinary life. They drove around Beverly Hills in her black pickup truck, going to the movies and eating out at regular diners. Nothing fancy for this pair. It wasn't long, though, before people noticed Billy Bob making some very out-of-the-ordinary requests. As hot as their sex life seemed to be, it apparently wasn't enough. Hotel staff complained that Billy Bob, whom they knew as a polite Southern gentleman, was acting totally out of character, hitting on girls in the hope, some observers believed, of encouraging a threesome with him and Angie. Aggressively sexual behavior was typical for Angie, as witnessed by numerous heterosexual women she had met. It was different for Billy Bob. He might have had a harem, but between the sheets, he was a conventional, one-woman guy. "She was into chicks and it seems that was his job, to bring her the girls," recalled one of Billy Bob's former lovers, speaking on the condition of anonymity. "While nothing came of it, it appeared she was trying to get a threesome going. He was hitting on girls for her pleasure. This was within a month of them marrying. People were horrified. It was the talk of the place." Psychologist Iris Martin sees Angie's behavior as "bizarre": "Angelina cannot connect with anybody emotionally. Nobody in their right mind gets married and then starts having threesomes. It doesn't make sense. It seems that he was not as exciting as she thought he was and so [she] lost interest."

Once back in London, Angie did not exactly morph into the ladylike Lara Croft. During preparation she encouraged her boxing trainer and stunt double, Eunice Huthart, then the women's world kickboxing champion, to get her first tattoo, and ignored her curfew in order to go see a group of Elvis impersonators at an off-the-beaten-track nightclub. For a girl who loved Madonna, Michael Jackson, and punk, Angie's willing embrace of one of Billy Bob's rock-and-roll icons had a touch of the Laura Dern school of romance about it. Just as Lara Croft would have turned up her finely bred nose at Angie's night out at the Jazzmines club in unfashionable Bromley in darkest Kent, so her screen character would have been unable to stomach her eating habits.

Angie frequently ignored the advice of her nutritionist and ordered her driver to stop at a McDonald's so she could get her fix of hamburger and fries. At the London premiere of *Gone in Sixty Seconds,* she turned up in leather trousers and a T-shirt, clutching a small bunch of flowers and wishing for all the world that she was somewhere else. No sooner had she made her way down the red carpet than she sneaked out of the auditorium in Leicester Square and went for a hamburger. "I was hungry and don't like to see myself on the screen all the time," she explained.

In the computer game, the voluptuous Lara Croft was a 36DD cup size, whereas at that time Angie was a mere 36C. The race was on to increase her ability to fill a bra. Teenage boys, who made up the bulk of the expected audience, notice these things. It ended as a compromise. Angie appeared on-screen as a 36D.

Even the Queen took second place to her cravings. In July Angie stalked out of the Cartier International Day polo match, held in the presence of Her Majesty and attended by British high society and international celebrities on the grounds of Windsor Great Park. She put down her glass of champagne, reportedly dismissed the likes of fellow actors Minnie Driver and Billy Zane as "pompous assholes," and ordered her driver to find her the nearest McDonald's. "I love Big Macs," she later explained. Her early departure from one of the highlights of the social calendar excited much irritated comment, model and polo player Jodie Kidd saying tartly: "Well, that's just typical. She's American, after all."

With principal photography beginning at the end of July, she had now to leave her trailer-park persona behind and start living to the manor born, in a baronial castle specially constructed on a soundstage at Pinewood Studios in north London. The start of filming also coincided with a personal celebration for the leading lady, who learned that she had finally been cast by director Oliver Stone in his latest movie, *Beyond Borders,* a high-minded romance set in refugee camps based on the work of Doctors Without Borders, an organization that won the 1999 Nobel Peace Prize. When she was first sent Caspian Tredwell-Owen's script during the filming of *Original Sin,* she had cried as she read the story of a well-to-do American socialite, Sarah Jordan, who falls for a dedicated doctor striving to save lives in Africa, Asia, and elsewhere. During their passionate affair she comes to see the world through the eyes of hard-pressed international relief workers.

In spite of her enthusiasm "to take the journey," Oliver Stone had other actresses in mind. When his first choice, Welsh actress Catherine Zeta-Jones, became pregnant, he turned to single mom Meg Ryan. Then Ryan dropped out, saying she didn't want to be away from her eight-year-old son for so long. This left the role free for Angie.

As with all his actors, Stone encouraged Angie, whom he describes as a "natural-born actress," to do her own research into her role. "He was one of the first people to tell me to start reading international papers and to educate myself," she recalls. While she was in London, he was visiting UN-run refugee camps in northern Kenya and the turbulent southern Sudan in order to learn firsthand about the dire conditions. "I want to make it as real as it can be," he said.

While preparing to dip her toe into the world of international relief, Angie first had to throw herself into the grueling twenty-week shoot for *Lara Croft: Tomb Raider*. She appeared in virtually every scene and performed her own stunts, which left her with torn ligaments and a battered, bleeding, and bruised body. "She was totally fearless. I had to decide how much jeopardy I wanted to put her in," commented director Simon West. On one occasion she was swinging on a moving log fifty feet off a concrete floor and asked to take off her safety harness—a request West denied. "If she fell, she would be dead. I didn't need that," he said, displaying the classic auteur's altruism.

One of the more telling—and quieter—moments in the action movie, which went on to shoot in Iceland, Cambodia, and Venice, was Jon Voight's turn as Lara's father, the late Lord Richard Croft. The interchange formed the emotional backstory to the movie, the whole adventure helping Lara find a sense of peace following the loss of her father. Angie personally approved the choice of her father to play the role, a far cry from her previous attitude toward being associated with him professionally. It was a sign of her confidence that she now overshadowed him as an actor, as well as a tentative personal reconciliation. The weeklong shoot with her father, scheduled for early October, had to be delayed when Angie flew to Los Angeles to be by Billy Bob's bedside after he was admitted to the hospital suffering a viral infection. At first it was thought that he had a heart complaint, an illness that runs in the Thornton family, his brother Jimmy Don having died of a heart attack at the age of just thirty. Such was the concern that President Clinton, a former Arkansas governor, personally called Billy Bob's mother, Virginia, to check on his condition. It helped that it was an election year; Billy Bob had recently appeared at a fund-raiser for Democrat presidential candidate Al Gore, then vice president.

When she returned to film the scenes with her father, Angie perceptively observed that their interaction was "a kind of goodbye in a strange way." As she said: "It was a hello and goodbye." Perhaps more accurately, it marked the ending of a period of her life. The movie has them professing sentiments about love and respect and lost time that appear to be both narrative-driven and reality-based. "I wanted to say a lot of those things to my dad," admitted Angie. "And he wanted to say them to me. And I wanted to hear them."

It seemed that father and daughter could connect through acting better than in real life, using words written by others but interpreted by them. Father and daughter did write a further scene, but it was never made. Angie finally got to hear what she had always wanted her dad to say. "I miss you and love you always and forever," Lord Richard tells Lara. In the movie he dies when she is still a child, just as in real life he left when she was still in the cradle. "The time was stolen from us, and it's not fair. I've missed you," she tells her father in a sequence in which he reappears in a tropical tent when the hands of time have been shifted backward. For his part, Lord Richard apologizes for leaving Lara. It was a profound moment. What daughter, however proud and haughty, would not melt in the face of her father's protestations of sorrow at the time stolen from them? "I am with you always, just as I've always been," says Lord Richard to his daughter in a final sequence before she bids farewell to his spirit. On camera Lara was duly dewy-eyed; offscreen Angelina was in tears.

"Jon and I could not stop crying," she later told TV reporter Ann Curry. "We'd have to stop takes. We'd walk on the other sides. We didn't talk in between takes. We met in that tent and we'd walk away and meet in the tent until the scene was completely over. Then we kind of hugged each other." On reflection Angie found it profoundly sad that the closest moment she ever had with her father was played out in public. It was also one of the rare times that she publicly acknowledged any positive influence he'd had on her life, telling the *Los Angeles Times:* "All my life my dad was always there for me, but I was very independent as well, and he'd always send me letters, books and information. And in the end we did the same thing with our lives—acting. So our scenes ended up becoming very personal."

For his part Jon Voight was thrilled that at last his professional dream had come true. He described the shoot as a "joyous" time, father and daughter laughing and loving together. "It seemed like the beginning—there was a little hope coming through at that moment in time," he later recalled.

He said hello, she said goodbye. "We seemed to understand each other and it was fun, but afterwards he returned quickly to old habits of being judgmental," she told writer Andrew Duncan. During the shoot Voight was worried about her stunts—"She's done things that I would never do and I wish she wouldn't"—and encouraged her to take up his health regime of yoga and vitamin supplements.

As working with her father had been a completion of sorts, it was the other man in her life she needed most, Angie convincing her husband to overcome his fear of flying—and genuine antiques—to join her in London. With a great effort of will—"It was a sign of how much he loved her," noted a friend of Thornton's—he endured the eleven-hour flight to Britain. Just so that the world got the point, she told the *Daily Mail,* "I need him in my bed. I told him I was going to lose my mind if he didn't get over here."

Such was the automatic association among Angie, Billy Bob, and sex that when they paid $3.8 million for the home of his friend Slash, from Guns N' Roses, it was immediately assumed that their huge basement had been converted into a sex dungeon. In fact, the onetime speakeasy was a music recording studio, perfect for Billy Bob to pursue his major artistic passion in life.

The real irony about their eleven-thousand-square-foot "love nest" was that their new neighbor was comedian Steve Martin, who Billy Bob had once feared would lure his fiancée Laura Dern away from him. Just three months on, Martin was no longer relevant to the script.

ELEVEN

Before, he was the sun, the moon, the stars and sky to Angie. Now he was no longer in her universe. Maddox was the new center of her life.

—INGRID EARLE, FRIEND OF BILLY BOB THORNTON'S

In late November 2000 the *Lara Croft* caravan left Pinewood Studios and moved to Cambodia for a two-week shoot during what is termed the "cool season," when temperatures drop to the high nineties. It was a visit—and a view into a previously unknown world—that changed Angie forever. Like many of her life-altering moments, it was a fluke. Originally filming was due to take place on the Great Wall of China or a faux fifteen-foot stand-in in Scotland. Cost and politics ended that plan; it was cheaper to set the exotic scene in Angkor Wat, a complex of sacred ancient temples surrounded by dense jungle, located 220 kilometers (135 miles) northwest of Cambodia's capital, Phnom Penh.

One of the archaeological wonders of the world, the Temple of Angkor Wat is a massive ring of sculpted sandstone structures, the blurred carved faces depicting legends of the once great Khmer civilization. Given Angie's love of symbol and ritual, the location must have been soul-stirring. It was a special privilege, too, Angie the first Hollywood star permitted on the grounds of this holy place since 1964, when Peter O'Toole filmed *Lord Jim*.

First, though, she and her film crew had to get there, trucking equipment from neighboring Thailand along a road only recently held by Khmer Rouge rebels and still pitted with potholes and land mines. Accompanied by the Royal Cambodian Army, the convoy of thirty trucks was forced to stop frequently so that soldiers could repair bridges and check for bombs.

Once Angie had reached the temple unscathed, the real work began.

She had to leap from twenty-foot walls, paddle a wooden canoe, and fight off the bad guys. At the end of a long day's shooting, she couldn't even bitch to her husband about her strained ankle, the bump on her head, and her pulled muscles. "The phone is a nightmare," Angie admitted. "When I finally get through to Billy, and you try to say something romantic you both end up saying, 'What? You said what? Oh forget it.' Trying to be sexy on a cell phone in Angkor Wat just isn't working."

At least she could still talk *about* him, her love life the lure for the intrepid journalists who hacked through the jungle to visit the set. "I'm obsessed with Billy. I always want more. I can't have enough of him," Angie told one unnerved reporter, sitting on the steps of her trailer, naked beneath a sheet she had quickly wrapped around herself after taking a shower. So close and yet so far away. Cut off from her man, yet feeling for the first time in her life supremely fit and healthy, immersed in a holy place complete with chanting Buddhist monks, and with the ever-present frisson of danger in this lush land, Angie felt a spiritual kinship to an exotic place and people, impoverished but still smiling. For Angie, who usually found connecting and feeling so difficult, this experience—albeit surrounded as she was by film folk and sleeping in an air-conditioned trailer with hot and cold running water—touched something inside her. She experienced what she later described as "an epiphany." Or, put another way, the mutable, impulsive Angie was about to shed yet another skin. "This has changed my life, being here in this country," she said when the Cambodia chapter wrapped. "The world is a lot bigger than I thought it was. There is a lot I have to learn." When she left, she was so touched by the people and the country that she cried for three days. She couldn't explain why, but the tears just kept flowing. "I didn't know what that country had gone through. I didn't learn about it in history. And they were so warm and so beautiful and so pure and honest. And the country, I just loved the country."

Back in London she continued her long-distance marriage, given every Friday off in order to share a few snatched hours with her husband in Los Angeles. "I spend twelve hours on a plane, fall into bed with Billy for ten hours, then it's straight back to the airport," Angie said. He had his own ferocious schedule, in December crisscrossing the States to bang the drum for *All the Pretty Horses,* his $45 million adaptation of Cormac McCarthy's stark, neo-Western novel, which was due for release on Christmas Day.

Taking a chapter from Angie's book of confessions, Billy Bob was generous with details about his private life that other, more prudent directors might keep to themselves. "I've screwed up so much, I've gotten into so much trouble over the years, and done weird stuff," he said. "Well, I'm afraid of the water. I can't watch movies before 1950 and eat at the same time. Don't even ask. I can't mention my children's ages or I think I'll put a curse on them. There's my well-known fear of antique furniture."

One of the stars of *All the Pretty Horses,* Matt Damon, shared the director's famous fear of flying. After appearing on *The Oprah Winfrey Show* in Chicago, the terrified twosome sat together on the five-hour flight back to Los Angeles. As Damon explained, "In Billy Bob's world, he is risking his life every time he gets on a plane. He'd much rather jump in front of a car because Billy Bob figures that way he might actually live." So the fact that he was prepared to fly to London to see Angie and stay at upscale hotels with antiques and silver cutlery was a sign of his true commitment. "He broke through barriers for her, he really did," observed a friend.

For her part she flew to New York to join him on the *Today* show to help him publicize his movie, the couple's behavior on- and off-screen belying any suspicions that their union was just a publicity stunt to sell *Gone in Sixty Seconds.* "I was unfocused my entire life, and so was Angelina," said Billy Bob. "Now we're both very clear and very focused. It took finding each other to make us that clear. I'm married to the love of my life." If that wasn't commitment enough, after the interview he raced down the corridor and launched himself into the arms—and lips—of his laughing wife.

To underscore the point further, Angie and her beloved were full of talk about renewing their marriage vows. Finally "family" seemed like a safe, warm place for Angelina, who confessed that she had found "a home" at last. Billy Bob talked about buying a farm and raising llamas, describing Angie as "a pretty regular gal." In turn, she liked to call herself "stepmom" to his sons, William and Harry. Of course the youngsters thought it was "cool" that Lara Croft was making them pancakes in their new house and reading them stories at bedtime. Even though her pancakes were, in Billy Bob's term, "strong," who cared?

Like her own mother, Angie did not cook, the quartet going for down-home cuisine in local West Hollywood eateries. "We eat a lot of ice cream and cereal, and when Billy sees me in an apron, he laughs," said Angie. She had not quite turned into a character in a Norman Rockwell painting: Her Christmas present to her husband was a framed message, "To the End of Time," which she nailed up over their bed. Naturally it was written in her blood. Some men get socks.

Sadly, the big turkey that Christmas was Billy Bob's labor of love, *All the Pretty Horses,* which opened to mixed reviews and indifferent audience numbers. Bitterly hurt by the rejection of a project he had truly believed in, Billy Bob retreated into his basement studio and took consolation in his music, shutting out the world. He vowed never to direct another movie, picking up the music he had started to lay down in Nashville as he worked to finish his debut album, *Private Radio.*

As he narrowed his horizons, Angie was opening up hers, researching her role for *Beyond Borders.* The project had already run into casting problems, with Kevin Costner, originally slated to play the renegade doctor who was Angie's love interest, being replaced by Ralph Fiennes. Although Costner's people blamed artistic differences for his departure, the word was that Angie thought the forty-five-year-old star of *Dances with Wolves* was too old to be her movie paramour. The irony was that her own husband was the same age as Costner, and the actor's then girlfriend was the same age as Angie.

Fiennes went to aid workers' demonstrations on handling life-and-death refugee crises; Oliver Stone continued his travels around camps in southern Sudan and Kenya; and Angie called on the United Nations High Commissioner for Refugees for information, reading pamphlets and books and scanning the Internet.

In many ways her character of Sarah Jordan was the perfect next step after Lara Croft. She was Lara with a social conscience, a real person out to do good, to help make the world a better place. Just as she had begun to morph into Lara during filming—director Simon West admitted "she was definitely thinking she was Lara Croft after a while"—Angie took her persona one stage further with Sarah; she was flesh and blood, not just a cartoon character.

In late January, however, Oliver Stone, whom Angie had come to see as a surrogate father, bowed out, complaining of the meager budget, inadequate prep time, and the looming possibility of an actors' strike. Angie was devastated. She loved her character and felt true kinship with the script and the story. She had already had discussions with the UNHCR about spending a couple of weeks visiting refugee camps to see for herself what life in them was really like. Now that plan seemed to be stuck in the sand.

For the first time in her life, however, the girl who had spent her career being told what to do by someone else slowly realized that she didn't need Oliver Stone or anyone else directing her life. She could go anyway. "Suddenly it dawned on me that just because I'm an actor, I felt like I needed a film to do it," she recalled. "I'm a person. Do it." She contacted the UNHCR in New York and discussed the possibility of visiting Sierra Leone and Tanzania under their umbrella. She was forthright, telling UN officials: "You might think I'm crazy. I'm an actress. I don't want to go with press. If you could give me access, allow me in on a trip so I could just witness and learn." There were two conditions: She insisted on paying her own way and on being treated like everyone else.

While Oliver Stone might have tipped his hat at her chutzpah, Jon Voight was concerned. With Sierra Leone in the midst of a rumbling civil war, he thought that Angie was deliberately putting herself in harm's way and contacted the UN to try to have the trip canceled. Officials pointed out that she was a grown woman and was visiting under escort. Typically, her mother was more passive, simply smiling through her tears. Before Angie left, Marche delivered a special message from James that alluded to her favorite childhood character, Peter Pan: "Tell Angie I love her and to remember that if she is ever scared, sad, or angry—look up at the night sky, find the second star on the right, and follow it straight on till morning."

Billy Bob shared her father's view, but he let her go ahead with her adventure. "He said he didn't think I'd be safe. But he didn't offer to come along, either. And so I left," she recalled.

As Angie, armed with pens and a notepad, went off to a war zone, her husband headed to the basement with his friend Randy Scruggs and wrote a love song for his bride. "It's basically the story of how we met," recalled Billy, who, with his friend, wrote the song "Angelina" in just a few minutes. Angie was on a very different path, briefed by UN officials when she arrived in Abidjan, Côte d'Ivoire, in late February about the blind bureaucratic reality facing refugees and asylum seekers. With no chance of romance in their battered lives, the picture of struggle and sacrifice was etched on the faces of those she met.

Shocked and upset by the human tumult she encountered, Angie observed that she felt like a visitor in a zoo. A petting zoo, at that; when she visited a refugee center in Freetown, the capital of Sierra Leone, a baby was unceremoniously placed in her arms. For Angie, who had never played with dolls and wasn't the cuddling type, this was a remarkable event. "No words could express how I felt," she wrote. At another transit camp children came running toward her. "Their tiny little hands grabbed on to mine. There was a child's hand around every finger of mine. I wanted to take each and every one of them home with me."

She was hungry to learn more, meeting the U.S. ambassador to Sierra Leone, veteran diplomat John Melrose, and other aid workers at the ambassador's residence on March 1, 2001. Before dinner she admitted to the seasoned Africa hand that the experience had really opened her eyes. Her naïveté was striking, but little different from the response of other well-intentioned Westerners he had met during his long career. "She had been doing food distribution the day before she came to dinner," he recalled. "She didn't realize these kinds of things were going on. However, when you are first exposed it is a rather powerful experience, and it can also be a very depressing one. She grew up with a much more sheltered existence and had not been exposed to anything like that. She was touched by it."

The impact was profound and immediate. A couple of weeks after that dinner, Melrose took a call from Angie's assistant about a program they had been discussing to teach former soldiers, mostly teenage boys, how to read and write. As that program was fully funded, he steered her toward a scheme to help "war brides," the girls taken by rebels and used as sex slaves, cooks, and human shields in battle. The idea was to house, counsel, and then teach these brutalized young women a skill or a trade so they could earn a living. Angie agreed to fund the whole program, donating just under $1 million on the condition that her gift be anonymous.

This spontaneous generosity was matched by her almost childlike response to the sights and sounds she had witnessed. She was like a character in a classic picaresque novel, the innocent at large. With hindsight, Angie would say that her first visit to refugee camps was monumental. "When I came back [to America] two weeks later, I was a very different person."

That was not how it seemed at the time. When she returned, she immersed herself in Hollywood froth, agreeing to play a ditsy TV reporter in a sudsy romantic comedy, *Life or Something Like It,* alongside Ed Burns. This was her replacement gig now that *Beyond Borders* no longer had a home. At the same time, she was in meetings to discuss Lara Croft merchandise, repeatedly sending back the prototype dolls with notes saying: "No. Boobs too big." Welcome back to the real world.

Before she flew to Seattle and then Vancouver to film the romantic comedy, she and Billy Bob managed their second wedding. It took place in their kitchen in April, in the presence of a woman from the multifaith, multigod Church of the Enlightenment, witnessed by Harry, their pet rat, and Billy's mynah bird, Alice. Instead of exchanging rings, they cut each other's fingers and sucked each other's blood. They were now officially blood brothers, even more so after Angie hired a doctor to extract her own blood, which she kept in vials in the minibar of her hotel during filming, awaiting the moment she might make a more meaningful wedding gift for her husband.

In May, for their first anniversary, Angie flew to Baton Rouge, where he was playing a prison guard and executioner in *Monster's Ball.* They were in full Gothic mode. They swapped vials of blood—Angie painting herself with her husband's blood—and she bought two grave plots so they could spend eternity side by side as well, along with a bench in the cemetery so they could sit together contemplating their future home. Not to be outdone, Billy Bob gave her a document signed and notarized in his blood saying that they would be married until the end of time. For good measure he created another message, once more vowing his undying love, which joined her bloody artwork above their bed. Finally, to seal the ritual of commitment, they added more tattoos to their crowded skin.

Beneath the frenzy of devotion, Angie was somewhat unsettled, knowing that her husband had a date with destiny—a graphic sex scene with Halle Berry, routinely described, along with Angie, as one of the world's great beauties. To ensure that her relationship with Billy Bob stayed on course, if not till the end of time then at least till the end of shooting, Angie deputed her now permanent bodyguard, Mickey Brett, to be with Billy Bob during filming. Nor did it hurt that her brother, James, had snagged a small part. They were her eyes and ears on set. Once a womanizer, always a womanizer. If Billy Bob was a reformed man, that would be good to know, too, especially as the scene would be shot just a couple of days before she headed back to Cambodia in mid-July on her second UN mission.

Angelina was not the only one concerned. Berry's husband, musician Eric Benét, insisted on a private screening so he could come to terms with his wife's having brutal, explicit sex with another man. He saw the version before a minute was cut from the final edit to avoid the dreaded NC-17 rating. "I had a screening just for him to let him deal with it," said Berry, who was paid only a modest fee for the shoot. Angie, though, had her game face on, seemingly untroubled by the vivid sexuality. "Lara Croft belongs to the world, I belong to Billy Bob," she said during publicity for her first big blockbuster, sentiments echoed by her husband. "She and I have a real strong relationship, and we're the best friends in the world," he observed.

For a time it seemed, too, that there was a genuine rapprochement between father and daughter. When Angie was filming the final scenes of *Life or Something Like It* in New York, her father and her husband stood in the wings watching her being shot, literally, in Times Square. When director Stephen Herek yelled "Cut," she raced to the sidelines to give her dad a big hug and Billy Bob a lingering kiss. Then it all began to unravel.

Voight took her to the airport for her flight to Cambodia, giving her a letter as he said goodbye. Letters were typical of how he communicated with her and others, allowing him to get his point across without any redefinition or argument. What she thought was a note containing fond sentiments, building on their "new deal," was instead, as she described it, a scathing indictment of her lifestyle. At a time in her life when Angie had finally heard what she wanted to hear from her dad, albeit in a movie—when she was feeling good about herself, mentally and physically, alive to bigger issues in the world than her own angst and pain, and in a marriage to a man who seemed to understand her—her father's missive seemed cruel and somehow pointless.

"All I can say is that the final letter I got, that was the final break," Angie said. "He handed it to me when I was on the way to Cambodia with the UN to go to a minefield for the first time. That's the day he handed me this letter to tell me I was a bad person."

Compared to negotiating the parental minefield, the United Nations proved an easier proposition. During the visit she met with UNHCR high commissioner Ruud Lubbers, UN secretary general Kofi Annan, and her hero, author and activist Loung Ung, whose book *First They Killed My Father* describes the period between 1975 to 1979 and the suffering her family endured under the brutal Pol Pot regime. They bonded during impromptu pit stops when they went to the bathroom together by the side of the road.

More important, Angie was like a kid in a candy store when asked to detonate a land mine with dynamite. "I must say it was a great feeling to destroy something that would have otherwise hurt or possibly killed another person," she noted in her journal. After the explosion, Loung told her how terrified she'd been the first time she was in America for Fourth of July fireworks. During the visit, Angie was formally asked by the United Nations to be a Goodwill Ambassador for refugees, although the announcement would not be made until a month later, on August 27, 2001, following a visit to Pakistan to see Afghan refugees. She was thrilled to accept, especially when she was informed that the UNHCR had a presence in 120 countries. "You have family wherever you go," she was told, a sentiment she found especially appealing as this was a perfect kind of family—noble, ever smiling, distant, transitory, and all but anonymous. It showed, too, how far she had come. Just a year before she had been struggling to come off heroin; now she was officially representing the voiceless and dispossessed.

The UN was equally thrilled to have her, senior UN officer Ron Redmond observing: "We are 100 percent convinced of her commitment. There was no contact with agents and no entourage—she travels by herself and gets dirty in the field with our staff. She pays for her own flights and accommodation, and went against advice from her own family to travel to Sierra Leone. Once there, she even traveled in a convoy with refugees returning to homes they had earlier been forced to flee—and that's a dangerous thing to do. She did it quietly and without fuss, not to win headlines for herself, but to play a positive role in issues that interest her. And we're happy to have her on board to reach segments of the population who don't know or care about the refugee issue." There was more good news: Her pet project, *Beyond Borders,* was finally on again with a new director and was scheduled to begin shooting in Montreal in December.

Just a few days later, on September 11, the political and charity landscape changed for good with the attack on the Twin Towers. Angie's donation of $1 million in response to the UNHCR's appeal for $250 million to meet the humanitarian catastrophe on the borders with Afghanistan and Pakistan was met with death threats, hate mail, and bilious derision. She was now seen in some quarters to be funding "the enemy."

While the media emphasized her work abroad, she and Billy Bob were quietly working on projects nearer to home. It was perhaps inevitable that the plight of the Native American struck a chord with the couple. He had roots deep in the Cherokee tribe, she a Bertrand family connection, albeit tenuous, with the Iroquois Indians. Not only had her father championed the plight of Native Americans, but on a more personal level, Marcheline's relationship with Native American poet and activist John Trudell had gone past the point of friendship, the couple enjoying a strong spiritual and emotional connection that endured and strengthened in spite of her health issues.

In some ways Trudell had qualities that may have reminded Marche of her ex-husband when she first met him—not that he would like to be reminded of that. Back then Jon Voight saw acting as an arm of activism, the art carrying the message. At that time Trudell was seen, at least by the authorities, as one of the most notorious political subversives in America, with an FBI dossier running to seventeen thousand pages. He led the Native American occupation of Alcatraz Island for twenty-one months in the 1960s, provoking condemnation but also a growing international awareness of government repression of tribal rights. In 1979, hours after he protested American government policy by burning a flag on the steps of FBI headquarters in Washington, Trudell's pregnant wife, three children, and mother-in-law died in a suspicious fire in his home on a reservation in Nevada. While accusing fingers pointed at government agents, Trudell never really recovered, pouring his wounded despair and scouring sorrow into poetry and song.

In October 2001, Trudell released his album *Bone Days*, which was recorded over two weeks in a Los Angeles studio and cited Angelina as executive producer. Billy Bob was among the large choir of folks who were thanked for helping bring the mixture of bleak poetry and song to a wider audience. While his own album took far longer to produce—Billy Bob's obsessive nature getting in the way of speed—he and Trudell were kindred spirits in the sense that music was simply another way to communicate a message. Billy Bob's album *Private Radio*, released in September, was an attempt "to speak [his] mind a little bit."

Billy Bob and Angie's commitment extended far beyond the recording studio. That same year, together with Marcheline and John Trudell, they set up the All Tribes Foundation to support and promote the cultural and economic survival of Native American peoples. With John Trudell as advisor, they focused on the Pine Ridge Reservation in South Dakota, site of the seventy-one-day standoff at Wounded Knee that led to the death of two FBI agents in 1973, where the Sioux Indian population had the lowest life expectancy anywhere in the Western Hemisphere. Within a couple of years the All Tribes Foundation—effectively Angie and Billy Bob's film money—had donated $800,000 in grants for programs to strengthen tribal ways of life and safeguard a future for Native American communities.

Although Angie was no longer looking for a Native American child, her most recent UN trip to Pakistan had reinforced her commitment to adopting. Rumors were swirling that she planned to adopt an Afghan child, especially when she and Billy Bob were spotted filling out documents at the Los Angeles office of Citizenship and Immigration Services.

Politically, however, the new Goodwill Ambassador had stepped into a minefield. For starters, the UNHCR opposed the adoption of orphaned children from Afghanistan, or any country in conflict. The reasons were pragmatic: It was common for families to be split up in the turmoil of war, only to be reunited afterward. Indeed, they were against foreign adoptions, period. "We try to find foster families within the country who are willing to take the children," said a UN official. "We also think it's better for the child to stay in the culture."

Nevertheless, Angie had her mind and heart set on adopting a child from the country that had had such an impact on her during the filming of *Lara Croft:* Cambodia. Despite his fear of flying—especially after 9/11—Billy Bob flew with Angie to Phnom Penh in November 2001 to look at orphanages with an adoption facilitator. For Billy Bob the plane ride was an act of devotion; for Angie it was the final chapter in a dream she had harbored for years.

Their first step had been to contact Seattle International Adoptions, run by two sisters, Lauryn Galindo, a semiprofessional hula dancer from Hawaii, and Lynn Devin, a former social worker. Theirs was the largest adoption agency in Cambodia, running orphanages and building schools as well as funding literacy and justice programs. As *Cambodia Daily* writer

Richard Sine noted in a profile of Galindo: "It is easy to see how someone like Lauryn Galindo can gain the trust of hundreds of adoptive U.S. parents, including Angelina Jolie. She moves with a dancer's grace, and she seems to radiate the compassion that draws so many parents to adopt in Cambodia in the first place. You can almost hear the U.S. parents breathe a sigh of relief: She's one of us."

Before Billy Bob and Angie boarded the flight to Cambodia, they would have undergone the agency's standard vetting procedure. Devin screened parents for suitability; Galindo chose children depending on availability and the parents' desires. Prospective parents paid on a sliding scale depending on income. A typical fee was $9,000—though Angie paid considerably more, unconfirmed reports speculating upwards of $100,000. The fees were split between donations to the orphanage and payments to government officials to facilitate processing; Galindo preferred to call this a system of "tipping" rather than bribery. While Angie has never spoken about the exact figure, Billy Bob later said that the couple set up their own foundation to build schools for deprived youngsters in the country.

Even by the odd standards of Billy Bob and Angie, Lauryn Galindo was a study in contrasts, her waist-length hair, gentle manner, and ethereal calm juxtaposed with her chauffeur-driven Mercedes with blacked-out windows that was always followed by a retinue of bodyguards in a Toyota Camry. With the country still recovering from a bloody civil war, Galindo's precautions were sensible—if slightly unnerving. As their unlikely convoy journeyed 150 miles northwest of Phnom Penh to an orphanage in Battambang, prospective parents could have been excused for thinking they were taking part in a kidnapping rather than an adoption.

At the orphanage Billy Bob and Angie met with numerous infants, but it was the last baby they saw, three-month-old Rath Vibol, who won their hearts. They both felt an immediate connection. Unlike most Western couples, who want to take home a baby girl, Billy Bob and Angie fell for a boy.

"It's the weirdest thing to go to an orphanage and know that you are going to be bringing a kid home with you," said Angie. "He was the last child I met. He was asleep and wouldn't wake up and at first I thought there was something wrong with him. They put him in my lap and I'd never held children, so I was scared that he wouldn't be comfortable with me, but he just stared at me for the longest time and then we relaxed and smiled at each other. He accepted me at the same time that I accepted him. He opened his eyes and it was like he chose me. I like to think we chose each other."

This was not typical Angie hyperbole but a common response of couples on the brink of adopting. Hollywood-based adoption facilitator Catherine Politte, who has been helping couples for thirty years, has frequently witnessed this uncanny, almost instinctive, bond. She says: "When Angelina met Maddox, she fell in love. He didn't seem as though he was from a different race or culture. Her heart was opened to this defenseless infant. I have seen it happen so many times."

Like his wife, Billy Bob fell in love with the country as well as with the baby boy, feeling humbled as he watched the poor and disabled coping with their meager lot. One incident seeing land-mine victims at work stayed with him. "There were these three guys carrying lumber. The one in the middle was blind and the two on each end didn't have arms. To watch them do that, smiling, open, friendly, without bitterness, really makes you rethink your complaints about your BMW seats needing reupholstering."

Enchanted by the country and the people, but most of all by their prospective son, Billy Bob and Angie instructed Galindo to put the wheels in motion to adopt baby Rath. Angie's long-held dream was now turning into reality: Angie and Billy Bob were becoming a family not just in word but in deed.

When they arrived back in Los Angeles in late November, they immediately began preparing for two different film projects, which they had arranged to be filmed in the same city, Montreal. It was a sign of their closeness—and their movie clout—that they could swing this. Angie was to start filming *Beyond Borders,* now with British actor Clive Owen playing her doctor lover, while Billy Bob planned to play a few local gigs to road-test his new album and then begin filming *Levity,* a somber movie about a killer's search for redemption, in January. Originally the Ed Solomon–directed movie was not due to start filming until April, but when Billy Bob realized that Angie was going to be in the same city, he insisted the filming schedule be brought forward so that he could be with his wife. "We always had a deal that we would never be apart for more than two weeks, and we've made a new deal—from now on it's one week," he explained. To further emphasize their love and fidelity, they agreed to exchange one home-made Christmas present each. Angie started knitting a scarf in their newly rented home in Montreal, but soon gave up. Instead she created a photo album of pictures from their respective childhoods, but spliced together to suggest that they had been united their whole lives. Only one picture was needed to complete the family album—that of baby Rath.

Then disaster struck. In December, just a few days after their return from the Far East, the American government suspended the issuing of visas for children adopted from Cambodia. The respected human rights and child welfare organization LICADHO had just released a damning report concerning the multimillion-dollar trade in Cambodian babies, including claims that children were sold by poor families and in some cases stolen. There were further allegations that unscrupulous middlemen sold these children to wealthy Westerners, mainly Americans, for a fat profit. At the center of this spreading scandal was Lauryn Galindo, currently fast-tracking a visa for baby Rath. LICADHO accused Galindo of luring young women to hand over their babies for temporary care in an orphanage, and then adopting them out without parental consent. The charity claimed to have extensive evidence against Galindo, including testimony by a woman who said she was offered $700 for three of her children.

While Angie acted in good faith, the newly minted UN ambassador risked accusations of going from tomb raider to womb raider. Like more than a hundred other American couples attempting to adopt Cambodian children, Angie and Billy Bob were placed in limbo, not knowing if their attempt to bring baby Rath back to America would be successful. It is not hard to appreciate Angie's agitation and heartbreak as the baby she had fallen in love with was seemingly snatched from her grasp. U.S. immigration services now had the task of carefully examining the circumstances concerning all 114 of the adoptions that had been under way before the visa ban. This was going to take time. Angie and Billy Bob would have to be interviewed and go through a home visit, during which they would be assessed as to their suitability as parents. Meanwhile, Lauryn Galindo, endlessly protesting her innocence, was able to give the couple some good news. By the New Year it seemed that baby Rath, whom they renamed Maddox, would be given a Cambodian passport with Angie and Billy Bob listed as his adoptive parents. Galindo herself arranged to fly Maddox in early

March from Cambodia to Namibia, where Angie was scheduled to be filming *Beyond Borders.* On that date with destiny they would become parents. There was still a catch. Maddox could not be taken to his new home until his U.S. visa was issued. That was a burden the couple were more than happy to bear.

Their secret plans led to a typically surreal Billy Bob moment with *Levity* director Ed Solomon, whose filming schedule called for Billy Bob to be on set until March 9. Billy Bob insisted he had to leave on March 1 for a vacation. Thinking that Billy Bob would shift his schedule, Solomon kept to his original plan, while Billy Bob refused to budge. Finally, Solomon, who had put up his house as collateral for the film, asked in desperation what was so important that Billy Bob couldn't spend a few more days in Montreal. Billy Bob would say only that he was going to Namibia on a desperately needed vacation with his family, keeping quiet about the imminent arrival of Maddox.

Finally Billy Bob agreed to stay in Montreal for a few days longer—if, and only if, Solomon could convince singer and actor Pat Boone, whom Billy Bob had never met, to accompany him on the long flight. With a house on the line and his project dangling in the breeze, Solomon picked up the phone and called Boone's people. Boone was having a root canal at the time, so Solomon left Boone's assistant his Montreal phone number and started thinking of how to explain to his six-year-old that his college fund had been squandered on a film.

Then the phone rang. It was Pat Boone. Solomon told him the story: the money, the filming schedule, the March deadline, and Billy Bob's wish to fly with the singer. Solomon recalls: "At the end of the conversation, Boone thought for a moment, then said: 'You know, if it means something to Billy Bob, and if it will help you keep your movie together—sure, I'll fly with him to Namibia.' To say I was flabbergasted would be an understatement."

During February, when Billy Bob wasn't filming, he was rehearsing with his eight-piece band for a couple of sold-out local gigs. At this time there were enough A-listers filming in town, including Brad Pitt, Anthony Hopkins, Drew Barrymore, Nicole Kidman, and Matt Damon, to make up a good-size crowd on their own. One night they were rehearsing when Bill Clinton showed up and played sax with Billy Bob's band. Sound technician Hugo Tardiff was impressed: "He was actually pretty good. Billy Bob was imitating Elvis for him." The two concerts meant a lot to Billy Bob; it was the first time he was able to try out material from *Private Radio*. A noticeable absentee was his wife, the excuse being that she was too busy filming to attend. That hurt him; he believed it was important for his partner to show her support when he was performing. It was one of the complaints he had made against Laura Dern. Now Angie was following the same path, from utterly worshipping and adoring the ground he walked on to being absent. What was going on?

He put these thoughts at the back of his mind as he took the long flight to Namibia, though without Pat Boone, as Billy Bob's schedule had changed anyway. He left Montreal on March 9, and a few hours later was holding his third son, Maddox, in his arms. Adoption facilitator Lauryn Galindo had flown halfway around the world to bring the eight-month-old baby to her most famous clients. It was a brisk handover at the airport and then she was gone, leaving Billy Bob and Angie with the first addition to their family. "A nurse came with Maddox and left ten minutes after handing him over," Angie said. "I stared at this little guy. I didn't know what to do. I called my mom. I remember saying: 'Do kids have two or ten bottles a day? I'm at a loss.'"

Their joy was short-lived. Once again her father had, in her eyes, put his foot in it by prematurely announcing that he had become a grandfather. On March 11, in answer to questions at an Academy Awards lunch in Hollywood, he told reporters that he was "thrilled," anxious to test his diaper-changing skills. Normally in a family, a new baby heals old wounds and resets the emotional clock. Not in Angie's world. She was furious. "I left him a strong message about how on the most beautiful day of my life, my first day with my son, he had cast this huge cloud. That day became about dealing with this thing that Jon had done." As Jon Voight had gotten the happy news from her mother, Angie told Marcheline never again to give her father details about her private life. Moreover, she vowed never to speak to him again.

Her response is interesting. There was no mention of "we," as in "Billy Bob and I, the parents of Maddox"; it was all about her. Her apparent overreaction to Voight's remarks, made in response to a question, also

211

demonstrates how edgy she was about keeping the adoption under the radar. Doubtless she feared that publicity might provoke further questioning—and delays—from U.S. immigration authorities, who were not as biddable as Hollywood producers.

The upshot was that Billy Bob and Angie hastily released a joint statement through Billy's Hollywood publicist: "It has been four months since we first met him. As usual in international adoptions, many background and other checks on both parents and child must be completed. He has finally received his passport, which is Cambodian. He officially became our son on March 11." The plan was for Angie to finish filming and then bring the boy home in May. "William and Harry are very excited to meet him."

Although they were still waiting for the American embassy in Cambodia to complete Maddox's visa, the signs were hopeful. Two days after their press announcement, the American ambassador to Cambodia, Kent Wiedemann, told the Associated Press that preliminary work had been done on the case and there was no reason to believe this was "a trafficked child." He cautioned, though, that the process could take "a couple of months." Hence the May schedule.

In the seaside resort of Swakopmund, Namibia, the new family retreated to their beach house, surrounded by bodyguards and security guards. Not that the local heavies had much of an idea who they were. When South African–based reporter Barbara Jones asked one sweltering guard who was inside the home he was watching, his offhand reply was unintentionally amusing. "There's an old guy in the house with some film star," he said nonchalantly. A few days later the "old guy," dressed in a baseball cap, headed to the tiny airport, where he told Jones that he and Angie were "cool" about the prospect of bringing up baby Maddox even though both parents were busy. "We're just going to do it. I'm going to turn down projects if Angie is working and she's going to do the same and we're going to try to be as good parents as we can."

He was putting a brave face on a rapidly changing situation. Inside their beach house, the woman who only a few months earlier had delighted at the prospect of being squeezed to death during their torrid lovemaking now plonked the baby between them. It was a not-so-subtle shift in the relationship. "Before, he was the sun, the moon, the stars and sky to Angie. Now he was no longer in her universe. Maddox was the new center of her life," said Ingrid Earle, a friend of Billy Bob's. The woman who had gone into a psychiatric ward in a frenzy of loss over the actor-musician was now addicted to baby Maddox. It was a fresh fascination, shifting through the emotional gears, first heroin, then her white knight, and now her complete devotion to the new little man in her life. Already a father of three children, Billy Bob was perhaps unfazed by the new arrival and the changing balance in their relationship, indulgent of Angie's messianic zeal for being a mother. After all, he had seen it all before. As far as Billy Bob was concerned, he was still very much with the program.

He next expected to see his bride and their son in Los Angeles in May after she had finished filming *Beyond Borders*. First, though, he had a little matter of a European and North American tour, starting in Dublin on April 1, to promote his first album. During his time in the Emerald Isle, he told local media that he hoped to spend a couple of days researching his Celtic ancestry, but most of all he was looking forward to taking some of the summer off so that he and Angie could bond with Maddox before he began work on his next movie, *Bad Santa*. Privately, though, he was getting worried. He was now hearing news about Angie and Maddox on the radio—not from his wife herself.

His tour was a modest success, winding up on May 28 in Toronto, the home city of air-traffic controller Sheila McCombe. Meanwhile, Angie, who took time off from filming to visit the Osire refugee camp near Winhoek, Namibia, where she donated 270 tents and other equipment, flew with Maddox to Thailand to wrap up the *Beyond Borders* shoot. Maddox enjoyed his first camel ride while Angie took a helicopter ride to visit nine thousand refugees at a camp in Tham Hin, west of Bangkok, Thailand, donating $100,000 and a sarong for each of the women.

These days it wasn't so much her films as her tireless charity work that was winning plaudits. UNHCR official Shannon Boyd praised her contribution to the global charity, saying: "She has become a key player in helping the office achieve its objectives of protecting refugees, assisting them, and winning public support for the respect of refugees' human rights."

Billy Bob had announced in April that Maddox had been granted a U.S. visa, Angie flying to Phnom Penh to complete the final formalities and arriving in Los Angeles with her boy in early June. She hadn't seen Billy Bob since mid-March.

They started off their reunion on June 3, the day before her birthday, with an almighty argument. From her side it was over allegations that he had been whooping it up on tour with other women. As far as he was concerned, he had no idea what the hell had gotten into her. The woman who had pledged to stay with Billy Bob until the end of time wasted no time packing a bag and moving out of their eleven-thousand-square-foot house. It is doubtful that William and Harry ever got to see their stepbrother. Billy Bob and Angie's parting was like their first meeting, dramatic and overblown. Now he knew how Laura Dern felt.

From Angie's perspective, this blowup had been brewing for months, the cracks in the façade first appearing when they moved out of their rented house in Montreal in March. "The marriage was already in trouble. It was obvious to both of us. I literally came back for one day, packed a bag and said: 'Goodbye.' It gave me a real sense of freedom," she said. Later she suggested that his infidelity during his tour was the turning point: "He hasn't been as honorable as he could be. I don't disbelieve the rumors. I don't think they are untrue." Fellow band member Michael Shipp dismissed the allegations as "horseshit," which, in any case, dated *after* the June 3 split. Angie was adamant: "I didn't see anything with my own eyes, but I could believe they are true. Let's just say that I'm not okay with certain kinds of behavior."

Clearly there were deeper conflicts behind the abrupt split. Billy Bob was obsessed with his music, while she was focused on Maddox. Her lexicon was that the new priority in her life was Maddox, completely and utterly. "Suddenly I had a baby and that child was the center of my life. Anything that took away from that or hurt that was going to have to go," she said. More than that, she felt he didn't appreciate or respect her charity work, needling her by saying that refugees and poverty were as common as the rain. "He's focused on his music and career," Angie said. "I'm focused on my baby. Maddox is so important to me. It comes down to what's important to you. Good for him. But I have other priorities."

As for Billy Bob, these accusations were all news to him. For a guy who had overcome his phobias, supported her charity work, set up joint foundations, tailored his career to fit in with hers, and encouraged her need to adopt, this was a bolt out of the blue. "I don't think either one of us knows why we split up. It was like, say you're going to a nightclub one night with your friends and you're in line and the next thing you know there are guys with helicopters and there's machine gun fire and you don't know what happened. And that's kind of what our breakup was like."

For a doting, adoring mother, her subsequent behavior was curious to say the least. She celebrated her twenty-seventh birthday by ditching her husband and then dumping her beloved boy with her mother and her brother, James—in Maddox's eyes two complete strangers—before catching a flight to Ecuador to spend a week visiting UN refugee camps. It seemed that once Angie had gotten the prize she had spent years planning for, her partner was superfluous, useful only insofar as his name on the adoption papers helped smooth the process. A single woman with a busy, full-time career and a well-known history of drug use might have had difficulty convincing even the most forgiving adoption agency that she would be able to give a baby from another country and culture the kind of constant support and care experts recommend. Having a husband helped.

For his part, Billy Bob embarked on the rest of his North American tour, the women he met a welcome distraction. So, too, were the long-necked bottles of Budweiser he now reached for with increasing regularity. As one "roadie" commented, "It wasn't like Billy Bob was having affairs on the road, but he was doing his rock-and-roll thing, letting the girls get up real close. He was not shooing anyone off." After reflecting on the split during her Ecuador trip, Angie told *USA Today:* "I'm angry. I'm sad. It's a very difficult and sad time. Sometimes, you don't see things coming, even though they are happening. It was a real deep connection, a deep marriage, so it's not that simple to say this or that one thing caused the problems."

Her status as a UN Goodwill Ambassador, however, made her a political target. In July, shortly after she appeared in a documentary alongside Nobel Peace Prize winner Desmond Tutu and UN secretary general Kofi Annan to commemorate World Refugee Day in June, a report in the Australian *Age* newspaper quoted human rights and child welfare agencies in Phnom Penh saying that Maddox had been bought from his destitute mother for $100 and that his adoption was only fast-tracked after substantial bribes were paid to senior government officials. "I am sure that this child was not a real orphan and was not abandoned," said Dr. Kek Galabru, head of LICADHO, whose report triggered the initial American visa ban. "A large number of them are not orphans. There are a lot of desperate parents who are willing to sell their children and some do it for as little as $50." These claims were never proven.

Meanwhile, U.S. officials were delving deeply in the world of Lauryn Galindo. During the two-year probe, investigators alleged that Galindo paid Cambodian child finders to purchase or steal children from their families, and conspired to create false identity documents for the children. Angie's response was to hire private detectives to look into allegations regarding Maddox's origins. However, the findings of her detectives were not made public, nor did she hand them over to prosecutors compiling the case against Galindo.

Some time later, Galindo pleaded guilty and was sentenced to eighteen months in federal prison on charges of conspiracy to commit visa fraud and money laundering, but not trafficking. Her sister Lynn gave evidence against her. "You can get away with buying babies around the world as a United States citizen," says Richard Cross, a senior special agent with U.S. Immigration and Customs Enforcement who investigated Galindo. "It's not a crime."

It seemed nothing was straightforward in Angie's world, the adoption of her beloved Maddox mired in years of controversy, both public and private. His arrival was a considerable factor in the breakdown of her relations with the two men in her life: her father and her husband. During the split from Billy Bob she had been playing her familiar game of hide-and-seek with her father, ignoring his phone calls and handwritten notes, still furious with him for telling the world about Maddox. On July 14, 2002, they had been separately invited to the Paramount ninetieth-anniversary celebrations in Hollywood, and Jon Voight planned to speak with his daughter about her lifestyle, her exhibitionism, and her erratic behavior. When he arrived at the event, he was as dapper as ever in a blue silk suit, but for once his smile was tight and his demeanor anxious. He spotted his daughter and made his way toward her through the throng of celebrities.

He later claimed that as he cried out her name, Geyer Kosinski, who transitioned from agent to manager as Marcheline's illness left her less able to cope with organizing Angie's life, blocked his way, telling him, "She doesn't want to see you." It could have turned ugly, as there is little love lost between manager and father. Kosinski remembers the incident differently, telling *Access Hollywood* that he interceded because Voight "aggressively, physically grabbed her against her will." Even so, the outcome was the same—another angry and frustrating stand-off between father and daughter.

Humiliated and scorned, Jon Voight pondered other ways to get through to his daughter. His next step was the gamble of a desperate man.

Angie, though, had other matters on her mind. On July 17, three days after her encounter with her father, she announced her divorce, leaving the man whom she'd credited with saving her life, a man whom she'd pledged to stay with until the end of time, without a backward glance. She had a new man in her life. While he couldn't walk or talk, he now meant the world to her.

TWELVE

For Angelina to adopt a child from another country is symbolic of how alien she feels. Metaphorically they are on the fifth floor. Worlds away.

—Dr. Franziska De George

It was just a regular day in his Burbank office for Pat O'Brien, the dapper, moustachioed host of *Access Hollywood*. Then his phone rang. On the line was Jon Voight, asking if they could meet privately. He said "Sure," and suggested they have a coffee at Nate n' Al's, a well-known casual meeting place for Hollywood movers and shakers. While O'Brien had met Voight a few times over the years, by no stretch of the imagination were they close. They were Hollywood friends, saying "Hi" to each other on the red carpet. "I had no idea what he wanted to talk about," recalls O'Brien about the encounter in late July 2002, days after Angie had announced her official split with Billy Bob Thornton.

O'Brien arrived at the deli shortly before Voight, and when the actor walked in, he got straight down to business. "I want to talk to you about my daughter," he said. "I'm brokenhearted. That's the reason why I'm here. I feel I can trust you as a journalist."

The TV host, who was a sports commentator before moving into TV entertainment, realized that Voight wanted to talk further. His antennae warned him to hold fire, to capture what Voight had to say on film. "Any chance you can do this on camera?" he asked. Voight nodded agreement. "That's what I want. I want to tell you about my daughter."

O'Brien returned to the office intrigued by exactly what was on Voight's mind. He remembered another time when he got a call out of the blue; it was from actor Michael J. Fox, who admitted on live TV that he had

Parkinson's disease and was bowing out of movies. O'Brien and his executive producer Rob Silverstein arranged to meet Voight in a suite at the Four Seasons hotel in Beverly Hills. While it was a two-camera shoot, which in television terms signifies that the interview is of some importance, O'Brien had no idea what he was getting into when he walked into the room. His questions were brief, O'Brien savvy enough to know when to stay quiet and let the star do the talking.

When O'Brien asked him why he was coming forward, Voight was immediately in full flow, explaining that while the public might see a poised, smiling actor who had enjoyed numerous successes, inside he was a broken man. "I've been trying to reach my daughter and get her help. I have failed and I'm really sorry. I haven't come forward and addressed these serious mental problems she has spoken about so candidly." It "pained" him deeply to see these unspecified mental problems paraded over and over again. "They're very serious symptoms of real, real problems, real, real illness."

He explained that her problems were in part drug-related and that over the years he had confronted her about her behavior, but with little success. As far as he was concerned, she had avoided facing up to these issues, more often than not shielded by her manager, Geyer Kosinski, whom he described as a "parasite." "I begged him to help many times and always he turned her against me," he said in a portion of the interview left on the cutting-room floor. (Geyer later sent him a letter threatening to sue him, but he never followed through.)

Nor did Voight absolve himself of blame, acknowledging the pain and hurt his affair with Stacey Pickren, whom he did not name, had caused the family. His ex-wife also had to share the burden of guilt, Voight said, accusing Marche of programming the children against him in spite of all his "repentance," combined with his efforts to be "an upstanding and strong example" for his kids.

While he emphasized Angie's drug taking as the main reason for her "real psychic pain," he also acknowledged her psychological damage. "There is something she has to work out," he said. "There is some trauma there."

Even though he had never held out much hope for his daughter's second marriage, he did concede that Billy Bob Thornton had had a positive impact on her attempt to get clean of drugs. Now that Angie was considered to be a role model, he was bothered about her possible influence on young people, pleading with her fans to send her their love and prayers. At this point he put his hand over his face and broke down in tears. It was an electrifying moment.

"All of a sudden he just broke down," recalls Pat O'Brien. "It was the dad in him coming out. This was his baby girl he was trying to save. He so wanted to reach out to her. She hadn't returned his calls and he didn't know where she was living. He broke down like a father who had not yet cried over the rejection by his daughter. I just sat there and stared at him. I didn't really know what to do. At that point I was no longer a journalist but one father to another who felt sorry for the guy. I put my hand on his knee and patted him to say: 'It's okay to cry.' The tears just came out." As he tried to compose himself, the veteran actor spoke of his greatest pain, not being allowed to see his first grandchild, Maddox.

When the cameras stopped rolling on the thirty-minute interview, the two men had lunch and swapped phone numbers. Voight went on his way, feeling that his mission had been accomplished. He couldn't have been more wrong.

The first indication of trouble was when Angie's lawyers, who were contacted before the Thursday-night broadcast on August 1, warned the TV show against even showing the material. "On no account can you run that interview," *Access Hollywood* was told. Angie, who was staying in a London hotel with Maddox as she prepared to reprise her role as Lara Croft, issued a formal statement: "I don't want to make public the reasons for my bad relationship with my father. I will only say that, like every child, Jamie and I would have loved to have had a warm and loving relationship with our dad. After all these years, I have determined that it is not healthy for me to be around my father, especially now that I am responsible for my own child."

Having seen her father break down in front of his eyes, Pat O'Brien was surprised by Angie's retort. "What shook me most about the whole episode was how cool her response was," he says.

If he had been in her hotel suite, he would have seen a very different reaction. She was incandescent with rage, shouting, cursing, and throwing cushions at her father's image on the TV screen. Her greatest fear was that her father's righteous intervention could lead to her son's being taken away from her. "It's horrible, it doesn't make sense," said the bewildered actress when first asked about the interview.

Voight had grotesquely misjudged the impact his words would have, not just on Angie but on his family and friends. As director Rob Lieberman, a friend for more than twenty years, observed: "Jon is a complicated, intense guy who is very thoughtful. I've scratched my head about him a number of times. Going on TV to talk about his daughter was not the greatest choice. He was desperate and trying to save his daughter as he saw it from drugs and bad choices."

Angie was right, however; it didn't make sense. He was once again treating her like a child—a daughter whose lifestyle had been a byword for independence: living with a boy at fourteen, moving into her own apartment at sixteen, making movies on her own at seventeen, buying her own place at nineteen, marrying for the first time at twenty and for the second time at twenty-four. In between she had become one of the world's best-known actresses and a UNHCR Goodwill Ambassador. In September, just a few weeks after the *Access Hollywood* broadcast, she became the first recipient of the Church World Service Immigration and Refugee Program Humanitarian Award. She was trying to be the good girl of her imagination. "No matter what he said, I realized that I was a good person, a good friend and a good mother," she said afterward.

Actor Nathan Lee Graham, who had worked with Voight on *Zoolander* a couple of years before, got a brief taste of why Angie might feel so aggrieved after a lifetime of never quite making the mark—at least according to her dad. Graham found Voight constantly judgmental, never encouraging or consoling. "His intensity was unnerving. He looked down on you like he had the answers and you didn't."

After some months of reflection, Angie told the TV show *20/20:* "I think he truly believes he's there to save me and my mother and my brother. And he's somebody who has an opinion about all of us and what we should be doing and who we are. I've been crazy in my life and I've been wild in my life. I've never been a bad person. I've never intentionally hurt other people just to hurt them. And I'm trying to do a lot of good things with my life."

If his concerns had some credence and credibility at one time, even Jon Voight would agree that Angie had clawed her way out of the pit of suicidal despair. It seems the years of hide-and-seek, of endless rebuffs in person or on the phone, culminating in her public rejection of him at the Paramount anniversary celebrations, had taken a heavy toll, tipping the balance in his own mind. While both Angie and Jon had used the media for years to communicate with each other, his latest TV confessional proved an intercession too far.

His timing could not have been worse. She was still upset, vulnerable, and emotional following the abrupt collapse of her second marriage, and her adoption of Maddox was under intense international scrutiny; she risked losing two of the most precious things in her life: her son and her position as a UN Goodwill Ambassador. During this time of turmoil Angie might have expected support from her father rather than public criticism.

"My daughter is very sad. It's a really tough time for her," Marche told *People* magazine. Certainly Voight's broadcast cast a shadow over Maddox's first birthday party a couple of days later, on August 5. Not that Maddox seemed to care. "Maddox was very happy playing with his birthday cake. But he was only interested in eating his broccoli," observed his proud grandmother.

As Jon Voight knew, his ex-wife was suffering her own health issues, still recovering from further cancer surgery and treatment. Since 1999 she had been in remission from cervical cancer, but in 2002 routine tests revealed that the cancer had returned, and her condition was treated with more surgery and chemotherapy. Her annual mammogram also revealed a malignant tumor that was detected early enough to be removed. "Every sunrise I experience is truly a gift," she wrote later.

Marche felt sufficiently robust to issue her own defense of her daughter. "I'm shocked," she said. "There's nothing wrong with Angelina's mental health. Mentally and physically, she is magnificently healthy." Certainly any problems, mental or otherwise, came as a surprise to *Lara Croft* producer Lawrence Gordon. "I have an excellent team around her," he said. "If there was a problem I would know it." Angie's mother, who had been the conduit of information between estranged father and daughter, now refused to speak to Jon Voight ever again, a pledge she resolutely kept. There was another reason behind her decision. Her relationship with Bill Day had regularly been undermined by the proximity of Jon Voight. Now that her love affair with John Trudell was flourishing, she wanted to give it a chance to grow without Jon's interference.

Not only was Jon publicly disowned by his ex-wife and daughter, but his son, James, also refused to have anything more to do with him, though they had always been closer than Jon and Angie. A committed Christian who for a time pondered becoming an evangelical preacher, even James could not forgive his father's behavior. Jon Voight now felt the full blast of the legendary Bertrand family freeze, his children and his ex-wife casting him into the outer darkness.

The rest of the Voights suffered, too; Marche stopped talking to or writing to any member of his family. For years she had been great friends with Joan Taylor, the first wife of Jon's younger brother, Chip Taylor. At a stroke she was out of her life. Joan continued to send family pictures as well as Christmas and birthday cards, but never heard a word from her friend again. It was as though she didn't exist.

To formally seal the family schism, Angie instructed her lawyer to legally remove "Voight" from her name. "He's not any more to me than a man who walks down the street," she said, indicating the depth of her anger. "I'm an adoptive parent so blood ties aren't what count."

The irony was not lost on her mother or on those who had known Angie since she was a youngster. Just as James was more like his mother, passive, introspective, and placid, Angie was strikingly similar to her dad. She shared not only his genetic flaw, a slight curvature of the spine, but also his full lips and high cheekbones. Like her father, she was wild, chatty, sexy, feisty, and a born debater who loved to argue a point. While her mother preferred to donate to causes—Angie inherited her impulsive generosity— Jon Voight had long been an activist. "I think celebrity is a gift," he once said. "You can do a lot of things with it and therefore you should be responsible. If I use it properly, I can help people": sentiments that found an echo in his daughter's work for refugees and other victims of society.

Of all the Voights, Angie inherited the straight-talking, loose-lipped nature of her crackerjack of a grandmother, Barbara Voight. One story straight out of the Barbara Voight playbook could have been about Angie. When her son took her to an Academy Awards ceremony, Barbara, then in her seventies, was complimented by James Bond himself, Sean Connery, on her silver dress. "Five bucks, five bucks," she said, pulling at the material. "Bought it from a secondhand store." Her genetic code, a breezy disregard of fashion and convention, seemed to have been passed on virtually intact to her granddaughter.

Angie continued to bridle at any comparison to her father or his family. After the O'Brien broadcast, she told one interviewer: "We're not similar people and we are not friends. In an argument we were always on opposite sides." In denying her father's existence, she was also denying herself. "Don't tell Angie that; she will go mad," Marche once warned her friend Lauren Taines, when they concluded that Angie was a true Voight.

While removing her father's name took but the stroke of a pen—she officially became Angelina Jolie in September 2002 after petitioning a Santa Monica court—it was a rather more painful process to etch Billy Bob's name out of her life, and her heart. She complained that it took five laser treatments to remove the tattoo of his name from her left shoulder; she then replaced his name with the global coordinates where Maddox was born. "The worst thing is the smell," she said. Fortunately the now infamous tattoo of Billy Bob's name beneath her bikini line had faded.

For his part, Billy Bob had the left forearm tattoo that once bore her name expunged. He observed later: "I had it covered up with an angel and it says 'Peace.' It's like, basically, my way of saying, 'No hard feelings.'" Then for good measure he buried the "vial of blood" in his backyard.

If only the tattoo left on his heart by his wild two-year ride with Angie could be removed so easily. To ease the pain and publicity, he cut the song "Angelina" from his band's playlist. He had been sober and off drugs for years, but now he was again drinking and smoking. "At the time, he was very depressed because he thought that the world would think he had left her and Maddox," recalled a close friend. "It just wasn't true. The fact was that she had no further need for him. She had resolved something inside herself and moved on."

For the last two years Thornton, at heart a homebody who lives for his music and art, had gotten himself into a freak show where he was exhibit A. While he had gone along with the overblown statements and sentiments—and contributed his fair share—he knew that the blood vials, the matching graves, and the endless sex talk were symptoms of her constant need for attention. "Shock value," he would tell friends, rolling his eyes in mock despair. "I went along for the ride." He understood Angie's motivation. During the early part of an actor's career, people only want the juicy and sensational. "So you play it up," he observed.

He later reflected to friends that the central difference between him and Angie was that he was an artist who had had to learn to cope with fame, whereas she was an actor who craved infamy. As his onetime girl-friend Sheila McCombe observed: "She fell in love with the idea of being with an artist and the reality was rather different. He is very smart and tal-ented but the downside is that he's a very heavy character." It was somewhat like the difference between Madonna and her first husband, Sean Penn. She dreamed of ways to feed the media beast, while he threw rocks at it.

Billy Bob had no regrets, though. "Most people can't talk me out of the house, but she did," he said. Not that the incorrigible horndog could be kept on the porch for long. Within days of the July divorce announcement, he was pictured in West Hollywood with model Danielle Dotzenrod, at twenty-three less than half his age, though he was adamant that he never cheated on Angie during the marriage. Riddled with anxiety and low self-esteem, he later explained to writer Barbara Davies that the reason for the split was in his head—not below the belt. "It was all down to my inade-quacy and fear. I was frightened of Angie because she was too good for me. She was too beautiful, too smart and had too much integrity. I felt small next to her and I just couldn't live with it."

It was not long before Billy Bob had resurrected his harem. Besides Dotzenrod, he was linked with country singer Deana Carter and his ex-wife Pietra, and in January he flew to Toronto to see Sheila McCombe. It was a woman who quietly flew below the radar, however, who truly cap-tured his heart. In early July he had begun work on *Bad Santa*. During filming, his regular makeup artist, Carrie Angland, introduced him to her sister, Connie, who worked in the background as a seamstress on movie sets. She was as far removed from Angie's life and lifestyle as one could get—which was probably half the attraction. At some point she moved in with him, and by late 2003 she was expecting his fourth child. As he ex-plained in an *Esquire* interview with Amy Wallace in 2005: "Sex doesn't have to be with a model to be good. As a matter of fact, sometimes with the model, the actress, the 'sexiest person in the world,' it may be literally like fucking the couch. Don't count out the average-looking woman, or even maybe the slightly unattractive woman, or the really unattractive woman. There may be this swarthy little five-foot-two stocky woman who just has sex all over her."

In August 2002, as Billy Bob was being photographed hand in hand with model Danielle Dotzenrod, Angie was six thousand miles away in London, reprising her role as Lara Croft for a reported salary of $9 million. The fast-paced hokum involved the frantic hunt for a Pandora's box that had the capacity to wipe out mankind. In her desperate search Angie jumped off Hong Kong's tallest skyscraper, fought killer sharks, and rode everything from a horse to a motorbike. The woman who climbed trees as a little girl observed: "This film brought out the tomboy in me."

Being newly single also brought out the animal in her. The panther was back on the prowl, explaining to *Marie Claire* magazine that one of the ten things she wanted to do before she died was tell her ex-husband Jonny Lee Miller that she still loved him. "But I think he knows," she said, declaring later that she hoped the two "might find a way back to each other."

She soon had the opportunity to tell him in person. According to the *Daily Mirror,* within days of checking into Claridge's hotel, Angie was, in scenes reminiscent of her pursuit of Billy Bob, bombarding Miller's production company, Natural Nylon, with endless phone calls, leaving her hotel name and room number. "Angelina has called up loads of times and sounded very distraught," a well-informed source was quoted as saying.

When Angie arrived in London, Miller was due to marry his sweetheart from school, blonde TV actress Lisa Faulkner, who had previously dated *South Park* creator Trey Parker. The couple, who had become engaged the previous May, were in the midst of planning a "fairy-tale" wedding in November. Within three weeks of Angie's arrival, the wedding was called off. Like Laura Dern, Lisa Faulkner never saw it coming. Faulkner was later photographed sobbing on a friend's shoulder, breaking down in tears during a shopping trip in central London. Remaining tight-lipped about the reasons behind their breakup, Lisa later tried to be philosophical: "The wedding was a huge part of my life, but I've got over it and am moving on. It just didn't work out. It has been tough, but I have no regrets about the split. Life brings up horrible things and you have to deal with them."

It was not long before Angie and Jonny picked up where they had left off, the actor squiring her around town for the next few months—when she was not visiting refugee camps or jumping off high-rise buildings in exotic locations. "I'm talking to Angelina on a regular basis," he told a society gossip writer, adding with a sideswipe at Jon Voight, "She's very well, and quite sane. She certainly bears no resemblance to the way she is depicted in the press."

In the first flush of their renewed romance, the couple was seemingly unconcerned about expressing their feelings in public, making out in the crowded dining room of Claridge's. A fellow diner at the hotel told the *Daily Mirror,* "They were all over each other. Angelina had draped herself over Jonny and they were giggling away. They seemed oblivious to the fact it was so busy. People were gawping at them." It was not just dinner dates; he also took her to watch the England vs. France international rugby union match at Twickenham, where she joined in singing the English rugby anthem, "Swing Low, Sweet Chariot." Such was their closeness that when she went on a land mines awareness course in Cheshire in northwest England as part of her work for UNHCR, she reportedly instructed her assistant to hold all cell phone calls except those from Miller.

It is not hard to understand why she was so keen to reconnect with Miller. In many ways they had never really been apart, Miller a friend and a shoulder to cry on even after their separation and subsequent divorce. Of all the men—and women—in her life, he probably seemed the most trustworthy. Unlike Mick Jagger and Billy Bob Thornton, who'd had to betray a partner to prove their devotion to Angie, Miller had never forfeited another to win her love. Until Lisa Faulkner. Perhaps, in a perverse way, his breakup with Faulkner was the final test, which, like all the other men in her life, he had failed. Abandoning his fiancée so abruptly in favor of Angie may have proved his dedication, but it also proved, in Angie's eyes, that he was no longer worthy. On some level he was now no better than her cheating father, her template for all that was wrong with men.

The only male who had never let her down—baby Maddox—shared her bed most nights. She poured all her love and devotion into the youngster she called "Mad," insisting on keeping him with her during the filming of the new Lara Croft movie. Over the course of the fourteen-week shoot, Angie and her son flew to Santorini in Greece, Hong Kong, Nairobi, Kenya, and north Wales, where an area of the Snowdonia mountain had been turned into a Chinese peasant village. It is not hard to imagine her distress when in mid-September 2002 the toddler managed to scald himself while staying in her suite in the luxury Seiont Manor hotel in Wales. He was rushed ninety miles by ambulance to the Alder Hey hospital in Liverpool, his mother fitfully sleeping by his bed at night and returning to film during the day as he made his recovery. She was exhausted, literally wrung out by the trauma of what at first seemed like a life-threatening injury. After her father's dire prognostications about her fitness to be a mother, this was the last thing she needed. The fact that she donated $80,000 to the hospital following his four-day stay was a sign of her relief. "Without a doubt, being a single mom is the hardest thing I've ever done," she ruefully observed.

As if juggling motherhood and a demanding, high-pressure job wasn't enough, she made it more difficult by trying to do everything herself. She found herself running on empty, on occasion falling asleep on the set. There was an emotional logic behind her behavior—child-care experts emphasize that parents who adopt foreign babies should spend as much time as possible with them, not only to help them bond but also to soothe any deep-seated fears of abandonment.

Meanwhile, she was already looking for a brother or sister for Maddox, admitting that she had completed the paperwork to adopt a baby from another religion and culture. As Dr. Franziska De George observes: "The motivation for Angelina to adopt a child from another country is symbolic of how alien she feels. Metaphorically they are on the fifth floor. Worlds away. She can identify with and responds to their feeling of alienation and abandonment, their helplessness and their pain. Cutting was a way of shifting herself out of her suffering, while adopting children shifts them out of their suffering. Adopting foreign children is her way of easing the suffering no one eased in her."

Maddox was the center of her universe. "I just can't bear to be away from him," she told writer Anna Day. "If that makes me a dull person, then so be it. He is my life. I want to be a great parent. I've done pretty much everything in terms of movies but the biggest challenge is raising a child." She added a tattoo in his honor, a Buddhist symbol and script branded onto her left shoulder blade. Thai artist Sompong Kanphai used the traditional long needles and hammer method, and Angie was obliged to kneel and fold her hands together in prayer during the long, painful process in a hotel room outside Bangkok. She saw it as a rite of passage for herself and a ritual of protection for her young son. In her mind Maddox gave her life meaning, a sense of purpose, and a richness and responsibility she had never known before. The days when she immersed herself in a role, living her character, were now over. Instead she steeped herself in her new incarnation as a mother. "There was a time I lived through my characters," she said. "I've now found that I prefer my life."

A home life, too. While the duo lived out of a suitcase for much of the year, Angie added to her existing portfolio of properties in Los Angeles and New York, buying a $3.4 million eight-bedroom converted farmhouse in Buckinghamshire, north of London, which she was then renting. Her new home, which had previously been rented by Tom Cruise and Nicole Kidman during the making of *Eyes Wide Shut*, was convenient because London was much nearer than the U.S. to the places in Africa and the Far East she wanted to visit in her work for the UN. At Christmas 2002, for example, she spent time with a group of women clearing land mines in Pristina, the capital of Kosovo, and in April she flew to Sri Lanka to see for herself the plight of refugees made homeless by the long civil war. She saw England, too, as a sanctuary. "I call England home," she observed. "Living in Europe makes me feel more connected to the rest of the world."

In time she would look for another home in mainland Europe, pondering the pros and cons of Spain or Italy. She also bought a twenty-one-acre plot of land in the Cambodian jungle in Maddox's name, the aim being for him to keep his connections with his home country. "He will have a very fortunate life and I want him to be responsible to his country, to know his language, his people, to do something to make it better for his people," she commented. "If he, at eighteen, said I don't want to go there I would have it out with him."

The contrast between their rural idyll in Buckinghamshire and the site in the Cambodian jungle, complete with forty-eight unexploded land mines and the occasional visiting tiger, where Angie built three simple wooden bungalows could not have been greater. One of the first visitors was her onetime lover Jenny Shimizu. "There's no special treatment there," said the former Calvin Klein model. "One electric light for each house. We play cards and go to sleep."

The endless traveling, ostensibly for filming, promotion, or her UN work, dovetailed with Angie's roaming personality, her restlessness one of the factors behind the breakups of her brief marriages. "I'm not very set-tled," she admitted. "The positive side of that is I'm on fire all the time, to try anything. The negative side is there isn't a lot of time for me to sit and watch a movie and hold hands. I tend to not be inside my relationships. I tend to be more focused on the world. It takes a certain kind of man to love those things."

Inevitably, any new man—or woman—would have to pass the Mad-dox test. Her new mate would have to be an "amazing" father, "indepen-dent, compassionate and strong." The real man of her imagination.

In London endless media speculation about her love life centered on Jonny Lee Miller, but the focus changed when she flew to Montreal in the spring of 2003 to work on *Taking Lives,* a thriller based on Michael Pye's novel. Playing an FBI profiler hunting a ruthless serial killer, she was linked to each of her costars: Ethan Hawke, Kiefer Sutherland, and Olivier Martinez. A classic example was when she and Maddox went to a Mon-treal Expos baseball game with various members of the cast and crew. She was photographed sitting or standing next to Hawke and Martinez, differ-ent tabloids plumping for one or the other as her new lover. While this unwarranted romantic juxtaposition irritated Australian singer Kylie Minogue, then the girlfriend of the French-born Martinez, it gave rangy blonde actress Uma Thurman, wife of Hawke and mother of his two chil-dren, rather more to think about. During the three-month shoot her five-year marriage steamed onto the rocks after Hawke was linked to Canadian model Jen Perzow. When the couple separated in September 2003, weeks after filming wrapped, Thurman's brother Mipam publicly threatened his brother-in-law, telling *People* magazine: "I want to kill him. I can't believe what he's done to my sister." His mood would have been even darker if he had known that Hawke had enjoyed a fling with Angie as well. Hawke's public pronouncements about Angie were clue enough. "She's ravishingly beautiful and never gets old and never gets boring. She is a really incredible woman, and I liked her," he said, which could hardly have been music to his wife's ears. "I knew about her affair with Ethan," recalls Lauren Taines. "At that time she hadn't seen anyone for quite a while."

During the publicity for *Lara Croft Tomb Raider: The Cradle of Life* that summer, however, she repeated that she was celibate like a mantra. "It's really funny that I'm still seen as a sex symbol considering I haven't had sex in a really long time," she said, amused at the idea that she was "dating everyone." When she left the cold climes of Canada in fall 2003 for the desert heat of Morocco and Egypt for the filming of *Alexander*, Oliver Stone's $160 million epic about the ancient warrior ruler, the burning question once again concerned Angie's love life. She was linked with her costars, Val Kilmer and Colin Farrell, as well as with Oliver Stone.

Farrell was playing Alexander, and even though, at twenty-eight, he and Angie were the same age, she was cast as his ruthless mother, Olympias. While Stone could see in Angie the "strong and determined" quality he wanted for his queen, he was intrigued by what would happen at the first meeting between screen mother and son. When they sat down for dinner at a restaurant in Manhattan, Stone recalls: "It was funny. He was all over her, he was like the Irish boy—he wasn't Alexander, he was just falling in love with her, couldn't help himself." He realized that he had made the right choice, as Farrell was behaving more like a baby, the infant to her mother. Both wild at heart, they discussed dating but decided they were too similar for a romance to develop. Angie said: "We'd go nuts." Even so, photographs of them together suggested a closeness and an intimacy that went beyond the professional. After all, why not? They were both unattached Geminis, single parents—he had a son by model Kim Bordenave—who were stranded in the desert. They shared, too, a love of tattoos, once spending hours touring Cairo in search of a tattoo parlor. She ended up with an Arabic script tattoo on her right arm that means "Determination." It covered up the energy waves tattoo she had done during her days with Billy Bob. "We knew there were going to be millions of rumors pouring out of this movie," recalls Rosario Dawson, who played Roxane, Alexander's chosen wife. "Nothing as good as what did happen, I have to say."

During the ninety-four-day shoot there were practical jokes aplenty—on one occasion Val Kilmer sent an unsuspecting Angie a snake in a basket—and late-night drinking sessions led by "The Regent," the cast's nickname for Farrell. Toward the end of the shoot in Thailand, he fell down the hotel stairs in a drunken stupor, breaking his ankle and wrist. "Colin came very close; he gambled," observed Stone indulgently.

As teasing as she was about her relationship with Farrell, Angie further intrigued her fans when she revealed that she had arrangements with a couple of men she knew well who met her in upmarket London hotels for afternoons of sex. It meant that she could enjoy herself without the need to interfere with her own family life. "It's an adult way of having adult relationships," she told the *New York Post*. Angie declined to name names, but clearly she and her former husband were great friends, so he was an obvious candidate. One man not on the short list was Billy Bob: "We're not friends. We don't even talk anymore," she said. As for her other lover, she admitted she had met him while married to Billy Bob and called him up out of the blue several years later when she came to live in London. Her mystery lover was in fact actor Ralph Fiennes, who had been penciled in to play the lead in *Beyond Borders* before withdrawing. "Yes, I knew about him," confirms a family friend. "She saw him occasionally."

Their clandestine meetings were held in smart London hotels, discreet and anonymous. At that time, Fiennes, eighth cousin to Prince Charles, was living with actress Francesca Annis, eighteen years his senior. They separated in 2006 after his reported affair with Romanian singer Cornelia Crisan. A year later, in February 2007, he was involved in another sex scandal when staff aboard a Qantas flight from Sydney, Australia, to Mumbai, India, caught the actor leaving the same airplane lavatory at the same time as flight attendant Lisa Robertson. After first denying allegations of a tryst, Robertson, thirty-eight, later confessed to having sex with the star of *The English Patient*, whom she had met only a couple of hours before. Fiennes, a UNICEF ambassador, was on his way to an AIDS awareness event. The charity kept him on; Qantas sacked Robertson.

Angie was able to switch back and forth from bad girl to the "other girl," swatting away inquiries about her sex life one minute, the next standing demurely on a podium in her capacity as UN Goodwill Ambassador. As she told writer Nancy Jo Sales about her forays to Washington: "When I'm here there's a side of me that I just get into focus. I get my notes, my pen. I get my head together. I do want to cover my tattoos, get into my suits, look clean, don't dress too sexy, and just try and present the woman that I'm not sure I am but would like to aspire to be." In June 2003, for example, she joined then secretary of state Colin Powell to launch World Refugee Day, and later stood with Senators Dianne Feinstein and Sam Brownback on Capitol Hill to publicly call on the U.S. Senate to support a bipartisan bill to reform the treatment of unaccompanied minors, including refugee children.

At that time, unaccompanied minors were held at detention facilities without lawyers or guardians to help them with complex immigration procedures, a fact that "really surprised" the Goodwill Ambassador. She told an audience of senators, officials, and media: "As Americans we defend our human rights, we defend our freedoms and we will help the innocent, especially the children, who need our support to protect their rights and their freedoms." Despite her lack of a college degree, Angie's profile and "heartfelt plea" on behalf of refugee children impressed legislators. At a private meeting with Senators Arlen Specter (a Yale Law School grad with "more political clout that some sovereign nations") and Hillary Clinton (an alumna of Wellesley and Yale Law School, and a former First Lady), Angie (a graduate of Moreno High) convinced the two political heavyweights to cosponsor the bill, which came into effect in October 2004. "Jolie seems much more at home these days talking to Powell about the refugee problems in Africa than sitting at the Dorchester hotel and promoting yet another of her movies," noted celebrity profiler Kevin Sessums.

The collision of her art and her passion came at the world premiere of *Beyond Borders* in New York in October 2003. Escorted by Jonny Lee Miller, Angie sat through the gala event, which raised $100,000 for UNHCR, in the presence of UN secretary general Kofi Annan and the UN High Commissioner for Refugees, Ruud Lubbers. A few days earlier Senators Edward Kennedy and William Frist had hosted a panel discussion in Washington on refugee-related issues, while in New York Kofi Annan gave the film a warm introduction.

Unfortunately, the movie itself was left behind in this caravan of self-congratulation, a refugee roaming the cineplexes looking for a home—and a half-decent review. The opening sequence, which showed an irate relief worker crashing a fancy fund-raiser to scold rich swells for enjoying themselves while their supposed beneficiaries were dying in Ethiopia, left Jack Mathews, of the New York *Daily News,* "squirming in his seat" given the fact that guests at the premiere itself had invitations to a posh post-screening party at the upscale Cipriani restaurant. "One might have trouble ignoring the irony," he observed, going on to describe the film as "awful." The title was a headline writer's dream: "Beyond Belief," "Beyond Dull," "Beyond Boring," "Beyond Redemption" . . . you get the idea. The high-minded movie made just $2 million in America and failed to find a distributor in Britain, with the UN-approved script by Caspian Tredwell-Owen widely derided.

Angie seemed to have swapped acting for earnestness—"wooden," a word never before heard about Angelina Jolie, an apt description of her performance. It was a movie she truly believed in and had worked hard behind the scenes to get to the screen. "Jolie's personal interest in humanitarian causes has been well documented," noted critic George Thomas. "Here, she shows precisely why you should never mix your work with your personal crusades."

Still, Angie's love-in with the United Nations continued. In the week of the movie premiere, Secretary General Kofi Annan personally presented her with the first Citizen of the World award given by the UN Correspondents Association for her efforts "to bring public attention to the plight of refugees across the globe, so that the world community will take action to help them." Only twenty-eight, she was justifiably proud of her achievement. "It means that I've done good work for an organization that I care a great deal about and that I didn't let them down. If I die tomorrow I can leave my son something that says I did something good with my life."

There is something endearingly naïve and innocent about her response, rather like that of a schoolgirl being given a gold star. The same quality of wide-eyed concern, a childlike wonder at man's inhumanity to man, runs like a thread through her book *Notes from My Travels,* published in October 2003, describing her visits to refugee camps in Africa, Cambodia, Pakistan, and Ecuador. In the 256-page paperback she paints a vivid and at times moving portrait of the lives of the refugees, particularly the children. "I wanted to take each and every one home with me," she wrote during a visit to a transit center in Africa. As well-meaning and eye-opening as her book was, it was still, as academic Jaimie Lee-Barron pointed out, rooted firmly in a traditional genre of travel writing in which the impoverished Third World is defined and described through the prism of the wealthy West, in this case a multimillionaire movie star.

With visits to refugees in Jordan and Egypt in December, Angie showed that she was not content to rest on her laurels, her goodwill missions invariably accompanied by large personal donations. During her visit to the SOS Children's Village in Amman, Jordan, she "adopted" a house of three girls and four boys, paying for their food, clothing, and education.

While she was happy to embrace the family of the world, this did not extend to her own father, who was reduced to congratulating her on her book through the media. Always dapper and outwardly cheerful, Jon Voight seemed to be covered in a cloud of brooding loneliness. He was often seen out and about in Hollywood; a regular at the Beverly Glen Deli, shopping in the Century City mall, and browsing through Book Soup on Sunset, looking for books for his friend singer Diana Ross, but always he was alone. His only consolation came from the tabloid magazines he once scorned. Now he read them avidly, searching for snippets about his daughter and grandson. He would become so overwrought reading these stories that at Prida, his regular hair salon, they hid these tabloids when he was coming in. There was a central emptiness in his life, a cheerless existence painfully exposed in a televised conversation with William Shatner in which he admitted that when he came home there was no one to greet him, turn on the lights, and make him feel welcome.

For a man who loved the idea of family—"I've stayed in touch with almost everybody I have worked with," he says—the estrangement from all those he loved and from the grandchild he had yet to meet was a constant torment. "There is a loneliness in my life," he later admitted to writer Tanith Carey. At Christmastime there was little to cheer about. Without his children, he no longer felt that life was worth living or had much meaning for him. Such was his anguish that, even though he was a lapsed Catholic, he contacted a priest in a desperate cry for help. It was clear that he wanted a reconciliation of sorts with Marcheline and, in some way, to reconstitute the family he had lost. The priest in turn spoke to Marche about her ex-husband's emotional state of mind. His ex-wife, then in remission from her cancer and in a loving relationship with John Trudell, was in no mood to offer Christmas cheer. The freeze was still on, forgiveness in short supply at the Bertrand inn.

Instead she asked Lutheran pastor Ken Anderson, the father of James's girlfriend, Rachel, to speak to her former husband. They met for dinner at a seafood restaurant in Hollywood, where Jon Voight poured his heart out, talking of his regrets about the past and his desire to have at least a sense of family. He felt his loneliness was literally killing him. They arranged to meet again in a restaurant in Santa Monica, this time Pastor Anderson's wife, Rosie, joining them, her jokes about what she called his "snake documentary"—the film *Anaconda*—helping to lighten the mood. As much as Jon Voight had been the heavy-handed father, always trying to run the lives of his wife and children, he cut a sad and somewhat pathetic figure. For all the achievements in his career he had lost what he held most dear: the love and respect of his children.

A few months later Angie was using the revolving doors to enter the Dorchester hotel in London when she spotted her father standing alone in the lobby. She continued to revolve, spilled out into the street, and quickly crossed town, where she checked into Claridge's. Her luggage came later. It was a metaphor of sorts, the UN ambassador spinning frantically around the globe, full of goodwill for the faceless and nameless but with none for her father.

THIRTEEN

Angie's personality type . . . doesn't present as crazy but as fabulous. She appears independent, rebellious, has got her shit together. That's her image. That's the persona she projected to hook him [Brad].

—A MEMBER OF BRAD PITT AND JENNIFER ANISTON'S CIRCLE

Of course she should have seen it coming. The moment Angelina Jolie unexpectedly arrived on the lot of *Friends*, Jennifer Aniston should have been on red alert. As Angie shook her hand, Jennifer could have been excused for wondering whether she was extending her long slim fingers in friendship or sizing up her next victim, like a hangman judging the length of rope needed for the drop. "Brad is so excited about working with you. I hope you guys have a really good time," Aniston recalls telling her.

If the memories of Laura Dern's tearstained face had faded, Aniston's friend Courteney Cox, who played Monica on the show, would have been quick to remind Jennifer of what Angelina Jolie could do. After all, when Billy Bob Thornton ditched his fiancée for Angie, Cox was one of the posse who raided his mansion one night to pick up her possessions. Not surprisingly, the Hollywood coterie around Dern viewed Angie with suspicion. "They gave her a lot of shade, a lot," recalls a onetime girlfriend of Angie's.

Then there were the warnings from Faye, the Iranian psychic whose advice guided the decisions of such Hollywood celebrities as Tamara Mellon, Kate Hudson, Goldie Hawn, and Jennifer. Jennifer would even consult her about whether to do a magazine interview. During their regular sessions, held in an anonymous Beverly Hills office building, Faye read the runes and felt the future. She didn't like what she saw, telling Jennifer that Angie was a "dark angel." In time Faye would no longer accept Brad Pitt as a client, the soothsayer smiling bleakly when acquaintances joked that she was the one woman in the world who had turned down Brad Pitt.

If those storm signals weren't enough, Jennifer knew full well that Angie put the "M" in Method acting; the part took over the personality. Such absorption had won her an Oscar. So the clue was in the title: *Mr. & Mrs. Smith*. Director Doug Liman wanted chemistry between his leading man and lady, with sexual sparks flying on-screen. If they caused a fire off set, who cared? He had it in the can.

Of course, Jennifer didn't see it that way. She could see that her husband was not that invested in the movie. He had previously pulled out of the troubled shoot when Nicole Kidman, who was originally scheduled to play the role, had other commitments, ironically to the movie *The Stepford Wives,* the dark tale of women who were slaves to their men. It meant that when the much-delayed shoot started in late November 2003, Brad would be in and out, filming intensely before going on to make *Ocean's Twelve* with his friend George Clooney.

After all, filming was in Los Angeles, just down the road from their Malibu home. What could go wrong? Jennifer could visit him on set, and he could come home some nights, and, besides, he was being paid $20 million for less than six months' work. For a time it did seem that the golden couple were indeed keeping romance alive. While Aniston was kept away from the set, "she'd send over little food things that she made for Brad's dinner," says a crew member. For his part, Pitt would occasionally request that his wife run an errand and then surprise her by arranging to have an old friend meet her.

What Jennifer didn't know was that Brad was one of the triumvirate of men—the other two were Johnny Depp and Willem Dafoe—whom Angie had watched and wondered about from afar. Thanks to her dad, she had already been introduced to Willem Dafoe, but had yet to meet Johnny Depp. As for Brad, he was the one Hollywood star she had seemed particularly curious about, asking those who had worked with him, "What is he like?"

Now she had the chance to find out for herself. When she got the rather desperate phone call from director Doug Limon while she was in London promoting *Lara Croft* redux, it seemed like fate. So many had fallen— Nicole Kidman, Cate Blanchett, and Catherine Zeta-Jones—but it was

Angie who was chosen. As scriptwriter Simon Kinberg later reflected, with hindsight Angie was the perfect choice to play one half of a pair of married assassins who discover that their next assignment is to kill each other: "You put a gun in her hand and you don't have to explain it. You believe that if she gets into a fistfight with Brad, she could handle herself."

Their first scene together, shot in November 2003 after the movie had been on the back burner so long it was in danger of turning into mush, is now a piece of Hollywood history. It was when, as they both later admitted after much denial and prevarication, they began to fall in love with each other. When their characters sat down for marriage counseling in the opening scene, it was pretty much the first time the two actors had laid eyes on each other. No rehearsal, no second thoughts, just two people who were awkward and cold and snarly—alive in the way of unhappy couples, or those struggling to cope with a visceral chemical reaction. Doug Liman knew he was taking a risk but gambled that their discomfort could lead to the kind of Hollywood alchemy film directors dream of.

"It was going to be rolling the dice," recalls Liman. "I decided I would take advantage of the awkwardness. They don't really know each other. They're not comfortable. Just sit them down, day one, first thing in the morning, and roll the camera. You can see right then and there, they had great chemistry."

The frisson between them continued. Just as in the early days Jonny Lee Miller and Angie competed to see who could Rollerblade fastest for their roles in *Hackers*, Brad and Angie went through a similar bonding routine for *Mr. & Mrs. Smith*—except with guns and live ammo. "We would go to rifle ranges and actually compete with each other," Angie later revealed. She preferred a pump-action shotgun, he a semiautomatic, the couple learning how to use their weapons as they made their way through obstacle courses, shooting at moving targets. "It made us trust each other quickly," she told *Vanity Fair*.

Even though Pitt had long been a target of her curiosity, he was an odd choice for Angelina. There is nothing especially dark, brooding, or wildly artistic about him. Quite the opposite; he would rather have a Bud than a blood vial. Even at thirty-nine, he was still a Hollywood pretty boy, a two-time winner of *People* magazine's "sexiest man alive" title, and half of a Hollywood golden couple. While Angie was undertaking missions for the

UN, he had a reputation for swilling beer, going for motorbike rides, and smoking dope. He was, as several actors who have worked with him attest, "a bit of a stoner," with a minor conviction for dropping his trousers and "mooning" a passerby in Santa Monica while under the influence.

In essence, Pitt was a corn-fed boy from the Midwest, the eldest of three children whose God-fearing parents, Jane and Bill, worked hard and prayed harder; they are still together after nearly fifty years of marriage. During his childhood in Springfield, Missouri, Brad grew up untroubled and unmarked: He was the class president, a sports hero, a drama king, and an all-around good guy, the most popular kid in school. If Angie was raised in Dysfunction Junction, Brad lived at the corner of Normal and Decent.

Like Angie, however, he suffered, as he admitted later, a "congenital sadness," always looking out, wanting and needing more but not quite able to put his finger on what "more" was. "The state of the world, the state of yourself, I don't know," he once said. Even his good looks troubled him; he was painfully aware that he got by as much on his profile as his personality. It was a topic he broached at length with his mother. The focus of this teenage angst was his church, and he eventually rejected the tenets of his Baptist faith. "It was a relief in a way that I didn't have to believe that anymore, but then I felt alone. It was this thing I was dependent on." His arguments must have carried weight inside the family. Months later they followed suit, now worshipping in a nondenominational church.

After studying journalism and advertising at the University of Missouri, he dropped out and headed for Hollywood, taking on a series of menial jobs, including dressing as a chicken, before landing a tiny role in *Thelma and Louise,* where he flashed his killer smile and showed his tight butt—and Geena Davis a good time. A million women around the world trembled at his beautifully masculine screen presence, and Brad Pitt became *Brad Pitt.* For his next major venture, *A River Runs Through It,* directed and narrated by Robert Redford, he effectively played himself: a handsome, adventurous, feckless, and doomed little brother in a family that loves him even if they don't quite understand him. School pal Chris Shudy called him after watching the epic and told him: "You're not even acting; it's just your home unit minus Julie [his younger sister]." While his career choices have deliberately taken him down the ensemble rather than the leading man route, his choice of lovers has placed him firmly on the Hollywood A-list. Like Angie, he has often said he falls in love with his leading ladies, who have included Juliette Lewis, who starred with him in *Kalifornia,* and Gwyneth Paltrow, who played his doomed wife in the macabre thriller *Se7en.* He was, though, insecure enough to veto the choice of an actor in one of his movies because he had dated Lewis after Brad, but you'd never guess it from the easy manner and megawatt smile.

Everyone bought into Brad as Mr. Cool and Mr. Charming, the perfect catch. A *Vogue* magazine cover story described Gwyneth Paltrow as the "luckiest girl alive" not just because of her talent and breeding but because of her boyfriend. They seemed the ideal Hollywood couple, Paltrow turning down the lead role in *The Avengers* so she could spend time with her fiancé on the set of *Seven Years in Tibet,* then filming in Argentina.

Hollywood gold quickly turned to pewter, Pitt abruptly ending their six-month engagement. Paltrow was left devastated and confused. There was, behind the "Aw, shucks, ma'am" persona, a streak of cold-eyed cruelty, or should that be calculation, in the corn-fed boy. As a mutual friend, a writer, explained at the time: "I think Brad Pitt has done Gwyneth Paltrow a real favor. It may not feel that way to Gwyneth now because the wound is new and raw. It's much easier to be broken up about something at twenty-three than it is to be broken up over a failed relationship at thirty-six with a bunch of kids in the picture." It was a prescient comment.

Looking back, Gwyneth now acknowledges that they had an unhealthy relationship, her emotional neediness first attracting and then repelling Brad, who morphed from caregiver to "couldn't care less." Instead the luckiest girl alive was Jennifer Aniston, who met Brad in 1998 on a blind date set up by their agents while she was licking her wounds after the end of her two-year live-in relationship with actor Tate Donovan. After an eighteen-month courtship, Pitt and Aniston married in a million-dollar wedding, complete with two hundred guests, fifty thousand flowers, four bands, and a gospel choir, in Malibu on July 29, 2000. It was a piece of terrific casting, he the handsome movie star, she America's favorite *Friend,* the gorgeous and funny girl next door. During the ceremony, Jennifer vowed to make Brad's favorite banana milk shake and Brad promised to find a balance on the thermostat. So far, so funny.

There was, though, one significant and deliberate omission from the jaunty celebrations: Jennifer's mother, Nancy Aniston, a clear sign that

Aniston, like Angie, owned real estate at Dysfunction Junction. Beneath the cute comic timing and the winning smile was an insecure, fragile young woman whose damage initially appealed to the dashing heroic protector in Brad. Abandonment underscored Jennifer's early life; she was just nine when her seventeen-year-old half brother took off for California and then, more devastatingly, her father, actor John Aniston, packed his bags and walked out the door of their Upper West Side apartment in New York. As Jennifer tells it, she came home from a birthday party to find the empty hangers in his closet, and didn't see Daddy for a year. Sensitive and anxious, Jen blamed herself for the split, believing she "wasn't a good enough kid." After a year's absence, she occasionally saw her father again, but by then, she "found it incredibly difficult," and her childhood memories "are mainly about just going from place to place, and taking care of adults."

She soothed herself by splitting off from harsh reality and throwing herself into the world of make-believe, winning a place at New York's so-called *Fame* school, the High School of Performing Arts. Hers is a familiar psychological journey. As James Lipton, the host of *Inside the Actors Studio*, never tires of reminding his audience, most actors come from broken homes. It gave her a brittle outer shell, grit, drive, street smarts, and, most important, talent that balanced her soft, needy center.

Nancy Aniston was bitter about her marriage breakup, codependent and needy to the point where Jennifer often felt that she was playing mother. When Nancy appeared on a TV show in 1996 and talked volubly about her now famous daughter, Jennifer considered her performance a betrayal too far. Not as far as her mother was concerned; three years later Nancy penned a self-serving memoir, *From Mother and Daughter to Friends,* that described her daughter as fearful, tremulous, and insecure, even as a baby. Just as Jon Voight and his daughter worked out their problems in the public arena, so, too, did Jennifer and her mother. It is the way of Hollywood.

Shortly after their lavish Malibu wedding, the world, or at least the world of celebrity-watching, was anxious to know when the golden couple would start a family. In this dreamy scenario, Jennifer seemed to be the perfect future mom, Brad describing her as being all about home, friends, and family. In spite of her difficult family background, she has a close circle of friends, several, like actress Andrea Bendewald, dating back to high school. "We all kind of crowd around her like moths to the flame," said Brad. "She's like a magnet; she brings a lot of people together that way. Jen's the fireplace; she provides the warmth."

The baby they lavished most attention on was the mansion designed by Wallace Neff in the 1930s for the character actor Fredric March, which they bought for $13.5 million in 2001. Though the house was move-in perfect, Brad, who has a passion for architecture, threw himself into renovating it, the couple gutting the ten-thousand-square-foot property. How to bring up baby exposed their differences—Brad austere and modernist, choosing hard edges and tough materials, Jennifer opting for comfy, shabby-chic, and homey living, what Brad called "grandma stuff." While he won the style war, at least she ensured that there was a nursery in their modernist mansion. Shortly before they moved in during the fall of 2003, Jennifer made nervous jokes about baby-proofing the stone floors and the unforgiving furniture he had chosen. As far as he was concerned, any offspring would have to learn to live with hard edges. "I have a different theory: you gotta fall down; you gotta learn," he said. If that didn't work, sell and move on. As a friend of the couple's observed some time later: "When Brad and Jen were in the marriage, having a baby was not his priority—ever. It was an abstract desire for him, whereas for Jen it was much more immediate." To some extent the house symbolized their marriage, all hard edges and soft center.

Similarly, their behavior at the premiere of her independent film *The Good Girl* at the Sundance Film Festival in January 2002 was a cameo in contrasts. While he joined his pals in whooping and hollering at the screen, she clung to him throughout, needy and clearly ill at ease. "She is incredibly insecure, run by abandonment issues, and cannot hold on to a guy because she engulfs them and they run for the hills," observed a psychologist who has met with Jennifer socially.

While their house reflected their emotional dynamic, their second offspring, Plan B Entertainment, displayed their joint ambition, the company coming into being when both actors were at turning points in their lives and careers. Jennifer's ten-year run with *Friends* was nearing its close, while Brad was nudging forty. The question loomed: "What next?" Through the vehicle of their new baby, they optioned some of the most interesting contemporary literature on the market, including *A Mighty Heart* by Mariane Pearl, the wrenching memoir of the abduction and subsequent beheading of her husband, Daniel, a *Wall Street Journal* correspondent, by Islamic extremists in Pakistan while he was investigating the background of the so-called shoe bomber. While Brad subsequently met and discussed the project with Pearl's widow, taking her to a U2 concert and dinner, it was Jennifer who harbored quiet dreams of playing the role of Mariane, who was pregnant when her husband was kidnapped. "I would love to think I could," she told *Vanity Fair* rather diffidently. Certainly the comedic actress who could raise a laugh with an arched eyebrow had her eyes on meatier material.

For Brad's fortieth birthday, on December 18, 2003, the meat was provided by celebrity chef Jamie Oliver, whom Jennifer had flown in from London along with his wife, Jools, to prepare a celebration dinner for a prince of Hollywood. The birthday boy, who had taken time off from the set of *Mr. & Mrs. Smith* to shoot a couple of final scenes for *Troy,* his sand and sandals blockbuster, was hardly effusive over his surprise party. Brad had considered buying a Rolls-Royce when he turned forty—then he got into energy conservation. "So I had a quiet dinner with my friends and my wife. It was a nice little dinner at home." It seems, however, that Brad, who had promised, "There's a midlife crisis on the way" was no longer into nice. "I'm sure there's some more rude awakenings yet to come," he said prophetically. "But I like it like that. I like the unknown. It's just more vibrant that way. It's fucking interesting, isn't it?"

What could be more vibrant than outgunning, outrunning, and outplaying the delectable Ms. Jolie? No more Mr. Nice Guy indeed. Angie was an intoxicating blend of sex siren, political activist, and yummy mummy. Of course the impish Maddox, with his helicopter necklace and ankle bracelets, was a constant presence, running around the set. He was the bait and the alibi. "They often relaxed on a patio that Pitt set up outside his trailer," says an actor from the film. "We called it Brad's grotto. Brad and Angelina were often out there while the little boy was playing."

Over the years Brad had done a lot of practice-daddying with his nieces and nephews, inviting the offspring of his brother, Doug, and sister, Julie, for summer vacations at Uncle Brad's beach house, where Aunt Jen would whip up killer barbecue and homemade salsa. During these sleepovers, he happily let his twin nieces paint his fingernails or climb all over him. So playing with Maddox came naturally. Sealing Jennifer's fate, Angie remarked: "I know if I ever saw a man be great with my child, that would be it for me." Not only was he a natural with Maddox, he spoke of his desire to have a large family mixing adopted and biological children. For Angie a light went on. "I ended up falling in love with a man who I think was destined to have children and suddenly one day it felt right and there it was."

During their conversations about family, life, and the whole damn thing, Angie artfully conjured up a different kind of perfect woman for the ever-restless Brad: maternal yet still dangerous, sexy yet a goddess. A woman with a sense of the bigger picture, able to pepper her conversation with references to "Bill," "Kofi," and "Colin." (That's Clinton, Annan, and Powell to mere mortals.) She came across as a strange exotic wanting to save the world's underclass and yet fill her life with children. And there was the gossip on set about her trailer, which was, as crew later noted, reportedly decked out with handcuffs, sex toys, whips, and the constricting paraphernalia of S&M. The corn-fed boy was toast.

"Brad was targeted," observes a psychologist who mingles in the Brad, Angie, and Jennifer circle. "He was bored, sick of Jen's neediness and tired of propping her up. I am sure that as soon as Jennifer heard the name Angelina Jolie she knew to her core that it was over for her and Brad. Angie's personality type is tremendously seductive, even for a professional counselor. They flatter, pay unbelievable attention, indulge your every whim. It is all about the dance. Her personality type doesn't present as crazy but as fabulous. She appears independent, rebellious, has got her shit together. That's her image. That's the persona she projected to hook him."

As she and Billy Bob had, Angie and Brad talked, connected, meant a lot to each other, but it was hands-off because, of course, he was a married man and she would never touch a married man. In interviews her mantra was that she was happy to be single, she had a son to raise, and no man would enter her life as a partner unless he deserved to be a father to such an extraordinary child. That she had a "bench" of lovers ready to discreetly bed her in anonymous hotels merely added to the allure. Those close to her insist that it was Brad who did the pursuing, not Angie. "He's not my type" was her refrain.

Perhaps the first sign, maybe the beginning of the end, came on January 23, when Brad found himself "too busy" to attend the last taping of *Friends,* the show that had been Jennifer's passport not only to international fame but also to a close and affectionate family. "I'm just hoping I get through that night," she told Diane Sawyer, cheerfully admitting that she cried every time she thought about The End. Knowing how upset Jennifer was and how much the show meant to her, friends and fellow cast members were amazed by Brad's no-show. "Busy working" was Jennifer's supportive if rather wan explanation. In fact, he was a thirty-dollar cab ride away on the set of *Mr. & Mrs. Smith* while she sniffled and sobbed her way through the final show, which was watched by fifty million fans on May 6. The breakup of her showbiz family brought back unhappy childhood memories. "That was really painful. It was a family, and I don't do great with families splitting up," said Aniston. "It was hard to have such a wonderful constant in your life, a place to go every day, and then all of a sudden it's not there."

As for Brad, she later recalled: "He just wasn't there for me," not just physically but emotionally. On Valentine's Day she was at the Berlin premiere of her movie *Along Came Polly.* He was working. At the Night Before the Oscars party on February 28, Jennifer was with her pals from *Friends.* He was working. A pattern was developing, which became public in April, almost five months into the protracted *Mr. & Mrs. Smith* shoot. The electricity and chemistry between Angie and Brad that so pleased director Doug Liman was now tabloid fodder, *The Star* claiming that the two were an item, which the couple staunchly denied. "Yeah, they have gotten close because they've been working together but that's it," said Brad's agent, Cindy Guagenti. Her comment reassured no one. As Suzanne Rozdeba, *The Star*'s entertainment editor, observed: "Brad and Angelina have kept it this tight little secret, but it brings more attention to it and people are dying to see this film now. They don't care about the plotline."

In what was to become a familiar routine, when the Brad and Angie rumor mill started churning, Angie got going with her good works, flying to Arizona in late April to visit child refugees who arrived alone in the United States without any legal assistance to guide them through the labyrinthine immigration process. She donated $500,000 to UNHCR to establish a National Legal Resource Center to provide lawyers for these lost, lonely, and frightened youngsters.

Her visit dovetailed nicely with a break in filming, Brad fulfilling his obligations to appear in *Ocean's Twelve* and to promote *Troy,* his first blockbuster movie. As the supportive wife, Jennifer was by his side on the red carpet at the premiere in New York and at the Cannes Film Festival in May. Angie was not far away, traveling to the French resort to promote the cartoon *Shark Tale,* in which she was the voice for—what else?—a sexy vixen fish. She was also there to help her brother, James, drum up support for *Breaking Dawn,* in which he had his first starring role, as a psychotic locked away in a mental institution. The idea for the low-budget thriller had come to director Mark Edwin Robinson after he listened to his father conduct interviews with the criminally insane at Patton State Hospital in San Bernardino, California. James spoke about his father's reaction to his first leading role: "I was notified that he said my performance was a masterpiece," he said. "To get that approval gives me a sense of peace. It's what I've always wanted to hear and never thought I would get." What was remarkable was that Jon Voight had even been able to see the movie; the $540,000 yarn was never distributed or critically reviewed.

In spite of parental enthusiasm, there was still no move toward a rapprochement, though Angie did make her peace with her second husband that summer, Billy Bob calling her to tell her that he was going to be a father again—his partner, Connie Angland, gave birth to a baby girl, Bella, in September. During their conversation they healed many of the wounds surrounding their abrupt breakup. That he had another child did show that he was, contrary to Angie's complaint, not averse to having children. More than that, they have remained friends. Billy Bob is always supportive when he speaks of her.

While Brad and Jennifer went through a marital ordeal by flashbulb at various European premieres of *Troy,* Angie was playing it cool. Almost too cool. Considering that this was the same girl whose frenzied search for an absent Billy Bob had ended in a mental hospital, it was interesting that she was always somewhere else when the media detectives were hot on the trail of Brad and Angie. While neither would ever admit it, it was almost as if Angie and Brad had worked out some kind of pact during those long, soulful tête-à-têtes on the set of *Mr. & Mrs. Smith.*

Jennifer had time on her hands now that *Friends* had ended, joining Brad in Rome during July for the *Ocean's Twelve* shoot. The couple was seen canoodling in the city of love, sharing ice cream and sweet talk. There were rumors that they were buying a vacation home on Lake Como near their pal George Clooney and speculation that they might move to London.

Even though Brad and Jen were clearly together and publicly affectionate, Angie simply sailed through the speculation, traveling the globe on behalf of the UNHCR, to Spain in June for World Refugee Day and later to the border between Chad and Sudan, where 160,000 refugees had fled the fighting in Darfur. In July she accepted honorary Cambodian citizenship, celebrating this signal honor by flying to her son's country to meet with tattooist Sompong Kanphai, who engraved a twelve-inch roaring tiger on her back.

Like her father, however, Angie was in danger of losing sight of what had propelled her to prominence in the first place and given her continued entrée into this club of world leaders—her acting ability. Even though she now liked to downplay her career, a salutary commentary in the influential *Empire* movie magazine may have given her—or her agent—pause. Critics were already preparing her box-office obituary, saying that since *Girl, Interrupted,* her movies had hardly set the world alight. "Among industry pundits dire warnings have been issued that if she doesn't have a major hit pronto the sweet glow of her 2000 Oscar win could be snuffed out and her exalted position as one of the highest paid actresses in Hollywood become a thing of the past." As far as pundits were concerned, she had not lived up to the crushing weight of expectations, her movie releases running the gamut from disappointing to outright disaster. Much, then, rested on the box-office success of *Mr. & Mrs. Smith.*

When filming restarted in August in Los Angeles and Italy, the studio was keen to emphasize the movie rather than the now-notorious real-life romantic subplot. Though paparazzi snapped pictures of Angie and Brad looking smitten, the publicity machinery tried to squelch the persistent rumors of an affair by saying they were simply acting in character. When filming moved to the Amalfi coast in Italy in October, the two were inseparable. Though they were in separate suites at the Hotel Santa Caterina, they ordered room service and dined together on Angie's terrace in between playing with Maddox. In Ravello, Angie surprised onlookers with her "utterly flirtatious" behavior, never walking past Brad without touching him or giving him a sultry look. Not surprisingly, alone in the couple's modernist mausoleum in Hollywood, Jen was said to be miserable, increasingly insecure and scattered.

Brad had little time—or possibly inclination—to soothe her. No sooner

Angie sent this striking Polaroid shot of herself in a cowboy hat and a wide-brimmed smile to her father as a Christmas card. It was a light-hearted moment during a photo shoot when she was having the name of her lover and future husband, Billy Bob Thornton, tattooed way below her bikini line. *Author's collection*

Angie was a regular visitor to Franklin Meyer's salon in the Chelsea Hotel. Here, her hair cropped short for *Gia,* she poses with a necklace of gold leaf and glass, which a record company executive traded for drugs. *Franklin Meyer*

Angie in 1998 at the Golden Globes, where she won her first-ever award, for her performance in *George Wallace.* During the course of the evening she shared a shower with *Titanic* star Leonardo DiCaprio, but he didn't float her boat. While she gained a trophy, she managed to lose a pair of diamond earrings that had been loaned to her.

Peter C. Borsari

While Angie was "married but dating," Jonny Lee Miller was regularly by her side. Even after they separated and divorced, the couple remained great friends. He was with her when she won the Golden Globe in January 1999 for her performance in *Gia*.

Jim Smeal/WireImage/ Getty Images

Before she won her Golden Globe for *Gia,* Angie promised to jump in the hotel pool afterward. She was as good as her word, after changing out of her silver Randolph Duke gown into a body suit. She was joined by her manager, Geyer Kosinski, Jonny Lee Miller, and James Haven. Then she pulled TV producer Jeremy Louwerse into the pool, where he managed to conduct an interview while chest-deep in water.

Chuck Ozeas

After weeks of nagging, tattoo artist Friday Jones finally agreed to Angie's request to have the name of her lover, Billy Bob Thornton, tattooed beneath her bikini line. Friday thought she would live to regret it. During the session, on October 6, 1999, an amateur photographer friend took a series of erotic Polaroids, the actress lying back languidly or indulging in mild bondage with tape as her tattoo artist worked. Angie says: "Usually all my tattoos came at a good time. A tattoo is something permanent, when you've made a self-discovery or something you've come to a conclusion about." *Author's collection*

When Angie won an Oscar for *Girl, Interrupted* in March 2000, it was her swooping, open-mouthed kiss with her brother that had the Hollywood crowd gasping for breath. While talk of incest was in the air, James Haven knew that his sister was wildly in love with Billy Bob Thornton, whom she saw later that night. Nonetheless, Haven, who was trying to kick-start an acting career, was forever tainted by that moment.
Gary Boas/Retna Ltd./Corbis UK Ltd.

"Hey, Angie, give us a little of that Billy Bob action," yelled photographers as the actor and his bride of four weeks smooched their way down the red carpet for the premiere of *Gone in Sixty Seconds* in June 2000. The couple gained instant notoriety not only for their revelations about their wild sex life but for wearing his-and-her blood vial necklaces.
Frank Trapper/Corbis UK Ltd.

Angelina and her mother, who was diagnosed with cancer in 1999, in Santa Monica a couple of days after Angie's second marriage in May 2000. Within days, Angie was on her way to London, where she starred as adventuress Lara Croft. Every day, wherever she was in the world, Angie phoned her mother, who was also her manager until she became too ill to continue. *Lucky Mat Corp./Getty Images*

Angie and her father at a press conference in 2001 to promote *Lara Croft,* in which Jon Voight played her father. It was a profound experience for both of them, though Angie complained later that he soon reverted back to his habit of being judgmental about her behavior. Angie displays a loving wariness toward her father, in contrast to her relaxed demeanor with her mother. *All Action General/ Press Association Images*

In Angie's eyes, Maddox, the Cambodian orphan she adopted in 2002, was the one man in her life who never let her down. His arrival changed everything, the catalyst that ended her brief marriage to Billy Bob Thornton and the missing link in her life that imbued her with an inner calm she had never felt before.
Author's collection

In order to honor Maddox's presence in her life, Angie flew to Bangkok for a tattoo engraved by tattoo master Sompong Kanphai. In July 2004 she had a second engraving on her back, a tattoo of a roaring dragon in celebration of being made an honorary citizen of Cambodia, Maddox's homeland. *AFP/Getty Images*

With his tongue out at photographers, Maddox seems to express how Angie feels inside. He was her surrogate, used to explain many of her actions and decisions. For example, before adopting Zahara, she said that Maddox had been "asking for an African brother or sister," and she opened her heart to Brad Pitt only after Maddox, after giving him the once-over, called him "Dad."

Matt Cardy/Getty Images

With three-year-old Maddox in her arms, Angie, as the UN Goodwill Ambassador for refugees, meets a patient at the Children's Cancer Center of Lebanon on Christmas Day 2004. Her work for the UN was inspired by the poverty she witnessed in Cambodia during the filming of *Lara Croft*, as well as by a subsequent visit to Africa.

Mahmoud Tawil/AFP/Getty Images

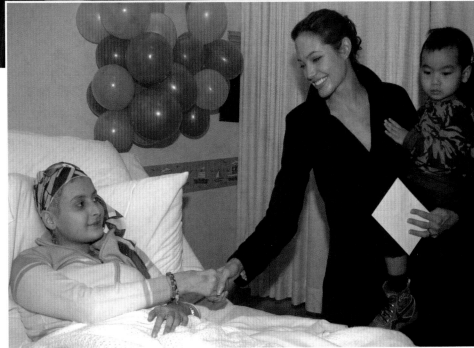

Angie takes a break from filming the second Lara Croft movie to attend a mines clearance and awareness day in northern England in October 2002. The year before, she had been asked to detonate a landmine with dynamite during a UN-sponsored visit to Cambodia. "It was a great feeling to destroy something that would have otherwise hurt or possibly killed another person," she said.

Jim Duxbury/Rex Features

Angie has always envied what she calls "the other girl," the wholesome blonde, the good girl, the girl next door, feeling that she was very different from these women. So her pleasure at being accepted by an august body like the United Nations and meeting with world leaders such as Secretary of State Colin Powell was all the sweeter. Here she is about to speak at the launch of World Refugee Day in Washington, D.C., in June 2004.

Mannie Garcia/Reuters/Corbis UK Ltd.

Angie has earned wide respect not only for speaking out on difficult issues but also for putting her money where her mouth is, donating approximately a third of her income to deserving causes. At a press conference in Islamabad, Pakistan, in May 2005, she spoke passionately about the plight of Afghan refugees who had been forced to flee their homeland and were living in temporary camps in northern Pakistan. *Anjum Naveed/ Associated Press/Press Association Images*

During a six-day visit to Tanzania in April 2003, Angie joined with children, orphaned by the fighting in neighboring Congo, who were traveling to a refugee camp for around 85,000 people. Saddened and visibly upset by what she saw and heard, she found time to play a game with youngsters under the Right to Play program. Later she donated $50,000 to a local orphanage. Abandoned and orphaned children touch her heart, striking a chord with the alienation she often feels about herself and her place in the world. *ABACA/Press Association Images*

The stance is awkward, the distance deliberate. Just two months after Brad Pitt announced his separation from Jennifer Aniston in January 2005, he and Angie, the woman believed to be the spoke in the marital wheel, appeared at a luncheon in Los Angeles to publicize *Mr. & Mrs. Smith,* the drama that first brought them together. They continued to give the impression that they were just good friends for some months afterward. *WireImage/ Getty Images*

Angie, pregnant with her first biological child, and Brad join the great and the good, including UN Secretary General Kofi Annan, left, at the World Economic Forum in Davos in January 2006. During their relationship the couple has been able to straddle the gap between tabloid tittle-tattle and high-minded public policy. *Fabrice Coffrini/AFP/Getty Images*

Relaxed and intimate, Angie and Brad enjoy a quiet drink in a Prague restaurant in May 2007 during a break in filming for the thriller *Wanted,* in which she played an assassin training the son of a fellow assassin in the profession's deadly arts. It was a break, too, from their growing family—and the ever-present paparazzi. *David Altman/Getty Images*

A brand, a corporation, and a charity powerhouse, Brad and Angie are considered one of the most influential couples on the planet. Restless, competitive, and volatile, they endeavor to juggle a family of six children, film careers, and a smorgasbord of charitable works. At the London premiere of *Beowulf* in November 2007, their union is neatly captured by photographer Rune Hellestad. *Rune Hellestad/Corbis UK Ltd.*

A star is born. Maddox shows off his sunglasses during a visit to Central Park, in New York City, while Angie shows off her second adopted child, Ethiopian-born Zahara, known as Zee. Each child has a nanny who speaks his or her native tongue, though inside Château Jolie-Pitt the *lingua franca* is French. *James Devaney/WireImage/ Getty Images*

Angie, out shopping with Shiloh and Zahara at a New York art shop, always wanted to adopt. She emulated dancer Josephine Baker, who famously had a rainbow family of twelve children who lived with her in a French château.

Abaca USA Street/
Press Association Images

When she was younger, Angie complained about endlessly moving around to different apartments. Actually she lived most of her young life on the same street, whereas her nomadic tribe of six children is fortunate to spend a week in one place, the couple determined to take the children along as they frenetically jet from red carpet premiere to refugee camp and film shoot. Here they are at the Chiba airport in Japan in January 2009, taking what Brad calls "the platoon" home to Los Angeles.

Masatoshi Okauchi/Rex Features

When she was a teenage goth, Angie had a crush on Johnny Depp, who starred in the cult movie *Edward Scissorhands*, about a weird outsider with scissors for hands. In *The Tourist*, shot in Paris and Venice in the spring of 2010, Angie had the chance to play alongside her idol. These days Angie is very much an insider, though still intriguing. The pose is reminiscent of Audrey Hepburn, but Angelina Jolie is unmistakably herself. *Lorenzo Santini/WireImage/Getty Images*

was he back home than he was out the door again. He accepted an invitation from U2 front man Bono to visit Africa and see for himself the poverty and AIDS epidemic sweeping the continent. It was a very high-powered introduction, Brad flying to South Africa with Virgin boss Richard Branson and visiting former South African president Nelson Mandela before moving on to Ethiopia, where he met orphans and AIDS victims, seeing the problems faced by some of the poorest nations on earth. However high-minded his intentions may have been, the media concluded that he was interested in these issues only because of his involvement with Angie.

While Brad was playing soccer in a dirt field with Ethiopian youngsters, Angie was back arm in arm with the other two men in her life, Oliver Stone and Colin Farrell. When *Alexander* was released in November 2004, the improbable screen mother and son toured talk shows in America and Europe promoting the $155 million blockbuster, which for all their efforts was a box-office flop, earning only $34 million in America. On November 16 Angie attended the Hollywood premiere with her brother, but this time the speculation was about Jolie and Farrell, the endless "Were they having an affair?" rumors quite enough to keep the gossip mill churning. That night James Haven brought along his fiancée, Rachel Anderson, whom he had met at an independent film festival in San Francisco in December 2002. He had asked her to marry him several months before, sealing their love not with a ring but with a glass slipper, as in her favorite Disney movie, *Cinderella*. On the evening of the premiere, Rachel, who was seated next to Angie, looked radiant in a bright red satin evening gown. Afterward James told her: "You were sitting next to one of the most beautiful women in the world and people only had eyes for you."

It was not surprising, then, that the talk at Thanksgiving dinner in Marche's suite in the Raffles L'Ermitage hotel, where she had moved at Angie's expense, was all about weddings, gowns, and bridesmaids. Not just the impending nuptials of James and Rachel but also of Angie's loyal assistant, Holly Goline. After dinner they all settled down to watch a video of the marriage in May of Holly and her husband, Mark, at Jekyll Island, Georgia, where Angie was bridesmaid and Maddox, who spent most of Thanksgiving dinner hiding under the table, the ring bearer. During the evening John Trudell presented Angie with an animal hide engraved and branded with a variety of Indian signs and symbols as a gesture of thanks for supporting and promoting his eponymous film, *Trudell,* due for release at the Sundance Film Festival in January 2005.

According to James, that dinner was the "best Thanksgiving" he had ever enjoyed. For once there was a real sense of family, nonjudgmental, giving, and loving. It was a special delight to see his sister so happy.

If fate had been different, rather than oohing and aahing over Holly's wedding video, the Thanksgiving party could have been cooing over Angie's second son. She had hoped to adopt again during a visit to Russia earlier in the month, but her plans had gone badly awry. Initially the aim was to adopt a little boy whom Angie had seen during a visit to Baby Home No. 13 in Moscow, an orphanage caring for developmentally challenged youngsters up to the age of four. She had, according to the *Daily Mail,* specifically asked for a "blonde, blue-eyed, Slavic looking boy"—observers noting the similarity in looks to her father and Brad Pitt. Apparently she fixed on a young Russian boy called Gleb.

Political considerations, however, were working against her plan. Her humanitarian visit came at a politically sensitive time. German chancellor Gerhard Schröder had recently adopted a three-year-old boy from St. Petersburg, but only after a personal intervention from Russia's President Putin. The notion that Russia was not able to offer a decent future to its own children was political dynamite. Hence the obstacles to Angie's plan, the head of the orphanage later stating that there was never any question of an adoption.

Clearly Angie had other ideas when she first arrived in Russia. As she later explained: "I was going to adopt this other child in Russia, but it didn't work out, so I may adopt another in about six months. I don't think Maddox is quite ready for a sibling yet." He was apparently ready enough at the start of November when she initiated the process. Maddox often came in handy as a lightning rod to deflect unwelcome scrutiny, Angie suggesting that many of her decisions—about love, about adoption, about her career—depended on the say-so of the three-year-old.

Children were very much on Brad's mind, too. In December, as part of the publicity for *Ocean's Twelve,* he gave a famous interview to Diane Sawyer in which he spoke about his life in the next three years. "Kids. Family. I'm thinking family," he said. Sawyer asked if he still was hoping for daughters, "little Jennifers" as he'd expressed it on previous occasions.

"Yeah," said Brad. "Jen and I, we're working something out." He then said girls might "crush" him and maybe all boys would be better. "Listen, I'll take them all at this point." Given the timing—the couple formally separated four weeks later—there is now the suspicion that he was papering the record to prepare for his separation from the nation's sweetheart. His narrative was that he wanted children, while Jennifer was reluctant, the conversation with Diane Sawyer the opening salvo in what was later seen as a subtle public-relations operation.

It was not that Brad and Jennifer lacked the support of friends and family. Even as the breakup neared, many people close to them held out hope that the marriage would survive. For what was to be their last Christmas together, Pitt's mother, Jane, who is a family counselor, and his sister, Julie, gave Aniston a ring monogrammed in the center with a "P." Afterward the couple headed to Anguilla with their close friends Courteney Cox, her husband, David, and their baby, Coco. New Year's Eve was spent at George's, a restaurant in Cap Juluca, where they met up with Uma Thurman, another woman who could tell Jennifer a thing or two about Angelina Jolie.

Once again above the fray and away from it all, Angie spent Christmas and New Year's with Maddox touring a children's cancer center and a refugee camp in Beirut. By contrast, Brad and Jennifer were photographed on the beach arm in arm on January 6, Brad wearing a T-shirt emblazoned with the word "trash." The next day, January 7, they announced their separation. Angelina was nowhere to be seen, in a different country and a different time zone, doing good works. She had the perfect alibi. They wouldn't find her fingerprints at the scene of this marital crime.

FOURTEEN

*If I find anyone getting a picture of Jolie, I will fucking smash some-
one to pieces. I'm not joking. I'll fucking put someone in the hospital.*

—BODYGUARD MICKEY BRETT

During the fall of 2004, MTV launched a new reality show, *Laguna
Beach,* about the lives of well-to-do, ambitious teenagers living in a
seaside town that had for years been a magnet for artists, writers, and filmmakers. Nothing in the show's plot could have matched what was really
proposed for the resort.

That August James Haven and his fiancée, Rachel Anderson, together
with her father, Ken, a preacher at the Evangelical Lutheran church in Cy-
press, and her mother, Rose, spent the day at Laguna Beach. They weren't
there to soak up the sun and the surf but to size up whether it was a suitable
venue for a wedding.

The original plan was for the couple to take their vows, barefoot on
the sand, as the bloodred sun set over the ocean. Soon enough, James en-
visioned a different scenario, a plan that would set the world on fire. With
his cockpit view of the developing relationship between his sister and Brad
Pitt, he of all people knew how serious they were about each other. Once
Brad was free, he could then formally commit to Angie. So at some point
the idea was born of a double wedding on the beach. After all, Angie had
frequently joked about marrying her brother; now she could stand beside
him as they took their vows—to other people. Certainly marriage was on
her mind, too, Angie admitting at the time that she was an "incurable romantic." "I would love to have a wonderful marriage that will last a very
long time," she told *Grazia* magazine.

There were just a couple of catches. Not only was Brad still married, but, given their celebrity, this simple ceremony would also have attracted a bigger crowd than the Super Bowl. While Brad and Jennifer had managed to keep their Malibu nuptials secure, others were not so fortunate. When Sean Penn married Madonna on a California cliff top he was so incensed by the "chopperazi," the helicopter-borne photographers, that he threatened them with a loaded pistol.

Doubtless James's simple plan would have crumbled to sand once security and safety considerations were factored in, but it does offer a window into the cautious double life Brad and Angie were leading at that time. In public Brad protested loudly that the end of his marriage had nothing to do with Angie, while his screen wife was equally adamant, saying that she would never have an affair with a married man after seeing the suffering caused by her father's adultery. "I have enough lovers; I don't need Brad," she argued.

The reality was that they were quietly planning a life together before Brad and Jennifer took that walk along the beach in Anguilla and announced their separation the following day. As for the Laguna Beach nuptials, they never got much farther than the back-of-a-napkin stage, but that had nothing to do with Brad and Angie. After dipping his toe in marital waters, James got cold feet and called off his engagement in July 2005, though he and Rachel remained friends for several years afterward.

As for Brad and Jen, they played the first weeks of their separation like an episode of *Friends*. Their joint statement left their fans wondering why they had split in the first place, the couple emphasizing that their decision was the result of much thoughtful consideration and had nothing to do with any third party, and that they remained "committed and caring friends with great love and admiration for one another." Although they stayed in their marital home for a time, they warned family and friends not to hope for a reconciliation. As friendly as things seemed—Brad and Jen were each spotted still wearing their wedding rings in January—Brad wasted no time in moving on.

With the ink barely dry on their separation announcement, Brad called his friend photographer Steven Klein and suggested a series of faux family portraits of Angie, him, and some hired child models that would represent the seamy reality behind the smiling image of a happy family. A style shoot like in *W* magazine, the bible of the New York fashion crowd, would really "throw this back at them," Brad argued—"them" being the paparazzi who dogged every move he and Angie made.

Meanwhile, Angie stuck to her own script, filming a documentary in Niger before heading to Davos, Switzerland, in mid-January to speak about refugees and humanitarian issues at the World Economic Forum. She was with world leaders in the Alps when her mother's first effort as a producer, *Trudell*, was screened at the Sundance Film Festival. The documentary, which had taken more than a decade to film and edit, received mixed reviews, seen as sincere but lacking dramatic focus.

In keeping with their "still friends" message, the Pitts threw open their home on February 12 for a birthday bash for Jennifer; guests included Gwen Stefani—now a great pal of Angie's—Gavin Rossdale, and Cindy Crawford. Before the Oscars in March, Mr. and Mrs. Pitt spent time together at industry events, including a party hosted by CAA agent Bryan Lourd at which Gwyneth Paltrow proudly showed off pictures of her baby daughter, Apple, to her former fiancé and his estranged wife.

Babies were on Angie's mind, too. On March 8 she told guests at a Washington Press Club luncheon that Africa was the focus for her next adoption. Once again it all came down to Maddox. "My son's in love with Africa, so he's been asking for an African brother or sister," she explained, describing his pleasure at walking around a market during a recent visit to Ethiopia.

It seems Brad was ready to adopt, too, he and Angie looking through pictures sent by the Wide Horizons for Children adoption agency, which specializes in Ethiopia. Both settled on a little girl, born on January 8, the day after Brad and Jennifer separated. They were told that her mother had died of AIDS and it was unknown if the baby, legally named Tena Adam but called Yemsrach, meaning "good news," by her mother, had also contracted the deadly virus. No matter; they wanted her anyway. As Angie later explained to writer Jonathan Van Meter: "We both had the same fear because she was sick at the time, and we both made the decision that no matter what, we were going to look after her."

While they stealthily planned their own family, Brad and Angie went ahead with his make-believe family a few days later, spending the four-day Easter weekend at a late 1950s condo in Rancho Mirage, where they posed with five little blond "Bradlets" as a dreamy, dysfunctional 1960s family, for pictures that would occupy sixty stunning pages of the June issue of *W* magazine. While the artistic intent could not be faulted, as an act of marital diplomacy it was a dagger to Jennifer's heart. Several months later she accused her ex-husband of missing a "sensitivity chip."

That weekend Jennifer had every right to feel sensitive. It was the date she filed for divorce. The night before she made it official, she visited her psychic, Faye, arriving in cargo pants, with no makeup and her hair pulled back. She looked like any other California girl and attracted little attention. The one jarring note was the distress etched on her freshly scrubbed face. When her lawyer called her the following day, March 25, Good Friday, to confirm that the divorce papers had been filed, she burst into tears and clung to her good friend Courteney Cox, spending the night at Courteney's Malibu home rather than at the empty house Brad had built.

Brad continued to move on. A couple of weeks later, he flew to Ethiopia with *Good Morning America*'s Diane Sawyer to show her the work of Bono's One charity and to talk about his own life for a TV special that would air in June, to coincide with the release of *Mr. & Mrs. Smith*. He explained that his nickname in Ethiopia was "Dabo," meaning "bread," as locals thought he was saying "bread" rather than "Brad" when he first introduced himself. While he talked movingly of the plight of youngsters in the country, the bread and butter of the interview concerned his private life. When Sawyer asked if he would ever adopt an African orphan, the actor was cagey. "I don't know," he said. "I'm certainly open to it. I think it's a beautiful idea. You know, especially meeting these kids firsthand. But at this point, I don't know."

As for Angie as home-wrecker, he kept to the party line, stating that she had had nothing to do with the end of his four-and-a-half-year marriage. Even as he spoke, a private plane was on the runway at Addis Ababa, waiting to fly him to Mombasa in Kenya, where he and Angie had secretly arranged a private rendezvous. It was Angie's idea; several weeks earlier she had instructed her bodyguard Mickey Brett to find a villa hideaway where she and Brad could enjoy a break together. For some reason, he chose the Alfajiri beach resort on Diani Beach on the Kenyan coast, a popular location for European vacationers. With regular international flights from London and other destinations, it was easily reached by the paparazzi.

So it proved. During the four-day break, long-range shots of the couple and Maddox playing on the beach made headlines around the world. It was reminiscent of similar pictures of Angie and Maddox playing alone in a park, taken within days of the split from Billy Bob Thornton, which presented a sympathetic image of Angie, the single mom focusing her attention on her son after the breakup. As *The New York Times* later revealed, those pictures were organized by Team Jolie, the photographer for *Us* magazine told when and where Angie and Maddox would be in the park.

The latest pictures had the hallmarks of a similar operation. Australian paparazzo Darren Lyons, owner of the London-based Big Pictures agency, happened to be in Mombasa when a suspiciously well-informed caller told him to be on the beach at a certain time and he would see something of interest. Right on cue, Angie, Brad, and Maddox appeared, Brad seeming like the perfect father figure, playing in the sand with Mad while keeping his hands off Angie. The visuals were consistent with their public utterances: "We're just good friends." When the pictures were published on April 29, the couple could fulminate about tabloid intrusion while presenting a platonic image, still able to keep everyone guessing about the exact nature of their relationship. Brad later complained to Diane Sawyer that he'd had no clue the pictures were being taken; otherwise he would have organized them himself and given the money—the pictures sold for more than $1 million—to charity. It seemed that Team Jolie and Team Pitt were not yet singing from the same public-relations hymnal.

Unfortunately, the "happy family" image went somewhat awry when security guards raced to their villa one evening thinking that a murder was taking place. One startled guest was quoted as saying: "The noise sounded like a wounded animal, like something being killed." It was, so it was claimed, Brad and Angie engaged in robust nocturnal activity, though even by Angie's high standards of exhibitionism this seems a tad extreme, especially with her bodyguard and Maddox nearby. Whatever the truth of the rather dubious story, it was soon part of the soap opera their lives were rapidly becoming. It was on this vacation that the nickname "Brangelina" was born—out of wedlock and proper syntax, but alive and kicking. How long the infant would last was anyone's guess.

Brad seemed to be in it for the long haul, and the couple was resolute in their message: "Trust us, the truth is what we say it is. Actions don't speak louder than words." In May he stayed with Angie and Maddox at her home in Buckinghamshire, where he joined her on outings to the local supermarket, took Maddox to school, and rode Angie's new motorbike around the grounds. Her bodyguard even arranged for photographer Steve Butler to take some discreet pictures of Brad on the property.

It was a tricky public-relations operation, Brad and Angie leading an increasingly threadbare double life, rather like the characters in their blockbuster. With the premiere of *Mr. & Mrs. Smith* looming in June as a summer "tentpole" release that was supposed to be a huge box-office draw for the studios, nothing could get in the way of focusing the public on the movie rather than the unfolding soap opera. There was even an attempt to coerce journalists to sign a legal agreement preventing them from asking personal questions of the lead actors, but that strategy quickly collapsed.

Studio executives were right to be nervous. They saw what had happened that May, when Tom Cruise jumped on Oprah's couch as he declared his love for Katie Holmes. It had left Steven Spielberg, director of Cruise's latest movie, *War of the Worlds,* pleading: "Talk a little bit about *War of the Worlds* because we're opening real soon." While Angie and Brad may have wanted to shout their love from the sofa tops, they had to keep their feet on the ground. With "Team Jennifer" T-shirts outselling "Team Angie" twenty-five to one, it was imperative that Brad and Angie stick to the script, telling the world that they were just good friends, leaving room for doubt.

There was now no doubt in Jennifer's mind, however, that she had been mistaken in believing her husband's assurances that he had been intrigued by but had not dallied with Angie. The evidence of a happy family beach vacation, a possible adoption, domestic bliss in Buckinghamshire, and an endless sexy spread in *W* even prompted Madame Tussauds waxworks to place Angie and Brad next to each other. The circumspect, forgiving Ms. Aniston finally had to accept the inevitable. What hurt most was not just the beach vacation, but stories that Brad and Angie were thinking of adopting a child.

She was way too late. By now Brad was known as "Dad" by one little boy, Maddox uttering that important word when they were playing cars on a hotel floor. It meant a lot to Angie, a sign that she was doing the right thing, Maddox once again both oracle and guide. "He just out of the blue called him Dad," she recalled. "It was amazing. We both heard it and didn't say anything and just looked at each other. And then we kind of let it go on, and then he just continued to do it and that was it. So that was probably the most defining moment, when he decided that we would all be a family."

A growing family. After fulfilling their publicity obligations for *Mr. & Mrs. Smith,* they flew to Addis Ababa, where, on July 6, 2005, Angie signed the adoption papers for a little girl she named Zahara. Brad was by her side, but as Ethiopia does not allow adoptions by unmarried couples, let alone by unmarried "friends," only Angie's name was on the official papers.

The next step was for the quartet, plus a nanny, to take a private jet to New York, where orphan expert Dr. Jane Aronson checked over Little Miss Jolie. While she was thankfully free of HIV, Zahara was in a fragile state, dehydrated, malnourished, and suffering from rickets. The following day she was admitted to the hospital with a potentially life-threatening case of salmonella poisoning, Angie keeping vigil by her bedside for a week as she slowly recovered. Zahara was not the only sick puppy. Brad, who had flown on to Los Angeles, was so ill that he checked himself into the hospital, suffering from viral meningitis.

On July 15, Zahara was given a clean bill of health and released from the hospital, spending another eight hours traveling to Malibu by private jet. Here she was reunited with her new "father," and settled in to real life with her brother, Maddox, who had thus far seen her only in institutions, first an orphanage and then a hospital where she was on an IV drip. The family bonding experience did not last long. At the end of the month, Angie, who had earned her pilot's license, flew Brad off in her own plane for a romantic weekend in Arizona. Zahara and Maddox, still feeling each other out, were left in the care of nannies. It was a significant weekend; under different circumstances he would have been celebrating his fifth wedding anniversary. Jennifer, meanwhile, spent that time with Brad's mother, Jane, a signal perhaps that Jane was not entirely enamored of her son's behavior.

After the couple returned to Malibu, Angie took Zahara back to New York for a further checkup with Dr. Aronson, who declared the child, now two pounds heavier than when she arrived in America, a "sugarplum": "She has gone from the depression of abandonment [after the death of her birth mother]," the doctor said, "to being completely and unconditionally loved and attached." Then the six-month-old returned to California to join her new brother for his fourth birthday, before taking off again in early August for Long Island, where Angie was shooting Robert De Niro's movie *The Good Shepherd,* a tale of betrayal and double-dealing during the early years of the CIA.

While young Zahara was certainly getting a taste of Angie's peripatetic lifestyle, her mother's movie choice was interesting. She played a woman who traps herself in a loveless marriage after stealing her man, a troubled spy hunter played by Matt Damon, from a deaf woman whom she considers inferior. There were arguably parallels with her behavior toward Jennifer Aniston, in keeping with the theory, articulated by Dustin Hoffman, Billy Bob Thornton, and others, that actors unconsciously choose their roles to reflect their personal journey. The overt appeal of the part was the chance to work with Robert De Niro. It was also, intriguingly, the first time she had acted with Timothy Hutton since their affair and near marriage.

While her role was significant, she was not the star of the film, giving her time to pack up the kids and join Brad in the backwoods of Alberta, Canada, where he was about to spend four months shooting *The Assassination of Jesse James by the Coward Robert Ford.* He was, of course, Jesse, not the coward. After a long prep period, principal photography was halted at the end of August 2005, as it was on *The Good Shepherd,* to allow actors to man the phones in a charity telethon to raise money for the victims of Hurricane Katrina, which devastated New Orleans and left thousands in Louisiana and Mississippi stranded and homeless. While Angie wrote to President Bush and influential congressmen and senators, Brad's involvement took a practical turn as he harnessed his contacts in the world of architecture to design sustainable housing in the worst-hit—and poorest—areas of New Orleans. His Make It Right initiative was eventually responsible for 150 environmentally friendly houses.

The delayed political and economic response to the hurricane was the talk of the inaugural meeting of the Clinton Global Initiative, a gathering of fine minds and original thinkers in New York in mid-September. Brad and Angie, still saying they were just friends, made a low-key appearance at the three-day forum, the couple somewhat self-conscious and deliberately keeping a distance from each other. As worldly as they were trying to become, neither Brad nor Angie was quite prepared for a crowd like this one. While there was a smattering of celebs, including Bono, Angie's former paramour Mick Jagger, and Barbra Streisand, it was a well-informed, high-minded group, focused on policy, not *People*. One former White House veteran recalls seeing Brad "standing in a corner by himself, clearly out of his depth." In general conversation, where he was often unsure of the politicians and countries under discussion, he made the sensible move and kept quiet. Angie, too, who was interested in the discussion on poverty, was scrambling to keep up with these eggheads, even though she had much more experience. Given the couple's record for rolling up their sleeves and pitching in, the verdict may have been a shade patronizing and professorial.

This was the very point made by Dr. Jeffrey Sachs, the youngest-ever professor of economics at Harvard University, a UN advisor on poverty, and an all-around policy wonk. That same week in September, he and Angie promoted their joint TV documentary, *The Diary of Angelina Jolie & Dr. Jeffrey Sachs in Africa,* about their visit to a group of villages in Sauri, western Kenya. Sachs admired Angie's readiness to get her hands dirty. "She waded right in," he said, adding, "She is becoming an incredible leader." Filmed in May 2005, the documentary demonstrated a successful experiment in social engineering, Sachs's so-called Millennium Project attempting to make the region self-sufficient in food, education, and welfare. As with the inauguration of the Clinton Global Initiative, the release of the documentary was timed to coincide with the 2005 World Summit at the United Nations.

Angie willingly used the example of her daughter to publicize the show, her life lesson demonstrating how a little can lead to a lot. Zahara survived, she told *Good Morning America,* while many others did not, going on to say that Maddox was very protective toward her. "They're the greatest little people I've ever met and they give me so much joy and I want to make a better world for them. I'm just grateful every day that I have the chance." Certainly the Angie and Zahara show had the desired effect, generating a spike of interest in adopting from Africa, the four agencies specializing in Ethiopia flooded with requests for information following the interview.

While the world focused on Zee, as Angie called her second adopted child, in September she was nursing a very sensitive secret. She was pregnant with Brad's child, the baby conceived before his divorce became final on October 2. Although that was reason enough to remain discreet, there were other factors, including family history—her mother miscarried her first child—as well as the convention that baby announcements are made only after the first trimester. Besides, she had a film to make and wanted no special favors.

When their filming commitments permitted, the happy couple spent most of their time together in Alberta, Brad hiring a big log cabin in the woods where they enjoyed the kind of privacy and respect from the locals that had been noticeable by their absence throughout their love affair. "Angie was pregnant. It was a very nice time for us," recalled Brad. "We stayed out in the woods by a river. So personally, it was a magical time." Although the paparazzi were kept well away from their backwoods idyll, they did attract unwelcome visitors. One day the couple and their kids were about to enter their cabin after a day's sightseeing—Maddox had enjoyed the local dinosaur exhibit—when they heard banging, shuffling, and grunting from within. Fearing they were being burgled, Angie and the children retreated to their 4×4 while Brad, king of the wild frontier, went to investigate. It was a couple of brown bears, attracted by open windows and the scent of food, playing havoc in the kitchen. Brad called the forest rangers, who, after shooing the bears away, lectured the couple on the need to keep the cabin secure.

These Beverly Hillbillies did, though, impress the locals in other ways, Angie described as "friendly and cordial," as the couple shopped at the local mall, ate in the food court, played on the indoor rides, and did what came naturally—made out in public. One shopper, Rosemary Austen, reported: "Brad and Angelina had a passionate, straight-out-of-the-movies moment when they shared a long kiss. Even though they had the kids in tow, it wasn't just a peck on the cheek. It was just how you'd imagine that couple kissing." They went on long motorbike rides together, stopping off at roadside diners and, when time allowed, spending the night in cheap motels—just as Angie did during the early days with Billy Bob.

There was one looming cloud on their horizon. While Angie and Brad had been told that Zahara was an orphan whose mother had died of AIDS, they learned that in fact the birth mother was alive. After their initial fears that she was going to claim her biological daughter, they discovered that the mother seemed to be pleased that her child had found a good home. Nonetheless, a court had to rule on the legitimacy of their adoption, and in late October Judge Dadnachew Tesfaye declared, much to Angie's relief, that she had done nothing wrong and that Zahara was her legal child.

It was a relief not just for Brad and Angie, but also for Dr. Jane Aronson; Angie, accompanied by her brother, James, was scheduled to be guest of honor at Dr. Aronson's first-ever fund-raiser, in aid of the Worldwide Orphans Foundation. At the New York gala, held in October, Angie announced her partnership with Aronson to build a pediatric AIDS center in Ethiopia. "I personally am not willing to wait any longer for action by the United States or any government while children are suffering and dying," she told the audience.

Now three months pregnant but still keeping the fact a secret, she made a curious admission to *People* magazine: "Most of the night I just thought about how quickly I want to adopt again," she said. "It's a very special thing. There's something about making a choice, waking up and traveling somewhere and finding your family."

It was as if she felt guilty that the baby she was carrying would take the place of a more deserving case. Yet the baby was planned, her mother suggesting that Angie's first biological child should be a Gemini. "She's really into astrology and thought it would be great to have a Gemini like me," Angie told friends. As ill as she was, Marche even suggested the child's name, Shiloh, presumably forgetting to mention that the original idea was Jon Voight's when they spotted a church bus in Georgia saying "Shiloh Baptist" during the making of *Conrack*.

As for Angie, she gave the impression that she wanted a biological baby only out of her love for Brad. Although she seemed dismissive, even neglectful, of her pregnancy, it was a huge leap of faith for Angie: a sign that she was willing to defy the Bertrand family curse of cancer and premature death by bringing a potentially genetically damaged child into the world. More than that, she was defying herself. For anorexics, pregnancy is dangerous, difficult, and emotionally challenging, with a high rate of postpartum depression. If anorexia is about control, then pregnancy confronts that mind-set head-on. Even if Angie's anorexia was greatly improved, she nonetheless would have been reminded of her struggles with body image and feelings of revulsion. For many anorexics, adoption is the recommended path to becoming a mother.

Angie seemed to respond to her pregnancy as she had to other traumas in her life, by disassociating and carrying on as if it weren't happening. Over Thanksgiving, she and Brad flew to Geneva and then to Kashmir in Pakistan to see for themselves the impact of the October earthquake, which had left at least seventy-three thousand dead and hundreds of thousands homeless. Chartering a helicopter to complete the arduous journey, the couple met with people facing a bleak winter in the mountains without adequate shelter.

They returned to their respective film sets, the wardrobe department on *The Good Shepherd* having to let out Angie's clothing in order to disguise her pregnancy. In early December, as shooting of *Jesse James* was about to wrap, Brad announced, to much congratulation, that he was about to become a dad—to Maddox and Zahara. While Angie's pregnancy was literally under wraps, the couple felt secure enough in the health of their unborn child for Brad to forge ahead and make the family whole by adopting. From the sidelines, Angie's father gave their informal union his own blessing. "I like the look of Brad and I always have done. He's a good fellow and he's very gifted."

Brad, though, was concerned about the mother of his child. She refused to slow down, bouncing around the country, eating badly, and sleeping poorly. In January she paid the price for her frenetic lifestyle, fainting on the set of *The Good Shepherd,* which was then shooting in the Dominican Republic. "I hadn't eaten for three hours. We were doing a Christmas scene sitting around this piano singing songs when the world just went completely black in front of me and I nearly threw up," she told writer Jonathan Van Meter. "They had to move me to the side, get me a nurse." She quietly told her director, Robert De Niro, that she "might" be pregnant, and he went off and got her a banana. One source was reported as saying: "She looks really frail and she's pale and gaunt. Brad has been trying to persuade her to go on bed rest, but she won't hear any of it."

Instead she maintained her hectic pace, flying with Brad from the Dominican Republic to Haiti to visit their friend musician Wyclef Jean and view the self-help projects encouraged by his charity, Yéle Haiti. Although the State Department had issued travel advisories against visiting this unstable nation, Angie was impressed by the pride and resilience of the locals. "You hear so much just about the danger and the fear and then you come here and you meet just an amazing people. Given just a little chance, and given a little help, this is going to be a great country."

The media focus, however, was not on the country but on Angie's countenance, the couple announcing her pregnancy on January 12, 2006. The first pictures of "le bump" were sold to *People* magazine, the funds going directly to Yéle Haiti. More than that, Brad was going to be a dad—officially. On January 19, 2006, he had formally jumped through all the hoops required to adopt Maddox and Zahara. They were now little Jolie-Pitts.

At the end of January, the couple flew to Davos, Switzerland, where Angie was again due to speak at the World Economic Forum. The days of skulking and pretending were over, Brad by her side as Angie met with UN secretary general Kofi Annan and other movers and shakers. They spent the next few weeks in Paris, where they discussed *A Mighty Heart,* the latest project for Plan B Entertainment, with Mariane Pearl, and Berlin, where Brad was working with an architecture firm on a "green" hotel in Dubai.

The attention in Paris was relentless, the family followed everywhere, from the amusement park by the Eiffel Tower to the famous Cirque d'hiver, and even to the playground where Brad took Maddox to test their new remote-controlled model cars. They did manage to escape for a few days, when the two novice pilots—accompanied by their Los Angeles–based instructor—flew the family to the south of France to check out secluded villas to lease.

They were adamant that they did not want the birth of their first child to turn into a circus or a repeat of the Kenyan beach vacation picture saga, where they shaped but did not manage the situation. This time they wanted complete control and would go anywhere in the world to find it. The couple decided that Namibia, the African country where Angie had filmed *Beyond Borders* and where she had first become a mother, would be ideal. It was a conscious choice, Angie argued. "We aren't completely insane. We looked for places that were not rife with malaria and dengue fever, and Namibia is good for that because it's so dry."

Angie had come a long way from her first visit to Africa, when she arrived with no cell phone, watch, or even makeup, her belongings thrown into a cheap duffel bag. This time they had the joint firepower to stage their own private African coup, the family arriving at Walvis Bay Airport by private jet. Before they set foot on Namibian soil on April 3, 2006, their bodyguard Mickey Brett had established a "no see" zone around the beach-front Burning Shore Beach Lodge, in the hamlet of Langstrand, which they had completely taken over for the duration. Green mesh netting was erected around the hotel to stop long-range photography. The popular oyster bar at the end of the pier nearby was closed down, to prevent any prying eyes from possibly seeing the couple.

Then the Namibian government agreed to enforce a "no fly" zone over the stretch of coast on which the couple's hotel lay. Journalists and photographers were not allowed into the country without the express permission of the celebrity couple. This edict, signed by Permanent Secretary Loini-Nyanyukweni Katoma, said that the Namibian government intended to support the Hollywood celebrities in their quest for peace and quiet. There was also the little matter of the marketing opportunity their arrival brought, as well as promised donations to the local hospital.

The few enterprising souls who made their cautious way to the remote resort found themselves confronted by Brett and a small army of body-guards, several of them former South African soldiers during apartheid. There was no goodwill from Angie's ambassador, Brett telling local photographers: "If I find anyone getting a picture of Jolie, I will fucking smash someone to pieces. I'm not joking. I'll fucking put someone in the hospital." During the eight-week-long game of cat and mouse, Brett's crew cordoned off roads, made nighttime searches of houses, and stopped suspect vehicles. At least one photographer was laced with pepper spray, others beaten up, and Brett himself was charged with assaulting a local restaurant owner. As a final throw of the dice, freelance photographer Steve Butler offered Brett £250,000 for the first picture of the baby. It was so much wishful thinking, Brett taping the conversation with the British paparazzo.

While photographers chasing big celebrity game generated little sympathy, Namibia's checkered history—it only became independent in 1990 after being a protectorate of South Africa during apartheid—made outraged locals particularly sensitive to their government's cession of authority to rich outsiders. "Never in my life have I seen two individuals exercise so much power here," commented Phil ya Nangoloh, executive director of Namibia's National Society for Human Rights. "They effectively captured the state." Local farmer Tomas Lorry was equally unimpressed, telling the

New Statesman: "The restricting of local and international press and this pseudo-royal attitude are the exact opposite of what Namibia needs. People who for years tried to build a democratic society can only shake their heads at this."

As for the couple at the center of the storm, Angie stayed in the hotel compound, having picnics on the beach with Maddox or, for a time, posing nude for portrait artist Don Bachardy, who flew in from Santa Monica to paint the expectant celebrity. Ironically, it was Bachardy who had sketched her father during his rehearsals for *Hamlet,* the play that ended his marriage. Brad slipped the media cordon to ride a dune buggy or take off into the desert on his motorbike, and hired a plane to practice flying, spending hours on circuits and longer flights over the coast.

During her eight-week confinement, the only journalist Angie agreed to meet was Ann Curry from NBC's *Today* show. While they walked around a nearby shantytown, Angie spoke not about her bump or about Brad, but about her advocacy of the Global Campaign for Education, which promotes education as a basic human right, with an aim of giving 100 million children in poor countries the chance to go to school. She expressed similar sentiments in a teleconference on May 26 with British finance minister, later prime minister, Gordon Brown, their conversation watched by international political reporters.

The next day, May 27, 2006, she and Brad climbed into a battered VW beach van with surfboards strapped to the roof while a convoy of 4×4's with blacked-out windows left from their lodge. The reason soon became clear. In the former German colony, an operation organized with military precision swung into action. Once the waiting paparazzi had been lured away by the decoy convoy, Mickey Brett, dressed as a beach bum, drove the couple, hiding behind the van's curtains, to the Cottage Medi-Clinic hospital in Swakopmund, where Angie's Los Angeles–based obstetrician, Jason Rothbart, whom they had flown in specially, was waiting to perform a scheduled cesarean section, as the baby was in the breech position. Brad was present throughout, cutting the umbilical cord as baby Shiloh Nouvel Jolie-Pitt, who weighed in at seven pounds, made a safe arrival. Angie's mother had her wish: Shiloh was born a Gemini and took her first name from the bus sign Jon Voight had spotted all those years ago.

While her brother was the first visitor to the hospital, Angie, who started breast-feeding within half an hour of Shiloh's birth, managed to call her mother with the good news. Marcheline was at Cedars-Sinai hospital undergoing further cancer treatment and, like Angie, was on morphine to control her pain. "We both laughed about that," Angie later recalled. Her mother was understandably thrilled. "My heart is overflowing with joy," she told *People*. "Maddox, Zahara and Shiloh are deeply loved children. They have very kind and caring parents who love and support each other in every way."

Marche had to wait until they returned to America to see her first biological grandchild, but the Pitts flew to Namibia to coo over the latest addition to the family and to celebrate Angie's thirty-first birthday on June 4. They had further cause for celebration: Brad's latest release, *Babel,* which he starred in with Cate Blanchett, had just won a prize at the Cannes Film Festival, Alejandro González Iñárritu taking the Best Director award.

Within days, Shiloh was set to work, earning more in her first month of life than many people do in a lifetime. Through her parents' friendship with Jonathan Klein, CEO of Getty Images picture agency, a breathtaking global deal was organized for the first pictures of Shiloh *en famille,* which raised an estimated $11 million for the Jolie-Pitt Foundation. In just two of the contracts, *People* paid $4.1 million, while the British celebrity magazine *Hello!* shelled out $3.5 million. The paparazzi went home sunburned, out-of-pocket, without even the traditional "All I got was this lousy T-shirt" memento for two months' worth of trouble.

On June 14 the family left their adopted country by private jet with a tailwind of thanks from the nation's president, Sam Nujoma. Alluding to the fact that for years Namibia was under UN mandate, he said: "You didn't just birth a child but a new era for our new country. If we are the UN's baby, then you, as one of its greatest supporters, are among its founding mothers." It was official: Angie was now the good girl, the clean girl.

Once back in America, Angie wasted no time before revealing her future ambitions, telling CNN's Anderson Cooper on June 20 that she and Brad planned to adopt their next child but weren't yet sure of the country. "It's gonna be the balance of what would be the best for Mad and Zee right now," she told him in an interview screened for World Refugee Day. It was somewhat odd that the new mother of a breast-feeding baby didn't mention Shiloh in this balancing act.

In fact, the couple had already decided on Vietnam as their next port of call, Dr. Aronson discreetly setting the wheels in motion for an adoption in a country where the tangle of red tape takes careful and time-consuming unraveling.

Meanwhile, Brad, now reprising his role for *Ocean's Thirteen,* was in full Mr. Mom mode, describing the joy of burping his new baby, the sore issue of diaper rash, and the best product to use for Zahara's tangled hair. Already Shiloh, just two months old, had made history by becoming the first infant re-created in wax by Madame Tussauds.

The happy family image was slightly marred by the ghost at the feast, Jon Voight. At a BAFTA tea party in Hollywood he wished Maddox a happy fifth birthday, then mistakenly sent good wishes to Shakira, the Latin American singer, rather than what he meant to say, Zahara, the granddaughter he had yet to meet. While there had been tentative attempts to heal the rift, notably when Brad was filming *Jesse James* in Canada, a truce was still far off. When Angie and Brad arrived at actor Scott Caan's birthday party in August, she refused to leave their limousine when she realized that her father was already inside the house.

The chances of bumping into her father, a familiar figure on the streets of Hollywood, were rather less when in September Angie and her family flew to Puna, India, where filming was soon to begin for *A Mighty Heart.* The obvious choice, Karachi, in Pakistan, where Daniel Pearl was kidnapped, was deemed too dangerous. It was a different working experience for Brad and Angie. They met as actors, and now Brad was a producer, Angie the leading lady, playing opposite Dan Futterman. For the newly minted mother, it was a stressful experience, both on and off the set. Director Michael Winterbottom's edgy documentary style meant that he kept the cameras rolling continuously, even when the actors went off to use the bathroom. It gave a sense of the frenzied and ultimately gut-wrenching emotion felt by Mariane Pearl as she approached the conclusion that her husband had been grotesquely murdered.

Not only was the shoot draining, but the attentions of the crowds and the paparazzi made every waking moment edgy and tense. At one point Angie's assistant, Holly Goline, sent a harassed e-mail to writer Jonathan Van Meter: "We are barely surviving India." As a brief respite, Brad took his partner for an overnight break at the nearby Taj Lake Palace hotel, one of the most romantic places on the planet. They drove to the lake in a vintage car, finally arriving by boat at the white marble palace that seems to hover above the water.

They were back to the madness all too soon. The behavior of their bodyguards did little to help the frenzied mood. As they soon realized, this was not Namibia, where strong-arm tactics went unchallenged. Mickey Brett and three colleagues were arrested after an altercation at a school where filming was taking place, the bodyguards accused of hurling racial and religious insults and making death threats to parents trying to pick up their children. No further action was taken. Wearing his producer's hat, and acutely aware of the $16 million Plan B Entertainment had sunk into the production, Brad called the incident "a horrible misunderstanding." This was the worst kind of publicity for such a sensitive film. He and Angie, who donated $100,000 to the Daniel Pearl Foundation on what would have been the journalist's forty-third birthday, October 10, were understandably disturbed. "I would never work with anyone [who] was derogatory to another man's race," said Angie, adding somewhat disingenuously, "I am of mixed race."

Once filming wound down, the couple made a Thanksgiving visit to former prison camps and detention centers in Ho Chi Minh City, formerly Saigon, in Vietnam. They roamed around on a moped, dined at wayside restaurants, wandered the thronging streets, and, more important, visited an orphanage on the city's outskirts where the latest member of their family, they hoped, was about to be discovered.

Just six months old, little Shiloh was about to get a playmate.

FIFTEEN

Don't let Jon in here.

—Marcheline Bertrand's last words

When former schoolteacher Johanna Silver Gordon died of ovarian cancer at the age of fifty-two, her younger sister Sheryl was not only heartbroken but outraged. Like millions of women, Johanna was not aware of the symptoms of ovarian cancer until it was too late. Sheryl vowed to change all that. In late 2002 she proposed Johanna's Law, to fund national outreach and education about the symptoms of gynecological cancer. After much lobbying, that legislation was signed into law by President George W. Bush on January 12, 2007. It was a personal triumph not only for Sheryl Silver but also for Marcheline Bertrand.

Marcheline and her partner, John Trudell, had set up the charity Give Love Give Life to organize support in the music and film community for Johanna's Law, arranging concerts and lobbying movers and shakers. With Trudell by her side, the days when Marcheline had been content merely to be a donor were over. Though Trudell did the heavy lifting, Angie's mother was now a committed activist for a cause she truly believed in.

At the time the law was signed, Marcheline was undergoing yet another course of chemotherapy at Cedars-Sinai hospital in Beverly Hills. While she was clearly ailing, she had shown remarkable resilience in bouncing back from this debilitating treatment over the years. When Marcheline's doctor told Angie that she had at least another six-month reprieve, it was a consolation of sorts. Rather than hovering by her mother's bedside waiting for the inevitable, Angie was able to get on with her life, though only up to a point—as TV host Ryan Seacrest found to his cost. When she and Brad walked the red carpet for the Golden Globes on January 15, 2007, Angie remained awkwardly silent when Seacrest lobbed her a typical question about her plans to increase her family. Brad eventually intervened, saying that they wanted to have a soccer team. Later, on his radio show, Seacrest complained about her behavior. "She clearly wanted nothing to do with me or my question or my answer or any of it." He was not the only critic, *The New York Times* describing her as a "sourpuss" during the red carpet walk. Clearly her attention was elsewhere.

It was not only her mother who was on her mind. Later that week Angie flew to Vietnam, ostensibly for a charity meeting to discuss helping subsistence farmers grow bamboo in the Mekong Delta, but also to advance the adoption proceedings for the new addition to their family, Pax Thien Jolie. She then joined Brad in New Orleans, where he was filming *The Curious Case of Benjamin Button,* the intriguing story of a man who ages backward, looking younger as he grows older. The couple had made more than a filming commitment to the Big Easy. Not only had Brad and Angie bought a $3.5 million house, but the architect-minded actor also continued to work on an environmentally friendly housing project to rebuild neighborhoods ravaged by Hurricane Katrina.

On Saturday, January 27, 2007, however, Angie had hardly had time to unpack her bags when she received the call that she had secretly been dreading. Her mother had taken an unexpected turn and was fading fast. Further chemotherapy was out of the question. Angie and Brad quickly took the four-hour flight from New Orleans to Los Angeles, but they were too late.

As Angie said later, her mother passed away an hour after they landed. With John Trudell and her son, James, by her side in a private room at Cedars-Sinai, Marcheline finally succumbed to the ovarian cancer she had battled for seven and a half years. It was just two weeks after Johanna's Law had been enacted.

Even though Angie arrived at the hospital too late to say a final good-bye, she took some comfort in knowing that her mother felt that the family was all together before she passed away. Tabloid speculation, therefore, that Marcheline's dying wish was for Angie and Brad ("an angel sent to look after you") to marry was cruelly inappropriate. In fact, for the last few days she had been heavily sedated and drifting in and out of consciousness, though she did have the strength to tell James, who was watching a TV documentary on Nazi Germany, to change the channel in the Jewish hospital.

Angie's most powerful memory of arriving at the hospital was seeing Brad put his arms around her brother, James, when James broke down in tears. Over the next few hours, Brad gently questioned the siblings about their mom, lightening the somber mood by getting them to tell amusing stories about her. "He was extraordinary," recalled Angie. "It was certainly one of the worst days of my life and then it was one of the most beautiful . . . realizing this is how family takes care of family. It was another gift she gave us." Not quite. In one of her last sentences before she died, she whispered: "Don't let Jon in here." There was no forgiveness for her ex-husband even as she breathed her last.

As brother and sister grieved, Brad took charge of the arrangements for the funeral and cremation. In a statement to *People,* brother and sister said, "There are no words to express what an amazing woman and mother she was. She was our best friend." There were many other tributes. Angie's godmother, actress Jacqueline Bisset, described Marcheline as "an enlightened spirit" who had "worked incredibly hard to raise both Jamie and Angelina and dedicated herself to their happiness." Her acting coach Lee Strasberg emphasized how she had given up her career to care for her children, describing her as "an unusually good person in the best sense of the word." There was a modest funeral service at the Holy Cross Mortuary in Los Angeles. Only John Trudell, Brad Pitt, and Marcheline's children were present. Others paid tribute to her many nurturing and life-enhancing qualities on a Web site dedicated to her memory.

As sweet, generous, and thoughtful as she was, the sad reality was that she died a rather lonely figure. Apart from John Trudell and her children, she had, for one reason or another, fallen out with many of her close friends and family in her waning years. It was a long litany that began when she was still in robust health. The first to go was her father, Rolland (although they later reconciled when he was suffering from terminal cancer), then her stepmother, Elke. Next out was her brother, Raleigh, followed by her sister, Debbie, along with Bill Day and close girlfriends like Jade Dixon and Belinha Beatty. Of course Jon Voight was cast out the day he gave his notorious TV interview in August 2002. Often the reasons were as trivial as a missed lunch date or a small unpaid debt. Even though they were ousted from Marche's life, they still loved and cared for her, appreciating the complexity of her character beneath the "Saint Marcheline" image. They were perplexed by yet indulgent of her behavior, always ready to forgive and forget. However, in her last years, the "Bertrand freeze," that stubborn inability or unwillingness to forgive, came more frequently to the fore.

As a result, there was general shock among those in her former circle when they heard that Marche had died. Indeed, the last word to filter out—via *Dances with Wolves* actor Floyd "Red Crow" Westerman, who was undergoing cancer treatment in the same hospital—had been that she was in remission. Bill Day, her former partner of eleven years, heard the news on his car radio while driving to Santa Monica, and was so stunned that he had to pull over to the side of the road. When he reached the seaside town, he climbed into an empty lifeguard station and gazed out at the ocean, reflecting on his life with Marcheline. "It was hard to believe she went through the slow agony of cancer death and didn't bother to let me know. I knew we had a bad ending, but we had a life together. I would have thought she would have wanted to forgive the past so that she could leave this planet in peace. But knowing Marcheline as I did, I also understood why she didn't. The freeze, the freeze, the freeze. God, I never hated it more than at that moment."

As phone calls were made among close family and friends, it quickly became clear that a whole slew of them had also been consigned to the spiritual deep freezer. Jon Voight was reduced to leaving a message of condolence on his son's answering machine, while Marcheline's sister, Debbie, like many others, heard about her death on the local news.

The fact that she had frozen out virtually all those who cared for her went a long way toward explaining James Haven's rather histrionic statement that he and his sister were now "orphans." Indeed, there were no adult members of the Voight or Bertrand family who were close to Marche's children. "She just became angry with everyone and shut them out of her life," recalled Bill Day. "Marche took it all away with her unresolved and unfinished. What hit me hard was not so much that she died so tragically, but that she died such a tragic figure. What a sad end comes to those who can't forgive, I thought."

For Angie, grieving over the loss of "her best friend," the only consolation was that Marcheline was now out of the pain she had endured for so long. In the weeks following her mother's death, Angie physically wasted away; as a onetime anorexic, not eating gave her control over her wayward emotions. Her brother spoke publicly about his fears for her well-being, saying that her profound sense of bereavement was affecting her health. Her work for the United Nations was also draining her physical resources. When the actress returned home from visits to refugee camps, she found it hard to eat out in expensive restaurants, knowing how little so many had to live on. Her brother, who accompanied her to several refugee camps, was also deeply affected. James, too, found it difficult to reconcile his life of plenty in a world of want, on one occasion abandoning his half-full supermarket cart during his weekly shopping trip and walking out of the store, repulsed by the groaning abundance that surrounded him.

Angie responded to her mother's death in the only way she knew how—by keeping herself busy. Just three weeks after Marche's passing, Angie was on the road again, spending two days in late February 2007 at the Oure-Cassoni refugee camp in eastern Chad, home to victims of the conflict in Sudan's Darfur region. "It's always hard to see decent people, families, living in such difficult conditions," said the UN Goodwill Ambassador, who had to cross the Sahara in a sandstorm in order to reach the 26,000-person camp. Several weeks after her visit, she and Brad Pitt, under the umbrella of the Jolie-Pitt Foundation, donated $1 million toward the humanitarian mission to assist more than four million people affected by the war in Darfur.

Just as satisfying for the girl striving to be "good" was an op-ed piece she penned for *The Washington Post* in late February, drawing on her experience to argue that there would be no permanent peace in Darfur until the perpetrators of the violence faced justice. For the first time she was referred to as a UN Goodwill Ambassador rather than an actor. At last she had broken free of the Hollywood ghetto, a fact underlined that month when she was nominated for membership in the prestigious Council on Foreign Relations, a think tank on international discourse that included four former secretaries of state as well heavyweights like Richard Holbrooke, Tom Brokaw, and Alan Greenspan. Her membership was confirmed that June.

Still, it was her private life, rather than her public works, that excited the most attention. On March 2, days after Angie returned from Darfur, Vietnam's top adoption official confirmed that the mother of three was about to add to her family. As Vietnam has a rigorous and complex adoption procedure, Brad and Angie had started the process the previous May, shortly after Shiloh's birth, their application shepherded by the Adoptions From The Heart agency. Since Vietnamese law makes it difficult for unmarried couples to adopt, Angie applied solo, though with her partner's full support, the couple agreeing that it would be good for their family to be ethnically balanced.

When they visited Ho Chi Minh City during Thanksgiving 2006, Brad and Angie had made a connection with a "shy but friendly" little boy, Pham Quang Sang, who celebrated his third birthday shortly after they distributed gifts to toddlers at Tam Binh orphanage. Abandoned at birth by his heroin addict mother, Pham Thu Dung, the youngster enjoyed a simple but familiar routine with 326 other orphans. All that was about to change.

So he wouldn't be alarmed, Pham wasn't told that he was about to meet his new mother—and brother and sister—until March 14, the day Angie arrived at the orphanage. Brad's filming commitments did not allow him to be present, so Maddox and Zahara were their mother's wingmen. The official handover in a room at the Department of Justice the following day didn't go quite according to script, the "rather shy and dazed" three-year-old bursting into tears in the presence of the world's most glamorous woman. While Maddox, now five, roamed around the nondescript room, the tearful Pham Quang Sang seemed bewildered.

Within a matter of minutes, he had entered a parallel universe. He had a new family, a new home, a new language, a new culture, and a new name, Angie calling him Pax Thien Jolie. The name Pax, Latin for "peace," was first suggested by her mother, while Thien traditionally means "sky" in Vietnamese. Suddenly he was scooped from a life of order and certainty to the pandemonium of "Angie's world," his new mother, brother, bodyguard, and others taking almost an hour to reach their hotel amid the scrum of paparazzi and the curious. At one point, in a desperate effort to slow the convoy, paparazzi threw their crash helmets under the wheels of Angie's car. The newly minted mother of four was acutely aware of the difficulties. "Photographs and press coverage will make him upset," she told the *Ho Chi Min Law* newspaper. "I'm very worried about that."

Aware, too, of the difficulties the youngster faced in adapting to a new country and a new language, Angie was committed to slowly building a bond of trust. During an interview with a Vietnamese journalist, she admitted that it would take her latest addition some time to realize that he now had a permanent family and that his life would not keep changing. To that end she stated emphatically that she had no plans to resume work. "I will stay at home to help Pax adjust to his new life. I have four children now, and caring for them is the most important thing for me at the moment. I am very happy to be their mother."

In spite of these assurances, the bewilderment on Pax's face was matched by the general unease in the media and in the wider public over the practice of celebrities—and politicians—swooping into Third World countries and walking away with orphans. Angie herself had entered the debate earlier in the year, when she questioned the decision by Madonna and her then husband, Guy Ritchie, to adopt a baby boy from Malawi, a country with lax adoption laws. "Personally I prefer to stay on the right side of the law," Jolie reportedly told the French magazine *Gala,* though she later made clear that she was "horrified" by the attacks on Madonna and Ritchie. Nor was Angie herself spared condemnation. Commentator Fiona Looney accused Angie of "choosing her babies like handbags." Upbraiding Vietnamese officials for a "terrible disregard" for Pax's emotional welfare, the *Daily Mail* columnist argued that just as it was cruel to change a dog's name when it was several years old, it was even worse for a confused little boy. Arizona-based columnist Tracy Dingmann, herself an adopted child, observed: "To me it looks like Jolie is collecting cute little brown kids like she collects tattoos," going on to quote Susan Caughman, editor of *Adoptive Families* magazine, who cautioned against adopting numerous children in a short period of time and out of birth order. To further add to the ethical debate about the adoption of Third World youngsters by rich Westerners, it was revealed that Pax's distraught mother, Pham Thu Dung, had kicked heroin—like Pax's adoptive mother—and was working in a shoe factory for fifty dollars a month. Though she was racked with guilt at giving away her son, she had no plans to reclaim him. She told her sister Pham Thu Trang: "I gave up my rights as a mother when I abandoned him. He is better off where he is. Now he has a life I could never give him." Instead this sad and forlorn figure followed his progress as part of the world's most famous rainbow family via the Internet or picture magazines—rather like his maternal grandfather. Within days of his adoption, pictures of Pax appeared on the covers of *People* and *Hello!* magazines in a deal worth a reported $2 million.

Perhaps anticipating the furor that would accompany her third overseas adoption, Angie's involvement in her latest movie, *Wanted,* was not formally announced until March 26—the naming of the director, Timur Bekmambetov, and the casting of the leading men, Morgan Freeman and James McAvoy, having been released in *Variety* the previous December. Indeed, during the film's promotion, McAvoy said he felt rather "intimidated" when told that his love interest was to be Ms. Jolie, implying that he knew of her involvement from the get-go. She was committed to a three-month shoot, flying to Prague in May and then to Chicago, where she played an assassin training the son of a fellow assassin in the deadly arts. It was the kind of stylish action adventure hokum she enjoyed, but she needed to be fit and focused.

After a long day's filming—which she saw as therapy after her mother's death—there would not be much energy left for mothering. Once *Wanted* wrapped, she was scheduled to star in Clint Eastwood's *Changeling,* the true story of a mother's ultimately hopeless search for her son abducted by a serial killer. After that, she was slated to be a voice in the epic cartoon *Beowulf* before starring in a film version of Ayn Rand's novel *Atlas Shrugged.*

If Angie could have spoken to her new son rather than using gestures, how would she have explained the disparity between her public statements in Vietnam that she was going to put her career on the back burner to focus on family and the fact that, even as she made the pledge, she was already contracted to work on a movie that started filming almost before Pax became familiar with the layout of his new home? On the level of short-term public relations, it was a way to dodge the bullets fired by the Vietnamese and international media concerned about Pax's welfare. Once on board the private jet that flew her and her family back to America, she knew she had lived to fight another day. Sweetened by the news that she and Brad had donated $100,000 to support the "Lost Boys" of the Sudan, the simultaneous announcement of her new movie passed largely without comment.

On another level, though, this was part of a pattern of behavior that gives an intriguing insight into Angie's psyche. As a working mother, she had no genuine need to dissemble. In her mind's eye, however, the image of motherhood was represented by her idealized vision of Marcheline's, giving up her career for the sake of the children. That was the narrative she—and others—believed, even though it was clearly untrue. Her mother continued to pursue an acting career and even moved to New York in the hope of attaining her dream. In her own way, Marcheline was a working mom. Yet this notion of the "domestic goddess" was the story Angie told herself and presented to the world not only about her own mother but about herself as a mother. As writer Susan Chenery observed: "There is something slightly preposterously pathological about all the things she is trying to be in her personal quest to be a 'good woman.' "

On an even deeper level, she was reliving the profound imprinted experience of abandonment that lay just at the edge of her consciousness. Known as "repetition compulsion," it is the state of mind represented colloquially by a phrase heard in families the world over: "If it was good enough for me, it's good enough for you." That is to say, many hurt or abused children grow up to impose similar hurt and abuse on their own children. And so the pattern repeats.

While Angie could not articulate the abandonment she felt in that stark-white nursery, it informed her adult behavior in a variety of ways. As a survivor of abandonment herself, she identified with those who had gone through the same experience, associating more deeply with her orphaned children than with her biological child. "I think I feel so much more for Mad and Zee because they're survivors, they came through so much," she told *Elle* magazine. "Shiloh seemed so privileged from the moment she was born. I have less inclination to feel for her. . . . I met my other kids when they were six months old, they came with a personality. A newborn really is this . . . Yes, a blob!"

Yet her relationships with both adults and children could be characterized as "Come here, now go away." A few examples should suffice: Within weeks of her marriage to Jonny Lee Miller, she began an affair with Tim Hutton; within days of marrying Billy Bob Thornton, she was on a plane to London to film *Lara Croft;* no sooner had she adopted Maddox than she ditched Billy Bob and left the boy with her mother and brother while she headed off to Ecuador; once Zahara was deemed out of danger in the New York hospital she began filming *The Good Shepherd;* and now with Pax she was flying to Prague for long days of filming—albeit with Brad and the children in tow. All the while she repeated the mantra of the need for family, of giving up work, of focusing on the children. Yet she was as much a savior as a mother. Nowhere was the disconnect between words and actions more apparent than with Pax. As her former babysitter Krisann Morel observes: "When I see how the children are being brought up by nannies while she is off filming, I see that she is repeating her own childhood without knowing it. Why adopt if you are not going to parent them?"

Angie was repeating her mother's cycle in other ways. Just as Marcheline broke Elke Bertrand's heart by stopping her from seeing her stepgrandchildren, so the pattern was renewed with Angie and her father. The famous Bertrand freeze had certainly found a home with Angie.

If Pax would have been confused by the behavior of his new mother, he would have been equally alarmed by the family she came from. This was clearly a family at war. In the same week as the announcement of her extensive filming schedule, his uncle, James Haven, whom he had yet to meet, launched a ferocious public attack on the grandfather Pax was not allowed to meet.

In an interview with British journalist Sharon Feinstein, James described Jon Voight as a "manipulative," abusive, and stingy father who left him with "horrible memories," especially about the way he treated his mother. Not only was Voight never around during his childhood, but he deliberately kept Marcheline short of money. This was not a one-off rant. James later told *Marie Claire* magazine: "I don't want to constantly berate my father but he put my mom through years of mental abuse and made me care especially for abandoned women and children. That is my religion—helping widows and orphans."

By contrast, James explained that he and his sister had nothing but wonderful memories of their mother. "Angie and I would walk in and comment on how we could smell things cooking and baking in the kitchen," he recalled. "She'd be in the middle of cooking and pick up a carrot and teach us about the vegetable or the fruit."

It is hard to know what to make of this narrative. Certainly those who knew the family were horrified at James's vituperation toward his father. So much of what he said was plain wrong. For starters, Marche never cooked. Ever. The nearest she ever got to cooking were the very rare occasions she made soup. The children did have a healthy, nutritious diet, but their meals came from high-end supermarkets, or their mother ordered takeout.

Then there was the nature of James's relationship with his father. Jon Voight had always seen James as more of a "buddy" than Angie. They played basketball together, James lived with him for a couple of years as a teenager, his father paid for him to attend the private University of Southern California and bought him a brand-new Porsche sports car when he graduated with honors as a budding director. Thereafter he bought him a condo in the same building in West Hollywood as his sister—she paid for her own, though her father acted as guarantor—and when he decided, out of the blue, to become an actor, his father took him around to every casting agent in Hollywood. Not exactly the behavior of a stingy, absent father.

For a time his father kept his counsel, but he later told *Life and Style* magazine that he believed the "trauma" of their mother's passing had deepened rather than healed the rift. "I find it very heartbreaking that my children want to paint a bad guy portrait of me. I feel it comes from the inability to let go of years of programmed anger from their mother, who understandably felt quite hurt when we divorced. In truth, I tried to give him [Haven] and their mother continuous love and support and large sums of money. God knows, for years I've tried to mend this relationship."

This family feud continued from beyond the grave. Marche's will, released on April 10, 2007, indicated her unending bitterness toward her ex-husband. In a handwritten note in the margin, she claimed that her assets included $180,000 in "unpaid spousal support." Even Marcheline's friends were baffled by this statement. For all his faults, Voight had religiously paid the agreed monies in spousal and child support even when his own earnings took a dive. He even continued to pay alimony to his first wife, Lauri Peters. Unnoticed in Marcheline's will was the $500,000 that had been accumulating interest ever since Jon Voight gave it to her for the house she never bought. The reason for Marche's continued animosity was clear, certainly in the eyes of her onetime friend Krisann Morel. "Jon Voight took away her fancy dream life, and she never got over that anger. It was so debilitating to carry that hatred around with her."

Nonetheless, Marcheline was still Angie's mother, her safe harbor, mentor, manager, best friend, and consoler in chief, the woman she spoke with every day. Angie's sense of loss was clear when she broke down during an interview on the *Today* show in May to promote *A Mighty Heart*. "Damn it, you got me crying," she told Ann Curry as she wiped away the tears, a spear of memory piercing her still-grieving heart. "I'm holding on to my family real tight at this moment—trying to be as good a woman as I can be." As she talked proudly to the media about her latest baby, the first serious film under the Plan B umbrella, it was clear that her mother's death was much on her mind. "This year I lost my mom. I've gone through a lot. I have four kids. I just finished breast-feeding. I do want people to understand that I am just trying to work through a very difficult year."

The film's producer, Brad Pitt, chipped in, too, revealing that Marcheline's death had one positive effect—it stopped them from fighting. "There's going to come a time when I'm not going to get to be with this person anymore," he said. "So if we have a flare-up it evaporates now. I don't want to waste time being angry at someone I love."

Doling out nuggets about Planet Brangelina, Angie admitted that she couldn't cook, said Pax was now the loudest, boldest member of the family, and stressed the importance of grandparents—Brad's parents, that is—in her children's lives.

Angie's powerful performance as Mariane Pearl was a triumphant return to form; she played the role of a woman who had become a close friend with a rigor and a passion that surprised even jaded skeptics. As film critic James Christopher wrote in the London *Times:* "The film belongs to Jolie. She won an Oscar for 1999's *Girl, Interrupted,* but this is by far her best performance, strong and true in every detail. Her total immersion in the role keeps the film from getting lost in the rush of details. Even after Daniel's death and subsequent beheading, Mariane holds Daniel's spirit close. Jolie sees to it that the humane and haunting *A Mighty Heart* honors that spirit." Chicago-based critic Roger Ebert found her performance "physically and emotionally convincing," saying, "She has a genuine screen presence. She holds the attention without asking for it." While the film just about broke even financially—returning $19 million worldwide on a budget of $16 million—it earned Angie twelve award nominations, including for a Golden Globe and an Empire Award from the same magazine that was writing her career obituary the year before.

Her life was now a juggling act; she was selling *A Mighty Heart* in New York, Cannes, and elsewhere; shooting up the bad guys in *Wanted* in

Prague and Chicago; and prepping for her upcoming role as telephone switchboard supervisor Christine Collins in *Changeling*, directed by Clint Eastwood, a man whom she would come to see as another surrogate father. Then there was the little matter of raising her first biological child and three orphans, only two of whom could speak passable English. Little wonder Brad seemed more and more to assume the role of wife to her busy executive husband. One week that summer she went from filming *Wanted* in Chicago until four in the morning to flying to Syria and Iraq in her role as UN Goodwill Ambassador and dashing to the Hamptons in a helicopter for a fund-raiser for Brad's New Orleans Make It Right project. As *The New Yorker* magazine described the superstar child wrangler: "His expression is sometimes that of a man who stepped out to hail a cab and got run over by a fleet of trucks." Like most parents, he discovered that the experience made him more focused and better organized. "It's the most fun I have ever had and also the biggest pain in the ass I have ever experienced," he said of his growing "cuckoo's nest." "I love it and I can't recommend it any more highly."

Indeed, the gridlock of Angie's life delayed arrangements for a memorial service for her mother, which finally took place at Roxbury Park, the site of so many family memories, on September 1, 2007. Of course, family politics played a central part; if Jon Voight came, would James, Angie, and John Trudell, whom Marche described in her will as "one of the loves of [her] life," boycott the event? In the end Angie was on her way to Venice for the film festival, where Brad's movie, *The Assassination of Jesse James by the Coward Robert Ford*, was a star attraction. Instead Jon Voight, John Trudell, and the other love of Marche's life, Bill Day, arrived for what was jokingly billed as the "Time to Bury the Hatchet Memorial." Marche's sister, Debbie, even had a gold necklace with an axe on the end specially made for the event.

Clearly Jon Voight hadn't gotten with the program. He appeared carrying a small rosebush and proceeded, as ever, to take over the event. Small talk was at a premium, Voight curtly asking Bill Day if he was now married and had any children. As Day, who is married and has no children, recalls: "He looked at me like: 'Well, don't try to put any claims on mine, pal, 'cause I ain't sharing. As far as I am concerned, when Marcheline died, you did too.'" After that inauspicious start, everyone, including friends like Lauren

Taines, Belinha Beatty, and Jade Dixon, as well as Debbie and Marche's brother, Raleigh, stood in a circle holding hands and fondly remembering Marcheline. Belinha Beatty made a point of saying that in spite of appearances to the contrary, Jon and Marche had worked out a loving resolution to their relationship and family life. In the end, Jon Voight, John Trudell, and Bill Day even posed for a photograph together taken by Raleigh's son, Francis. (Sadly, six months later Raleigh, too, was gone, succumbing to cancer in February 2008.)

There was one incongruous note: A couple of paparazzi were spotted hiding nearby. A few days later, a picture of Jon and the rest of the family appeared in a magazine. The suspicion was that Jon had alerted the media so that he could use the pictorial evidence to argue that if he was as bad as he was portrayed by his children, why was the rest of the family prepared to be with him? As one participant noted: "In the world of Voightville, the shit never ends."

SIXTEEN

I have watched this family at war for decades. There comes a time to forgive and forget.

—BILL DAY

When Angie began filming *Changeling* in October 2007, she remembered her mother in her own way, carrying a picture of her in her costume handbag as she played the grievously wronged character of Christine Collins, a telephone switchboard supervisor whose son was abducted and killed. If *Wanted* was her escape from grief, then *Changeling* was a catharsis, a profoundly healing experience. She found herself drawn to Collins, as her quiet but resilient personality reminded her of "the kind of femininity that [her] mother had, that modern women don't have so much."

Shortly after filming began, she discovered that she was pregnant, just before she was due to shoot harrowing scenes in a mental hospital ward. On several occasions filming was delayed because she felt sick or faint. In her heart she believes the highly charged nature of the story about a mother's search for her abducted son actually contributed to the pregnancy. "I was so emotional about children that I think something in me kicked into gear," she recalled. It was, though, a shock to learn that she was pregnant with twins. Brad and Angie's much-talked-about "soccer team" was coming along sooner than ever expected.

That November it was her second adopted child, Ethiopian-born Zahara, rather than any speculation about her condition, that was the focus of attention. It was "revealed" that Zahara was the daughter of a rape victim and not an orphan at all, the world's media taking two years to notice

Judge Dadnachew Tesfaye's ruling in October 2005 that the adoption was legal even though Zahara's birth mother was still alive. In fact, Mentwabe Dawit, who was unable to support her sick daughter, was thrilled that Zahara had the chance of a new life. "My baby was on the verge of death. She became malnourished and was even unable to cry," Mentwabe told reporters. "I was desperate and decided to run away, rather than see my child dying." Her distraught mother, Zahara's grandmother, searched for her for a month and eventually put Zahara up for adoption in the belief that her own daughter had died or at the very least would not be found. In her hometown of Awassa in southern Ethiopia, Mentwabe kissed a picture of the actress for the cameras. "This is to show I have no ill feelings towards her," she said. "I think my daughter is a very fortunate human being to be adopted by a world-famous lady. I wish them both all the success they deserve." While the Ethiopian adoption agency said that the process was "legal and irrevocable," it was now established that at least two of the three children Angelina had adopted had birth mothers who were still living, while her first adopted child, Maddox, was procured by an agency in Cambodia with a reputation for buying babies from impoverished families. The response from U.S. immigration officials was that there was no case or reason to believe Maddox was anything but a true orphan.

Pregnant and impregnable, Angie sailed through this latest storm like some Hermès-clad galleon, impervious to rumor and criticism, glowing with beatific radiance. No longer the druggie goth, she had transformed herself into an earth mother, a modern-day goddess, voluptuous, bold but good, dispensing largesse wherever she went: In 2006 alone she gave more than $4 million to various charities, a sum matched by Brad. Even jibes from Jennifer Aniston barely scratched her image of untroubled serenity. The veil of deceit Brad and Angie had erected to keep their true relationship a secret was beginning to fall, each of them admitting, with startling if belated candor, just how far back their relationship went. Brad told *Rolling Stone* magazine that his favorite movie was *Mr. & Mrs. Smith:* "Because you know . . . six kids. Because I fell in love."

Jennifer considered Angie's comments about the fact that she "couldn't wait to get to work every day" during the making of *Mr. & Mrs. Smith* to be very "uncool," rubbing fresh salt in the wounds of Brad's betrayal. "There was stuff printed that was definitely from a time when I was unaware that it was happening," said Aniston. Her childhood friend, actress Andrea Bendewald, was blunt, telling *Vanity Fair:* "It was extremely hurtful to Jen that he was seen with another woman so quickly after they were separated." Most painful were the rumors that Jennifer wanted a career more than a child, forcing Brad to find a mate who wanted a family. As an unnamed friend told the magazine: "So is there a part of Brad that's diabolical? Did he think, I need to get out of this marriage, but I want to come out smelling like a rose, so I'm going to let Jen be cast as the ultrafeminist and I'm going to get cast as the poor husband who couldn't get a baby and so had to move on?"

At one point all those evasions and denials could have come back to haunt Angie's image, but it now seemed so last year. Angie had bigger and more important matters to attend to: launching a new United Nations campaign, Nine Million, to improve education for children around the world, meeting with the British foreign secretary, David Miliband, in November to discuss "global diplomacy," and joining Undersecretary of State Paula Dobriansky on a visit to Baghdad in February 2008 to learn more about the plight of the two million youngsters under the age of twelve who were made homeless by the war. During the visit to the Green Zone, Angie met with the top U.S. commander in Iraq, General David Petraeus, and Iraqi prime minister Nouri al-Maliki as well as senior Iraqi migration officials, calling for a coherent plan to allow refugees back to their homes. "There's lots of goodwill and lots of discussion, but there seems to be just a lot of talk at the moment, and a lot of pieces that need to be put together. I'm trying to figure out what they are," she said, penning another op-ed piece for *The Washington Post* on the issue.

Her condition did eventually catch up with her. On April 8, 2008, while on a panel discussing education in Iraq at the Council on Foreign Relations in Washington, she got some unsolicited feedback. "I felt kicking suddenly!" said Jolie, then thirty-two. She was still able to present a Vital Voices Global Partnership Award to her friend journalist Mariane Pearl. The kids might be kicking, but she wasn't stopping. A month later she was back along the now-familiar corridors of power with her brother, lobbying movers and shakers on behalf of the charity Global Action for Children.

Of course, Angie wouldn't be Angie if she wasn't able to pass on what was going on between the sheets during her pregnancy. "It's *great* for the sex life," she said. "It just makes you a lot more creative. So you have fun, and as a woman you're just so round and full." Rather than welcome their twins in America, the couple decided on France, partly inspired by Marcheline's dream of living there one day. Angie took lessons to try to master the language, while she and Brad rented and months later bought Château Miraval, an 880-acre property on the Riviera where showbiz neighbors included Johnny Depp and his partner, Vanessa Paradis. In May, after attending the film festival in Cannes, where they stayed with Microsoft billionaire Steve Allen and dined with *Changeling* director Clint Eastwood and Angie's onetime courtier Mick Jagger, they decamped to the secluded villa, which came complete with marauding wild boar—and rather less tame paparazzi. There the impatient brood waited for the big day, an event described by the local newspaper, *Nice Matin,* as "the most important since man walked on the moon."

It was normally a giant leap for Angie to remain in one place for a week, let alone be confined to a hospital for three, taking small steps around her suite of rooms. On July 12, 2008, after two frustrating weeks in the hospital, she gave birth by cesarean section at the Fondation Lenval hospital in Nice. Knox Léon arrived first, Vivienne Marcheline second, the babies weighing in at five pounds each. Brad, who helped Dr. Michel Sussmann during the thirty-minute operation, cut the umbilical cords. The doctor noted that the parents were calm, laughing and joking but deeply moved by the moment.

With the world's media camped outside, Knox and Vivienne instantly became the most valuable properties on earth, worth far more than their weight in gold. In fact, their images were jointly sold to *People* and *Hello!* for $14 million—the most expensive celebrity pictures ever taken, the money going to the Jolie-Pitt Foundation. Angie did most of the negotiations herself, according to *The New York Times,* the deal contingent on the U.S. magazine, which enjoyed its highest sales in seven years, never saying a bad word about her or her family.

As the family themselves had generated much of the negative media, it was a case of pot and kettle. There were, though, some moves toward an amnesty in the war of the Voights. Thanks to a friend's detective work, Jon Voight had found the whereabouts of James's new apartment in Sherman Oaks and had driven over to see him. Even though he had said hurtful things about his father in the media, James tends to be rather passive and nonconfrontational. This quality enabled him and his father to smooth over their public differences, the duo going to watch an L.A. Lakers basketball game in early June before James flew to be by his sister's side for the last weeks of her pregnancy. The arrival of the twins, combined with Jon's upcoming milestone—his seventieth birthday was in December—impelled friends and family to make an extra effort to warm the frozen relations between father and daughter. Director John Boorman made a personal plea to them to heal the breach. He was not the only one, the eventual result being a short telephone conversation around Jon's birthday. Others, like Krisann Morel, who hadn't seen Angie since she was a babe in arms, could only sit on the sidelines and watch with frustration. "Her view of her father is partly informed by the poison fed to her by her mother. It breaks my heart to see Jon denied access to his grandchildren."

While Jon, increasingly aware of his own mortality, indicated his willingness to get on the next plane to France if there was a chance of seeing his six grandchildren, Brad's parents were invited over to see the new arrivals—and to help out with the other kids. Help was indeed needed, the family having expanded by five children in just three years. During the long summer vacation, Jane Pitt was a familiar figure in the local stores, a handful of euros in one hand, her granddaughter Shiloh in the other, buying groceries for the château. Her parenting style, with set mealtimes and bedtimes and no nonsense, would have been a distinct contrast to the "no boundaries" approach promoted by Angie's mother and the new mother herself: the Midwest meets Hollywood.

Angie based her child-rearing methods on what she could remember—or what she told herself—about her mother's skills. Like Marcheline had when the children behaved themselves, she gave them sticker stars that they could later exchange for treats. Naturally, given the background of the parents, home life revolved around arts and crafts and dramatic play. So when the kids reportedly threw hair dye around the bathroom and stained the walls, Angie justified it as "creative expression," but the owners reportedly complained later about the mess. As for Jane Pitt, presumably she spent much of the summer biting her tongue.

Angie did, however, portray herself as a traditional parent, too, telling *Vanity Fair*: "You end up hearing yourself saying all those clichéd parent things: 'I don't care who started it, but I'm here to finish it.' I really can discipline the kids when I need to."

Those who visited the château were not entirely convinced. According to tabloid reports, breakfast took place at all hours of the day, Maddox, at six, allowed to use the stove to make his own concoctions, including macaroni and cheese with apple, toast, and pizza. After he had finished shooting his siblings with arrows from his catapult or toy guns—his mother also gave in to his entreaties and took him shopping for knives—he surfed the Internet looking for "weapons" or slumped in front of the TV watching *SpongeBob SquarePants* while his dad, usually in another room, sat glued to *The Ultimate Fighter*. Bedtime, like breakfast, was whenever, Brad putting the kids into their own beds only after they were well asleep.

Otherwise they all slept together. The overall impression was one of structured chaos, a happy family squirming and struggling in a huge nine-foot-wide bed, especially on weekends, with Brad making airline reservations and reading scripts in between changing diapers. "We're very hands-on parents, believe me," Angie told writer Martyn Palmer.

Besides Angie's brother, James, and Brad's parents, they did have other hands to help: nannies from Vietnam, the Congo, and the U.S.; four nurses; a doctor on permanent call; two personal assistants; a cook; a maid; two cleaners; a *plongeur*, or busboy; four close-protection bodyguards; and six French former army guards patrolling the extensive grounds. The staff all stayed in a nearby hotel. However harassed Angie and Brad may have felt with six children, they still had a way to go to match Angie's inspiration, dancer Josephine Baker, who raised twice as many orphans, also with the aid of a huge staff, at her home at Château des Milandes in the Dordogne.

There was one significant figure missing from this domestic caravan: the stocky figure of Mickey "Snowy" Brett, Angie's loyal bodyguard for the last eight years. When she first met him for the filming of *Lara Croft* she arrived in London with just a duffel bag. Now she needed a coach to move her family and entourage. Brett's departure showed how the wind was blowing inside the château of Brad and Angie. For all the chatter that Brad was just minding the kids while Angie got on with men's work, the boy from Springfield was not quite the grinning pussycat he seemed.

For years Brett and Angie had enjoyed a father/daughter relationship, the muscular East Ender, with a reputation for using threats in confrontations with photographers, regularly treated to her overblown generosity. Over the years she had given him lavish bonuses and, on one occasion, a Cartier watch. When Brad arrived on the scene, all that changed. For Christmas 2007 Brett got a pair of slippers. It was a not-so-subtle way of suggesting that Brett no longer occupied the position of prominence he had once enjoyed.

There were three of them in this relationship, and it was, to coin a phrase, "a bit crowded." Brad was asserting his rights as top dog, the alpha male who would brook no rival. Someone had to go, and it wasn't going to be him. According to Brett, the actor demeaned him by sending him to sex shops to buy face masks and other rubber paraphernalia for the kinky pair. Brett was outraged at this humiliating treatment—it was almost the first story he told casual acquaintances. Seeing the writing on the wall, Snowy melted from the scene, believing that Brad, brooding and moody, was not the man to make Angie as happy as she deserved to be.

As with Brett, so with Angie's brother, Brad keeping a wary eye on his day-to-day involvement with his family. While he welcomed James's help, Brad was not enthusiastic about swapping one intrusive male in the family mix for another and kept the boundaries clear. He apparently vetoed James's desire to be in the delivery room when his sister gave birth. In his position as family patriarch—unsurprisingly, one of his favorite shows is MTV's *Run's House,* about the chaotic family life of rapper and hip-hop pioneer Joseph Simmons—he questioned Angie's insistence that James adopt children of his own. As James had no permanent relationship or job, Brad didn't think adoption was a realistic option for him, someone he described as an "overgrown kid." To date, James has still to adopt.

While the Bertrand matriarchs have tended to rule the roost in their families, this is not the case with Brad and Angie. Theirs is a competitive relationship, a constant vying for supremacy. At the "boy racer" level they chased each other on their motorbikes, while Brad was so desperate to get his own private pilot's licence—like his partner—that he took endless flying lessons from the Nice airport so that he could take her for a joyride. It bugged him that she had earned both British and American certifications while he struggled to certify to fly planes in America, where the rules are less rigorous.

The couple share, too, an innate restlessness—"My theory is be the shark, you've got to keep moving," says Brad—their edgy energy funnels into their good works and creativity as well as their highly sexual relationship. As with her other lovers, Angie's public displays of affection can be embarrassing in the company of friends. When they fought, which was often, he would go off on his motorbike to cool down while she called his parents, brother, sister, and everyone she knew to find out where he was.

At heart, though, they were a couple of guys, and while Brad was the more likely to have a beer and shoot the breeze, it was a matter of debate on any given day as to who was wearing the trousers. Even with such a combustible, volatile, passionate yet seemingly compatible relationship, the arrival of the twins changed their lives much more than they anticipated. Like she had during the adoption of Pax, Angie spoke often and publicly about reining in her workload and focusing on her family. "My kids are my priority so it's possible from now I will make fewer movies. I may stop altogether," she told Italian *Vanity Fair*. It was a similar refrain with the BBC and others. Her mantra was: "I don't plan to keep acting very long. I will take a year off. I have a lot of children. I have a big responsibility to make sure that they're growing right and that they have got us there for them."

Yet just five weeks after giving birth, still struggling to properly breastfeed—though that didn't stop Brad from taking black-and-white pictures of her doing so for his friends at *W* magazine—she was in talks to replace Tom Cruise in the spy thriller *Edwin A. Salt*. After Cruise dropped out, writers busily reworked the lead character to be female, Angie set to portray a CIA officer falsely accused of being a Russian agent. (The movie was renamed *Salt*.) Once more there was a gap between her words and her deeds, a dissonance that she herself had grown up with. As ever, once she had taken the new chicks under her wing, Angie was desperate to fly the coop and leave Brad literally holding the babies. Her pattern seems to be one of possession and abandonment, endlessly reworking a deep-seated psychological script based on her own childhood experiences. Apparently, her psychic emptiness, the void she often talked about, could not be filled for long—even by a new arrival. As one observer with an inside track on the couple said: "He got stuck with the nanny role. She told him she was going to be a mom and not do all those movies. Yet she did movie after movie. In his mind she broke that sacred contract, to have children and be a family together." In fairness, though, as one of the highest-paid female stars in Hollywood, with a $15 million price tag, a relatively short time at the top, and a lot of hungry mouths to feed, who could blame her for cashing in?

There was more than cash at stake with the arrival of Knox and Vivienne. Quite simply, Angie struggled. In her mind's eye she had, as a typical Gemini who craves symmetry and a twin, a vision of introducing an African brother or sister to match with Zahara. Viewing her burgeoning family like a latter-day Noah's ark or even a cake, she called bringing another orphan into the family mix "layering in." Every time she visited a refugee camp or an orphanage she was racked with enormous guilt that she couldn't do more by rescuing another child from poverty. Those close to her believed that she was focused on adopting a child from the African state of Zimbabwe, currently suffering widespread starvation under the repressive regime of Robert Mugabe. An adoption agency in South Africa had been briefed on her requirements. Indeed, when the then Opposition leader, Morgan Tsvangirai, was injured in a car crash that killed his wife, it was reported that one of the first messages of condolence came from Angie.

Her surprise pregnancy put an end to that dream—for the moment. It was one of the reasons, friends said, that she initially found it difficult to bond with Knox and Vivienne. Later she warmed to Knox because he was the more fragile and struggled with his breathing. Still, though, she aimed to adopt an African orphan to bond with Zahara, but Brad, knowing her propensity to adopt and then take off, was more circumspect. He felt it sensible to consolidate for at least a year before "layering in" another slice of baby cake.

If her failure to honor their "contract" was a brooding undercurrent, then Brad, too, was equally culpable. As she recuperated from giving birth, Brad was smoking pot and downing five bottles of rosé with Quentin Tarantino, who visited the château to try to convince Brad to appear in his World War II drama, *Inglourious Basterds*. At the start of the evening, Brad said he couldn't possibly take on the role of Nazi hunter Aldo Raine. By the time the sun rose over the vineyards, the drunken couple had sworn eternal friendship and Pitt had signed on for Tarantino's army.

When the family moved to Berlin for the start of the shoot in September, the frat-house atmosphere continued after the cameras stopped rolling,

Brad joining the guys for beers and banter. Every week Tarantino hosted a film night. One time Brad took Maddox along to see the spaghetti Western *The Good, the Bad, and the Ugly,* starring a now-familiar face, Clint Eastwood.

The family and staff had only just settled into their huge rented villa in the Wannsee neighborhood of Berlin in October when they picked up again and flew to New York for the premiere of *Changeling.* Then they all returned to Germany before once again flying to New York, where Angie was promoting her latest movie. "It's a rule of ours we keep the platoon together," Brad explained.

With probably one of the largest individual carbon footprints in the world, Angie believed that the children actually enjoyed their globe-trotting lifestyle, bouncing from châteaux, to villas, to rented houses and sometimes their own homes in New Orleans, New York, and Los Angeles. "Sure, I am still restless," she said. "But do you know that my kids are the same way? We were in France these last few months and after a while they started asking when we could get back on a plane."

Their apparent enthusiasm contrasts with Angie's own childhood memories and complaints that she was constantly on the move and never had a permanent home. Yet she lived on the same street for most of her life, moving to Snedens Landing outside New York for just a few years before returning to California to finish her schooling in Beverly Hills. There are those in her circle who believe she is, however unconsciously, using her children as a shield; she is the one who cannot bear to stay anywhere for long, to dare to make anywhere "home." Her apartment at the Ansonia in Manhattan never felt permanent, with nothing in the fridge and half-unpacked suitcases in the living room. Certainly Maddox, now nine, is at an age when he wants to play with other youngsters. Life in Angie's traveling circus, albeit in private jets and luxury limousines, will at some point be seen by him and his siblings as a deprivation, stopping them from joining in with the crowd.

Angie, though, is not stopping anytime soon. Her peripatetic lifestyle is much more than films and promotion; she is now part of the furniture in the world of international relations and humanitarian aid. Recognized as one of *Time* magazine's one hundred most influential people of 2008, she formed a substantive part of a major paradigm shift in Hollywood, where activist actors were becoming the rule rather than the exception. While Hollywood's helping hand was nothing new—Audrey Hepburn was a tireless Goodwill Ambassador for UNICEF—the confluence of so many celebrity voices on thorny issues like the killings in Darfur focused the public and ultimately the administration on taking a tougher stance with the Sudanese government. Angie, now dubbed the Mother Teresa of Hollywood, was a leading light in this process. She earned praise from JFK's onetime speechwriter, Ted Sorenson, who sat in an audience of policy wonks and power players, including General Wesley Clark, at the Council on Foreign Relations in October 2008, when she spoke about the need for peace with justice in places like Darfur. "Frankly I came a skeptic, but am leaving impressed," he said. It seemed the days of "mist reading," when journalists tried vainly to decipher what she was trying to say, were over.

SHE'S ACTUALLY SMART, said the headline in the *Daily Beast* blog, the patronizing tone drawing ire from Nicholas Kristof, a Pulitzer Prize–winning journalist who specializes in global conflicts. "Until we have an administration that cares about these issues, we have to accept moral leadership where we can find it—and that includes celebrities who care," he wrote, singling out Bono, Ashley Judd, Ben Affleck, Mia Farrow, and of course Angie as examples of stars who shine a light on subjects politicians often shy away from. The role of the celebrity advocate is increasingly influential, their participation essential in bringing difficult issues into the mainstream of the American conversation. They are global politicians, without a party or a manifesto, and, unlike the Hollywood activists of Jon Voight's youth, they have deep pockets and access to the corridors of power.

While Angie was speaking on global issues, for once the spotlight was on her father. During the presidential election, Jon Voight, a guest at the 2008 Republican National Convention, launched a savage attack on Democratic candidate Barack Obama, the media, and what he described as the nation's "lunatic fringe." He then went on to provide the voice-over for a promotional video for Republican vice presidential nominee Sarah Palin. If he was trying to woo his children, he was hardly helping his cause. James, a pro-Obama activist who considered running for office himself in Nevada or California, was furious with his father for his outspoken attacks on the man who became the next president.

Angie, who privately dismissed Sarah Palin as setting back "the cause of women a century," was much more circumspect in public about her political affiliations. She was aware that as a UN lobbyist she would have to curry favor with whichever party was in power if she wanted to be an effective voice on the Hill. It was one of the reasons why she was a registered Independent, although, in keeping with her strong Voight genes, she admitted that she and Clint Eastwood, a noted Republican, saw eye to eye on numerous issues. She even initiated a truce with her father, calling him around his birthday on December 29 and making occasional contact thereafter. It was an uneasy peace, most conversations confined to the children and what books they were reading.

Angie and Brad had campaigns of their own to wage after they were both nominated for Oscars, she for her understated but powerful performance in *Changeling,* and Brad, who had just turned forty-five, for his role as a man who ages in reverse in David Fincher's *The Curious Case of Benjamin Button.* In their game of one-upmanship, even though Brad had now been nominated for the second time, it was his partner who had won an Oscar for *Girl, Interrupted.* While she noted with an unconcerned shrug that her late mother had somehow misplaced her Oscar, she and Brad were quietly assiduous in schmoozing the red carpet during the awards season, glad-handing one and all at ceremonies in Hollywood, London, and elsewhere. The Oscars epitomized the Angie and Brad brand, a schizophrenic mixture of glamour and grit, the couple flying to the Thailand/Myanmar (formerly Burma) border shortly before the awards ceremony. There they met with Rohingya refugees, a minority community denied citizenship in their own country by the brutal military dictatorship. Their stories were heartbreaking; a month before, the Thai military had towed six boats carrying Rohingya refugees out to sea, and five of the craft had sunk, leaving hundreds drowned. In her capacity as UN Goodwill Ambassador, Angie asked the Thai authorities to accept Muslim migrants fleeing the tyranny of their next-door neighbors.

Within days of leaving this living hell, they were back to a different surreality, walking the red carpet for the Academy Awards, once again ignoring TV host Ryan Seacrest. Indeed, it was these wild swings in her life that inspired Angie to ask twenty-seven friends, including Jude Law, Hilary Swank, Colin Farrell, and Jonny Lee Miller, to film what they saw at the same time at different locations around the globe. Her ex-husband found himself, perhaps symbolically, allocated a minefield. The resulting documentary, *A Place in Time,* Angie's directorial debut, captured something of these extremes, of radically different lives, cultures, and experiences.

On Oscar night in March 2009, Angie and Brad were front and center in their real-life soap opera. All eyes were on the celebrity couple as much for their dramatic potential as for their Oscar-nominated acting chops. They sat in the front row, just feet from the podium where Jack Black and Jennifer Aniston were presenting the animated feature award. Would she, could she, would they, could they . . . look at each other, that is? In the end Jen fluffed her first lines and smiled in the general direction of her nemesis and her former husband while Brad and Angie laughed at the rehearsed banter onstage. It was left to the professional mist readers in the tabloids to divine that Jen's smile was "only for Brad."

For all their efforts, the couple left empty-handed, Sean Penn winning the Oscar for his role in *Milk* and British actress Kate Winslet for hers in *The Reader.*

It was back to work: Angie filmed the action drama *Salt,* helmed by Phillip Noyce, who had worked with Angie on *The Bone Collector,* in Washington, New York State, and Manhattan; while just down the road, Brad reprised his starring role as Mr. Mom at the couple's rented estate at Oyster Bay on Long Island. An early riser, he liked to make breakfast for the children before taking them to school. Just a normal stay-at-home dad, except locals noticed that moms bussing their kids to and from Maddox's school seemed to be wearing higher heels and more makeup than usual. He took the attention in stride, Brad and the kids regulars at Dunkin' Donuts, the local pizza parlor, and Borders bookstore, while he took the boys to Niagara Falls, bike riding, and to the local mall. Even so, this was Mr. Mom with a difference: Brad met with President Obama and Speaker of the House Nancy Pelosi in March to discuss how to do more to aid the victims of Hurricane Katrina, and later that month talked with Newark mayor Cory Booker about a potential partnership to build housing projects in New Jersey.

As worthy as these causes were, the story that got the most attention concerned the night Angie arrived home unexpectedly at their Long Island mansion. When she walked through the door, she found a scene of devastation, the kids causing mayhem, the TV blaring away, and Brad upstairs, beer in hand, slumped on the bed. She gave him hell. "Will you please respect the fact that I am working right now?" she was reported as shouting. "All you have to do today is watch the kids. Will you please do it?"

Sadly, the story, as much as it consoled working mothers worldwide to hear that even the sexiest woman on the planet had trouble keeping her lazy, good-for-nothing partner in line, was dismissed as nonsense by Team Jolie-Pitt. Nevertheless, it seemed to have the ring of truth, and Brad's behavior was probably one of the few things Angie and Brad's ex-wife would ever agree on. His laid-back approach informed Jennifer's thinking about having children. "She didn't want to be stuck at home with a baby while he behaved like a forty-two-year-old adolescent, partying, smoking, and working out," recalled a friend. Angie confessed that if Brad defied her, she was likely to fly off the handle. "Then I can get so angry that I tear his shirt," she told *Das Neue* magazine.

While the cozy image of domestic disharmony added to the gaiety of nations, there were more troubling whispers. Angie, clearly painfully thin and very pale, was spending much of her time holed up in her suite at the Waldorf-Astoria in Manhattan, seemingly ignoring Brad and her children. She had done the same before when filming *A Mighty Heart,* leaving the kids with Brad and their platoon of nannies while staying in a hotel in Beverly Hills. At that time she explained that in order to perfect Mariane Pearl's French accent and inhabit her new character, she needed time away from her madding crowd of kids. It was reminiscent of her mother's desire for "me time," leaving James and Angie in the company of nannies while she read self-help books, reviewed her astrological chart, and wrote poetry.

This time Angie had a simple explanation for her absence from the rented family home. Her film work was so utterly demanding—the mother of six spent her days jumping through windows and off bridges, cars, and subway trains—that she didn't want to arrive home exhausted and unable to give the children her full attention. "She doesn't want to be irritable and short-tempered around the kids while she is totally focused on the part," noted a close friend. After all, she had given Brad space when he was working with Tarantino in Berlin on his bloody war movie.

There were times Brad became the punching bag for her frustrations, Angie picking fault with the way he was handling the children as a way of venting her own tired anger. In their flashpoint arguments she would hurl insults at him and dare him to leave the family. For his part he found this rapid escalation of their fights to be frustrating and irritating. Whether she meant what she said or not, Brad made it clear that he was in it for the long haul. He wasn't going anywhere soon.

Angie took out her frustrations on others, too—much to the delight of director Phillip Noyce. Inside the Waldorf-Astoria hotel, Angie was in the mood to kill. In between organizing playdates with stunt coordinator and martial-arts expert Wade Allen, who is the father of two sons, she was kicking the bad guys to death. Her director wanted Angie's character, CIA agent Evelyn Salt, to show a cruel, vicious streak, and he wanted the fight sequences to be correspondingly "street and grungy." This was something of a private joke between Angie and the stunt team. She had appeared in a mockumentary, *Sledge: The Untold Story,* about a fictitious stuntman whose claim to fame was introducing dance into screen fights. In a spoof interview about the stuntman, Angie deadpans: "We're all going to have to dance. . . . I hate dance." There was no dancing in her latest movie; in one sequence, which she rehearsed in the hotel suite, Angie performed what is known as a "stutter step" in front of a prone assailant. In the moments from looking at the guy to kicking him, Angie's attitude suggested, "I'm going to hurt you because I want to and I can." Fellow assailant, stuntman Rich Ting, lying prone on the floor, watched the move and thought: "This girl is vicious— and very sexy." Then, in between rehearsals in April she would be on the phone to Brad, asking after the children before continuing her one-woman killing game. As they rehearsed she got so up close and personal with Ting, a Calvin Klein model, that he moved away. "What's wrong? Do I smell?" she joked.

While she was easygoing in rehearsals, on the day of the shoot, it was a different Angie who appeared on set, surrounded by bodyguards and a fluttering entourage. She had her game face on. The days of yelling and clearing her throat to get in character were long gone, Angie laid-back but ready for action, playfully hitting Ting in the face with her gun and saying: "Good morning. How are you? We are going to have fun today."

After twenty-five takes, Noyce was happy but Angie was perplexed that the crew was giving Rich Ting a hard time. She discovered that he was due to fly to Vietnam on a modeling assignment and his agent didn't want his face messed up in the fight. Her own face lit up when talk turned to Vietnam, the actress speaking enthusiastically about the country and giving him a list of friends who would show him around. Ting was amazed that the leading lady would take this trouble. "In this industry courtesy is uncommon, but she is so gracious," he says. "Unlike many others, she has not gone Hollywood; she has gone global."

During filming she stopped kicking the bad guys long enough to extend the hand of friendship to one of the good guys in her life. In January Bill Day received a call out of the blue from Angie, asking to meet up. It had been fourteen years since they had last met, but her schedule was such—her assistant, Holly Goline, breaks up her day into thirty-minute segments—that they didn't come face-to-face until April. He arrived at the Long Island set to be met by a heavily made-up woman in a blonde wig.

"You look just the same," she said as they hugged in the middle of the warehouse set. "Wish I could say the same for you," he joked, pointing at the wig and the costume. After she did a couple more takes of the scene, they went back to her trailer, where he met Shiloh and Zahara and they ate lunch, caught up on old times—and laid to rest some ghosts. He was keen to clear up the past, explaining that he met his wife, Caroline, long after he and Marcheline had split up. As he suspected, Marcheline had explained their breakup differently, telling the children that he had cheated on her. That wasn't the case, as everyone in their circle knew at the time. In fact, Marcheline was so over Bill that she was dating a divorced father of four daughters shortly after they parted—something Bill had only learned recently. Angie made it clear that she bore him no ill will. She wanted to forgive and forget, eager to meet Caroline and to move on. Angie even arranged a birthday surprise for her brother a couple of weeks later in early May, Bill the special guest at a discreet lunch in a Manhattan hotel. Once again Bill explained the reasons behind the breakup with their mother. James was more skeptical, still believing the story their mother had told them fourteen years before. Like his sister, he had subscribed to the Bertrand freeze, sticking with his mother, right or wrong. During the three-hour lunch there was a dawning recognition that their mother's version of events was not necessarily the truth, a grudging acknowledgment that her assessment of others, notably their father, had colored their perceptions since childhood. As James described his mother's last days, he was even able to joke that at least her last words were only about his father and not about Bill as well. These encounters seemed to mark a turning point for Angie and James, a tacit admission that they had been party to an illusion and that they, unlike their mother, had the capacity to forgive.

This friendly but important reunion was soon tarnished when *Now,* a British tabloid magazine, fabricated a story saying that Angie had had an affair with her mother's boyfriend when she was sixteen, citing this author as the source. This was news to me, and of course totally untrue. For Bill it spoiled what had been a happy reunion, leaving him "seriously depressed." The whole incident could be seen as a metaphor for Angie's life, a life of illusion and delusion further distorted by a tabloid prism.

In May Angie left this monstrous world of make-believe behind for grotesque real life, flying to Holland to spend time at the International Criminal Court in The Hague. There she attended the trial of Congolese warlord Thomas Lubanga Dyilo, charged with war crimes, namely, using child soldiers in bloody tribal conflicts during 2002–2003. His was the first international trial focusing solely on child soldiers. In the courtroom Angie was given a long, unnerving, hard-eyed stare by the suspected mass murderer. Afterward she praised the child soldiers who were prepared to give voice to the horrors they had witnessed: "After watching the proceedings from the viewing booth, I stood up and found Thomas Lubanga Dyilo looking at me. I imagined how difficult it must be for all the brave young children who have come to testify against him."

A couple of days later, Angie found scrutiny of a very different sort much easier to bear when she and Brad strolled down the red carpet at the Cannes Film Festival amid a flurry of flashbulbs for the premiere of *Inglourious Basterds.* It was the couple's first appearance in public in three months. Angie, looking like a latter-day goddess in her slit-to-the-thigh Versace gown, with her partner dressed in a slick tux, put on a suitably amorous show to silence the Greek chorus of doom. It was a chance, a friend noted, to indulge in "cuddles and old-fashioned romance."

Not for long, though. The *National Enquirer* gave Angie an early birthday surprise with the headline that she and Brad had officially split. After she wiped away the birthday cake Brad smushed into her face when he arrived unexpectedly on the set of *Salt* on June 5, she reflected that there was some truth in the story. They were indeed splitting—but not intentionally: Brad was heading to Los Angeles in July to make Steven Soderbergh's baseball drama, *Moneyball,* while Angie continued with *Salt* in New York. Then Brad was scheduled to spend months in the Mato Grosso region of Brazil to film *The Lost City of Z,* the story of the vain search for a legendary city by British surveyor Colonel Percy Harrison Fawcett during the 1920s. Brad was growing his beard in preparation. Layer into that creative mix the fact that Geyer Kosinski had successfully concluded a deal with the author Patricia Cornwell for the movie rights to her bestselling series about medical examiner Kay Scarpetta and it was clear that the couple had a creatively overflowing plate. Even with the best intentions, their ideal scenario of one movie on, one movie off—which Angie and Billy Bob tried in their early days together—wasn't working out as they would have liked. The last-minute cancellation of *Moneyball* by Columbia Pictures at a cost of $10 million gave them breathing space, the couple spending part of the summer in their Los Feliz home.

Even though she now had the time, Angie did not take the opportunity to watch her first-ever screen performance in Hal Ashby's comedy *Lookin' to Get Out.* She missed an emotional evening at the Billy Wilder Theater in Westwood on June 29, her father breaking down in tears as he spoke of a father's search for his daughter. Voight was relating the untold story of the director's cut of the film, which was first discovered by Ashby's biographer Nick Dawson. The fact that Ashby had a daughter whom he had never been able to bring himself to meet added greater poignancy to the scene between the six-year-old girl played by Angie and her biological father, played by Jon Voight as a ne'er-do-well hustler. As Voight told the audience: "He walked to Leigh's door many times. I truly believe he just couldn't cross the threshold because he didn't know if he'd be proper as a father because fatherhood was so questionable to him."

The audience of friends and colleagues shuffled uncomfortably in their seats as they recognized that the weeping Voight was really talking about his own pain and disconnection from his daughter. For example, he was not invited to the twins' first birthday on July 12, though Brad's parents flew in from Springfield for the occasion. Forgiveness stretched only so far.

Within days Angie was off on her travels again, visiting Amman, Jordan, with Maddox in late July for the Twenty-ninth International Arab Children Health Congress, before making her third trip to Iraq, praising the efforts of the American troops while, once again, pinpointing the plight of the country's homeless. Back in Los Angeles, she spent much time taking flying lessons, doing circuits or taking short flights to places like Las Vegas. Flying set her free; it was her escape from earthly cares. Once off the ground—astrologically she is an air sign—she was in her natural element, unfettered and unencumbered. There is no earth in her star sign.

On the ground she was chained to her image; goddess, savior, and, ironically, earth mother. Whether she wanted to or not, she had to be or at least give the impression of being supermom, especially as Brad was now fully formed in the public imagination as Mr. Mom. She had always said she wanted the man in her life to be a great dad, the kind of father she wished she'd had. During the publicity for *Inglourious Basterds,* Brad waxed lyrical about the delights of fatherhood, how he enjoyed growing older and being a domestic god. "I'm a dad now; my partying ends at six P.M.," he told the *Daily Mail,* while his costar Eli Roth revealed another dimension of the screen idol, describing how he used baby wipes to freshen up if he didn't have time for a shower. Roth explained: "After a scene, Brad had to get next to me for a close-up shot, and he said: 'Damn, you're ripe.'" Roth replied: "I didn't have time to shower." Brad gave him a tip: "Baby wipes, man, baby wipes. I got six kids. All you've got to do is just take them, a couple quick wipes under the pits. I'm getting [peed] on all day. I don't have time to take a shower."

The story captures the earthy good nature of a man who can still cause maternal hearts to flutter. While he talked volubly about his life as a father, there wasn't much talk of "we," as in Angie and him. With Brad now positioned as Mr. Mom, it appeared that the onus was on Angie to join him on Happy Family Airways rather than seem to fly solo. After all, she had what she always wanted—or told herself that she wanted. Be careful what you wish for.

In the fall of 2009, whether consciously or not, she set herself a test, signing on for a romantic thriller, *The Tourist,* directed by Oscar winner Florian Henckel von Donnersmarck. The plot revolves around an "extraordinary woman," Elise, played by Angie, who deliberately crosses the path of an American tourist visiting Venice to mend a broken heart. The tourist, played by Johnny Depp, pursues their romance, which culminates with the couple making passionate love in the shower. While a Depp-Jolie pair-up had been dreamed about by producers and studios over the years—

there was even talk of their playing Cathy and Heathcliff in *Wuthering Heights*—it was also a long-cherished ambition of Angie's to work with her teen idol. Once again Billy Bob Thornton's dictum that actors choose the parts that reflect where they are in their lives seemed to have resonance.

Those who have known Angie for years anticipated trouble. Johnny Depp, notes a family friend, is very much her type: wild, artistic, and intriguing. In her mind he falls somewhere between Billy Bob and Brad Pitt, creative but not weird, natural but not insane. Elusive, too, engaged at one time to Winona Ryder and to Kate Moss—which may help explain Angie's antipathy toward both women—but now living with French singer and fashion muse Vanessa Paradis, with whom he has two children. People who know Angie well believe that in days gone by she would have made a play for Depp. For her to live out her fantasy on film rather than in real life might be the resolution of this emotional conundrum.

"Angie is a free spirit; you cannot tame her," says a friend. "If she could get something going with Depp, she would leave Brad. She has always had a crush on him, always admired his quirky roles and his looks." Astrologically, though, there is little connection between Depp's and Jolie's charts; there is much more between Brad's and Angie's.

Certainly an affair would be box-office poison for Angie, especially as she has been comprehensively outmaneuvered by Brad, who seems, at least in the public mind, to be the more stable, responsible, and hands-on parent. Brad cut off any likely romantic concerns at the pass, reportedly insisting, against Angie's wishes, that he and the children join her for the three-month shoot in Venice and Paris. Before filming began in February 2010, Vanessa Paradis parked her tanks on Angie's lawn, declaring in *People* that even after twelve years she was "still deeply in love": "[Johnny] makes me happy. We are many things—we are together and, in a way, one person," she said.

If the interview was a marker, it was placed just in time, Angie telling Germany's *Das Neue* magazine in December that she did not consider fidelity "absolutely essential" in a relationship. "It's worse to leave your partner and talk badly about him afterwards. Neither Brad nor I have ever claimed that living together means to be chained together. We make sure that we never restrict each other."

Angie seemed to be sending out a signal, her semaphore interpreted by the media as indicating storms ahead. Those storms were not long in coming.

Hotel worker Anna Kowalski, who worked on Angie's floor at the Waldorf-Astoria, accused the actress of cheating on Brad with one of her dialect coaches. She told *In Touch* magazine that after a late-night visit from the coach she found Angie's hotel room littered with sex toys, a black rubber sheet, and empty vodka bottles. While the film's chief dialect coach, Howard Samuelsohn, dismissed the claim as "bullshit," Kowalski further claimed that Angie and Brad rarely interacted when they were in the suite together. "I didn't see any kind of connection between Pitt and Jolie," said the maid, who had been fired by the hotel.

While the tittle-tattle of a hotel worker was one thing, the front-page story in the *News of the World* on January 24, 2010, claiming that the couple had seen divorce lawyers and had signed a £205 ($320) million deal to split their assets and share custody of their six children was quite another. The story, which detailed the couple's initial visit to the lawyer's office in December and their subsequent agreement, which was signed in January, set off a furious spin cycle of speculation that sucked in even staid TV, radio, and print outlets. The whirr of further evidence included the information that Brad had paid $1.3 million for a bachelor pad—complete with cave—near his existing property in Los Feliz; that he had been absent from the Screen Actors Guild Awards when the rest of the cast of *Inglourious Basterds* was present; and that he was apparently overheard at a four-hour dinner at Alto restaurant in Manhattan telling Angie that she needed psychiatric help. (Given the distance between tables, this would have been difficult.)

One intriguing question that hung in the air was why they would need to see a divorce lawyer when they were unmarried. According to her circle, the reality was that they had gone to a lawyer in order to formalize arrangements for their children should anything happen to either of them. Since common-law marriages are not recognized in California, it made sense to have some paperwork relating to the children. Angie was notoriously slack in this regard. When she was married to Jonny Lee Miller, the couple had never bothered to sort out a prenuptial agreement. After Angie's career took off, it was her mother who took the initiative to see a lawyer to draw up legal papers so that Angie was protected in the case of divorce. On February 8, 2010, Brad and Angie took legal action against Britain's biggest-selling Sunday newspaper for making "false and intrusive allegations."

While the physical and emotional demands of filming *Salt*—reshoots were still going on in January—had undoubtedly strained their partnership, and the looming prospect of working with Johnny Depp had given Angie pause about her past obsessions and future direction, the couple pulled together for a cause they both held dear, helping the homeless and injured following the devastating January 2010 earthquake in Haiti, a country they had just recently visited. Not only did they donate $1 million to Doctors Without Borders—on top of the $6.8 million they had given away during 2009—but Angie, in her capacity as Goodwill Ambassador, was soon on the ground seeing for herself the progress made by relief efforts.

During the two-day visit, when she visited SOS Villages for orphans and a Doctors Without Borders hospital, Angie spoke to CNN's Christiane Amanpour. The conversation reflected how far and how quickly she had come, Amanpour overtly recognizing her influence on the national and international stage. "You have a huge amount of power at your fingertips because of who you are. You have the ability to sway people." Implicit was the fact she had broken free of Hollywood typecasting, a screen siren defined not by what she wore but by what she said. As activist John Trudell notes: "Her intelligence is the core of her substance. Looks and sexuality are the surface of who she is." Today she is a role model for a different kind of woman: unconventional yet traditional, a homemaker but a marriage wrecker, nurturing but self-destructive. In fact, a classic Gemini. She is able to have it all without, seemingly, paying a price.

Yet she is still paying a price in a currency that she barely understands, repeating a script from her childhood that she only briefly glimpses. There are signs, though, that she is venturing onto the path of forgiveness, inviting her father to join her family in Venice in February after flying to Dublin to watch his friend John Boorman receive a lifetime achievement award. It is possible that the long winter freeze is ending and a familial thaw has begun. Her mother would not have approved, just as she would not have countenanced Angie's meeting with Bill Day. Perhaps Angie is starting to become her own woman. As Day observes: "I have watched this family at war for decades. There comes a time to forgive and forget." Breaking free of the narrative of the past, understanding the truth of her journey, is Angie's next big challenge.

As a free-spirited woman, she has constructed a gilded cage for herself, surrounded by the vulnerable, the needy, and the dispossessed, with an ever-expanding family and a partner who, in sickness and health, clearly shares this brave adventure with her. There is no easy escape and there are few opportunities to cut and run. Angie, this creature of air, has deliberately anchored herself in the reality of a partnership and family life. On her body is a quotation from Tennessee Williams that reads: "A prayer for the wild at heart, kept in cages." In truth, she should add: "Of their own making."

ACKNOWLEDGMENTS AND SOURCE NOTES

When I first saw Angelina Jolie at a film premiere for the Peace One Day charity at New York's Ziegfeld Theater in September 2005, the response to her reminded me how people behaved when the late Diana, Princess of Wales, walked into a room. Unlike the royal demographic, though, the women in this audience looked as if they had just stepped off the catwalk or come from making a keynote business speech, while the guys had that Brad Pitt vibe going on. Yet when Ms. Jolie walked into the theater in a long silver dress, all conversation, BlackBerry and other, came to a halt as sophisticated heads craned to get a better look. For some reason, she sat a couple of seats away from me, and I can confirm that the physiognomy and the rest of the bits did not disappoint.

The takeaway from the evening was twofold: How sad to think that the goals of a charity whose raison d'être is to encourage the human race to stop killing one another for one day a year seemed so far off; and what on earth was the quietly charismatic Angelina doing at such a function?

At the time, I was researching a book on Tom Cruise and was based in Beverly Hills. Most mornings I ran around Roxbury Park, one of the few spots of public green in an otherwise palm tree–lined concrete desert. Little did I realize that this modest oasis of grass and roses held a major clue to the secret that is the extraordinary life of Angelina Jolie. While I wrote my biography on the couch-jumping actor, Angie did what stars do: twinkle—but also give birth, adopt a child, and visit places like Peshawar, in the bandit country between Pakistan and Afghanistan. Now a virtual no-go zone, even in those days Peshawar was hardly a place for hardened charity workers, let alone bona fide Hollywood movie stars.

I was intrigued to know more. At first viewing, Angelina Jolie seems to be a young woman who has lived in plain sight: an actress happy to talk about her love life, sexual preferences, drug use, tattoos, and why she kissed her brother on the lips in public. Secrets and Angelina Jolie don't usually fit in the same sentence. Like other savvy Hollywood stars, she has shaped, often unintentionally, the landscape of her life to fit our expectations of how a celebrity behaves. It works.

Yet the true story of Angelina Jolie remains largely uncharted territory. Her statements are taken at face value, her stories uncorroborated. As a result, Kipling's "six honest serving men," What, Why, When, How, Where, and Who, have worked overtime on sorting the fact from the fiction of her extraordinary life. How did this woman who was a self-confessed drug user become a leading light in the United Nations? What lay behind this restless need to adopt children? And what with the cutting, the kissing, and the coke? Why Billy Bob? And when Brad Pitt?

It soon became clear that her life had been marred and scarred by the marital rift between her parents, a schism that had shaped her view of herself and informed her subsequent actions. Perhaps more than many others', Angie's story owes much to the character and nature of her parents, actor Jon Voight and Marcheline Bertrand, their lives defining who she is and, perhaps more important, how she sees herself.

Within a few weeks of starting my research, I discovered an extraordinary story about Angelina, a fresh and compelling narrative that perhaps only impinged on the edge of her consciousness and yet defined who she is and how she subsequently behaved. The facts I uncovered and the circumstances surrounding them meant that I knew more about Angelina's life, what formed her, what drove her, than she did herself. It unlocked the door to understanding the dynamic yet enigmatic character of one of the world's best-known and possibly best-loved actresses.

Angie's story is essentially a synthesis of revelation and interpretation, uncovering new material about her life while trying to place her journey in the context of what she says, what she believes, and what she does. Words and actions rarely act in concert. Picking a path through the shifting sands of words, actions, belief, and fact has been the most ticklish aspect of this journey. I have enjoyed the company of many guides, some of whom have become good friends. While they have been generous with their memories and insights, the conclusions and interpretation, however ill-judged, are my responsibility alone.

Although Angie is one of the most picked-over celebrities of the modern age, for the most part I have relied on original research and interviews with contemporaries, or at the very least tried to place Angelina Jolie's own words in a coherent framework. In Hollywood nothing is ever quite as it seems.

This is very much a family story, the history of the Voights and Bertrands, which forms the spine of Chapter 1, shaping Angelina's destiny. In this endeavor I was helped by the insights and memories of Don, Shirley, and Chuck Peters, Esther Kasha, Karen Kaptor Jasnoch, Denise Horner-Halupka, Marianne Follis Angarola, Adrianne Neri, Marilyn Knickrehm, and the research of Riverdale historian Carl Durnavich, who placed the history of the Bertrand family in context.

To understand the trauma of Angelina's childhood, the voice of Krisann Morel, who was effectively her nanny for two years, along with others who asked not to be named, was crucial. They provided the key that opens the door into Angie's troubled soul. In this traumatic period, which occupies Chapters 2 and 3, I am grateful for the reminiscences, too, of actor Jeff Austin, publicist Deborah Kolar, director Robert Lieberman, family friends Randy Alpert and Susie Kantor Szarez, as well as director John Boorman, whose conversation and book *Adventures of a Suburban Boy* (Faber and Faber, 2003) provided much insight. Angie's former school friends from El Rodeo and Beverly Hills High and other contemporaries were full of stories, though several, even at this remove, were nervous about being identified. My thanks therefore to Brian Evans, Bernard Hallet, Eddie Horowitz, Michael Hsu, and Windsor Lai.

I am eternally grateful to Bill Day, who was Marcheline Bertrand's partner for eleven years, and Lauren Taines, who was a close friend of both Marcheline's and Jon Voight's for thirty-five years, for the ribbon of fact and anecdote that is a both a bracing antidote to the conventional view of Angie's parents as well as an important window into her young life.

In describing Angelina's early career, I was guided by the thoughts and recollections of photographers Robert Kim and Sean McCall, makeup artist Rita Montanez, instructor Kent Sterling of the Arthur Murray dance studio, cameraman Mark Gordon, director Michael Schroeder, and actors Karen Sheperd and Ric Young. The suicide of Julie Jones is based on the official autopsy report as well as background briefings from John Connolly and her friends. Jim Cairns, pathologist and former deputy chief coroner, Ontario, gave a specialist's insight into the incident. As for the bizarre story of the theft of garbage left outside the home of Jon Voight's manager, this is centered around off-the-record, and almost straight-faced, interviews with two of the conspirators. Angie's work on *Hackers* and *Foxfire* was based on conversations with fellow actor Michelle Brookhurst, camera crew, agents, production staff, and others speaking on the condition of confidentiality. Andy Wilson, the director of *Playing God,* had a wryly cynical take on Hollywood, as befitting a man raised in a circus.

The period from the making of the movie *Hell's Kitchen* in 1997 to Angie's marriage to Billy Bob Thornton in 2000 was a haze of drugs, dramatic awards, and rock and rollers, most notably her relationship with Mick Jagger. I spent a fascinating day with her former dealer Franklin Meyer, looking over his extensive video and picture collection, inhaling only his memories of Angie and other well-heeled customers to his salon at the Chelsea Hotel. Inevitably, many of those involved wish to remain in the background. Or have forgotten they were there in the first place. This was, though, a creative time for Angie, when she starred in *Gia, Girl, Interrupted, George Wallace,* and other works. My thanks to drummer Joey Covington, TV producer Jeremy Louwerse, tattooist Friday Jones, and other anonymous sources for helping to ink in this period. John H. Richardson's February 2000 profile of Angelina Jolie in *Esquire* gives a sense of where her head was at, while the July 2001 *Rolling Stone* portrait of Angie and Billy Bob by Chris Heath can be read as performance art as much as an interview. Celebrity writer Jonathan Van Meter's conversations with Angie are always revealing.

Angie's time with Billy Bob Thornton, her involvement with the United Nations, and her eventual adoption of a Cambodian orphan, Maddox, in 2002, marked a turning point in her life. I would particularly like to thank Ingrid Earle for her insights and enthusiasm in helping to uncover sources, as well as Rachel Flanagan, Heather Hope Howard, Melissa

Howard, Sheila McCombe, and Penny Thornton. *Levity* director Ed Solomon's story about Billy Bob Thornton, Pat Boone, and the flight to Namibia captured the actor/musician's enduring quirkiness.

With regard to Angie's work with the United Nations, the Honorable Joseph Melrose, former United States ambassador to Sierra Leone, was very helpful in describing her first UN tour, while career aid worker Annick Gillard Bailetti described in detail life in refugee camps. Joanna Piucci, manager, Messengers of Peace & Special Projects Advocacy & Special Events, Department of Public Information at the United Nations in New York, and Patrick Hayford, director of the Office of the Special Advisor on Africa (OSAA), explained the role of a Goodwill Ambassador. Angie's observations about her visits to refugee camps in her book *Notes from My Travels* (Pocket Books, 2003) provide the perspective of an innocent abroad to the problems of the planet, while the discourse by her sometime traveling companion Jeffrey Sachs, titled *Common Wealth: Economics for a Crowded Planet* (Penguin Books, 2008), gives a more scholarly outlook.

On the vexed matter of adoption, I have consulted with a number of sources both specifically involved with Angie's adoptions and with the general difficulty of Westerners adopting children from developing countries. Adoption facilitator Catherine Politte was most helpful, as was Kate Adie, whose book *Nobody's Child* (Hodder & Stoughton, 2005) is highly informative. In relation to Operation Broken Hearts, the case against Seattle International Adoptions, which facilitated the adoption of Maddox, I would like to thank U.S. Assistant Attorney Jim Lord, who prosecuted, and Lorie Dankers, spokesperson for the Department of Homeland Security and Immigration and Customs Enforcement in Seattle, which investigated the case. I consulted research papers by Kevin Browne and others on international adoptions and orphans in Europe and the so-called Madonna effect.

Fresh information and insights into the now-notorious interview Jon Voight gave about his daughter in 2002 were provided by TV presenter Pat O'Brien, though it is a pity his memories of Hunter S. Thompson and Timothy Leary didn't make the cut. Another time. Pastor Ken Anderson helped place this public melodrama in human context, while actor Nathan Lee Graham and others who wished to remain in the background walked me through the fallout. The reissue of Hal Ashby's *Lookin' to Get Out* in

June 2009 provided another setting to witness this estrangement. Nick Dawson's biography *Being Hal Ashby: Life of a Hollywood Rebel* (The University Press of Kentucky, 2009) had eerie parallels with Angie's own story.

Once Brad Pitt moseyed into town like some Wild West gunslinger, shutters were slammed shut, eyes averted, and Hollywood folk circled the wagons. It will, however, be clear that I have managed to ride shotgun and talk on a background basis with people who worked on *Mr. & Mrs. Smith,* who moved in the Malibu circle of Brad and Jennifer Aniston, and shuttled between Davos and Washington as part of the international humanitarian circuit. They know who they are and my thanks to them. Nancy Aniston's self-serving autobiography, *From Mother and Daughter to Friends* (Prometheus Books, 1999), makes the perfect case for why children should be allowed to divorce their parents.

The extraordinary invasion of the African country of Namibia by Team Jolie for the birth of Shiloh was well described by the combatants, some of whom lived to fight another day. My thanks to Barbara Jones, Cornall De Villiers, Steve Butler, and Donna Collins. Marina Hyde's book *Celebrity: How Entertainers Took Over the World and Why We Need an Exit Strategy* (Harvill Secker, 2009) provided covering fire.

In the 24/7 tabloid hysteria that is the world of Brad Pitt and Angelina Jolie, it is difficult to hear the quiet voices of reason, so my thanks to Mich Ahern, Alan Hamm, John Bell, Sharon Feinstein, Tim Miles, and others for calming the cacophony. My thanks to John Trudell for his observations about Angie's luminous personality, while Bill Day's insights into Marcheline Bertrand's death and his subsequent meeting with her daughter and son, James, provide a telling bookend to the drama of her life. Rich Ting revealed what it was like to work with Angie as the tabloids yelled outside.

In understanding such a complex and sometimes troubled character, the professional insights of psychologist Iris Martin and contemporary psychoanalyst Dr. Franziska De George, as well as the observations of interventionist Candy Finnigan and Dr. David Kipper, have been invaluable in appreciating Angie's personality. My thanks to them all, as well as to other professional care workers who chose to remain anonymous.

On this journey a detailed timeline has been the rope that has helped guide me through the fog of words and stay on the path to understanding.

Time and again a clear chronology of Angie's life has provided insight, and I would like to thank my researcher Bronwen Tawse for her dogged work, Peter Bahlawanian for technical services, as well as Gabriella Kantor for emerging with truffles from unlikely places. While Dr. Johnson, the pioneer of biography, might not have approved, Facebook proved an essential research tool. Who knew?

At St. Martin's Press my editor, Hope Dellon, performed miracles with the manuscript, showing a deft and sensitive touch, publisher Sally Richardson bravely backed a hunch, and publicity director John Murphy was, as ever, full of brio and boundless enthusiasm. Thanks, too, to my agent, Steve Troha, for getting a green light for the project.

Give it up as well to the king and queen of bling, Bruce and Lori Halprin, for their generous hospitality at their Calabasas palace, to Aaron at the Sunset Marquis hotel for mixing the drinks, and the Dave Matthews Band for providing the sound track.

Finally, my undying appreciation to my partner, Tracy Nesdoly, for her indefatigable research, her smart and telling insights, and the bonniest of bon mots. Just don't mention the timeline.

As they say in the movies, it's been emotional.

—Andrew Morton
New York
April 12, 2010

INDEX

317